W9-DAS-816 01/2012

VOLUME 4:
THE CARNIVAL WARS

PALM BEACH COUNTY
LIBRARY SYSTEM
3650 Summit Boulevard
West Palm Beach, FL 33406-4198

VOLUME 4: THE CARNIVAL WARS

Story By
Serena Valentino

Art by
Harley Sparx

Introduction by
Jennifer de Guzman

Pin-Ups by
Jennifer Feinberg
Pluto
Tammy Lee

Created by
Serena Valentino &
Ted Naifeh

Editiors
Julia Dvorin,
Jennifer de Guzman &
Eric Russel

Published by *SLG Publishing*

President & Publisher
Dan Vado

Art Director
Scott Saavedra

Editrix-in-Chief
Jennifer de Guzman

Drector of Sales
Deb Moskyok

Public Relations Coordinator
Mike Moss

Production Assistants
Eleanor Lawson

Lovingly dedicated to:
My Husband Eric
My Sister Jesse
& Our Lovely Readers
-Serena Valentino

To my lovely boyfriend, and sometimes girlfriend,
RED.
-Harley Sparx

SLG Publishing
P.O. Box 26427
San Jose, CA 95159-6427

GloomCookie Volume Four: The Carnival Wars collects issues 18-23 of the SLG Publishing series *GloomCookie*.

www.slavelabor.com
www.gloomcookie.com

First Printing: October 2005
ISBN 1-59362-022-5

GloomCookie, created by Serena Valentino and Ted Naifeh, is ™ and © 2004-2005, all rights reserved. Art is © Harley Sparx, 2004-2005. No part of this publication may be reproduced without the permission of Serena Valentino & SLG Publishing, except for purposes of review. Printed in Canada.

GloomCookie's Uncanny Charm
by Jennifer de Guzman

Years ago, I had a nightmare that, in the retelling, simply does not sound as if it should be as frightening as it was. In the nightmare, I was trying to call my husband. The calls were getting through to him, but it was the *wrong* him, another version who was confused about who I was and what I wanted. My own confusion and frustration soon turned to horror. What if the person I knew was gone? What if I had been cut off from the reality I knew and had to start over in a new life in a new reality where everything was set just a bit *off* from the way I knew it? What has stayed with me for all this time is the creeping eeriness of what was happening to me in that dream. It was what Freud (if you'll excuse the reference) called *unheimlich*. Uncanny. Not the terror of the unknown and unknowable but of what is frighteningly unfamiliar in a setting or situation that is otherwise utterly mundane.

This is exactly the feeling that Serena Valentino taps into in *GloomCookie*. Sebastian, the most quiet of the "GloomCookies," must learn to navigate a life that is a series of changing realities. There are realities where he has a girl-eating monster under his bed, where his girlfriend is not his girlfriend but his sister instead, where one of his friends dies, where this friend is resurrected. Sebastian can never be sure anything he knows is truly real — not memories of his past, not the love of his friends and family — or if it is an illusion of his own creation. And the reality that seems the most real to him is unraveling in a horrific war that only he can end.

The war is truly terrible, and I couldn't think of anyone better than Harley Sparx to draw the beasts, monsters and colorful and creepy characters who fight in it. But she and Serena shine in the scenes of humor and friendship, as well. They have to. Because without the anchor of his friends in San Francisco's goth scene, Sebastian's struggle for reality is meaningless. The GloomCookies — the sassy Chrys, the lovely Lex and even the clueless Vermilion — are what hold Sebastian's reality together, as well as *GloomCookie* itself. They're what drew me to *GloomCookie* when I first saw issue one at Comic-Con, years before I started working at SLG, and they're what keep readers coming back to this truly unique, charming and uncanny comic.

On a personal note, I have to add that I feel incredibly lucky that my reality and Serena's happened to cross. Her talent, intelligence, imagination and sass are unmatchable. What's funny is that Serena and I were in parallel universes for a while: We lived in the same town for a time (she did Rocky Horror in what is now the Afghan movie theater, but my mother would have never let me go to *that* kind of thing!); she was friends with my husband's brother; her sister and I went to the same high school at the same time. And as corny as it sounds, *GloomCookie* was the comic that got me reading SLG's comics. So, really, Serena is responsible for part of what my reality is today. Uncanny, isn't it?

Jennifer de Guzman is the editor-in-chief at SLG Publishing. She still has a copy of GloomCookie #1 that Serena signed for her at the 1999 San Diego Comic-Con. What a fan girl!

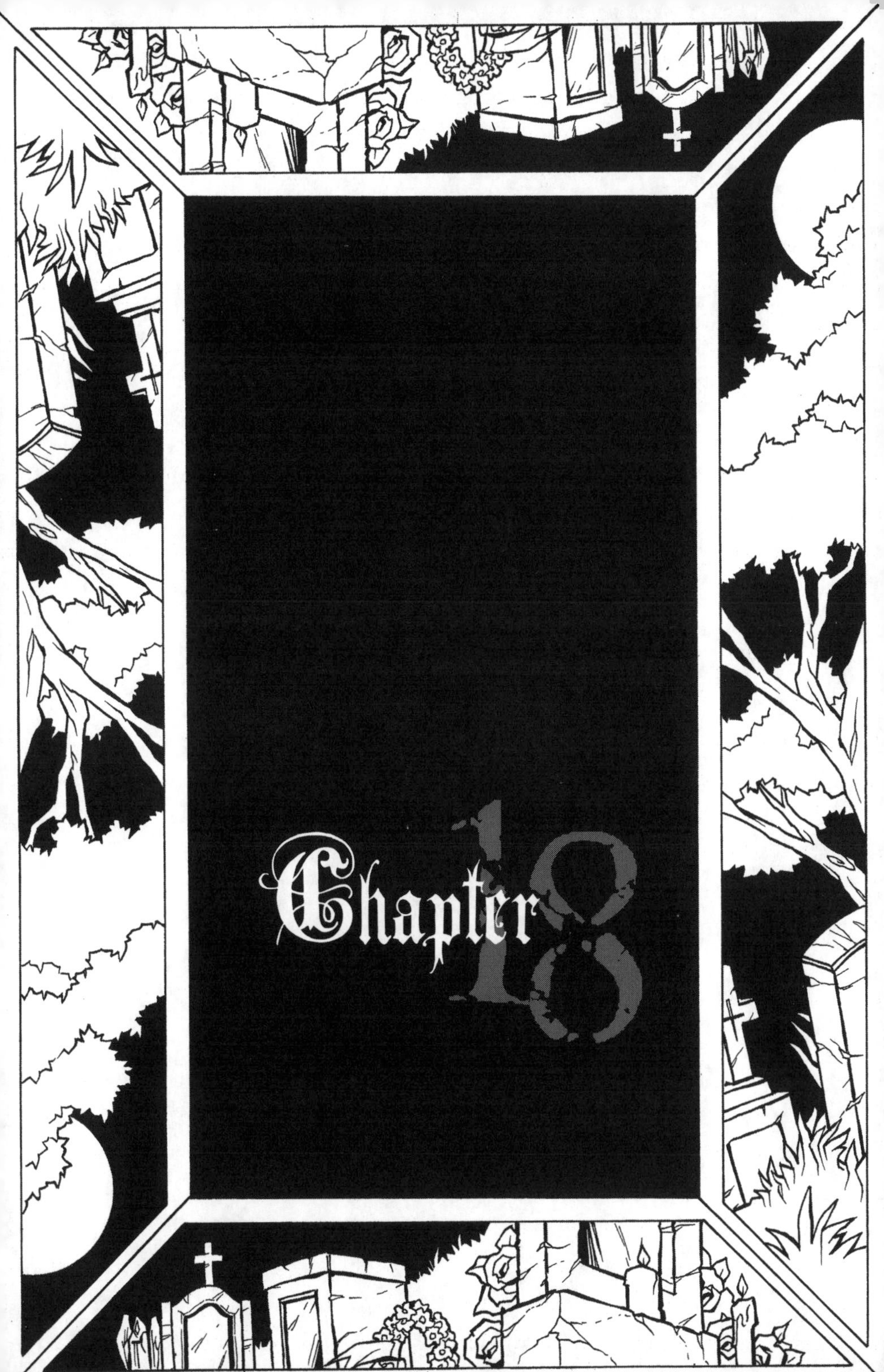
Chapter 18

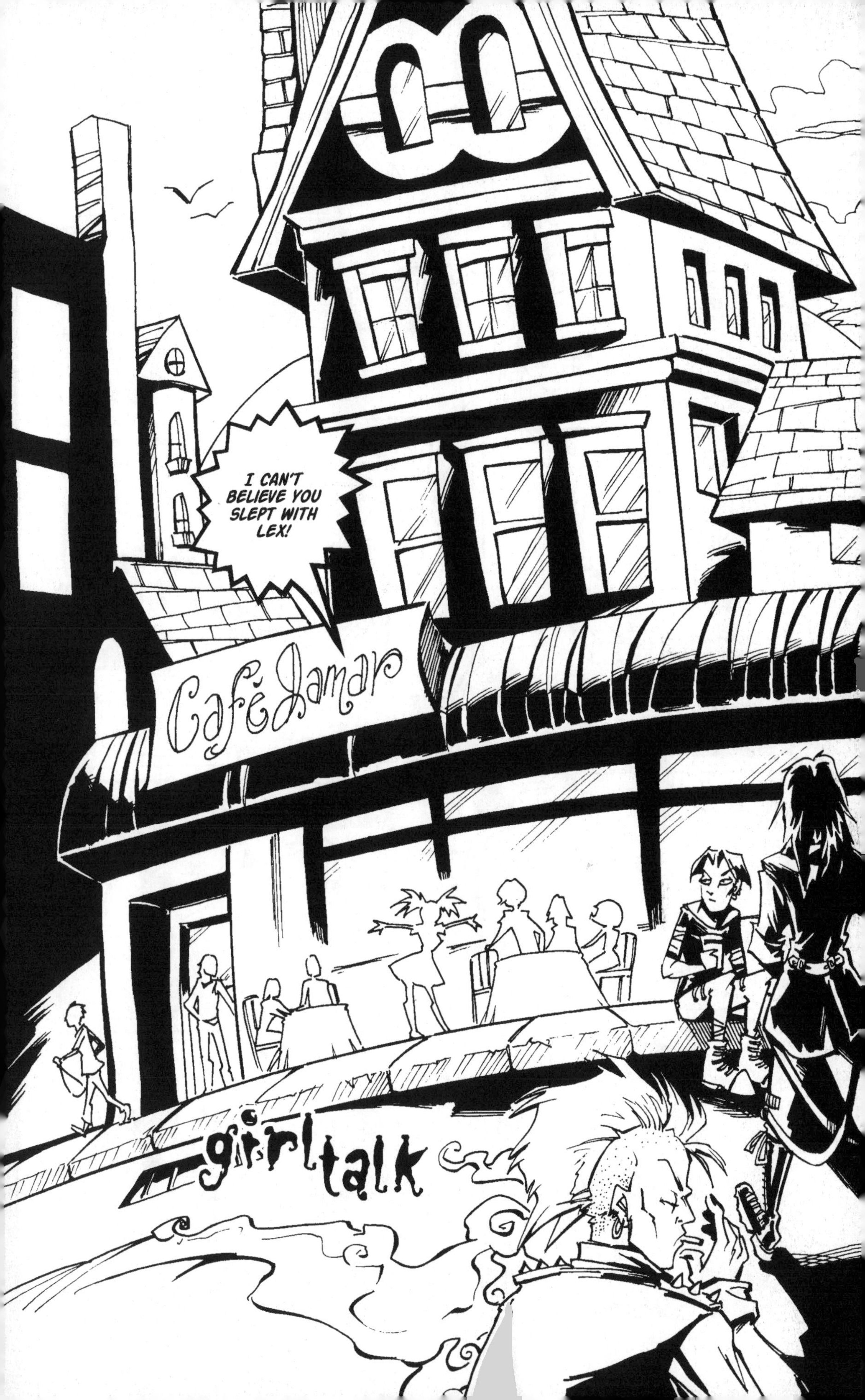
I CAN'T BELIEVE YOU SLEPT WITH LEX!
Café Jamar
girl talk

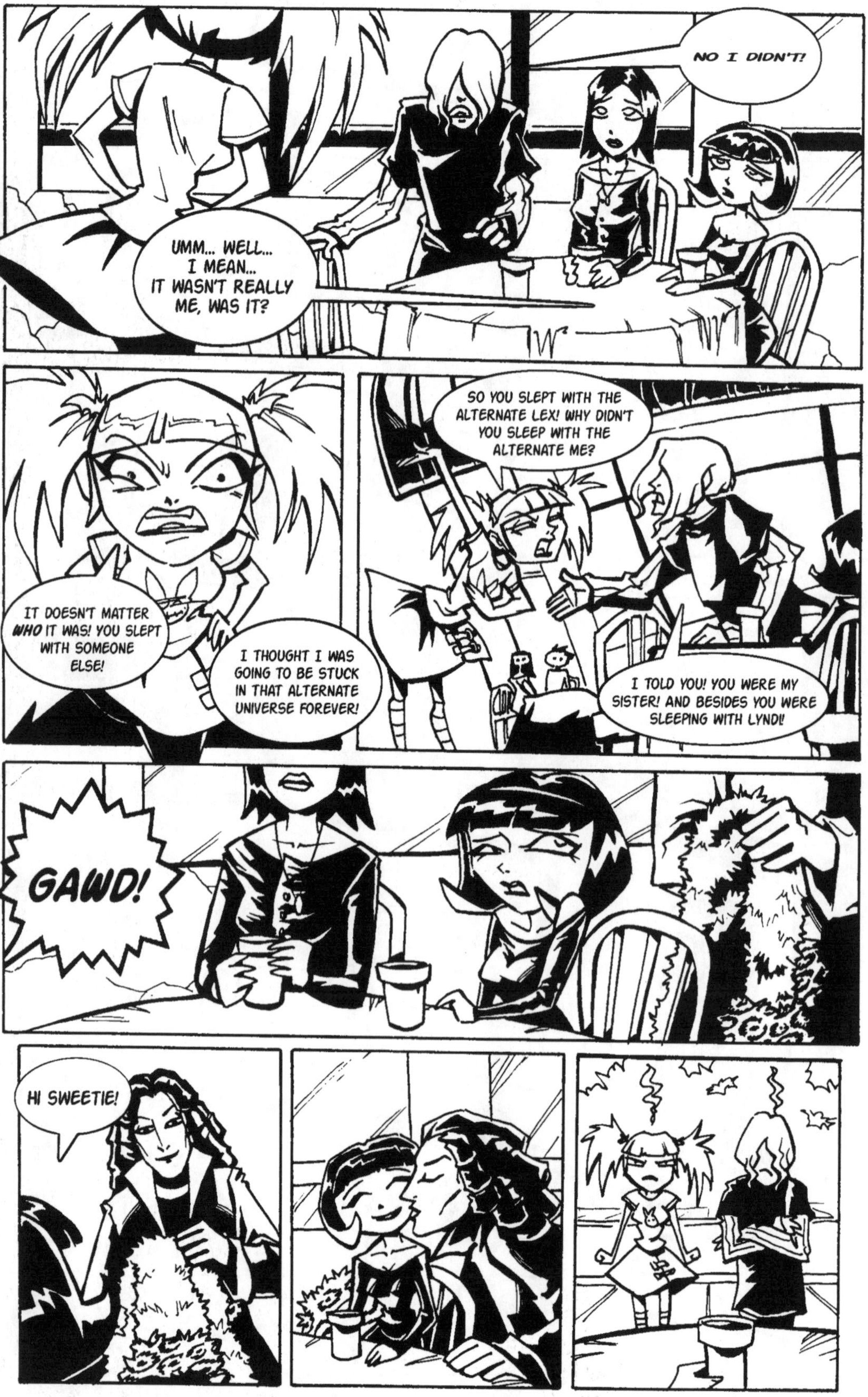
NO I DIDN'T!
UMM... WELL... I MEAN... IT WASN'T REALLY ME, WAS IT?
IT DOESN'T MATTER WHO IT WAS! YOU SLEPT WITH SOMEONE ELSE!
I THOUGHT I WAS GOING TO BE STUCK IN THAT ALTERNATE UNIVERSE FOREVER!
SO YOU SLEPT WITH THE ALTERNATE LEX! WHY DIDN'T YOU SLEEP WITH THE ALTERNATE ME?
I TOLD YOU! YOU WERE MY SISTER! AND BESIDES YOU WERE SLEEPING WITH LYNDI!
GAWD!
HI SWEETIE!

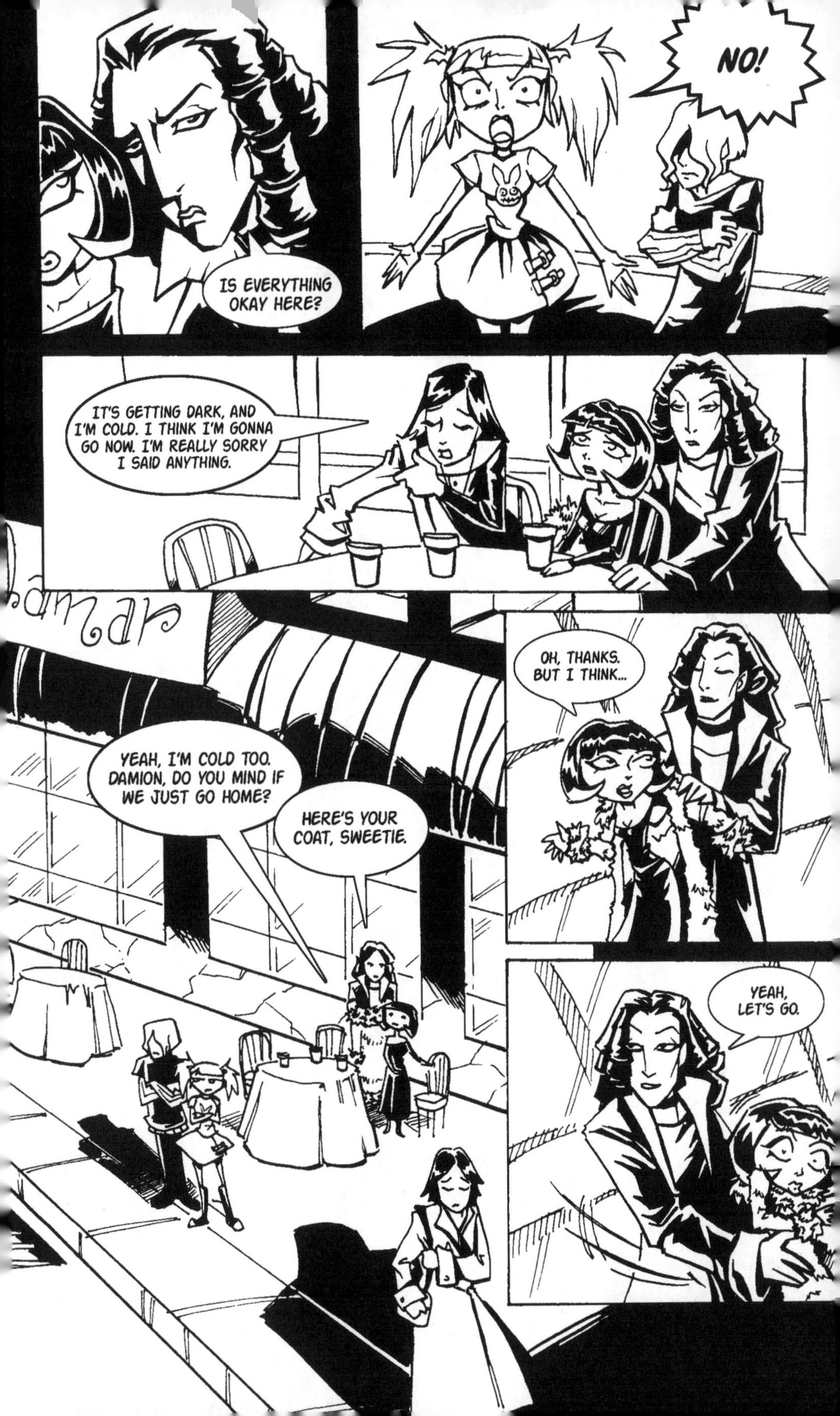
IS EVERYTHING OKAY HERE?
NO!
IT'S GETTING DARK, AND I'M COLD. I THINK I'M GONNA GO NOW. I'M REALLY SORRY I SAID ANYTHING.
YEAH, I'M COLD TOO. DAMION, DO YOU MIND IF WE JUST GO HOME?
HERE'S YOUR COAT, SWEETIE.
OH, THANKS. BUT I THINK...
YEAH, LET'S GO.

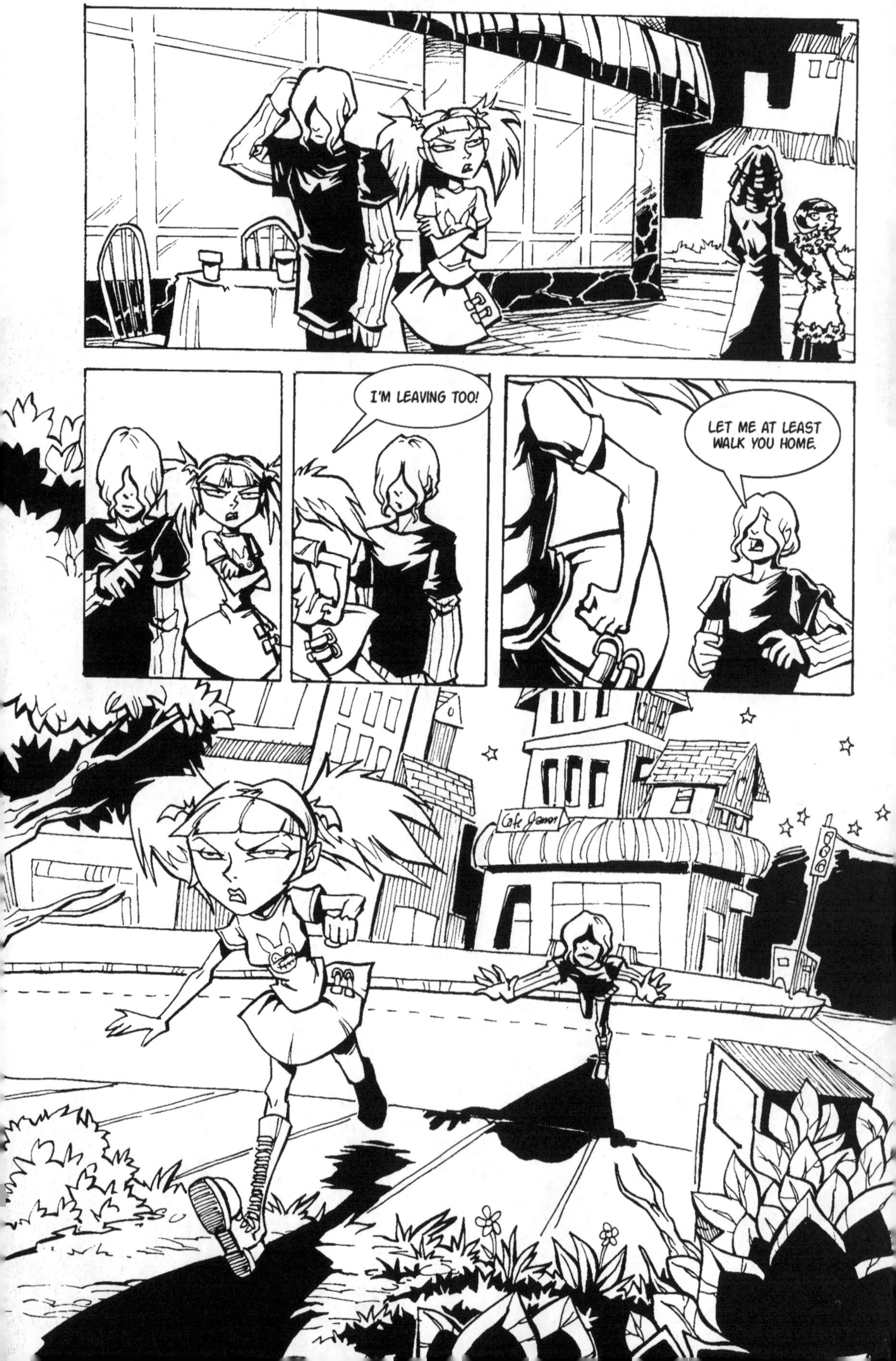
I'M LEAVING TOO!
LET ME AT LEAST WALK YOU HOME.

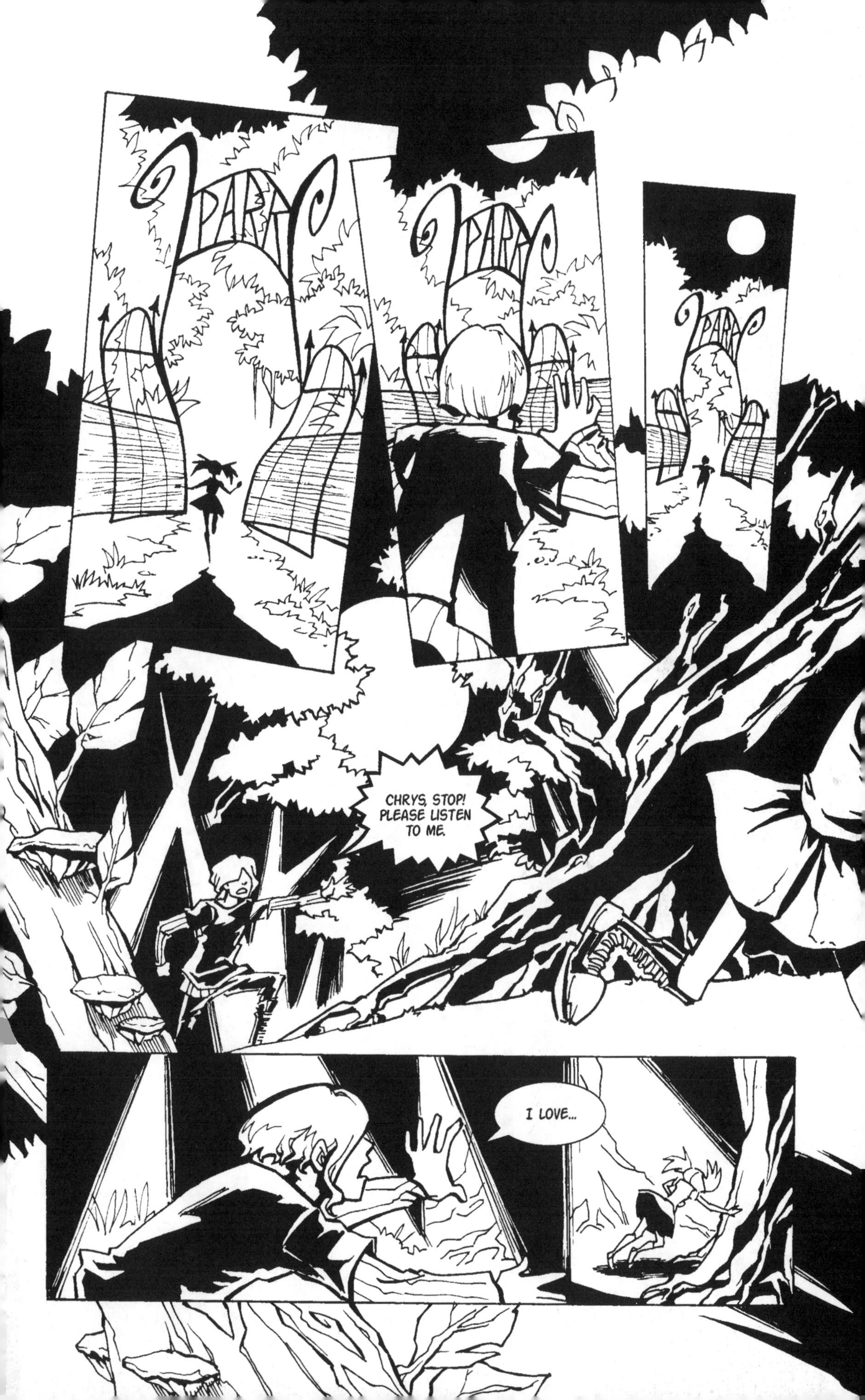
PARK
PARK
PARK
CHRYS, STOP! PLEASE LISTEN TO ME.
I LOVE...

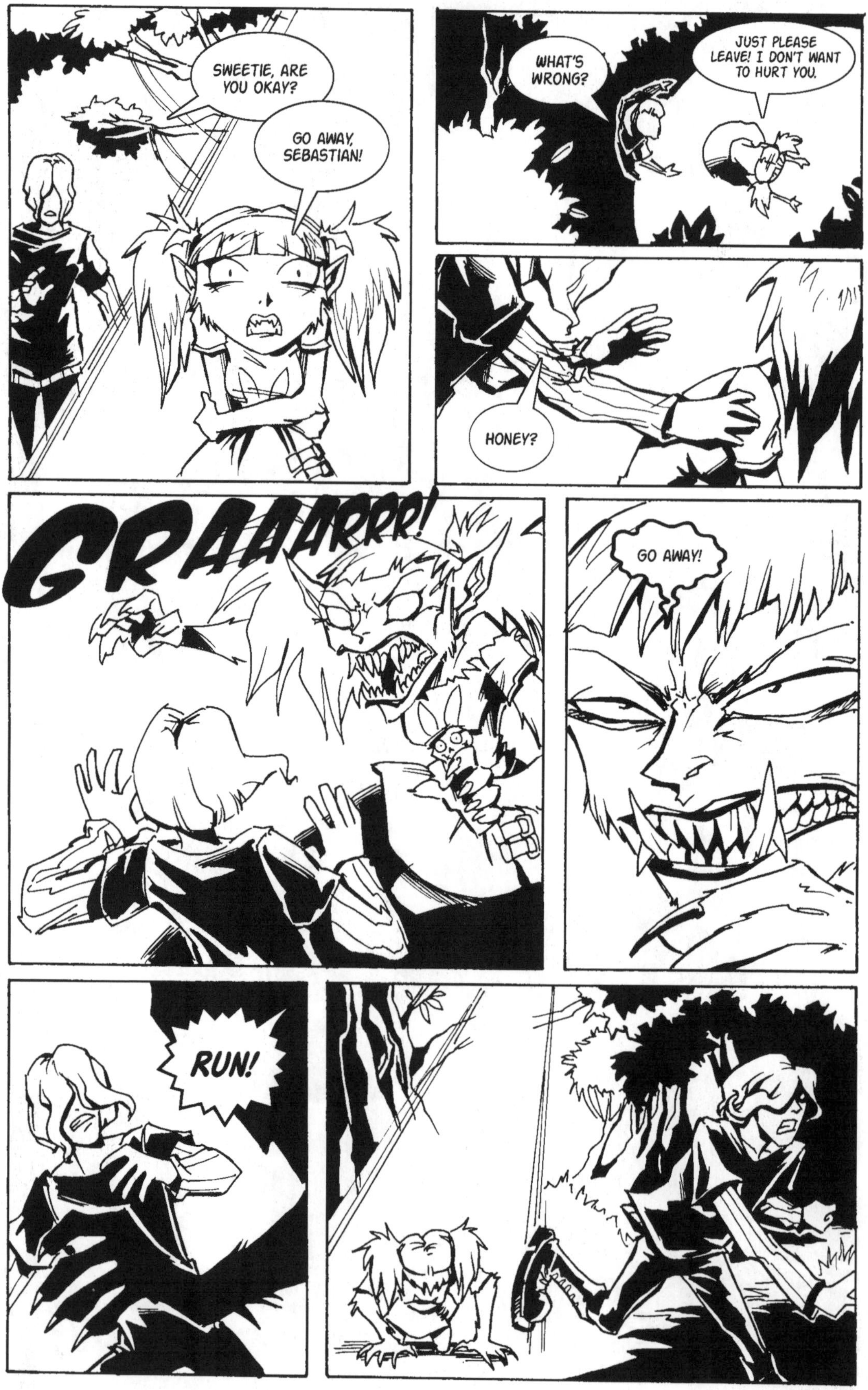
SWEETIE, ARE YOU OKAY?
GO AWAY, SEBASTIAN!
WHAT'S WRONG?
JUST PLEASE LEAVE! I DON'T WANT TO HURT YOU.
HONEY?
GRAAARRR!
GO AWAY!
RUN!

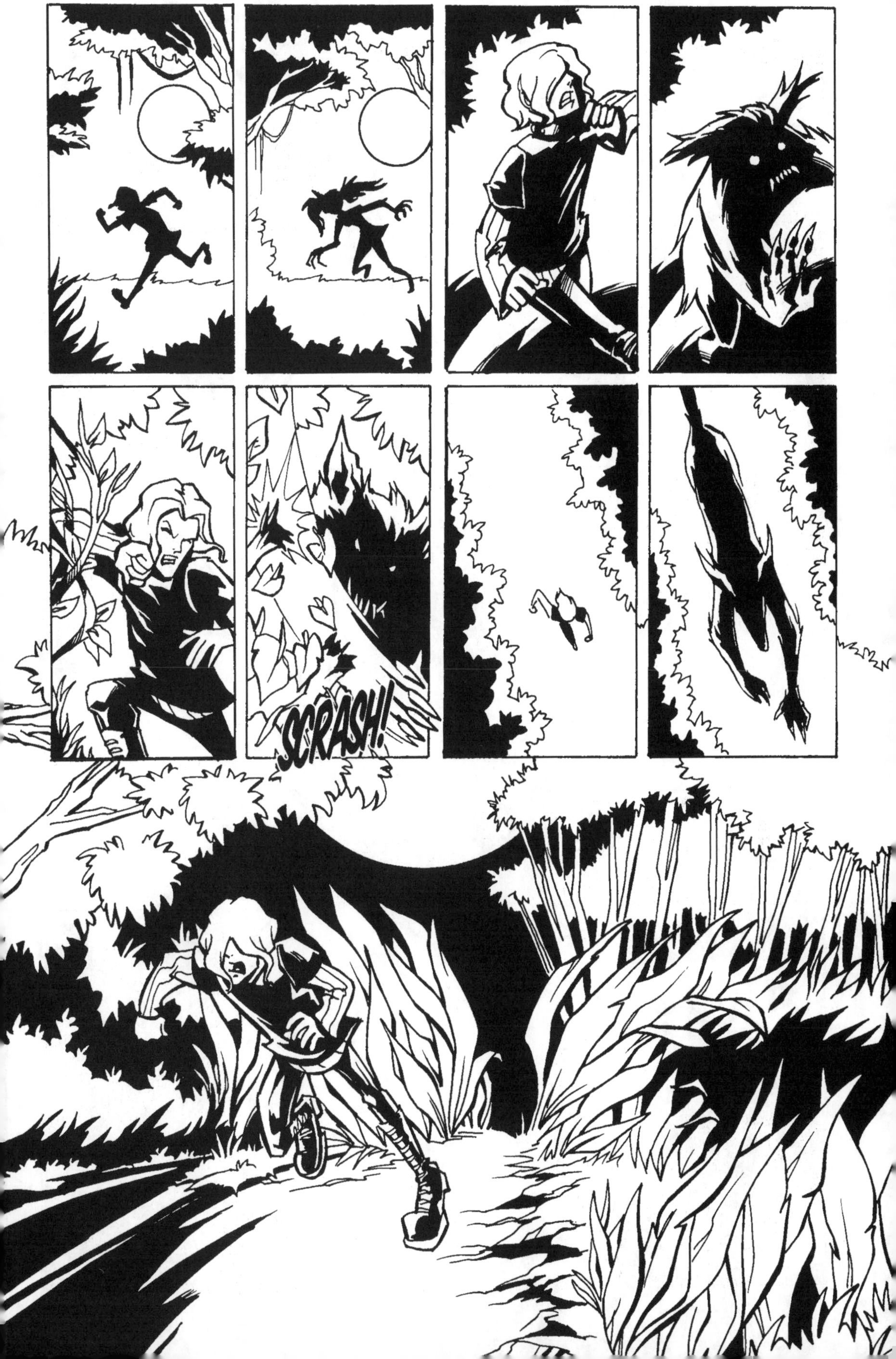
SCRASH!

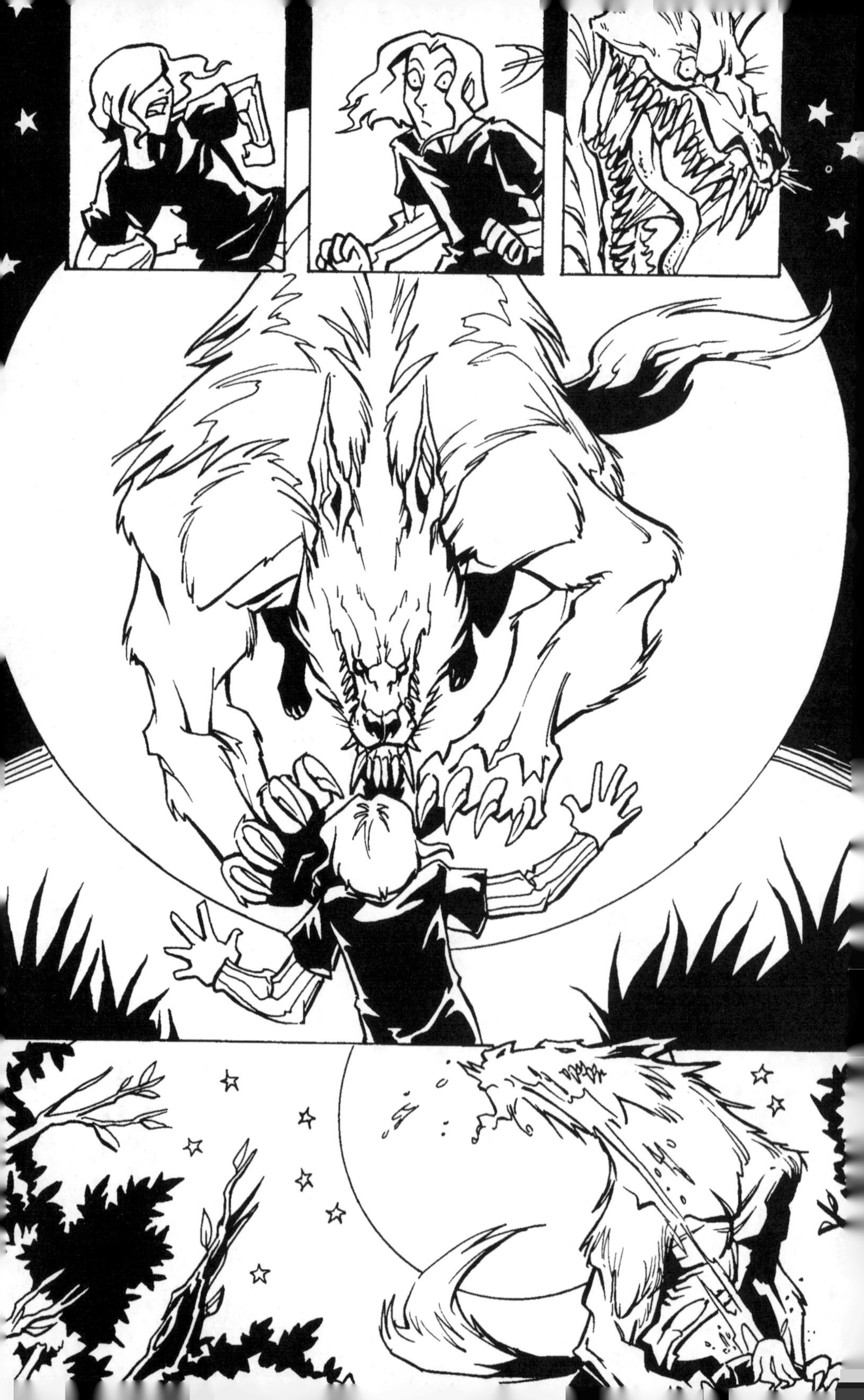

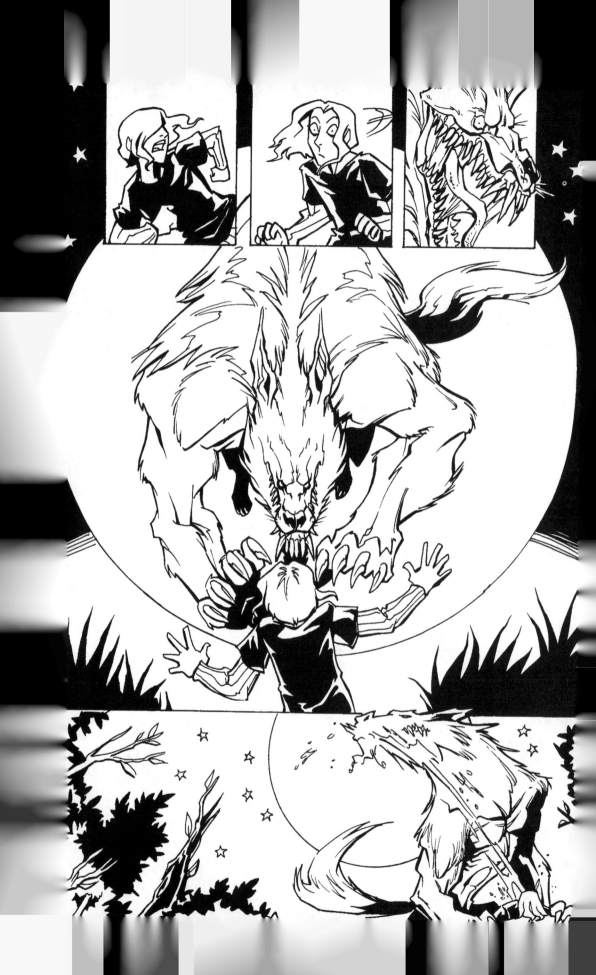

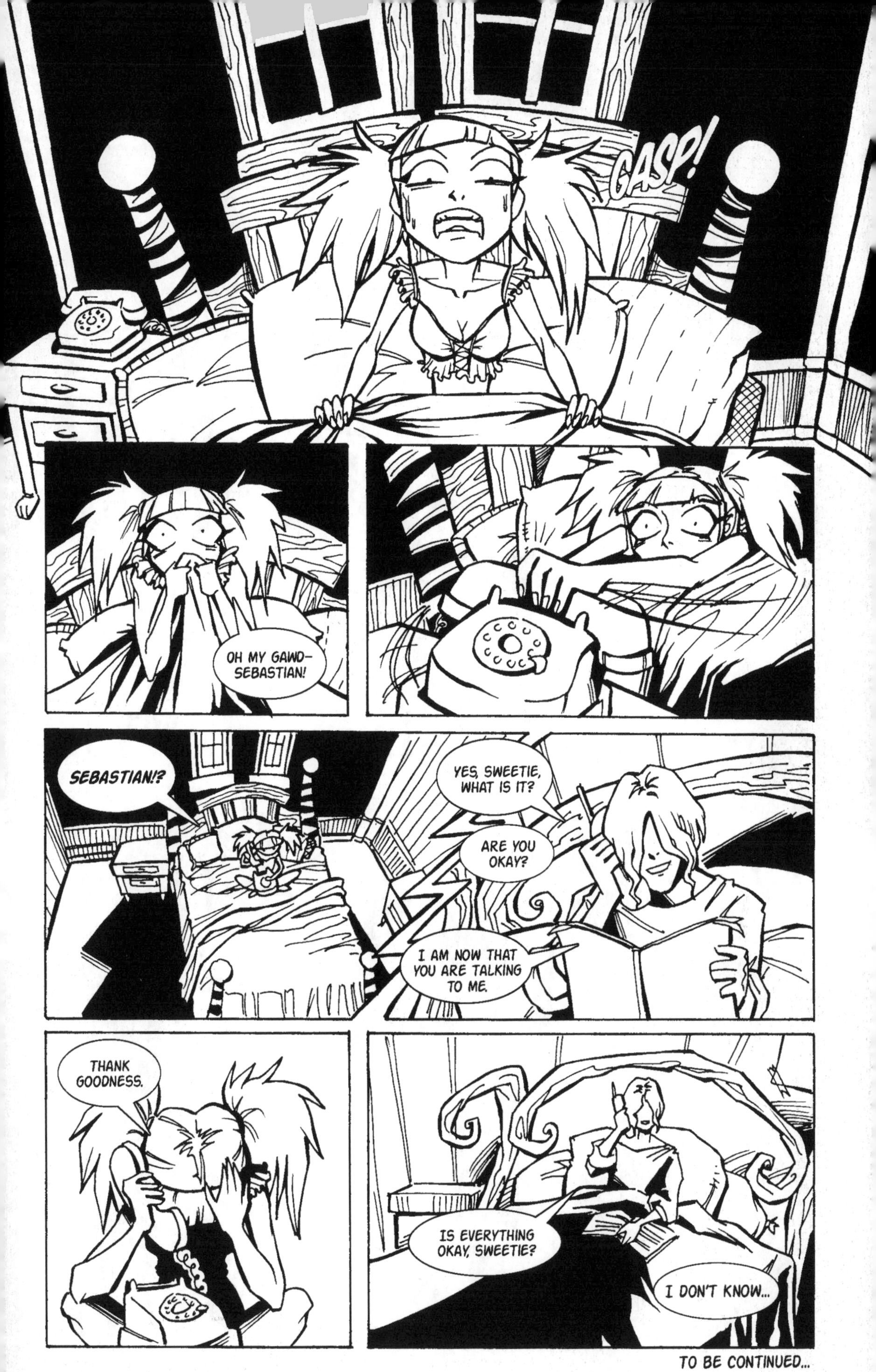
GASP!
OH MY GAWD-
SEBASTIAN!
SEBASTIAN!?
YES, SWEETIE, WHAT IS IT?
ARE YOU OKAY?
I AM NOW THAT YOU ARE TALKING TO ME.
THANK GOODNESS.
IS EVERYTHING OKAY, SWEETIE?
I DON'T KNOW...

TO BE CONTINUED...

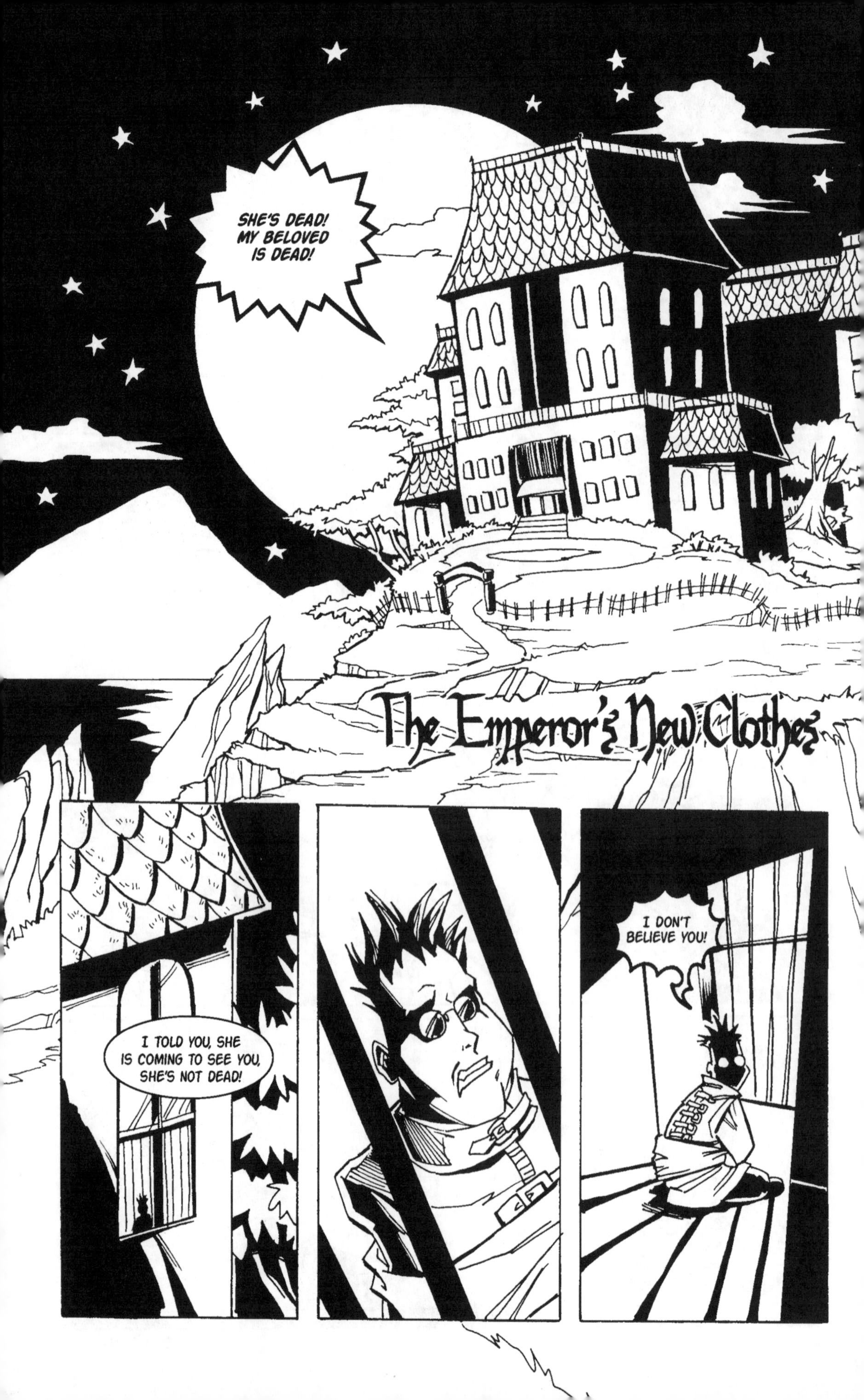
SHE'S DEAD! MY BELOVED IS DEAD!
The Emperor's New Clothes
I TOLD YOU, SHE IS COMING TO SEE YOU, SHE'S NOT DEAD!
I DON'T BELIEVE YOU!

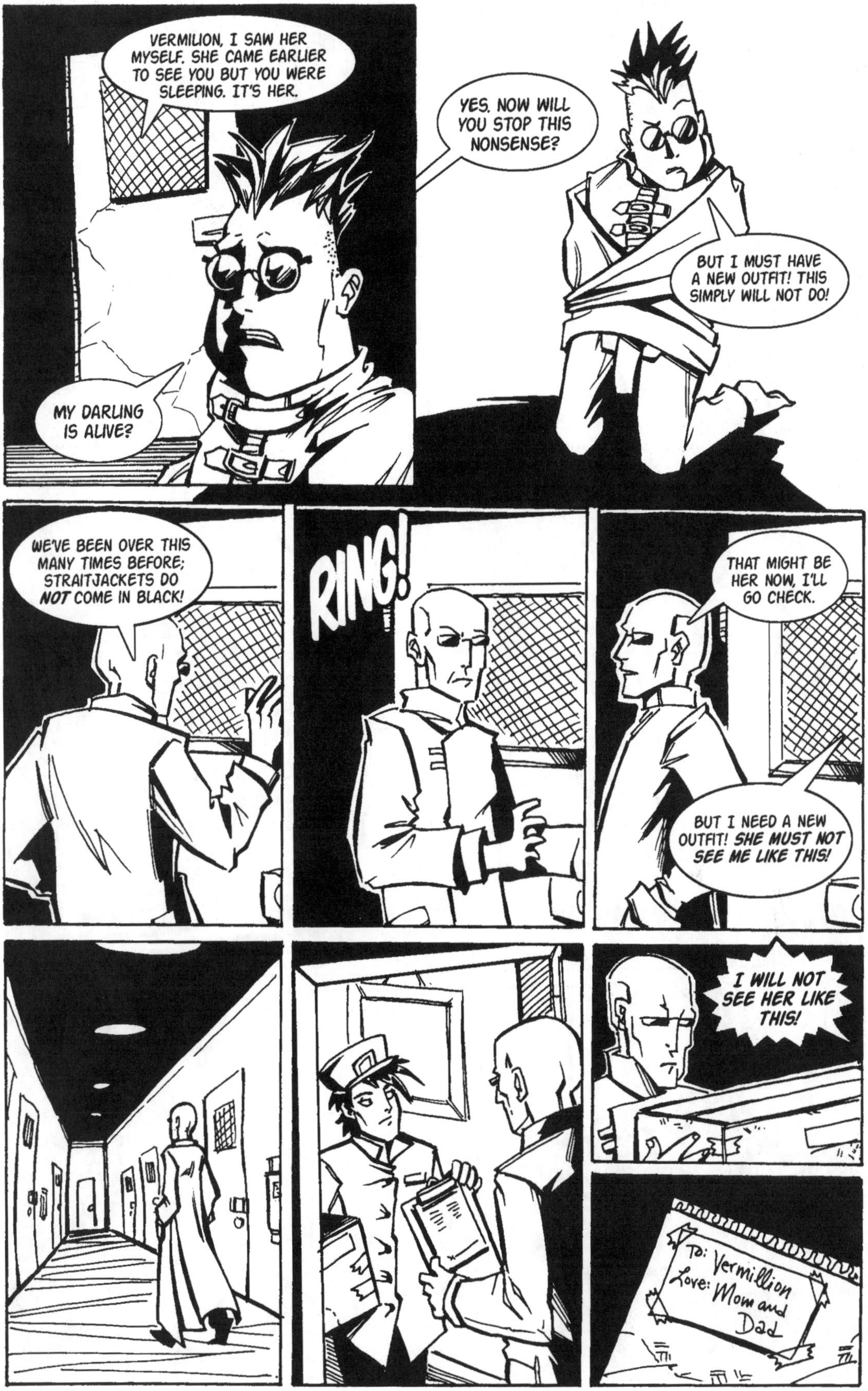
VERMILION, I SAW HER MYSELF. SHE CAME EARLIER TO SEE YOU BUT YOU WERE SLEEPING. IT'S HER.
MY DARLING IS ALIVE?
YES. NOW WILL YOU STOP THIS NONSENSE?
BUT I MUST HAVE A NEW OUTFIT! THIS SIMPLY WILL NOT DO!
WE'VE BEEN OVER THIS MANY TIMES BEFORE; STRAITJACKETS DO **NOT** COME IN BLACK!
RING!
THAT MIGHT BE HER NOW, I'LL GO CHECK.
BUT I NEED A NEW OUTFIT! **SHE MUST NOT SEE ME LIKE THIS!**
I WILL NOT SEE HER LIKE THIS!
To: Vermillion
Love: Mom and Dad

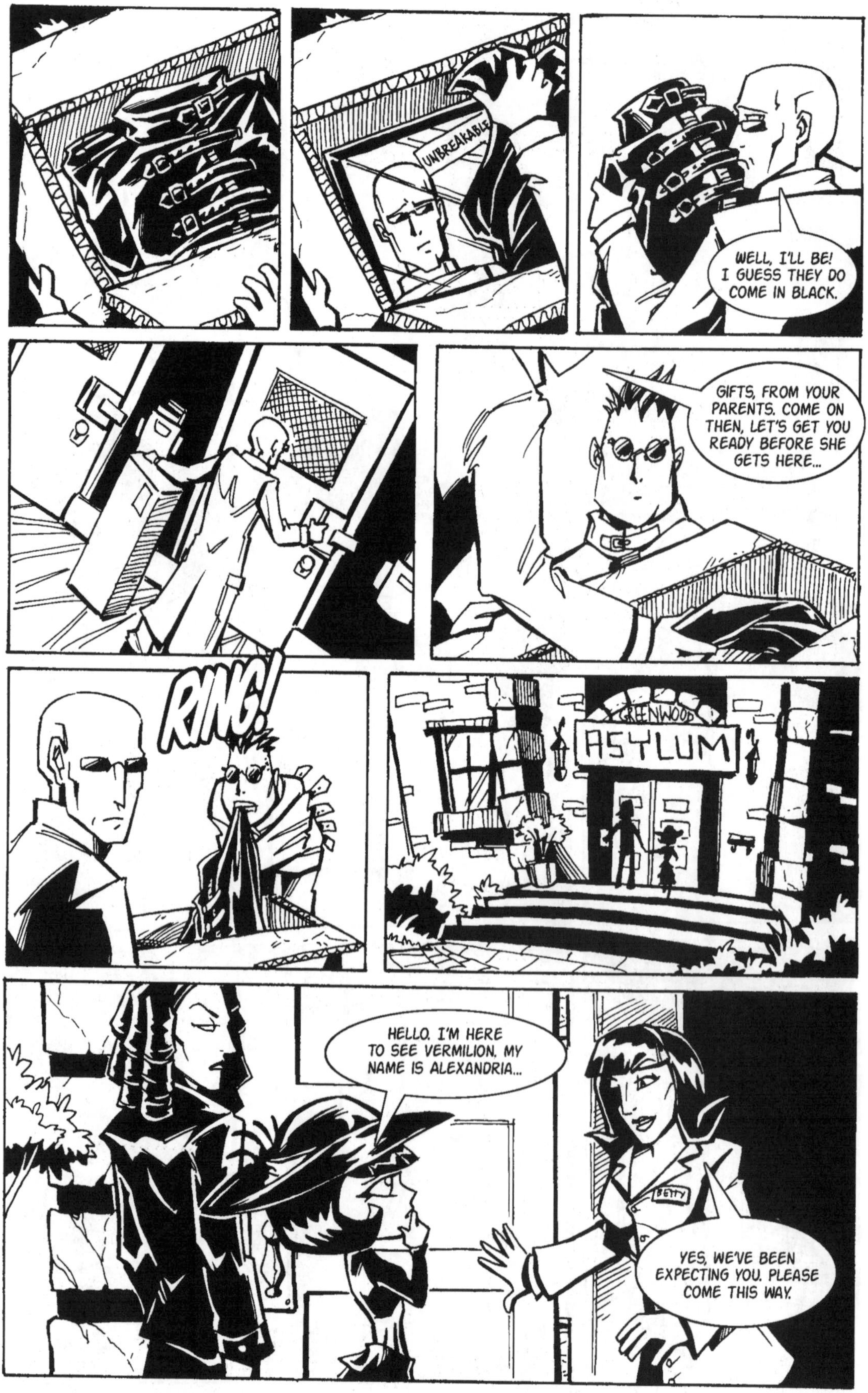
UNBREAKABLE
WELL, I'LL BE! I GUESS THEY DO COME IN BLACK.
GIFTS, FROM YOUR PARENTS. COME ON THEN, LET'S GET YOU READY BEFORE SHE GETS HERE...
RING!
GREENWOOD
ASYLUM
HELLO. I'M HERE TO SEE VERMILION. MY NAME IS ALEXANDRIA...
BETTY
YES, WE'VE BEEN EXPECTING YOU. PLEASE COME THIS WAY.

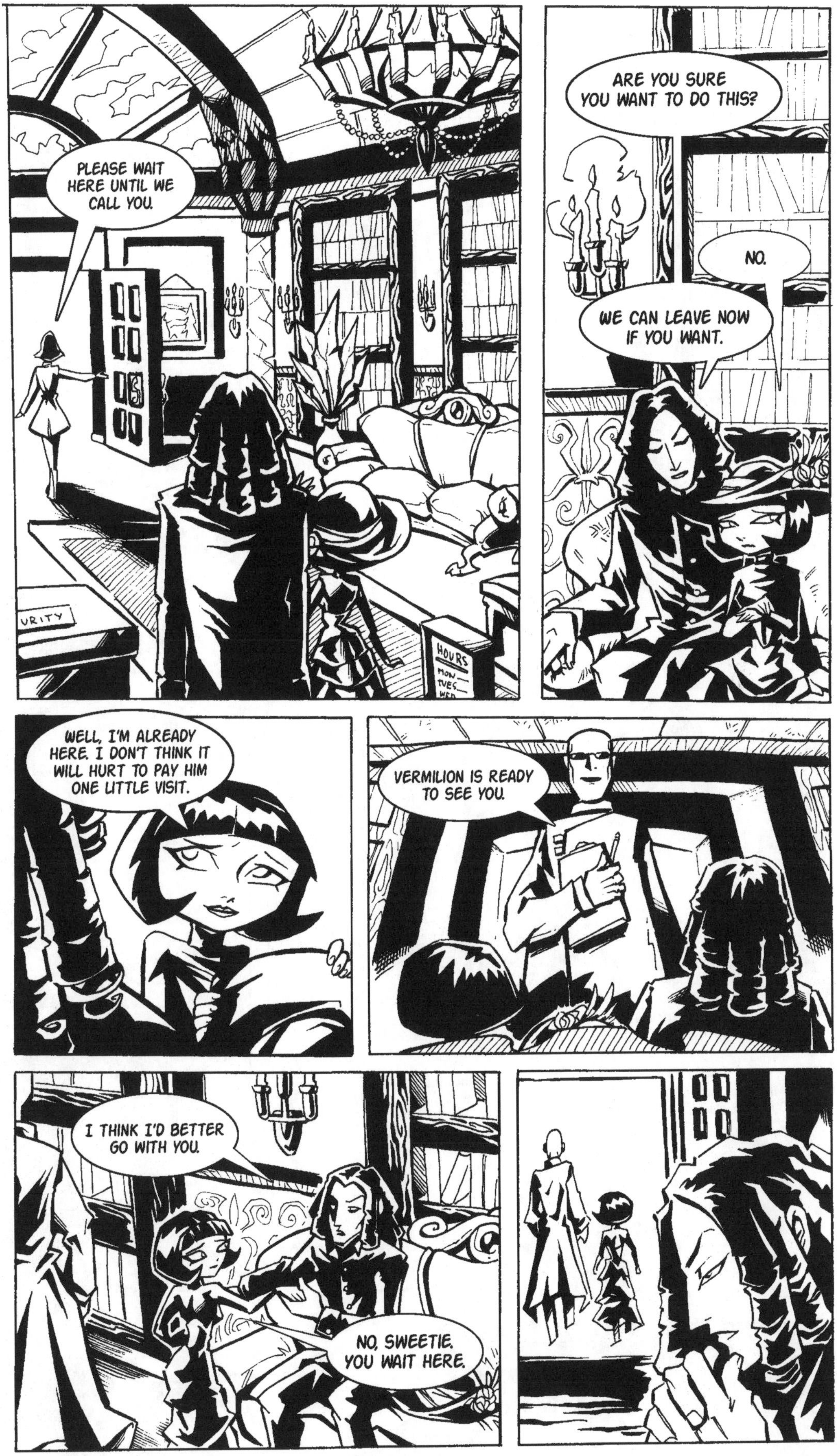
PLEASE WAIT HERE UNTIL WE CALL YOU.
URITY
HOURS
MON.
TUES.
ARE YOU SURE YOU WANT TO DO THIS?
WE CAN LEAVE NOW IF YOU WANT.
NO.
WELL, I'M ALREADY HERE. I DON'T THINK IT WILL HURT TO PAY HIM ONE LITTLE VISIT.
VERMILION IS READY TO SEE YOU.
I THINK I'D BETTER GO WITH YOU.
NO, SWEETIE. YOU WAIT HERE.

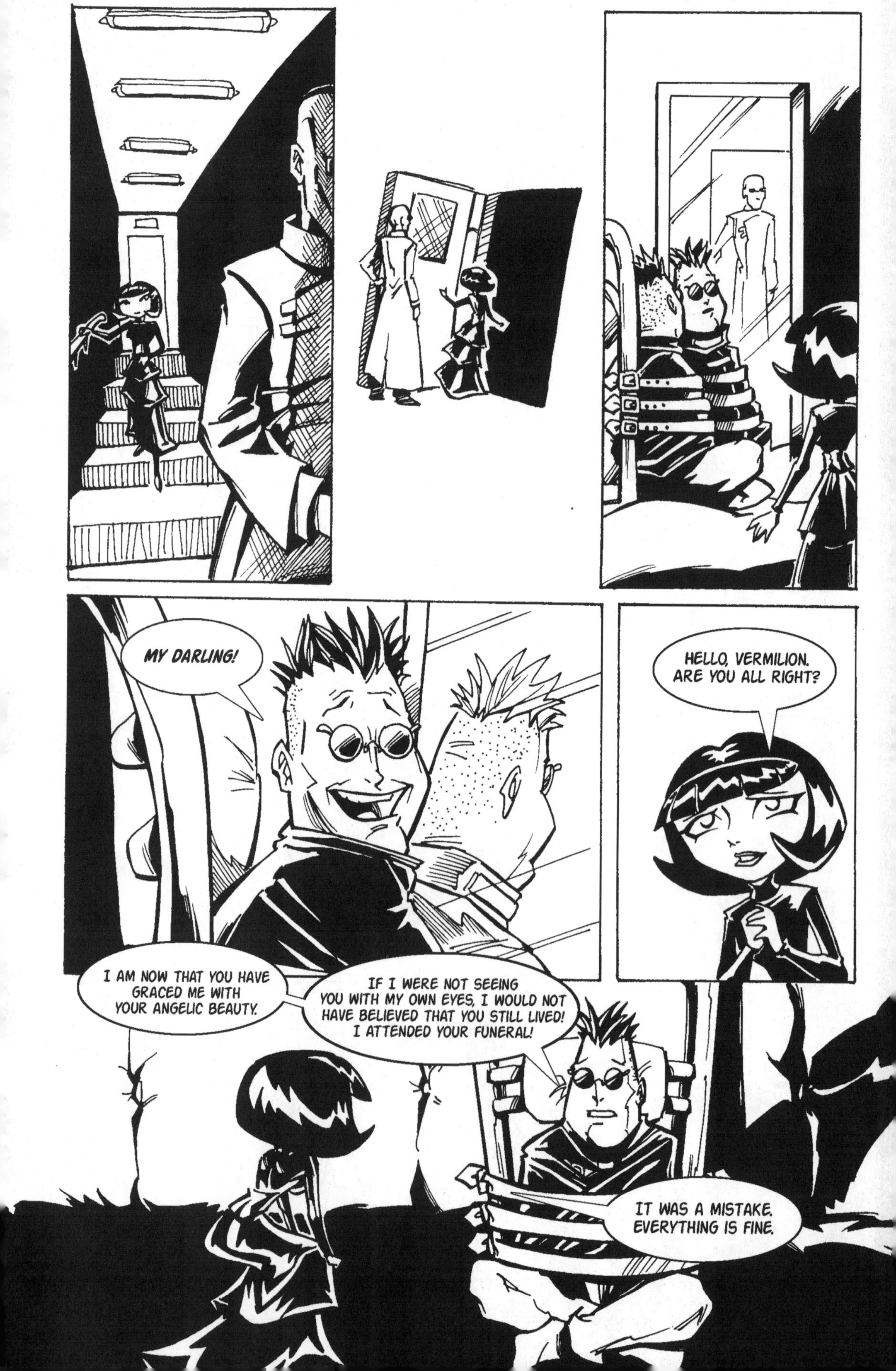
MY DARLING!
HELLO, VERMILION. ARE YOU ALL RIGHT?
I AM NOW THAT YOU HAVE GRACED ME WITH YOUR ANGELIC BEAUTY.
IF I WERE NOT SEEING YOU WITH MY OWN EYES, I WOULD NOT HAVE BELIEVED THAT YOU STILL LIVED! I ATTENDED YOUR FUNERAL!
IT WAS A MISTAKE. EVERYTHING IS FINE.

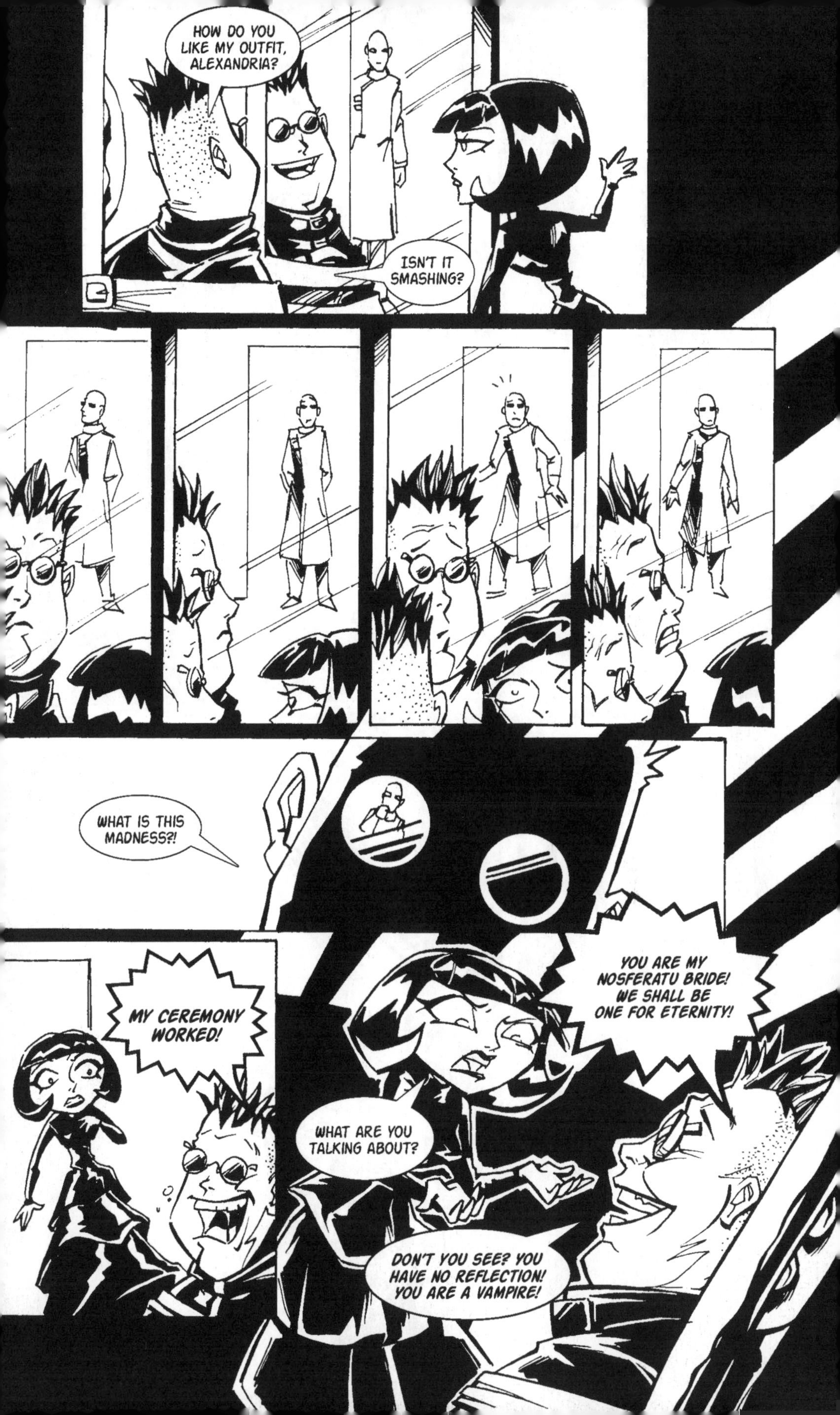
HOW DO YOU LIKE MY OUTFIT, ALEXANDRIA?
ISN'T IT SMASHING?
WHAT IS THIS MADNESS?!
MY CEREMONY WORKED!
YOU ARE MY NOSFERATU BRIDE! WE SHALL BE ONE FOR ETERNITY!
WHAT ARE YOU TALKING ABOUT?
DON'T YOU SEE? YOU HAVE NO REFLECTION! YOU ARE A VAMPIRE!

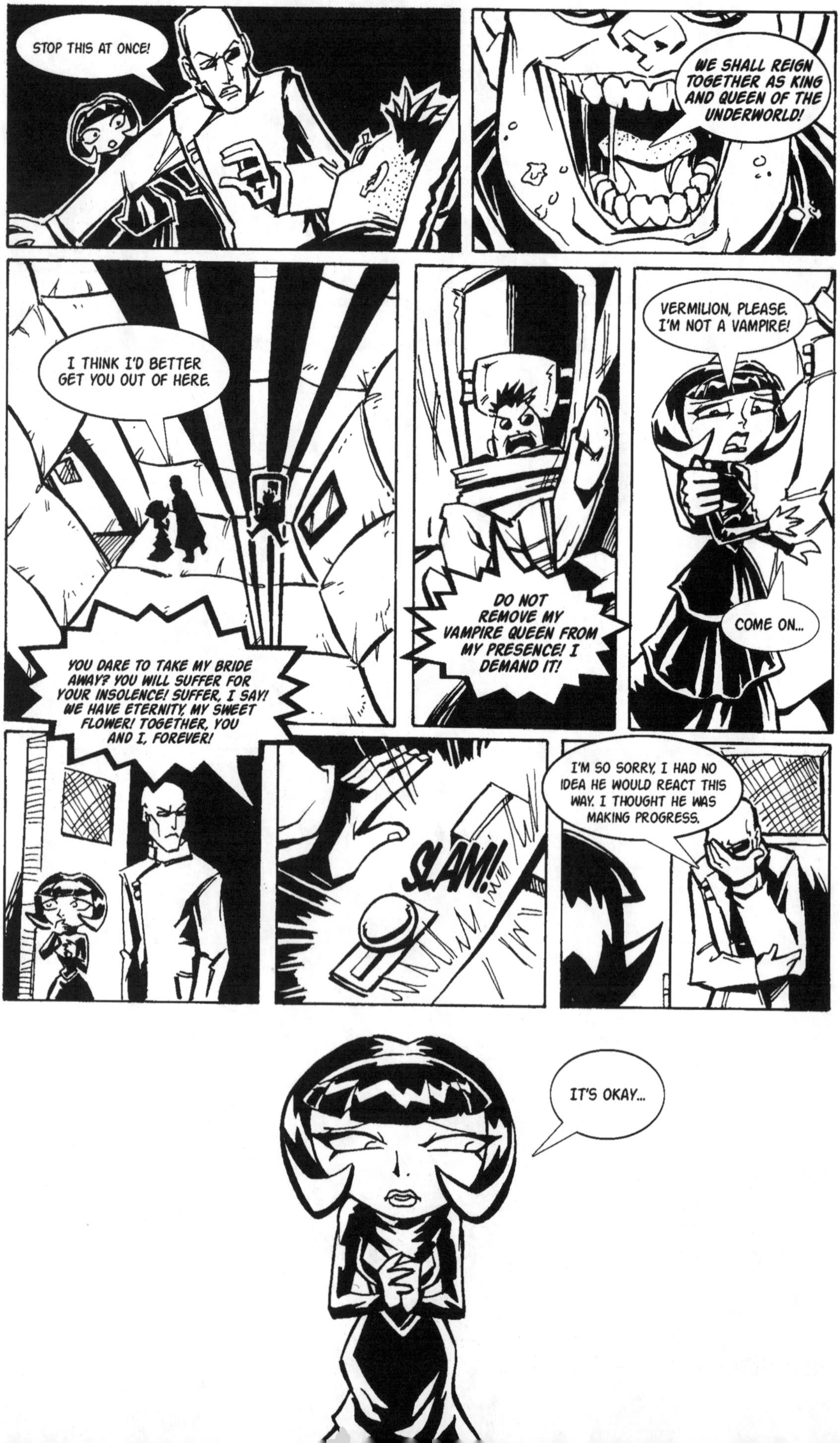
STOP THIS AT ONCE!
WE SHALL REIGN TOGETHER AS KING AND QUEEN OF THE UNDERWORLD!
I THINK I'D BETTER GET YOU OUT OF HERE.
YOU DARE TO TAKE MY BRIDE AWAY? YOU WILL SUFFER FOR YOUR INSOLENCE! SUFFER, I SAY! WE HAVE ETERNITY, MY SWEET FLOWER! TOGETHER, YOU AND I, FOREVER!
DO NOT REMOVE MY VAMPIRE QUEEN FROM MY PRESENCE! I DEMAND IT!
VERMILION, PLEASE. I'M NOT A VAMPIRE!
COME ON...
SLAM!
I'M SO SORRY, I HAD NO IDEA HE WOULD REACT THIS WAY. I THOUGHT HE WAS MAKING PROGRESS.
IT'S OKAY...

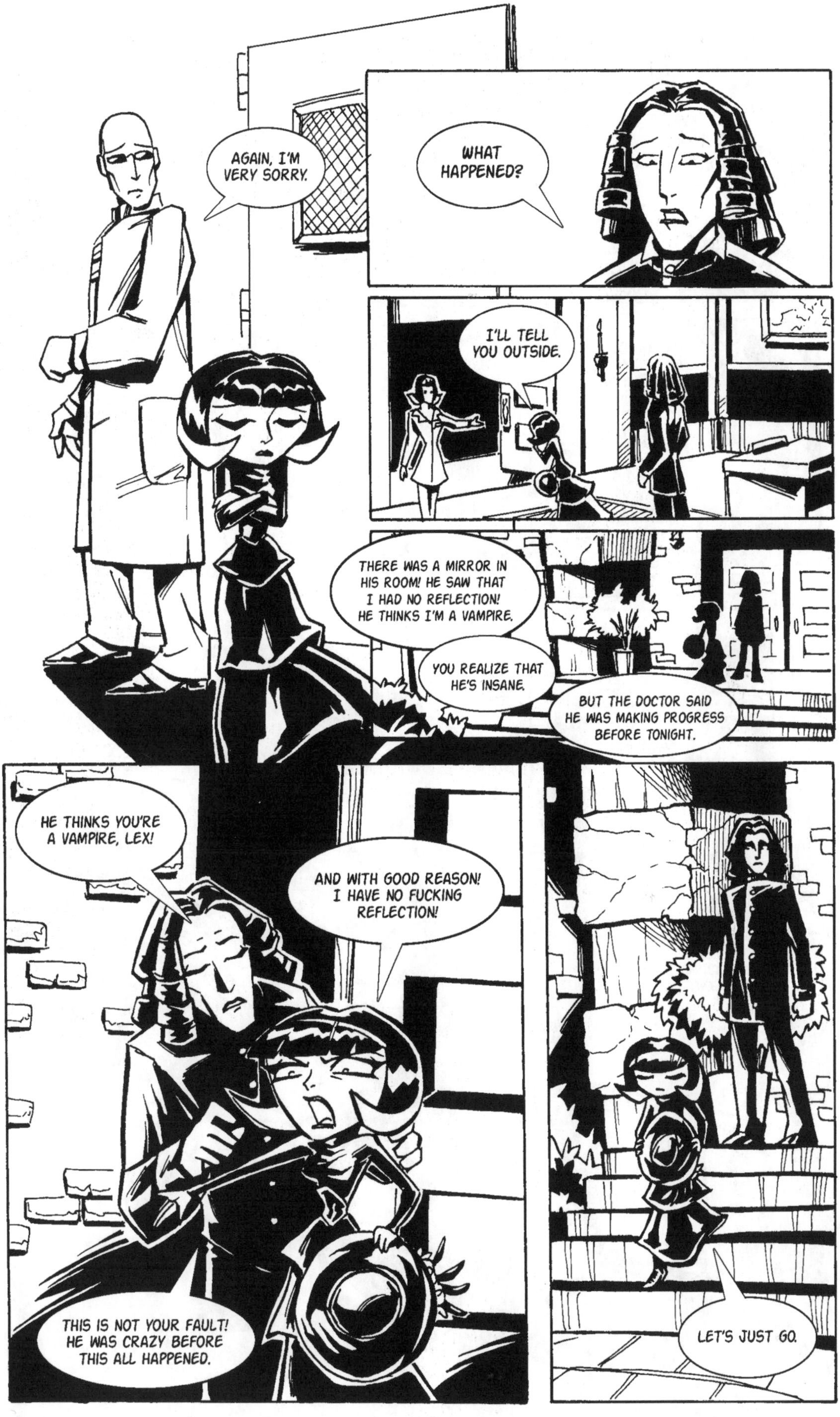
AGAIN, I'M VERY SORRY.
WHAT HAPPENED?
I'LL TELL YOU OUTSIDE.
THERE WAS A MIRROR IN HIS ROOM! HE SAW THAT I HAD NO REFLECTION! HE THINKS I'M A VAMPIRE.
YOU REALIZE THAT HE'S INSANE.
BUT THE DOCTOR SAID HE WAS MAKING PROGRESS BEFORE TONIGHT.
HE THINKS YOU'RE A VAMPIRE, LEX!
AND WITH GOOD REASON! I HAVE NO FUCKING REFLECTION!
THIS IS NOT YOUR FAULT! HE WAS CRAZY BEFORE THIS ALL HAPPENED.
LET'S JUST GO.

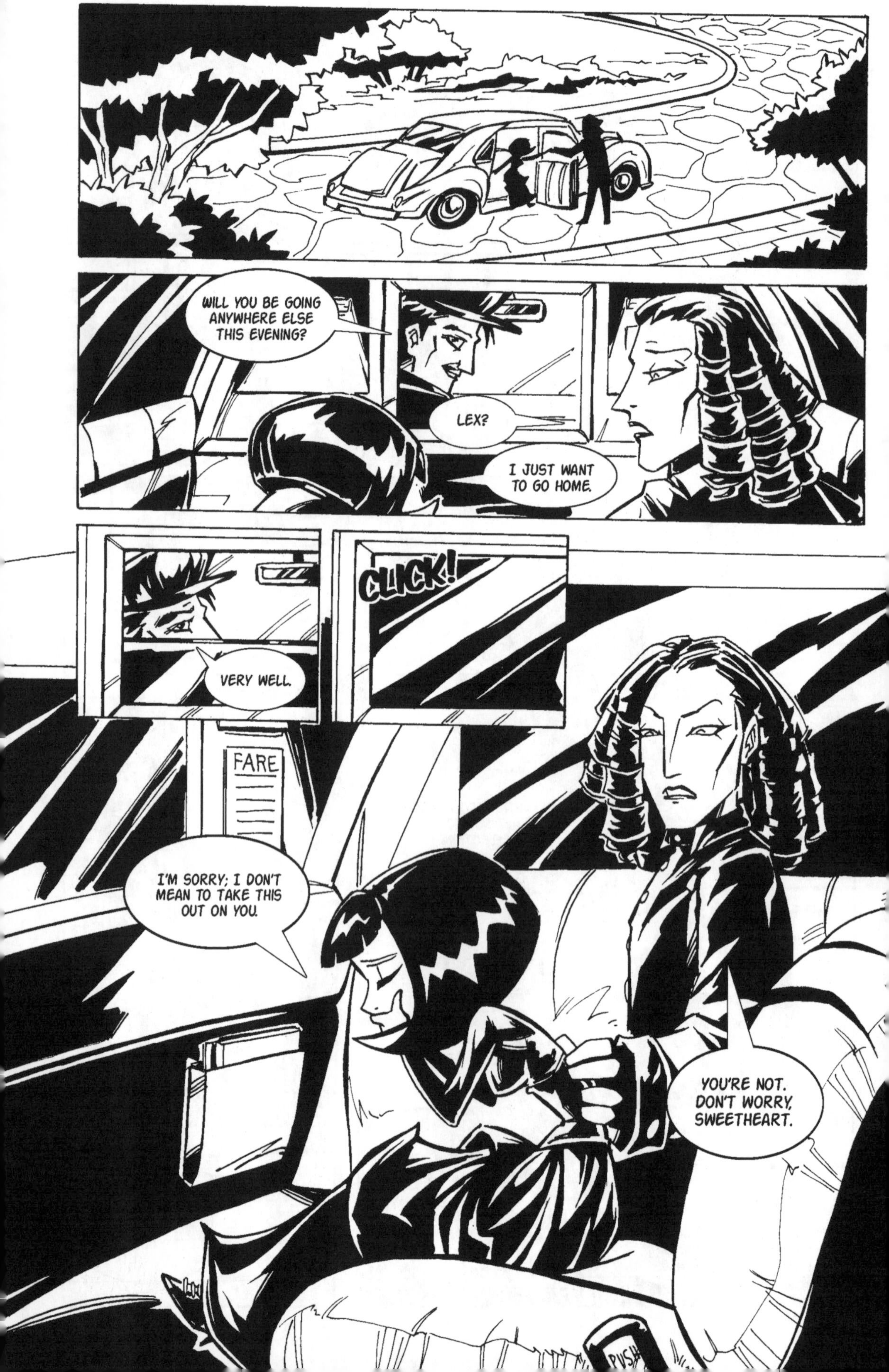
WILL YOU BE GOING ANYWHERE ELSE THIS EVENING?
LEX?
I JUST WANT TO GO HOME.
VERY WELL.
CLICK!
FARE
I'M SORRY; I DON'T MEAN TO TAKE THIS OUT ON YOU.
YOU'RE NOT. DON'T WORRY, SWEETHEART.
PUSH

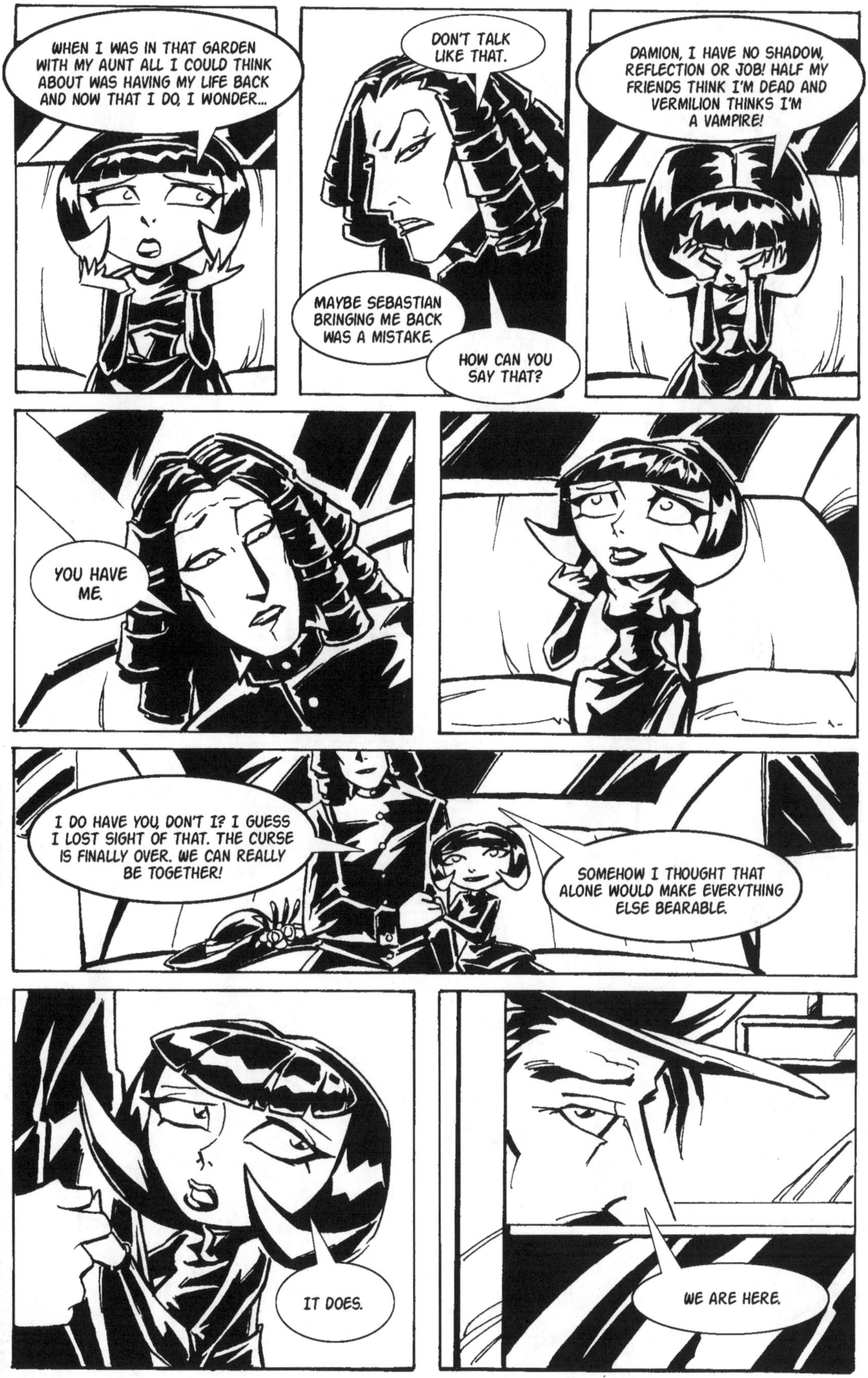
WHEN I WAS IN THAT GARDEN WITH MY AUNT ALL I COULD THINK ABOUT WAS HAVING MY LIFE BACK AND NOW THAT I DO, I WONDER...
DON'T TALK LIKE THAT.
MAYBE SEBASTIAN BRINGING ME BACK WAS A MISTAKE.
HOW CAN YOU SAY THAT?
DAMION, I HAVE NO SHADOW, REFLECTION OR JOB! HALF MY FRIENDS THINK I'M DEAD AND VERMILION THINKS I'M A VAMPIRE!
YOU HAVE ME.
I DO HAVE YOU, DON'T I? I GUESS I LOST SIGHT OF THAT. THE CURSE IS FINALLY OVER. WE CAN REALLY BE TOGETHER!
SOMEHOW I THOUGHT THAT ALONE WOULD MAKE EVERYTHING ELSE BEARABLE.
IT DOES.
WE ARE HERE.

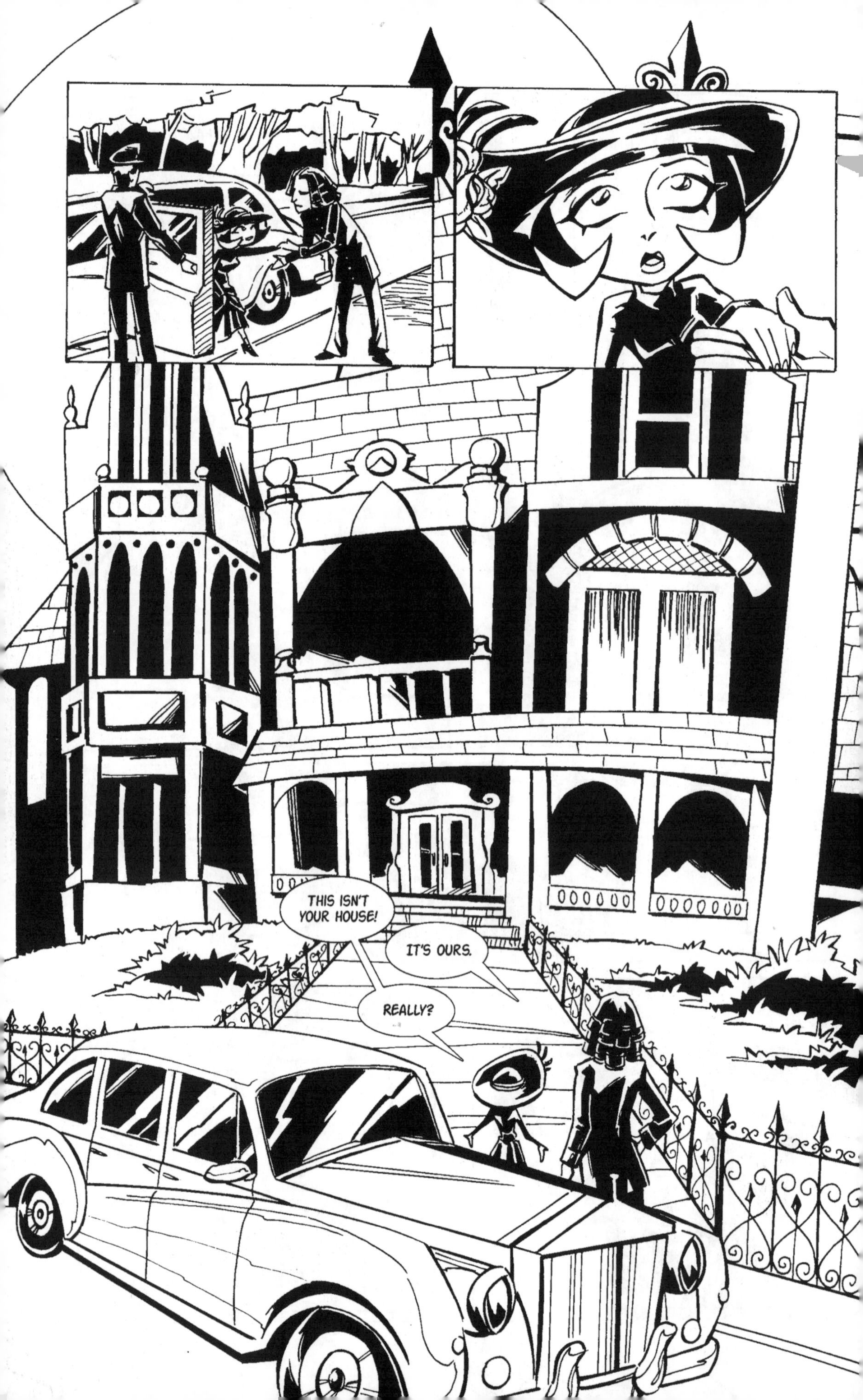
THIS ISN'T YOUR HOUSE!
IT'S OURS.
REALLY?

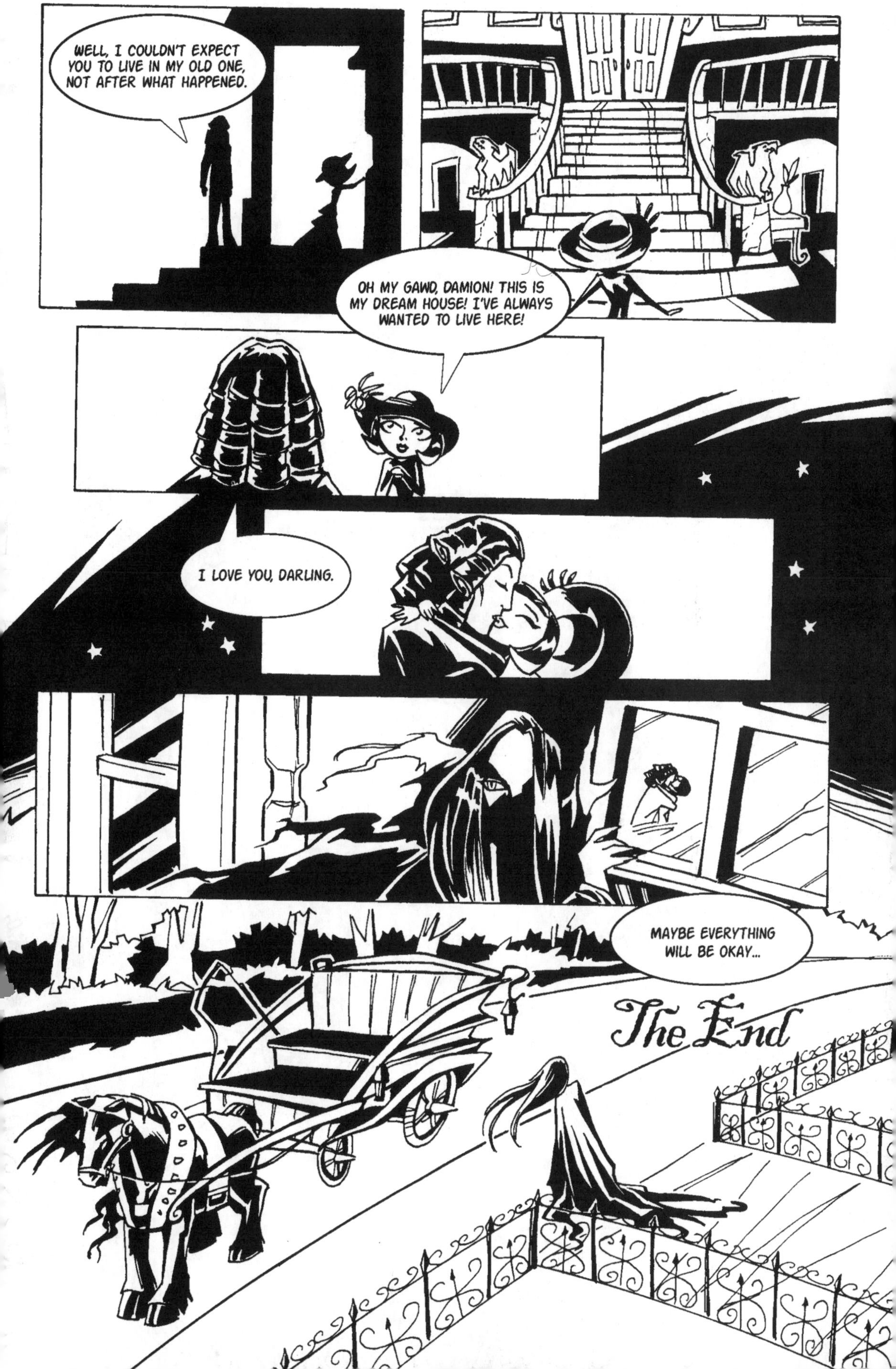
WELL, I COULDN'T EXPECT YOU TO LIVE IN MY OLD ONE, NOT AFTER WHAT HAPPENED.
OH MY GAWD, DAMION! THIS IS MY DREAM HOUSE! I'VE ALWAYS WANTED TO LIVE HERE!
I LOVE YOU, DARLING.
MAYBE EVERYTHING WILL BE OKAY...
The End

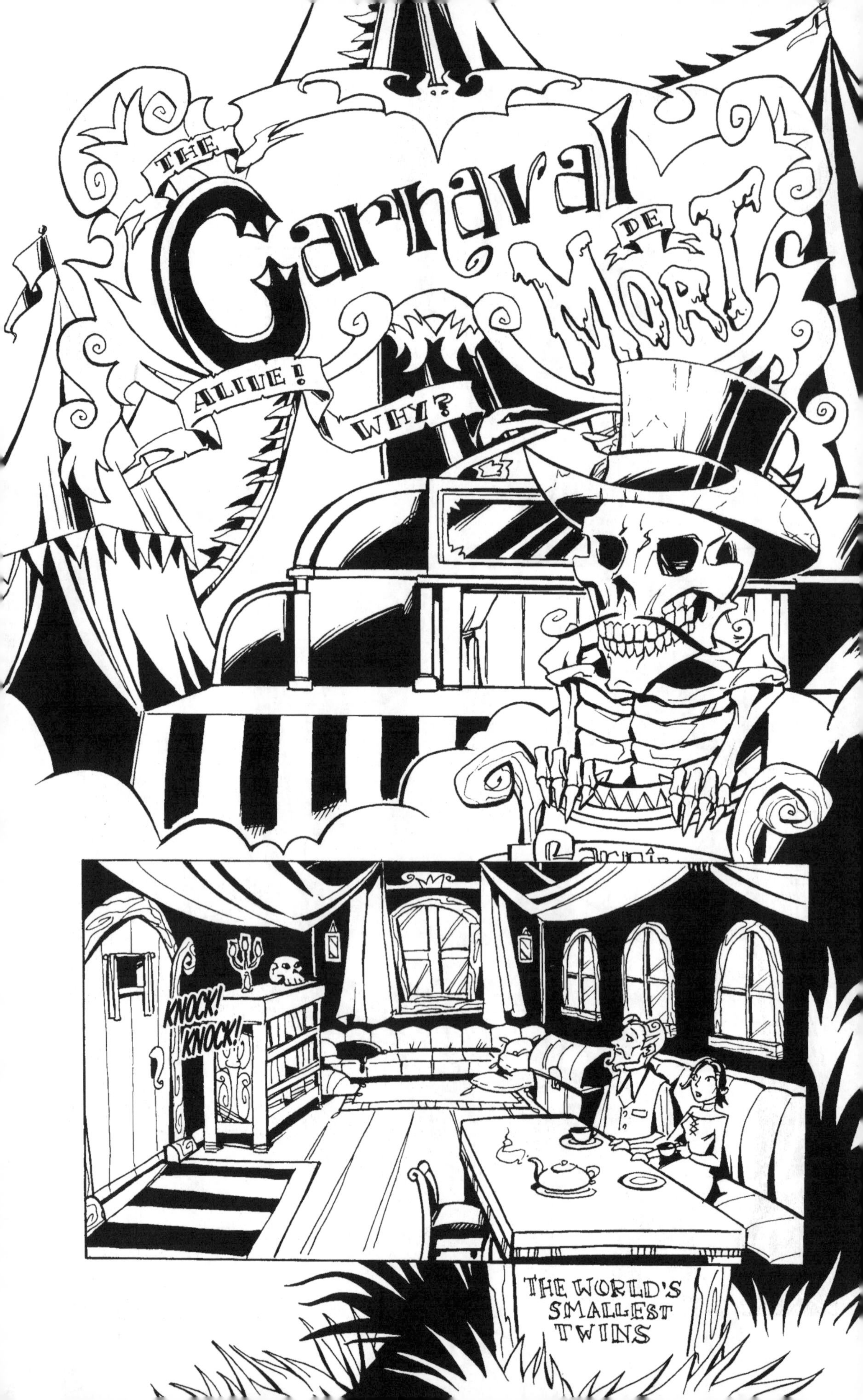
THE
Carnaval
DE
MORT
ALIVE!
WHY?
KNOCK!
KNOCK!
THE WORLD'S SMALLEST TWINS

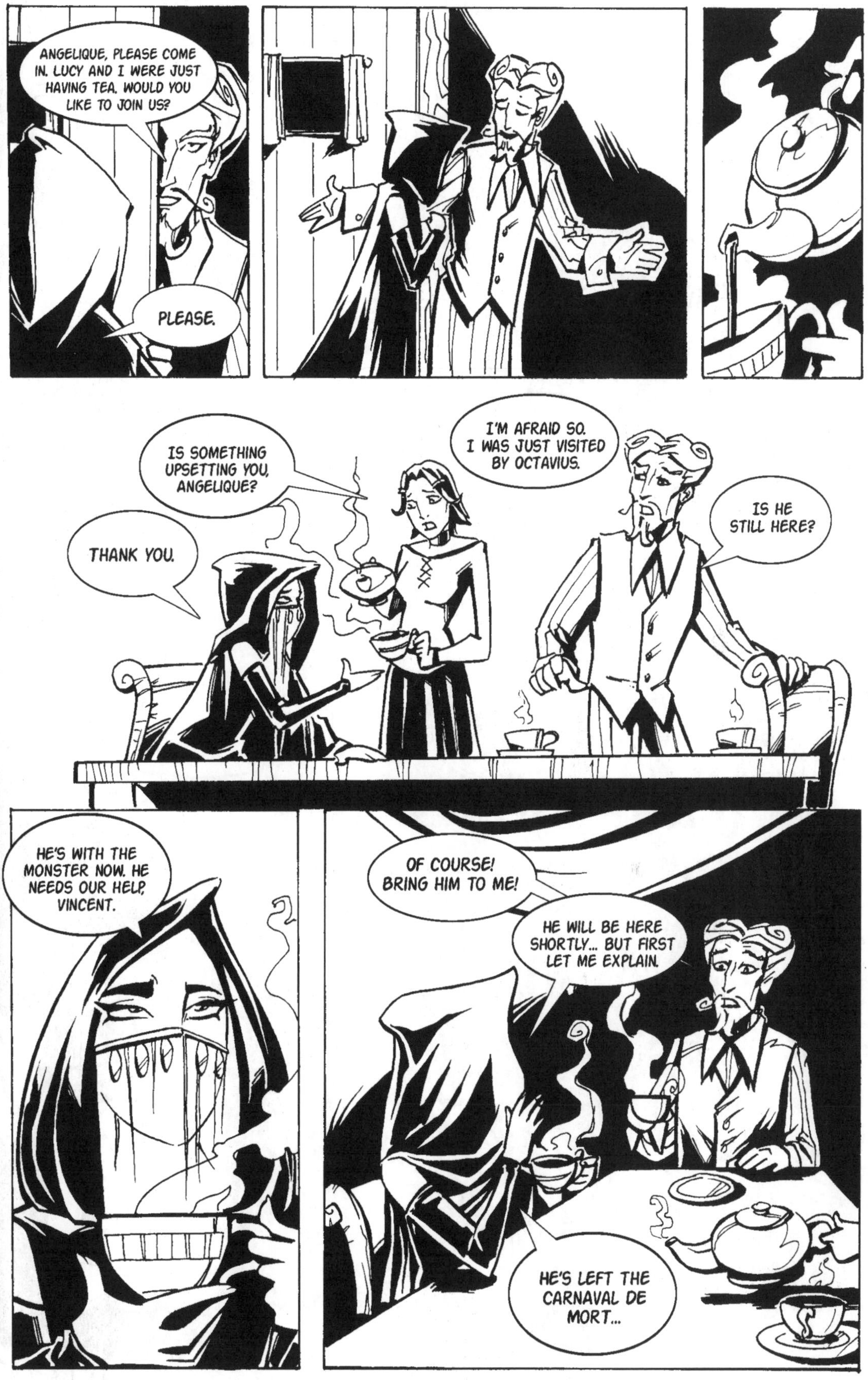
ANGELIQUE, PLEASE COME IN. LUCY AND I WERE JUST HAVING TEA. WOULD YOU LIKE TO JOIN US?
PLEASE.
THANK YOU.
IS SOMETHING UPSETTING YOU, ANGELIQUE?
I'M AFRAID SO. I WAS JUST VISITED BY OCTAVIUS.
IS HE STILL HERE?
HE'S WITH THE MONSTER NOW. HE NEEDS OUR HELP, VINCENT.
OF COURSE! BRING HIM TO ME!
HE WILL BE HERE SHORTLY... BUT FIRST LET ME EXPLAIN.
HE'S LEFT THE CARNAVAL DE MORT...

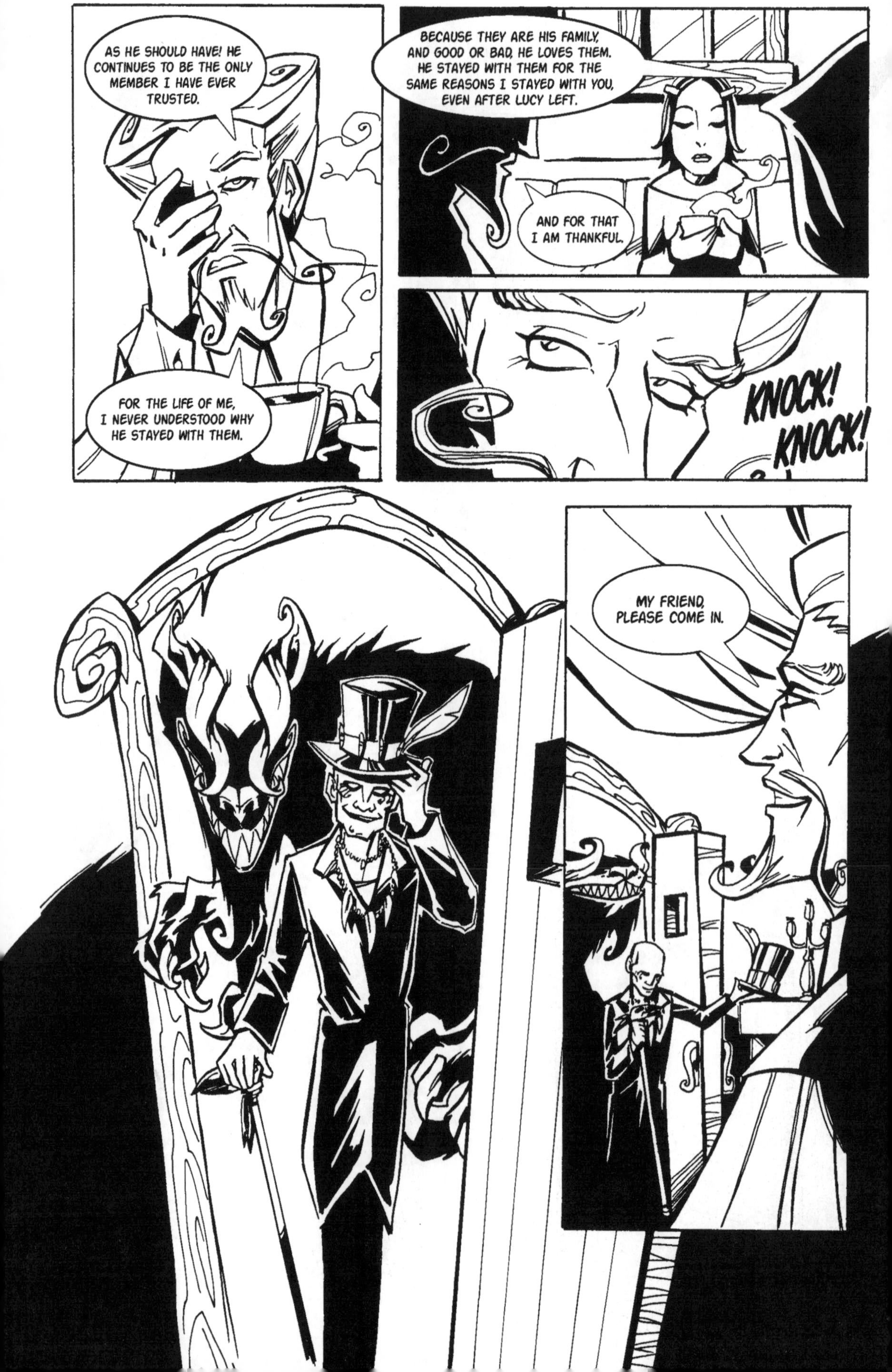
AS HE SHOULD HAVE! HE CONTINUES TO BE THE ONLY MEMBER I HAVE EVER TRUSTED.
FOR THE LIFE OF ME, I NEVER UNDERSTOOD WHY HE STAYED WITH THEM.
BECAUSE THEY ARE HIS FAMILY, AND GOOD OR BAD, HE LOVES THEM. HE STAYED WITH THEM FOR THE SAME REASONS I STAYED WITH YOU, EVEN AFTER LUCY LEFT.
AND FOR THAT I AM THANKFUL.
KNOCK! KNOCK!
MY FRIEND, PLEASE COME IN.

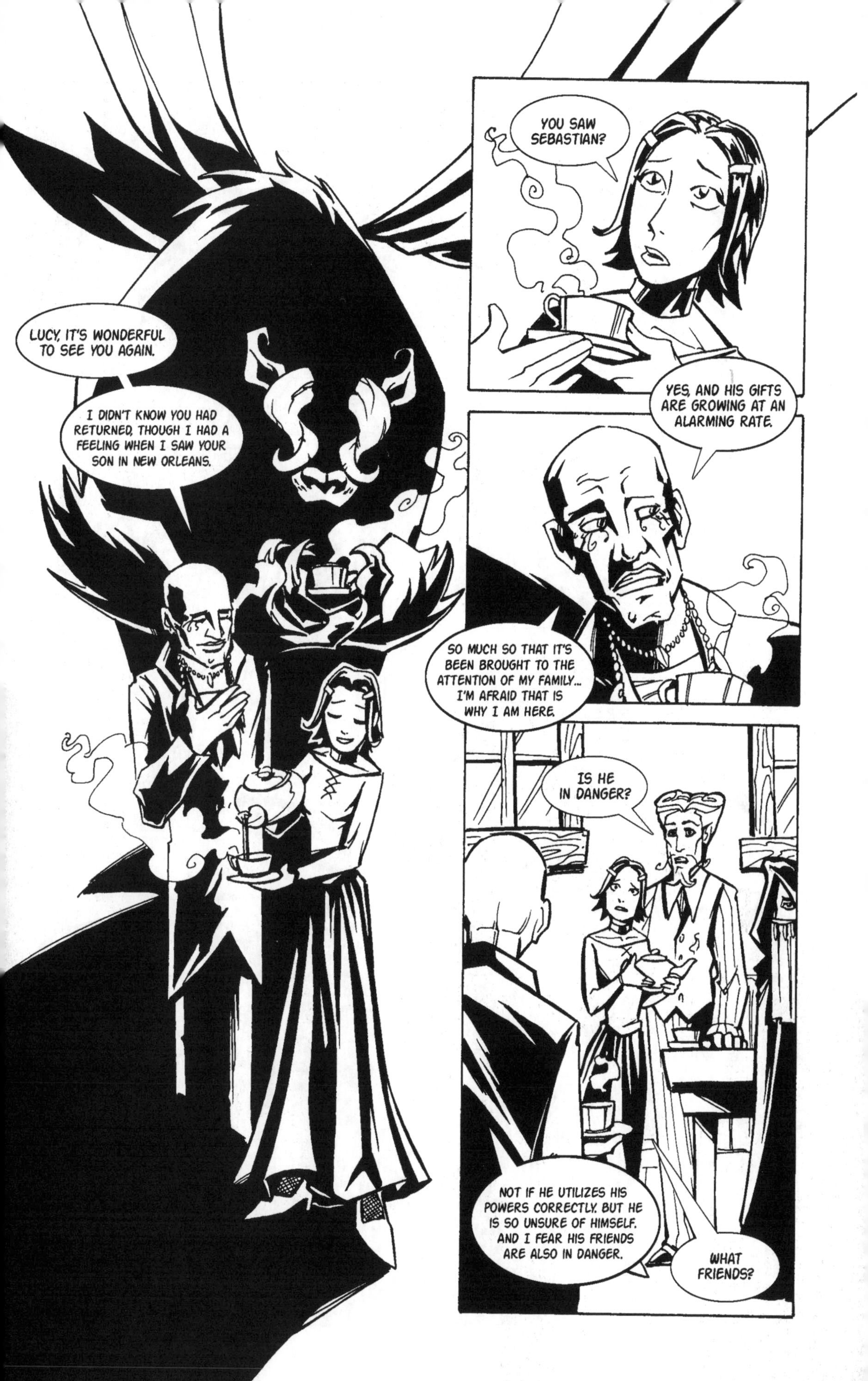
LUCY, IT'S WONDERFUL TO SEE YOU AGAIN.
I DIDN'T KNOW YOU HAD RETURNED, THOUGH I HAD A FEELING WHEN I SAW YOUR SON IN NEW ORLEANS.
YOU SAW SEBASTIAN?
YES, AND HIS GIFTS ARE GROWING AT AN ALARMING RATE.
SO MUCH SO THAT IT'S BEEN BROUGHT TO THE ATTENTION OF MY FAMILY... I'M AFRAID THAT IS WHY I AM HERE.
IS HE IN DANGER?
NOT IF HE UTILIZES HIS POWERS CORRECTLY. BUT HE IS SO UNSURE OF HIMSELF. AND I FEAR HIS FRIENDS ARE ALSO IN DANGER.
WHAT FRIENDS?

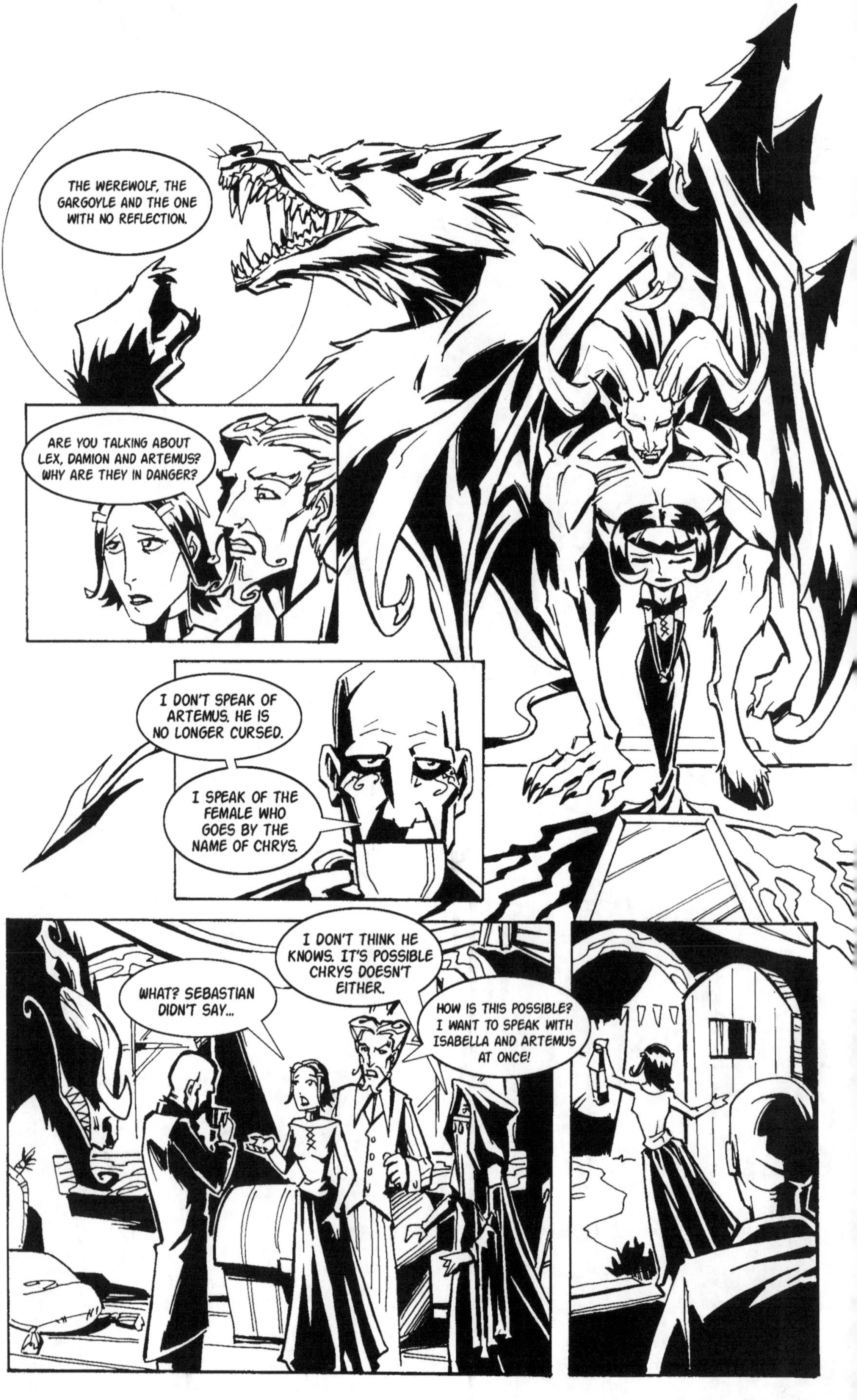
THE WEREWOLF, THE GARGOYLE AND THE ONE WITH NO REFLECTION.
ARE YOU TALKING ABOUT LEX, DAMION AND ARTEMUS? WHY ARE THEY IN DANGER?
I DON'T SPEAK OF ARTEMUS. HE IS NO LONGER CURSED.
I SPEAK OF THE FEMALE WHO GOES BY THE NAME OF CHRYS.
WHAT? SEBASTIAN DIDN'T SAY...
I DON'T THINK HE KNOWS. IT'S POSSIBLE CHRYS DOESN'T EITHER.
HOW IS THIS POSSIBLE? I WANT TO SPEAK WITH ISABELLA AND ARTEMUS AT ONCE!

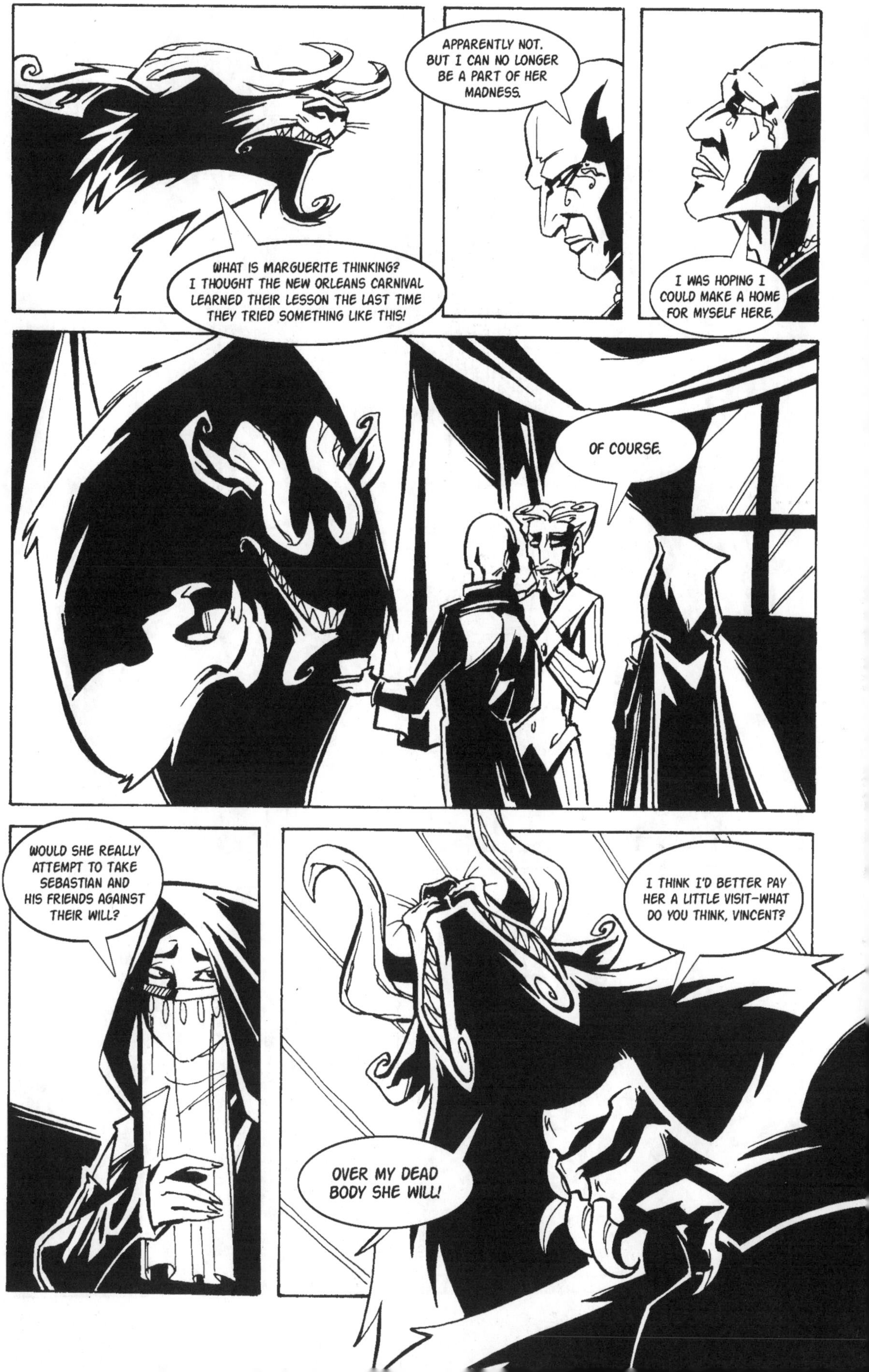
WHAT IS MARGUERITE THINKING? I THOUGHT THE NEW ORLEANS CARNIVAL LEARNED THEIR LESSON THE LAST TIME THEY TRIED SOMETHING LIKE THIS!
APPARENTLY NOT. BUT I CAN NO LONGER BE A PART OF HER MADNESS.
I WAS HOPING I COULD MAKE A HOME FOR MYSELF HERE.
OF COURSE.
WOULD SHE REALLY ATTEMPT TO TAKE SEBASTIAN AND HIS FRIENDS AGAINST THEIR WILL?
I THINK I'D BETTER PAY HER A LITTLE VISIT—WHAT DO YOU THINK, VINCENT?
OVER MY DEAD BODY SHE WILL!

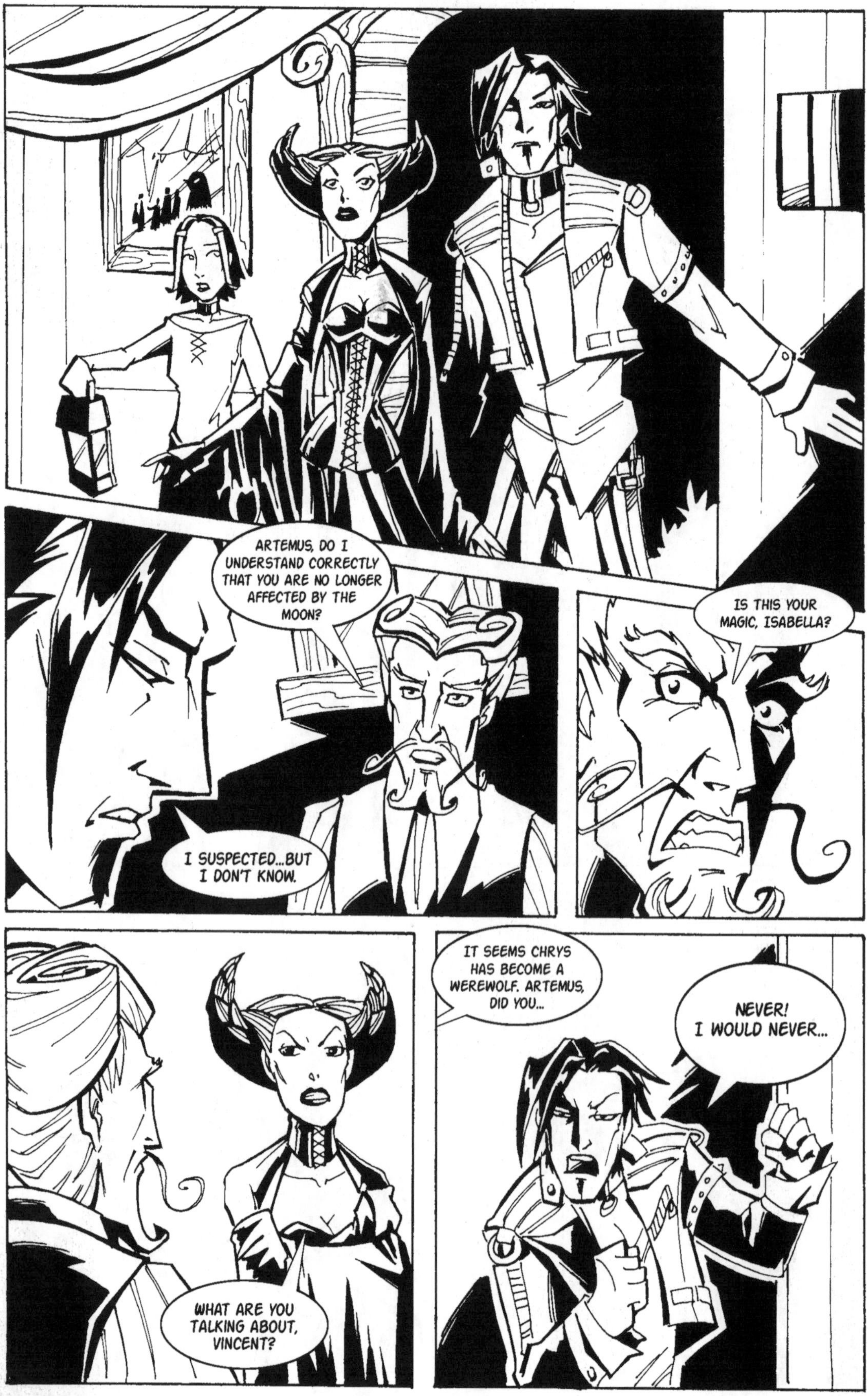
ARTEMUS, DO I UNDERSTAND CORRECTLY THAT YOU ARE NO LONGER AFFECTED BY THE MOON?
I SUSPECTED...BUT I DON'T KNOW.
IS THIS YOUR MAGIC, ISABELLA?
WHAT ARE YOU TALKING ABOUT, VINCENT?
IT SEEMS CHRYS HAS BECOME A WEREWOLF. ARTEMUS, DID YOU...
NEVER! I WOULD NEVER...

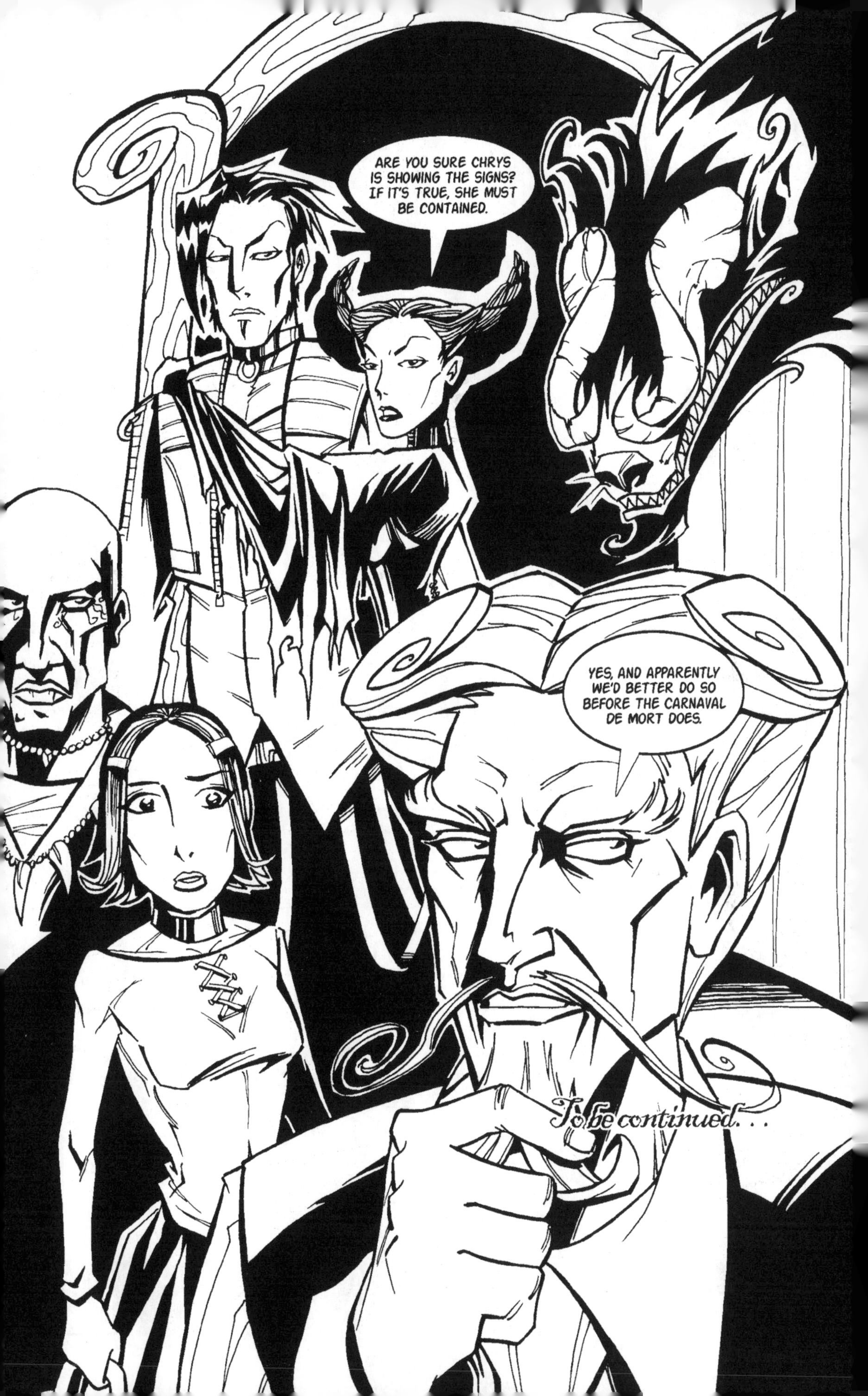
ARE YOU SURE CHRYS IS SHOWING THE SIGNS? IF IT'S TRUE, SHE MUST BE CONTAINED.
YES, AND APPARENTLY WE'D BETTER DO SO BEFORE THE CARNAVAL DE MORT DOES.
To be continued. . .

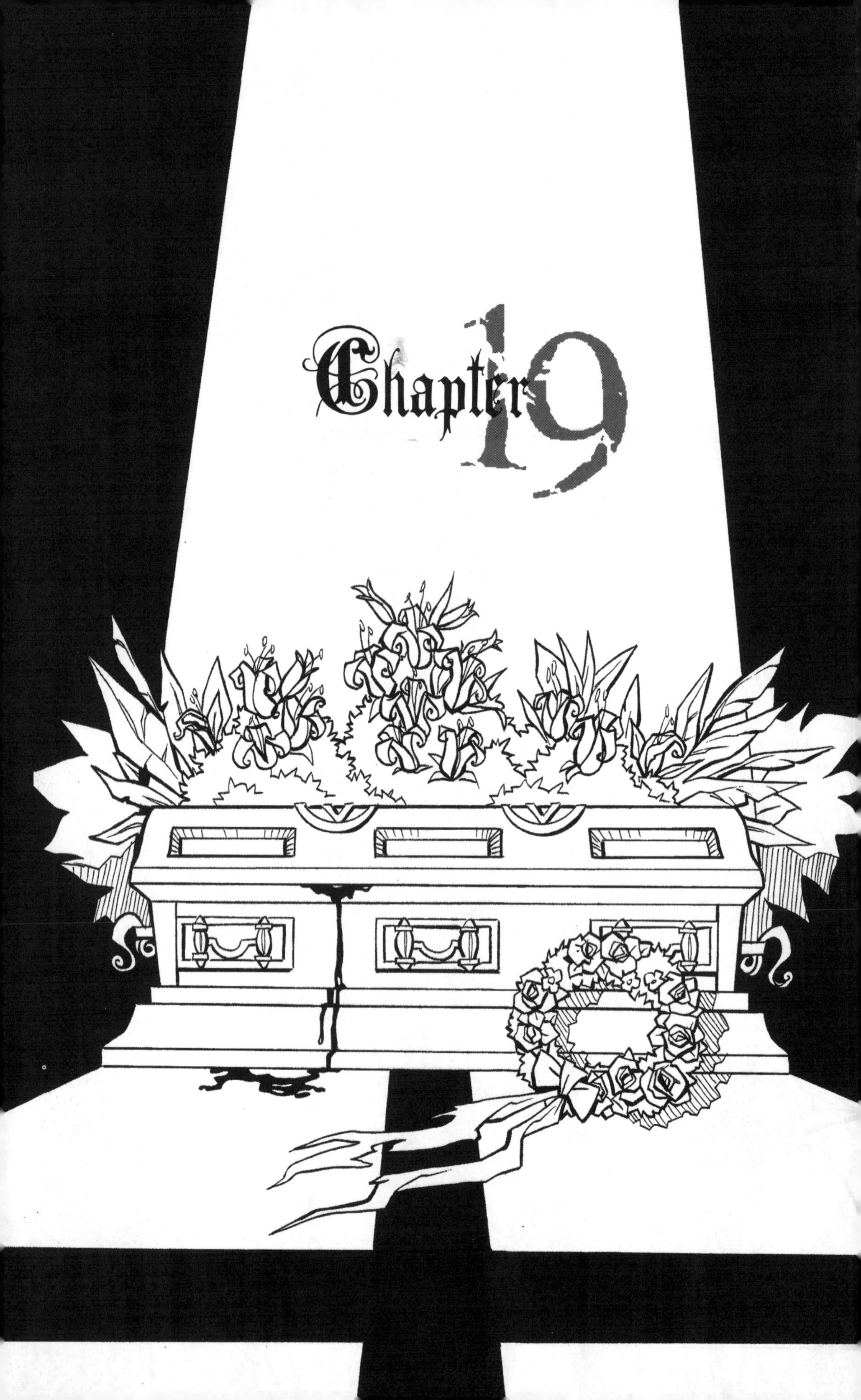
Chapter 19

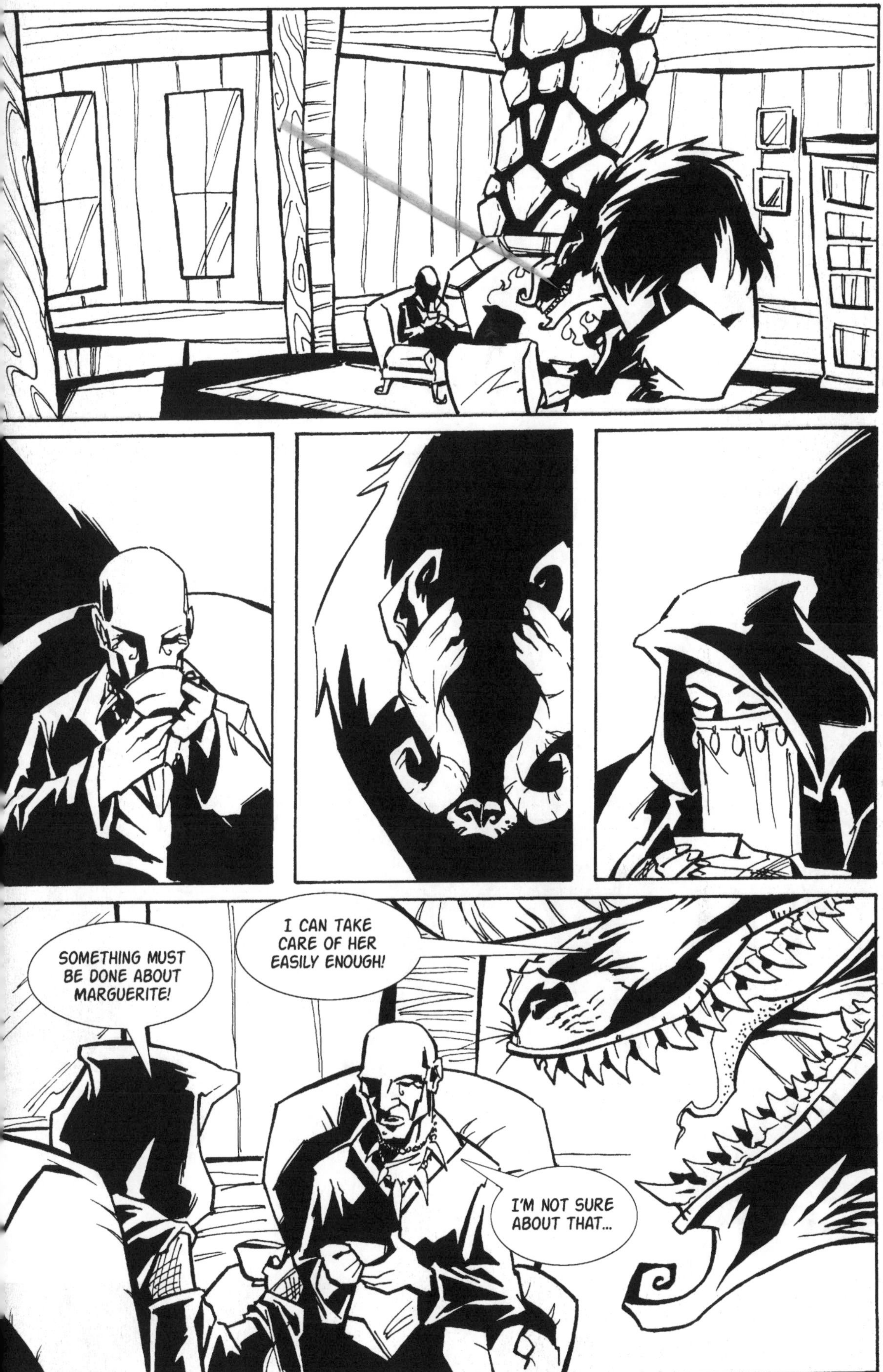
SOMETHING MUST BE DONE ABOUT MARGUERITE!
I CAN TAKE CARE OF HER EASILY ENOUGH!
I'M NOT SURE ABOUT THAT...

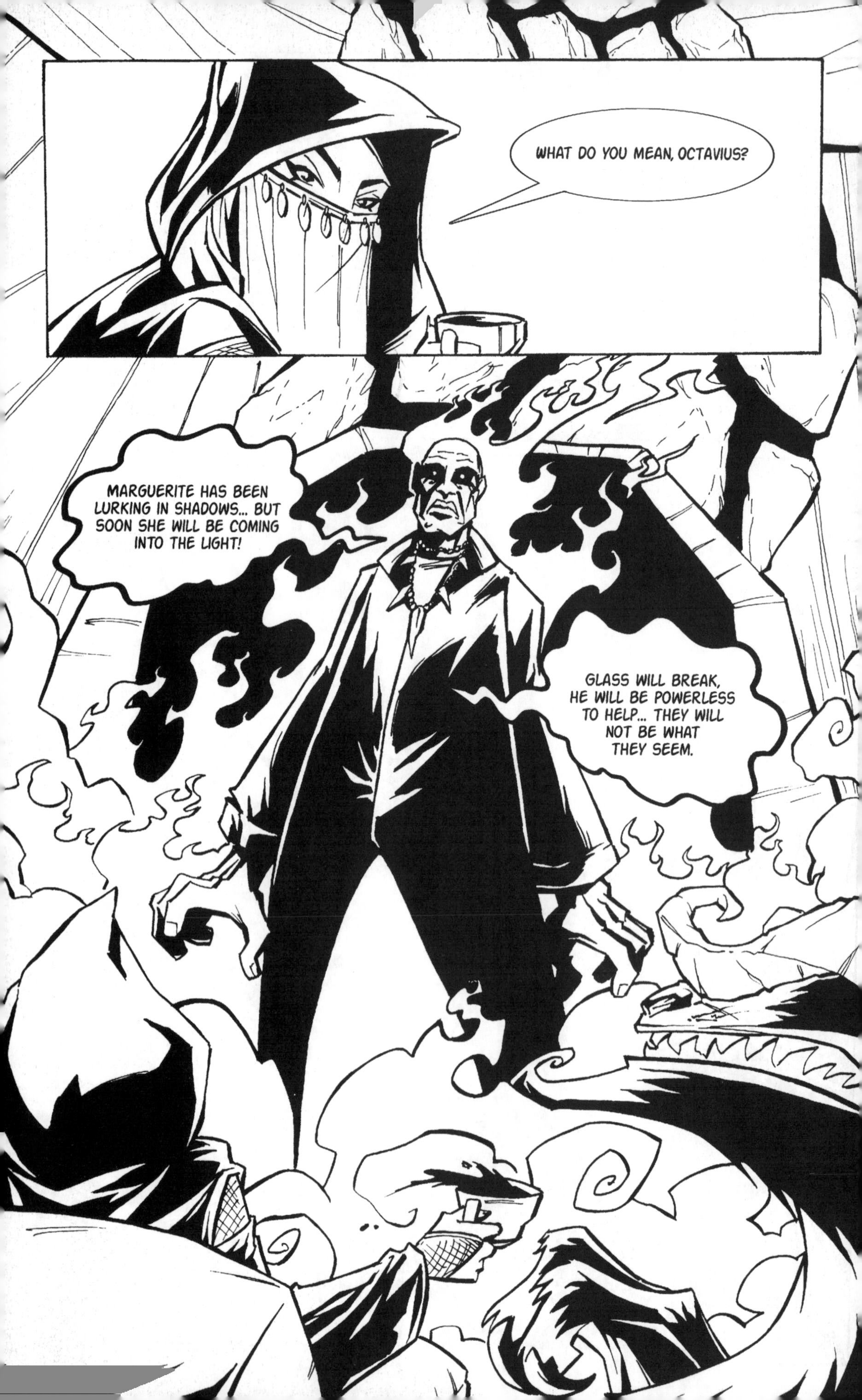
WHAT DO YOU MEAN, OCTAVIUS?
MARGUERITE HAS BEEN LURKING IN SHADOWS... BUT SOON SHE WILL BE COMING INTO THE LIGHT!
GLASS WILL BREAK, HE WILL BE POWERLESS TO HELP... THEY WILL NOT BE WHAT THEY SEEM.

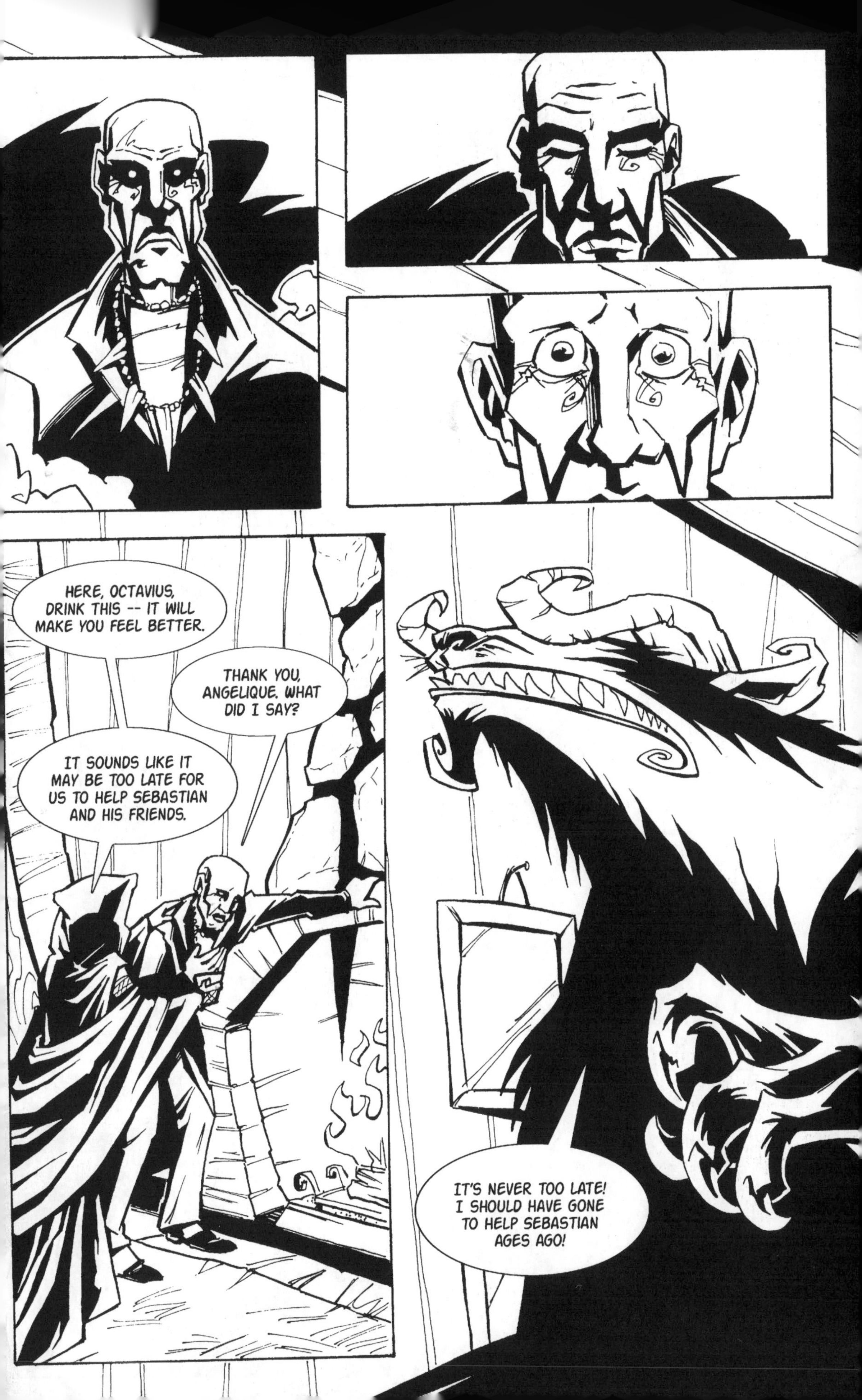
HERE, OCTAVIUS, DRINK THIS -- IT WILL MAKE YOU FEEL BETTER.
THANK YOU, ANGELIQUE. WHAT DID I SAY?
IT SOUNDS LIKE IT MAY BE TOO LATE FOR US TO HELP SEBASTIAN AND HIS FRIENDS.
IT'S NEVER TOO LATE! I SHOULD HAVE GONE TO HELP SEBASTIAN AGES AGO!

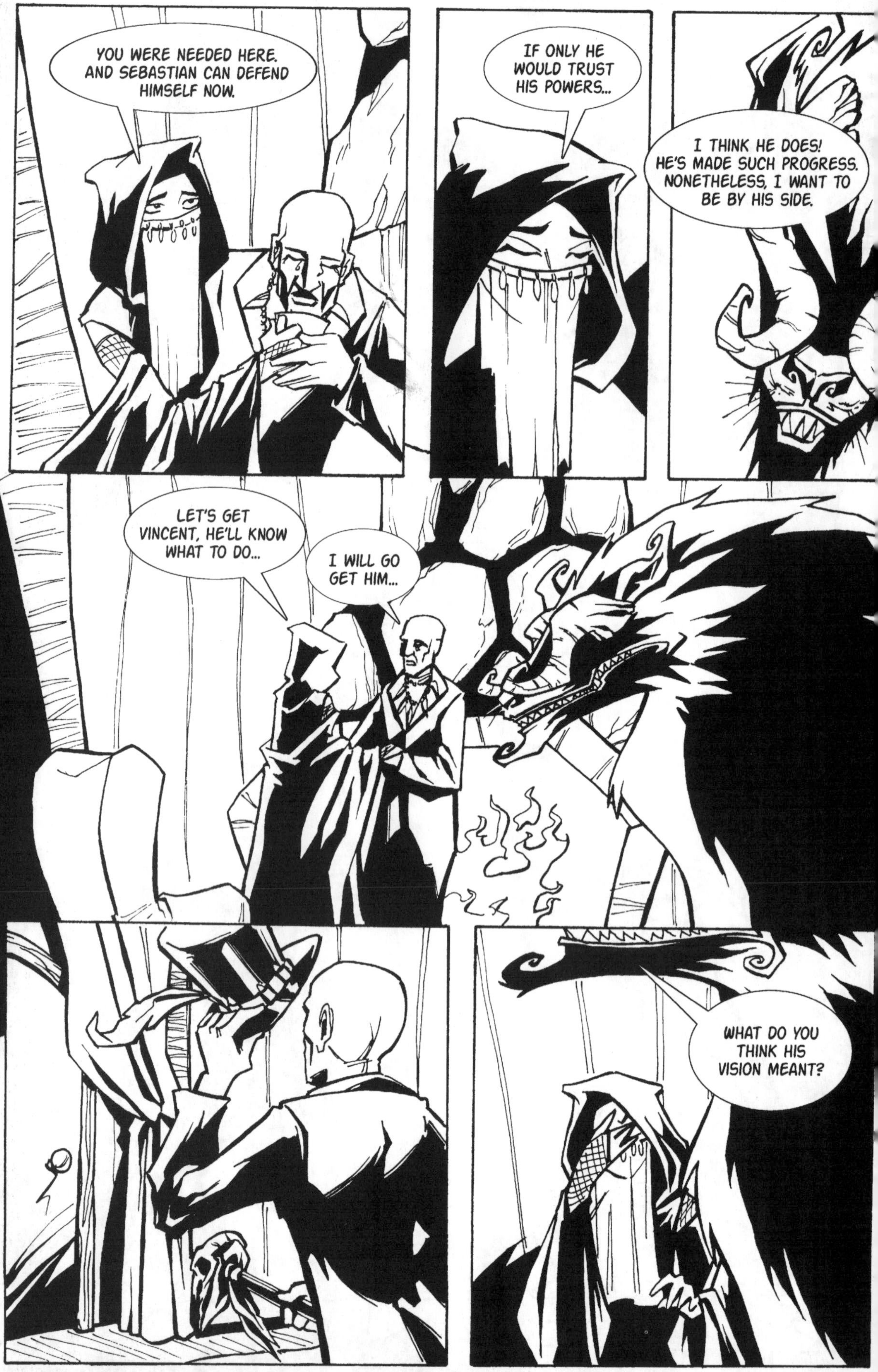
YOU WERE NEEDED HERE. AND SEBASTIAN CAN DEFEND HIMSELF NOW.
IF ONLY HE WOULD TRUST HIS POWERS...
I THINK HE DOES! HE'S MADE SUCH PROGRESS. NONETHELESS, I WANT TO BE BY HIS SIDE.
LET'S GET VINCENT, HE'LL KNOW WHAT TO DO...
I WILL GO GET HIM...
WHAT DO YOU THINK HIS VISION MEANT?

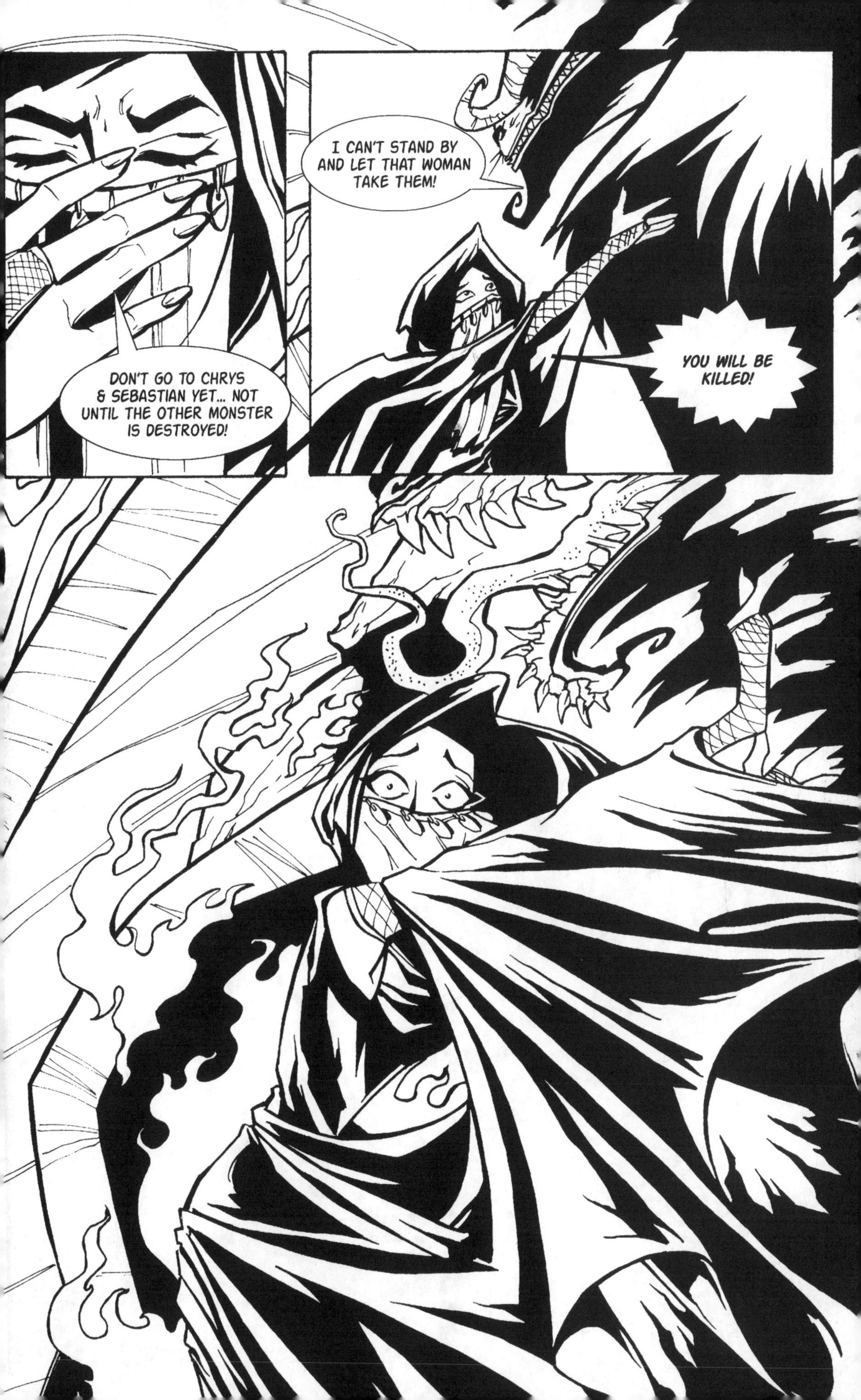
DON'T GO TO CHRYS & SEBASTIAN YET... NOT UNTIL THE OTHER MONSTER IS DESTROYED!
I CAN'T STAND BY AND LET THAT WOMAN TAKE THEM!
YOU WILL BE KILLED!

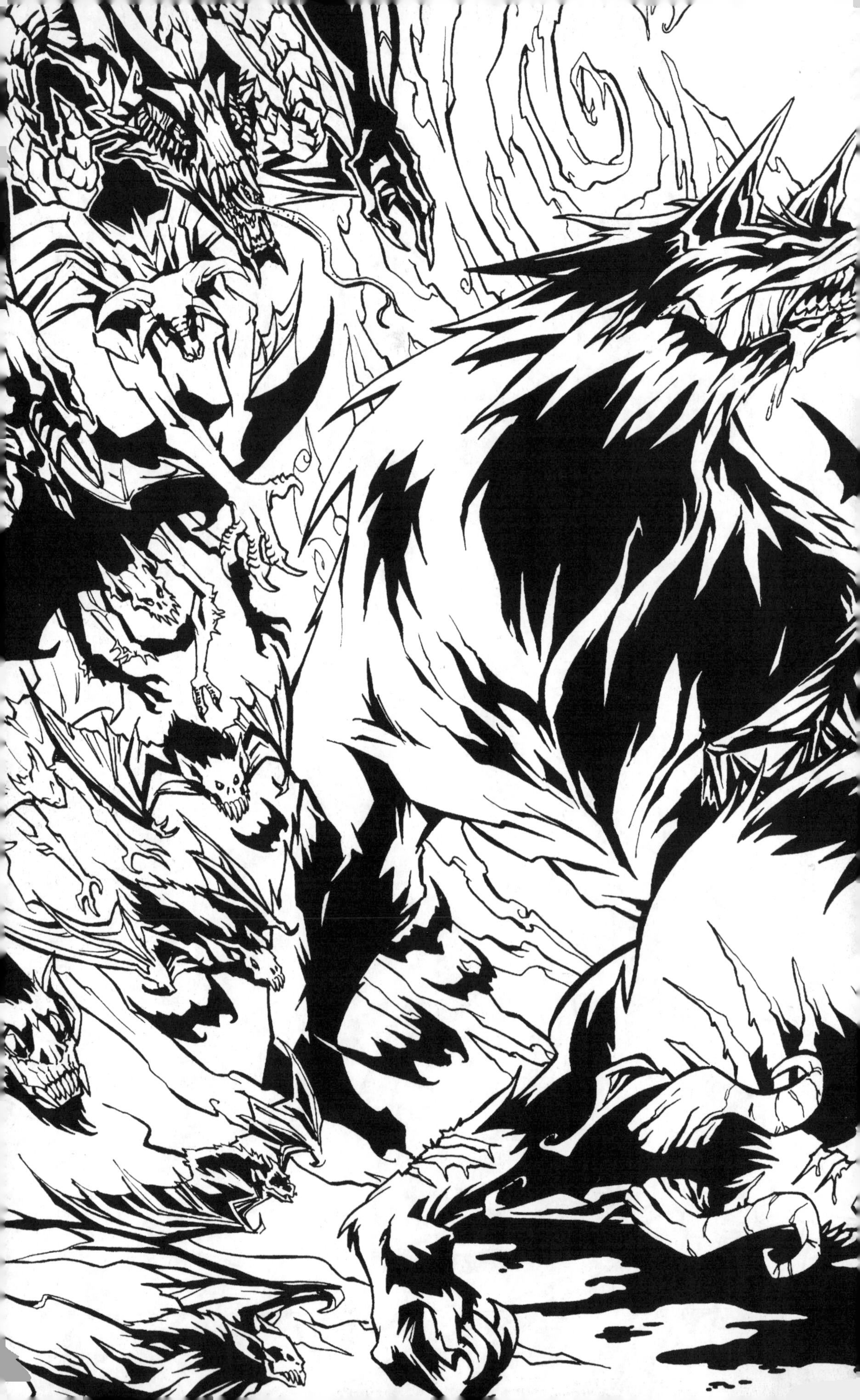

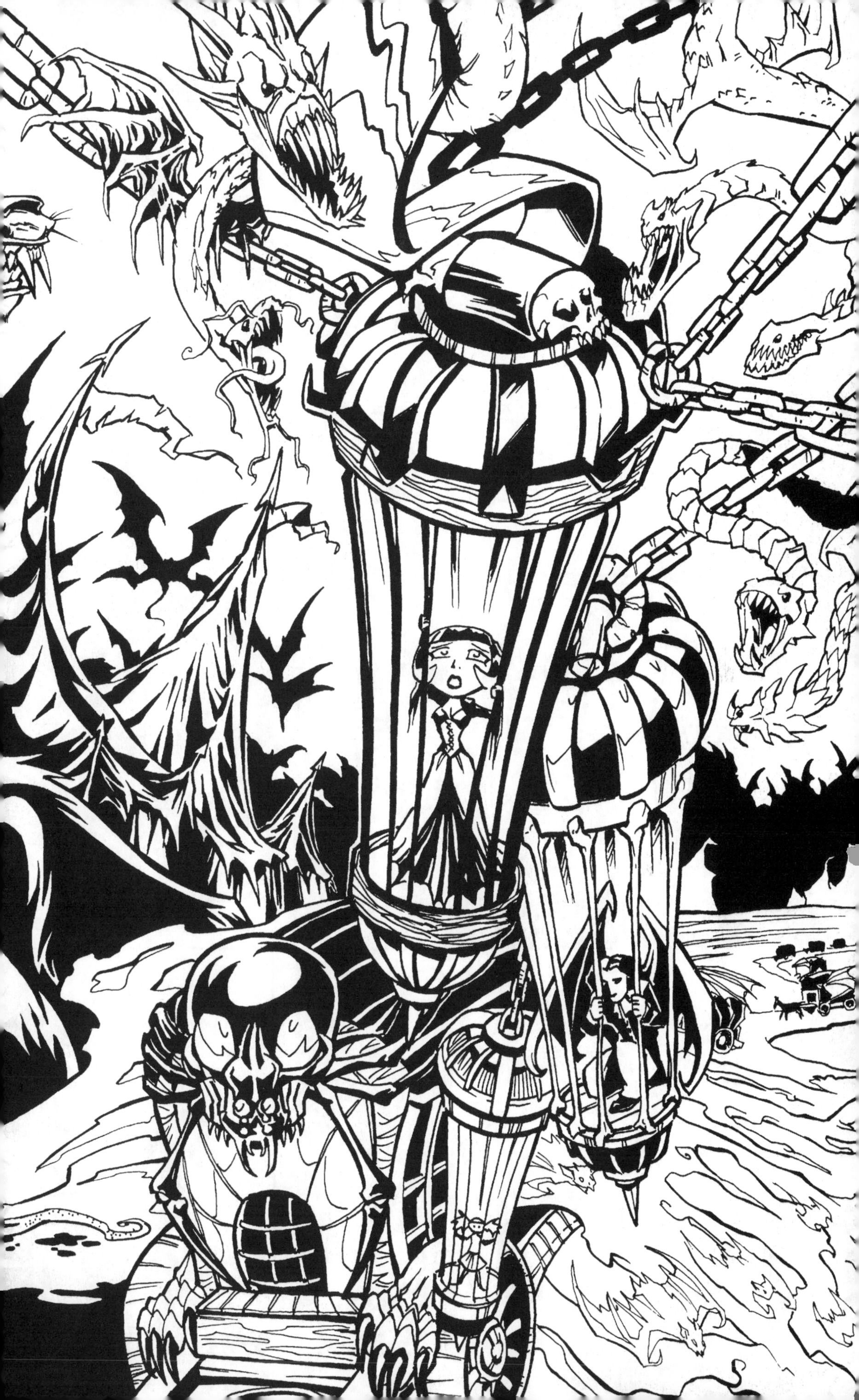

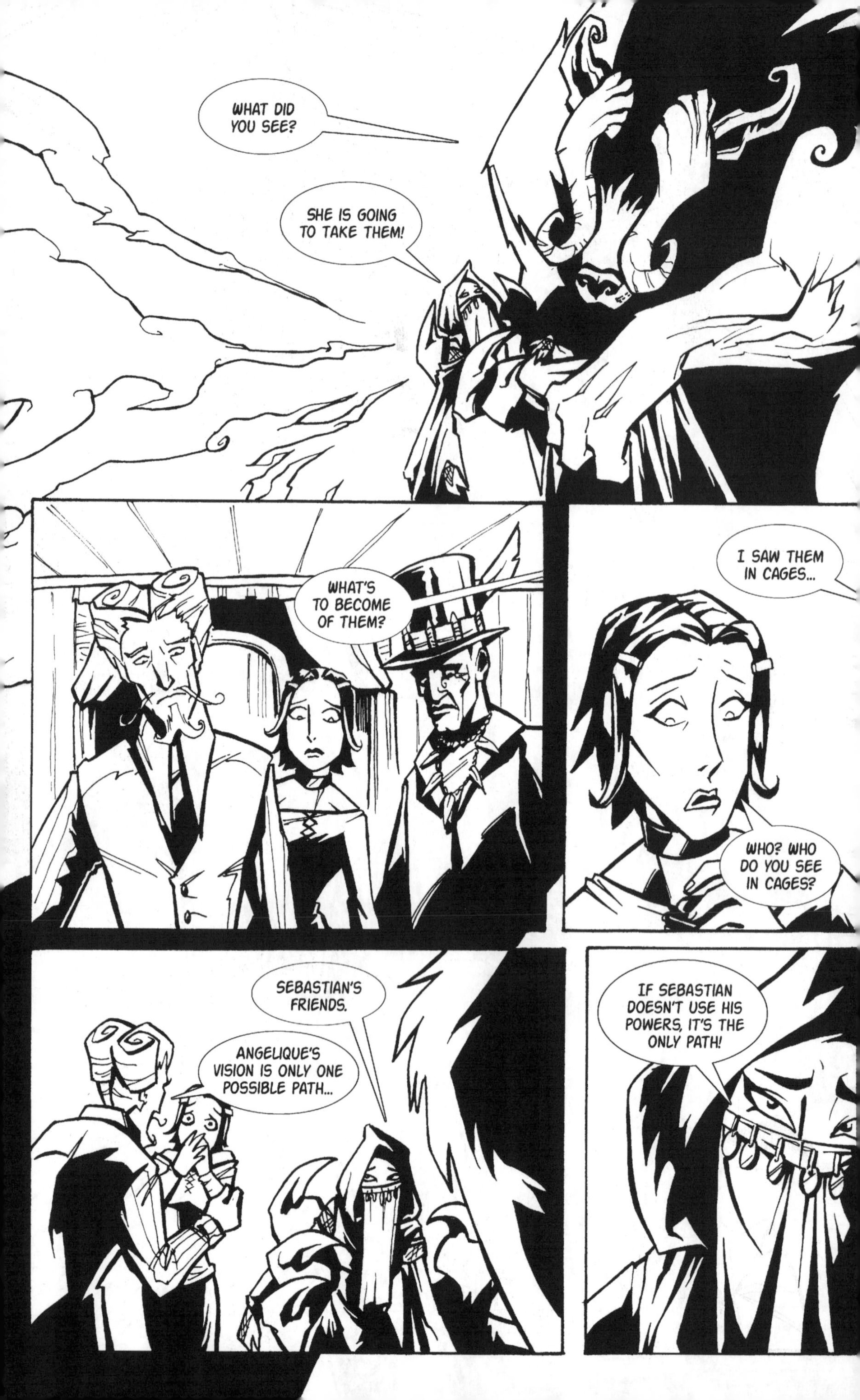
WHAT DID YOU SEE?
SHE IS GOING TO TAKE THEM!
WHAT'S TO BECOME OF THEM?
I SAW THEM IN CAGES...
WHO? WHO DO YOU SEE IN CAGES?
SEBASTIAN'S FRIENDS.
ANGELIQUE'S VISION IS ONLY ONE POSSIBLE PATH...
IF SEBASTIAN DOESN'T USE HIS POWERS, IT'S THE ONLY PATH!

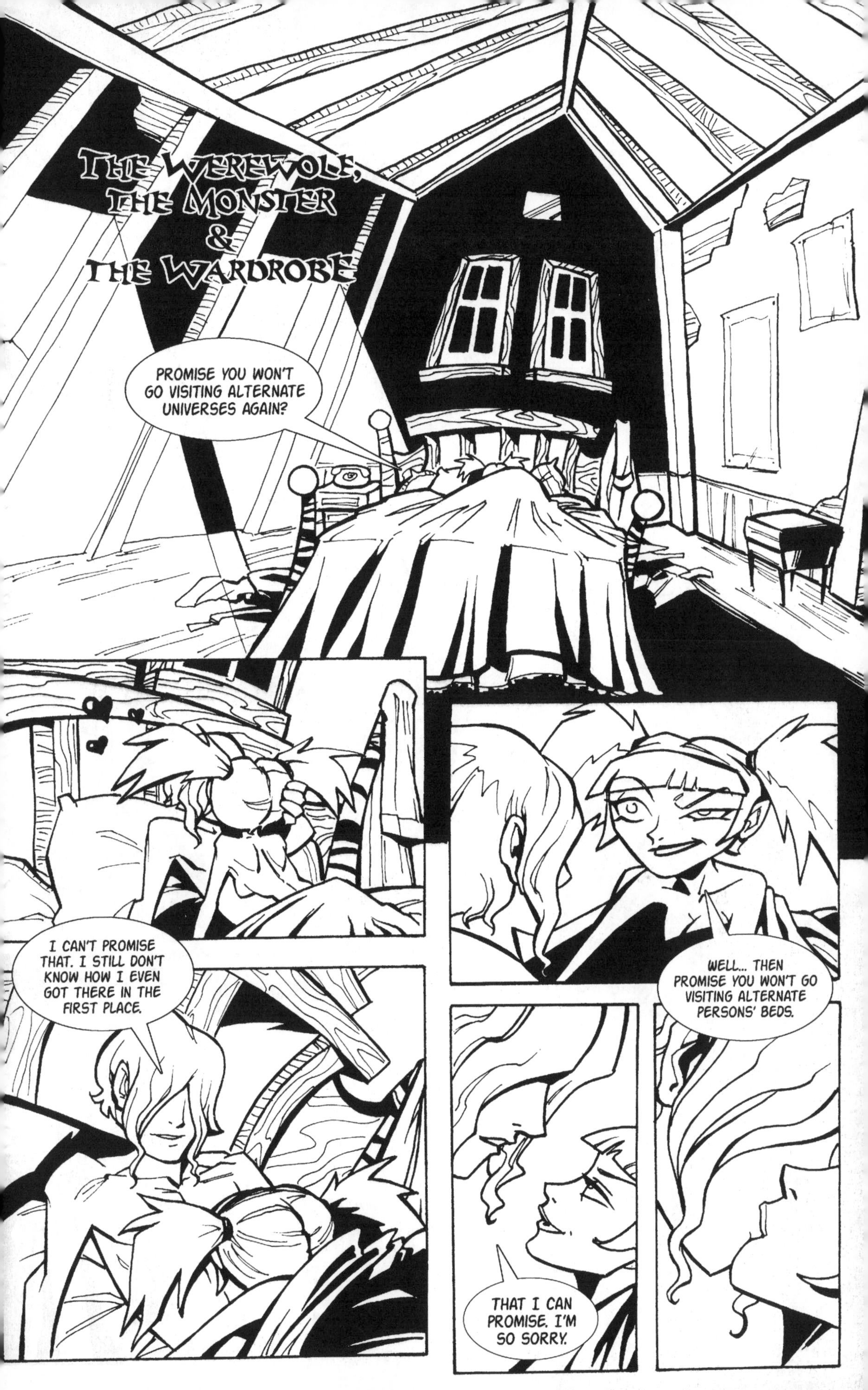
THE WEREWOLF, THE MONSTER & THE WARDROBE
PROMISE YOU WON'T GO VISITING ALTERNATE UNIVERSES AGAIN?
I CAN'T PROMISE THAT. I STILL DON'T KNOW HOW I EVEN GOT THERE IN THE FIRST PLACE.
WELL... THEN PROMISE YOU WON'T GO VISITING ALTERNATE PERSONS' BEDS.
THAT I CAN PROMISE. I'M SO SORRY.

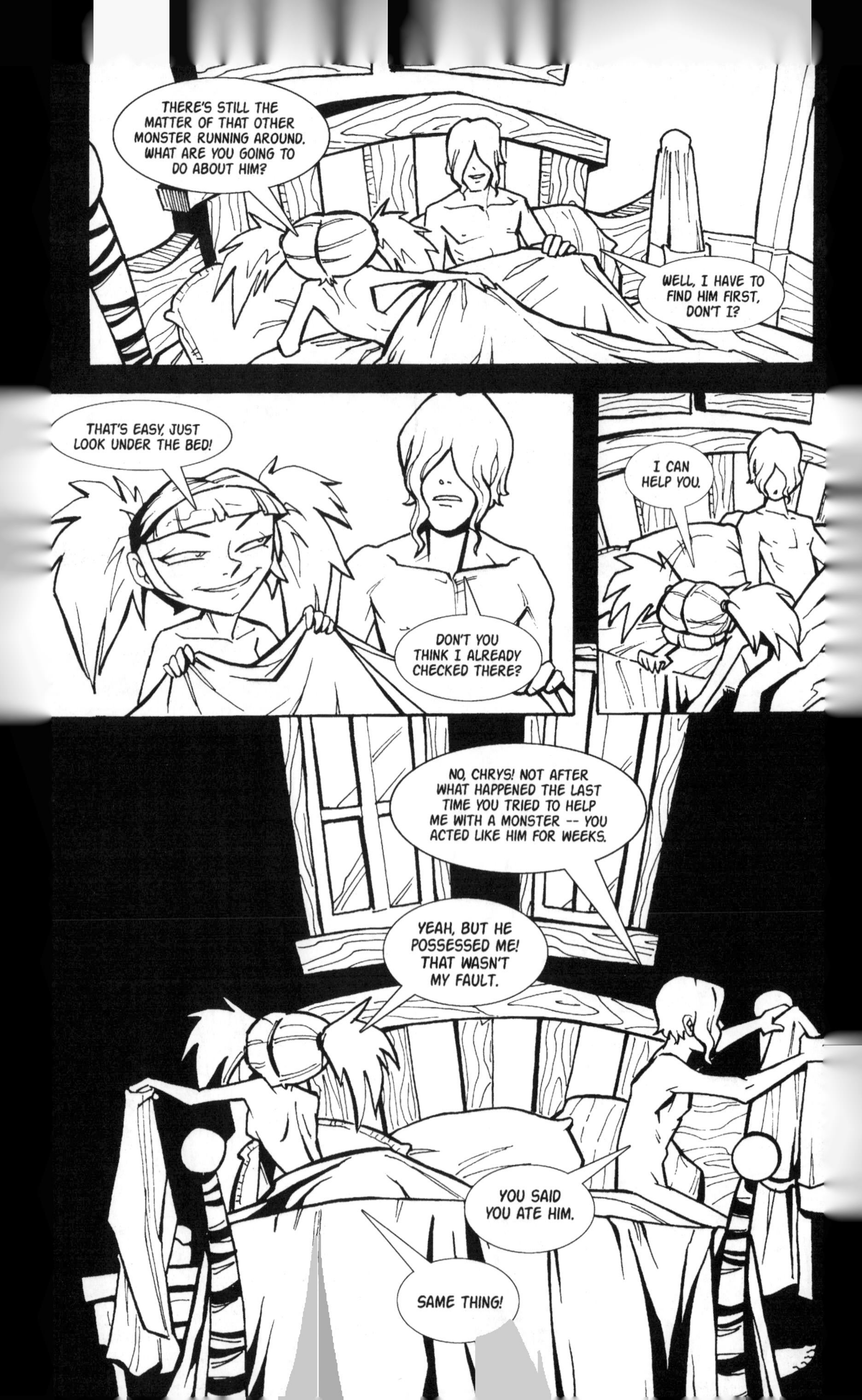
THERE'S STILL THE MATTER OF THAT OTHER MONSTER RUNNING AROUND. WHAT ARE YOU GOING TO DO ABOUT HIM?
WELL, I HAVE TO FIND HIM FIRST, DON'T I?
THAT'S EASY, JUST LOOK UNDER THE BED!
DON'T YOU THINK I ALREADY CHECKED THERE?
I CAN HELP YOU.
NO, CHRYS! NOT AFTER WHAT HAPPENED THE LAST TIME YOU TRIED TO HELP ME WITH A MONSTER -- YOU ACTED LIKE HIM FOR WEEKS.
YEAH, BUT HE POSSESSED ME! THAT WASN'T MY FAULT.
YOU SAID YOU ATE HIM.
SAME THING!

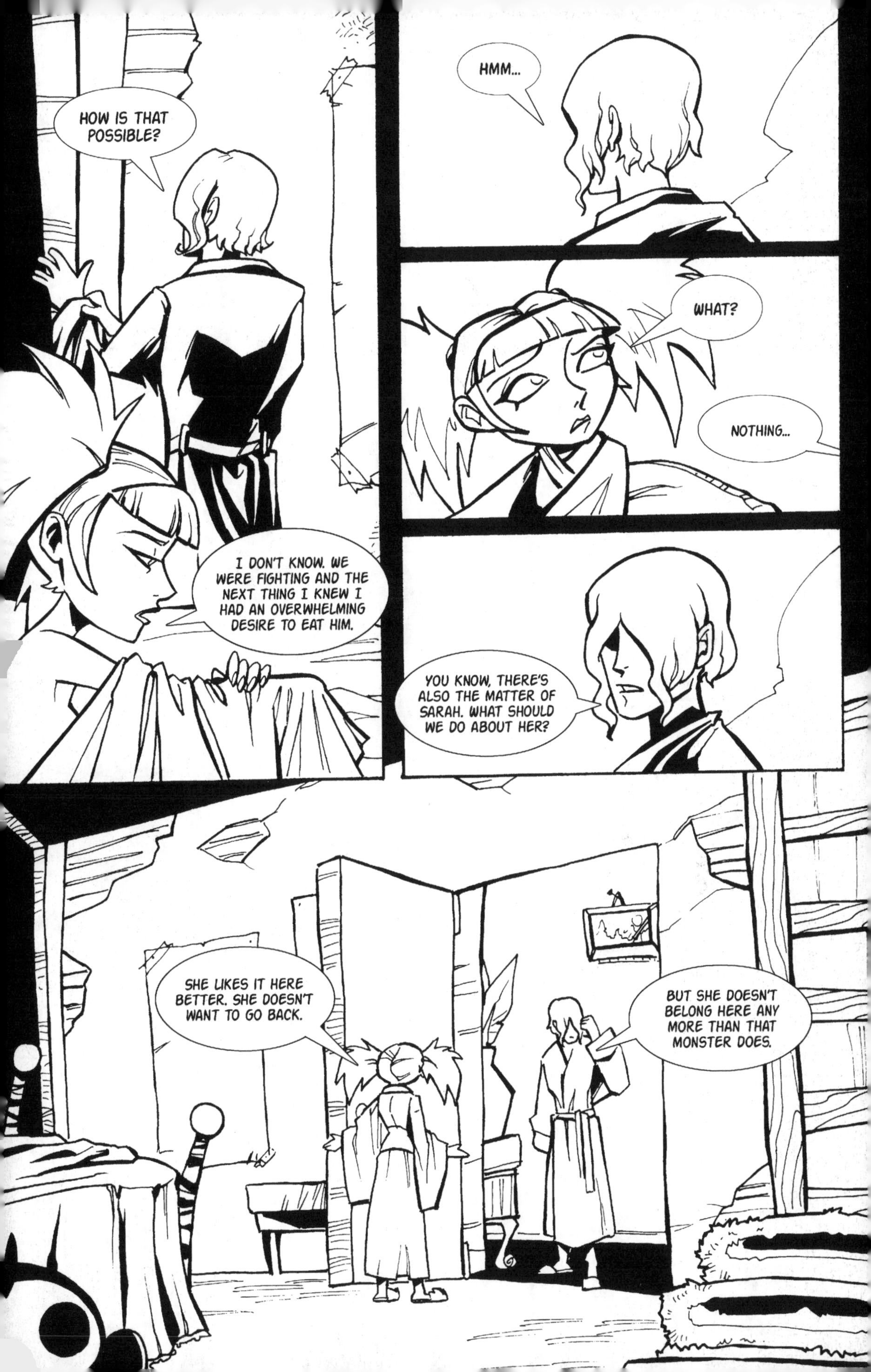
HOW IS THAT POSSIBLE?
HMM...
WHAT?
NOTHING...
I DON'T KNOW. WE WERE FIGHTING AND THE NEXT THING I KNEW I HAD AN OVERWHELMING DESIRE TO EAT HIM.
YOU KNOW, THERE'S ALSO THE MATTER OF SARAH. WHAT SHOULD WE DO ABOUT HER?
SHE LIKES IT HERE BETTER. SHE DOESN'T WANT TO GO BACK.
BUT SHE DOESN'T BELONG HERE ANY MORE THAN THAT MONSTER DOES.

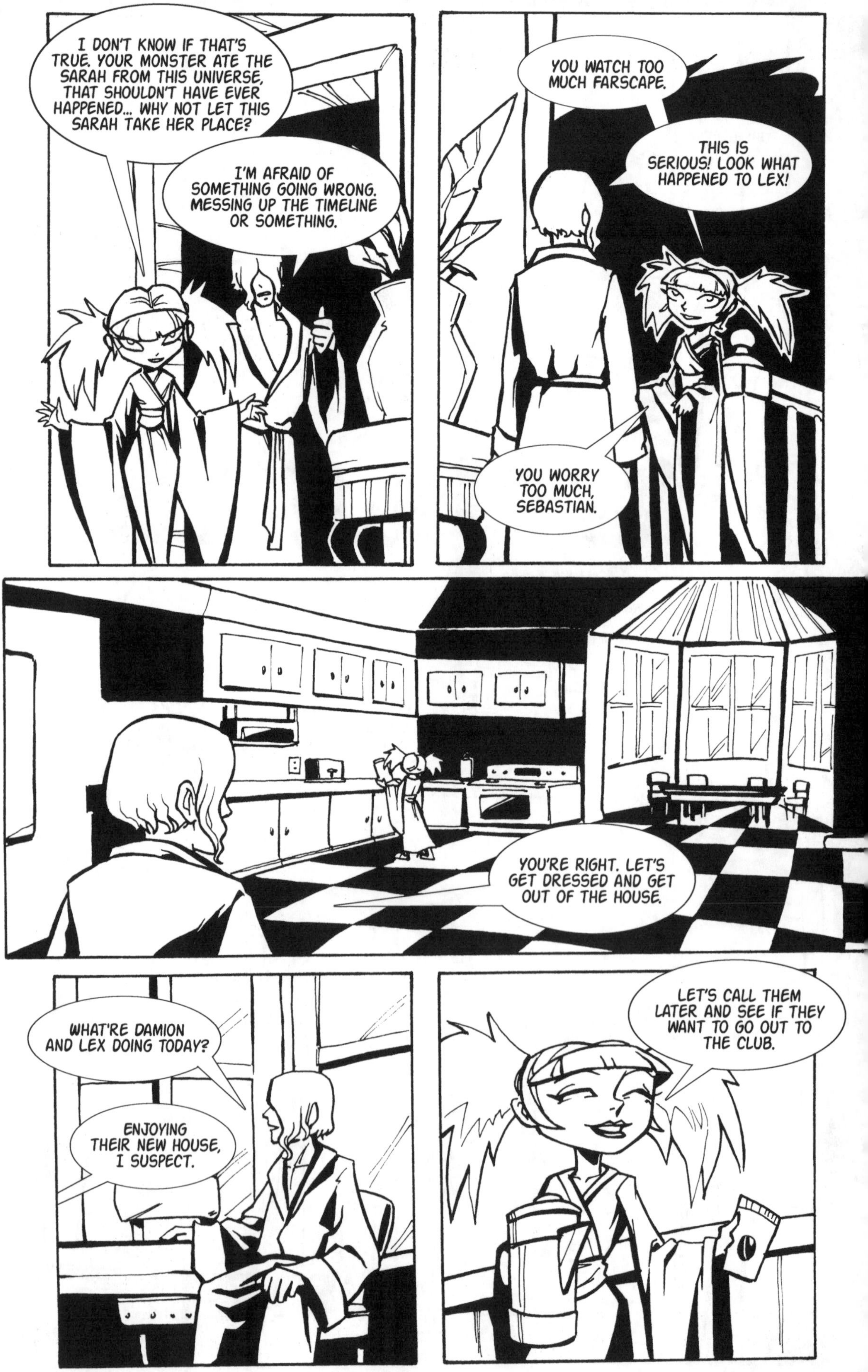
I DON'T KNOW IF THAT'S TRUE. YOUR MONSTER ATE THE SARAH FROM THIS UNIVERSE, THAT SHOULDN'T HAVE EVER HAPPENED... WHY NOT LET THIS SARAH TAKE HER PLACE?
I'M AFRAID OF SOMETHING GOING WRONG. MESSING UP THE TIMELINE OR SOMETHING.
YOU WATCH TOO MUCH FARSCAPE.
THIS IS SERIOUS! LOOK WHAT HAPPENED TO LEX!
YOU WORRY TOO MUCH, SEBASTIAN.
YOU'RE RIGHT. LET'S GET DRESSED AND GET OUT OF THE HOUSE.
WHAT'RE DAMION AND LEX DOING TODAY?
ENJOYING THEIR NEW HOUSE, I SUSPECT.
LET'S CALL THEM LATER AND SEE IF THEY WANT TO GO OUT TO THE CLUB.

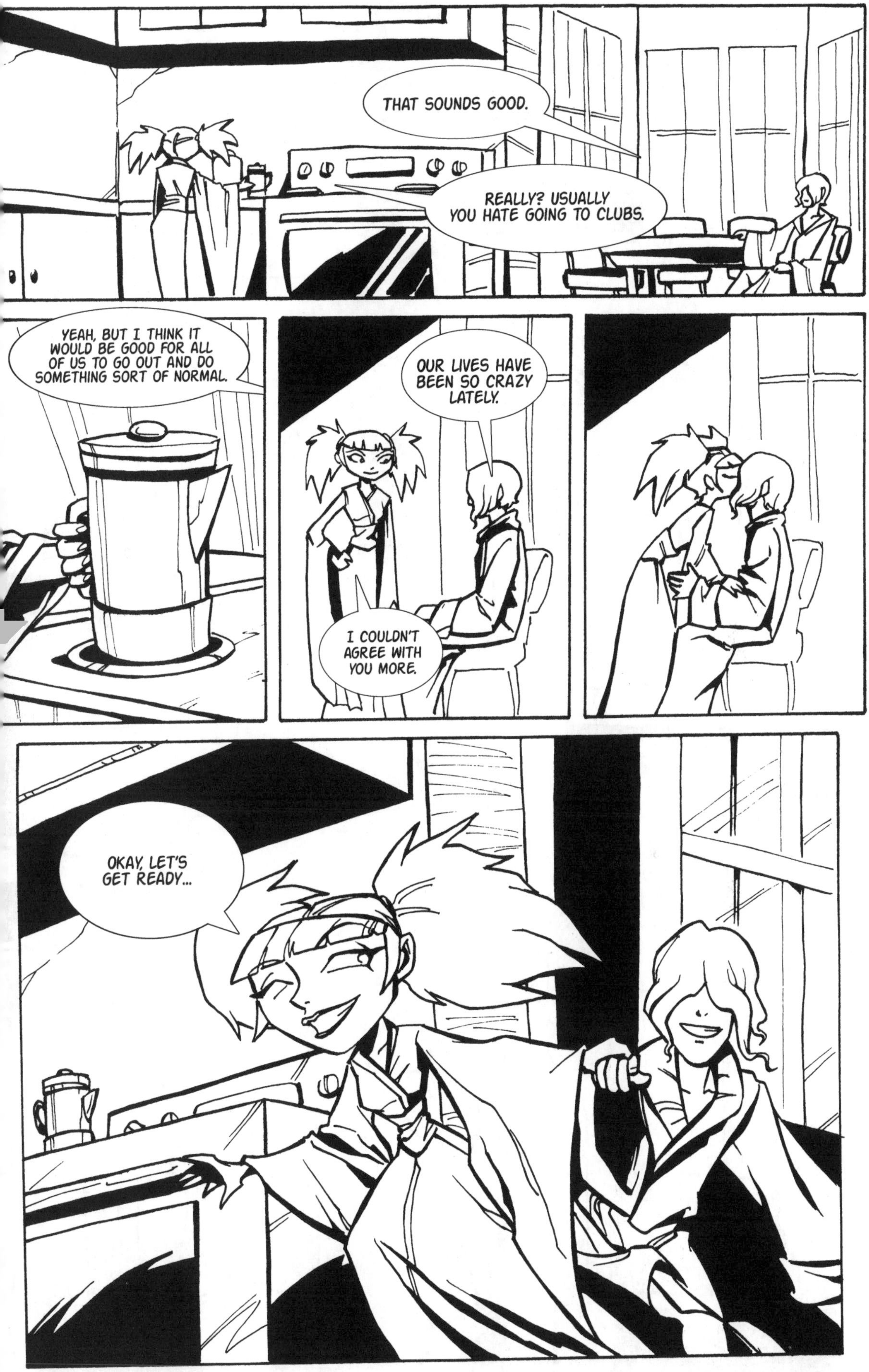
THAT SOUNDS GOOD.
REALLY? USUALLY YOU HATE GOING TO CLUBS.
YEAH, BUT I THINK IT WOULD BE GOOD FOR ALL OF US TO GO OUT AND DO SOMETHING SORT OF NORMAL.
OUR LIVES HAVE BEEN SO CRAZY LATELY.
I COULDN'T AGREE WITH YOU MORE.
OKAY, LET'S GET READY...

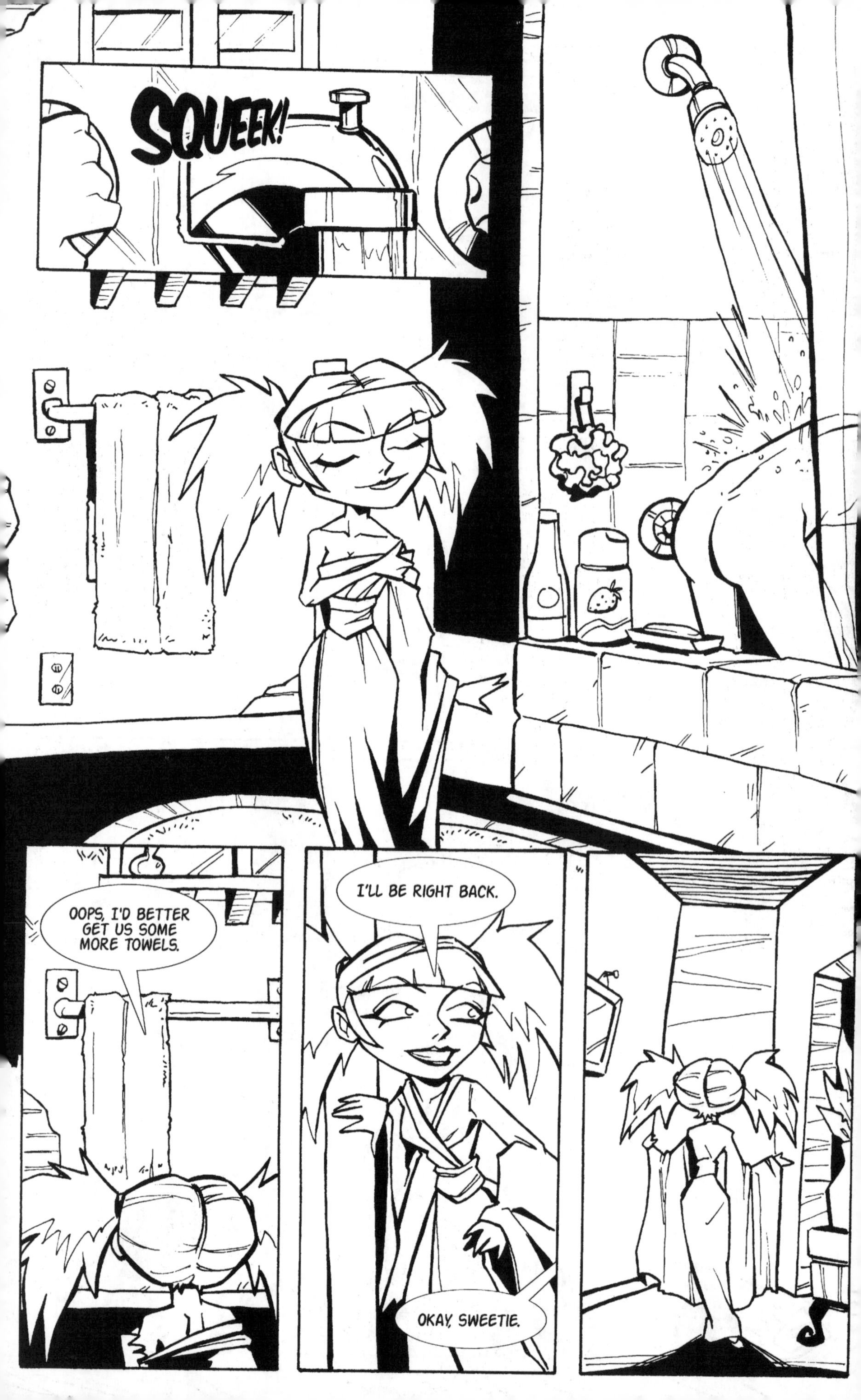
SQUEEK!
OOPS, I'D BETTER GET US SOME MORE TOWELS.
I'LL BE RIGHT BACK.
OKAY, SWEETIE.

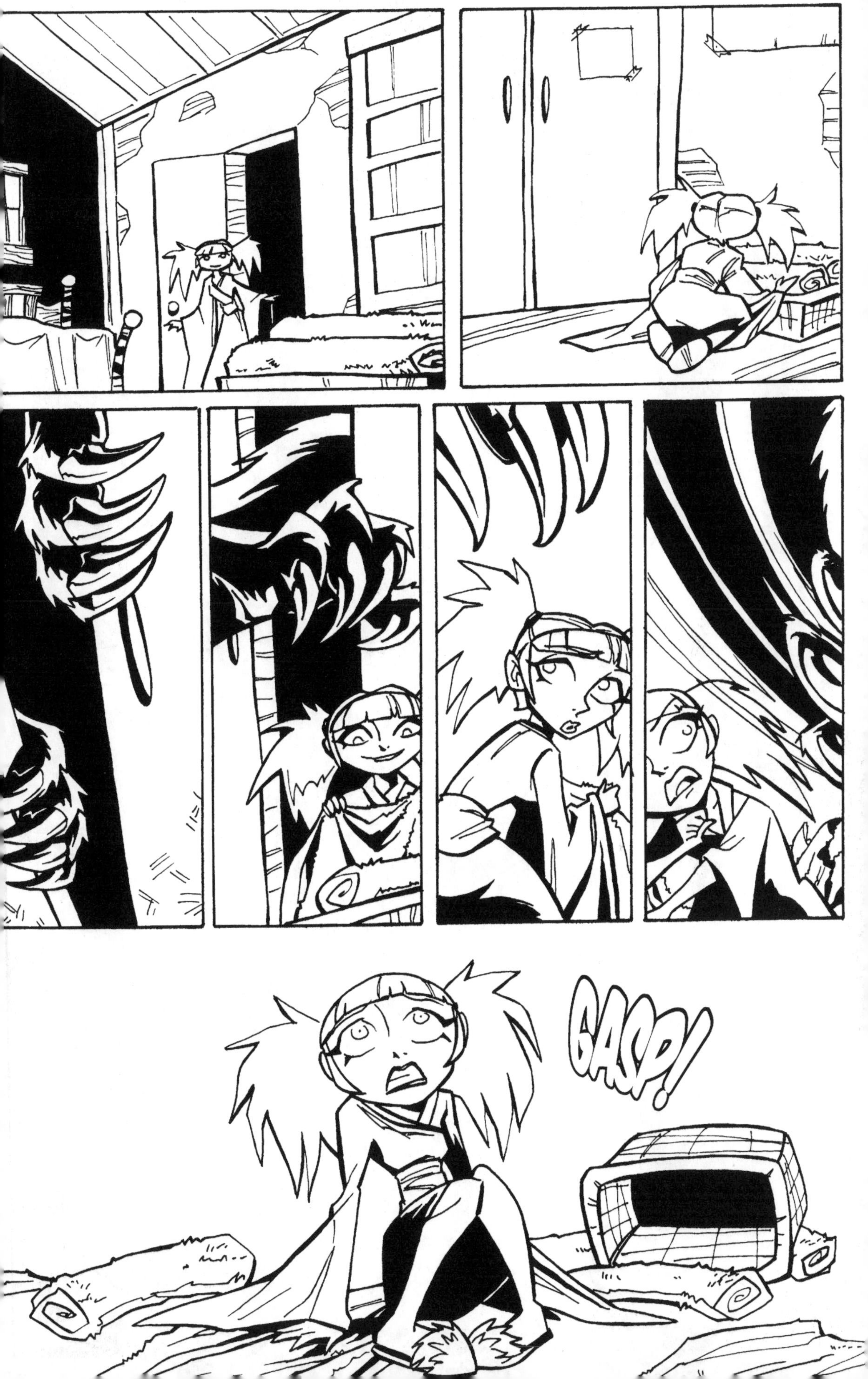
GASP!

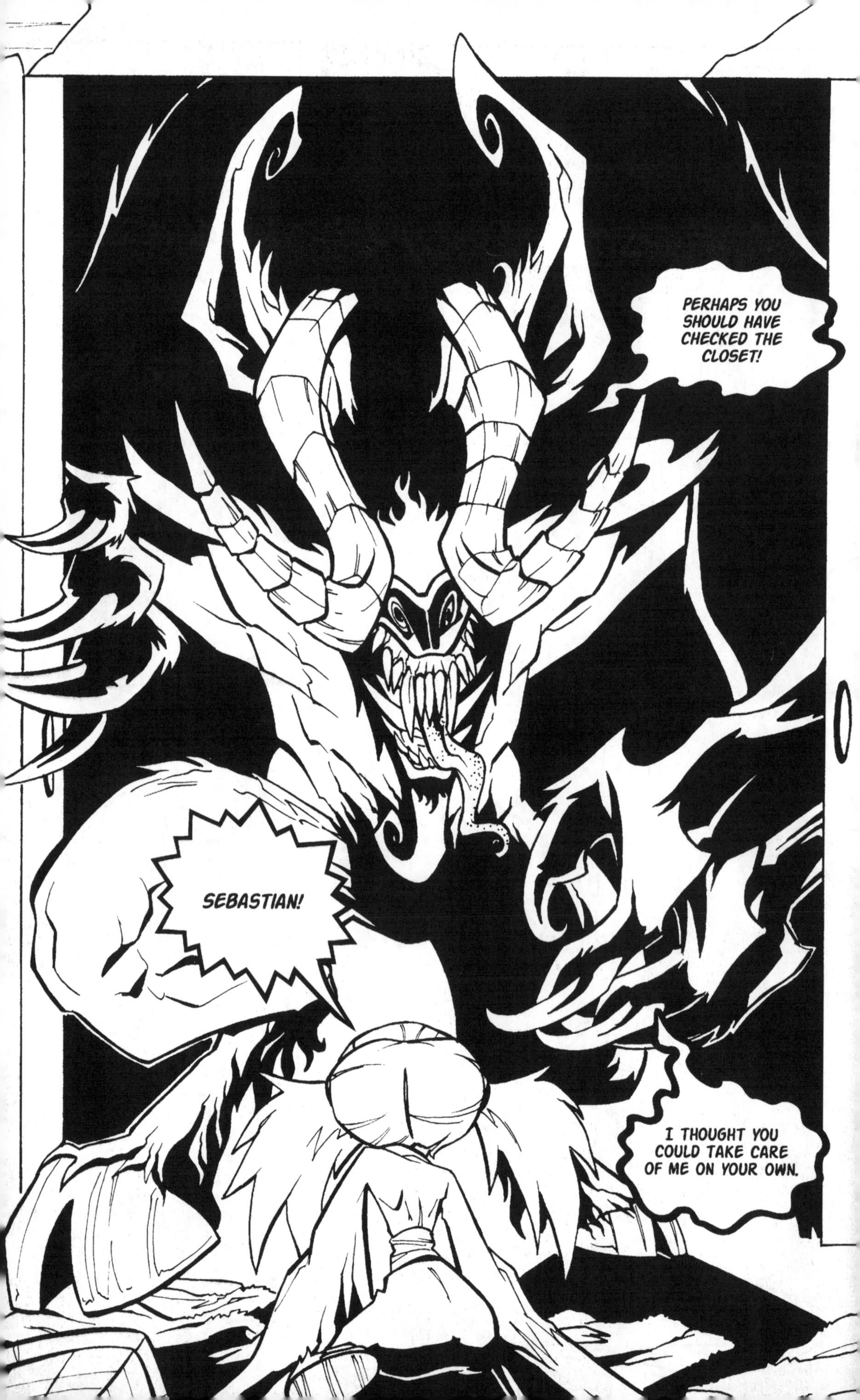
PERHAPS YOU SHOULD HAVE CHECKED THE CLOSET!
SEBASTIAN!
I THOUGHT YOU COULD TAKE CARE OF ME ON YOUR OWN.

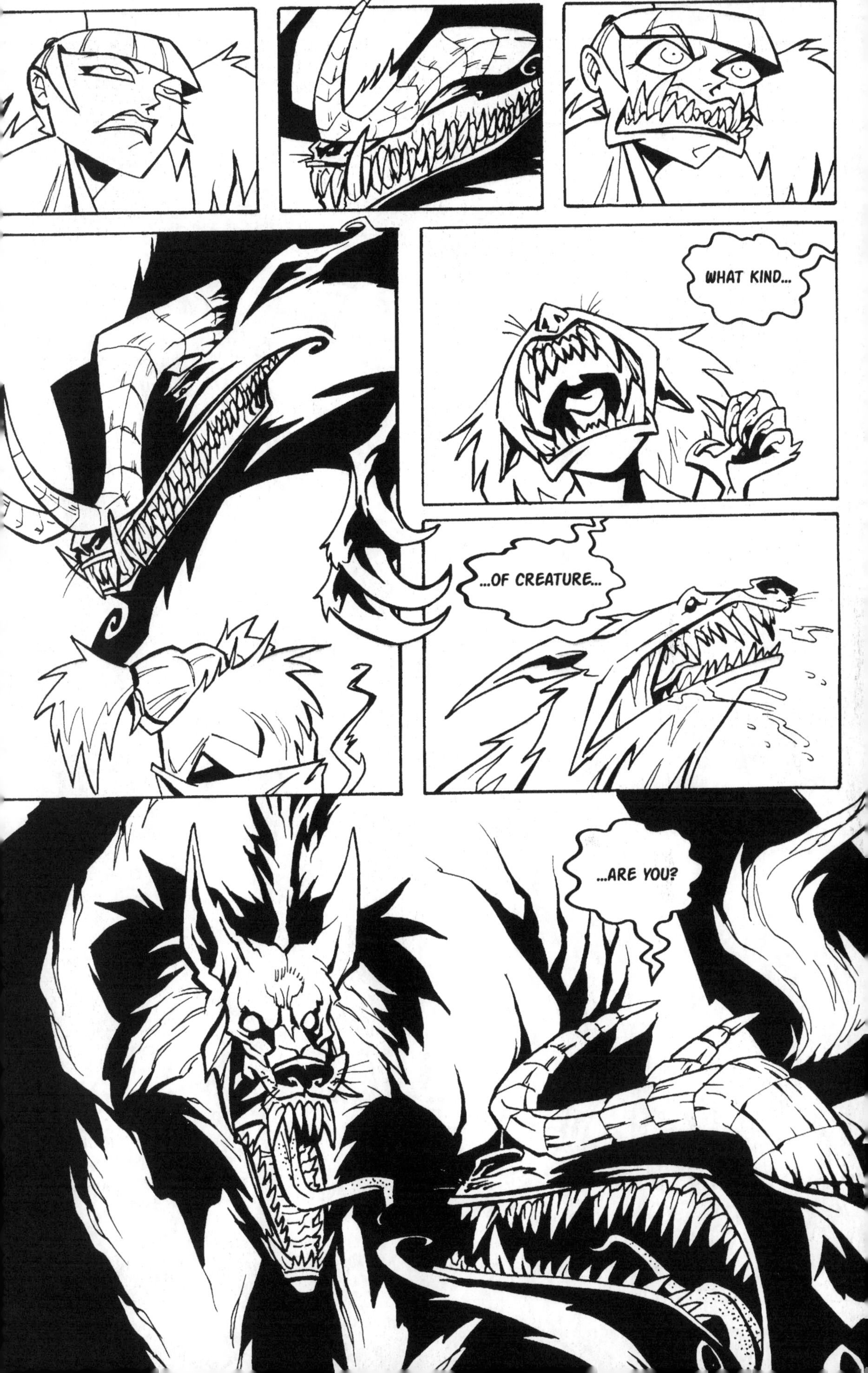
WHAT KIND...
...OF CREATURE...
...ARE YOU?

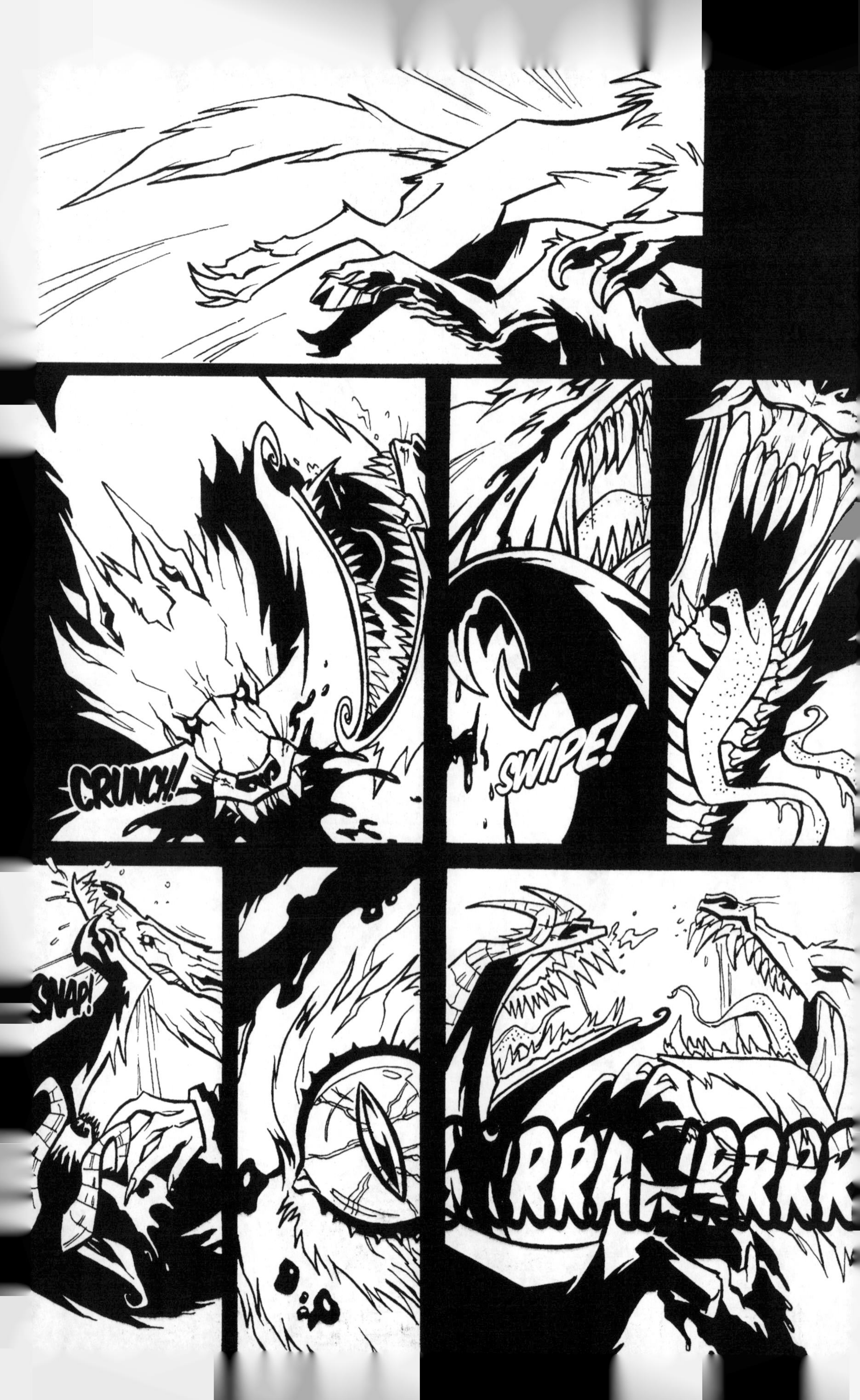
CRUNCH!
SWIPE!
SNAP!

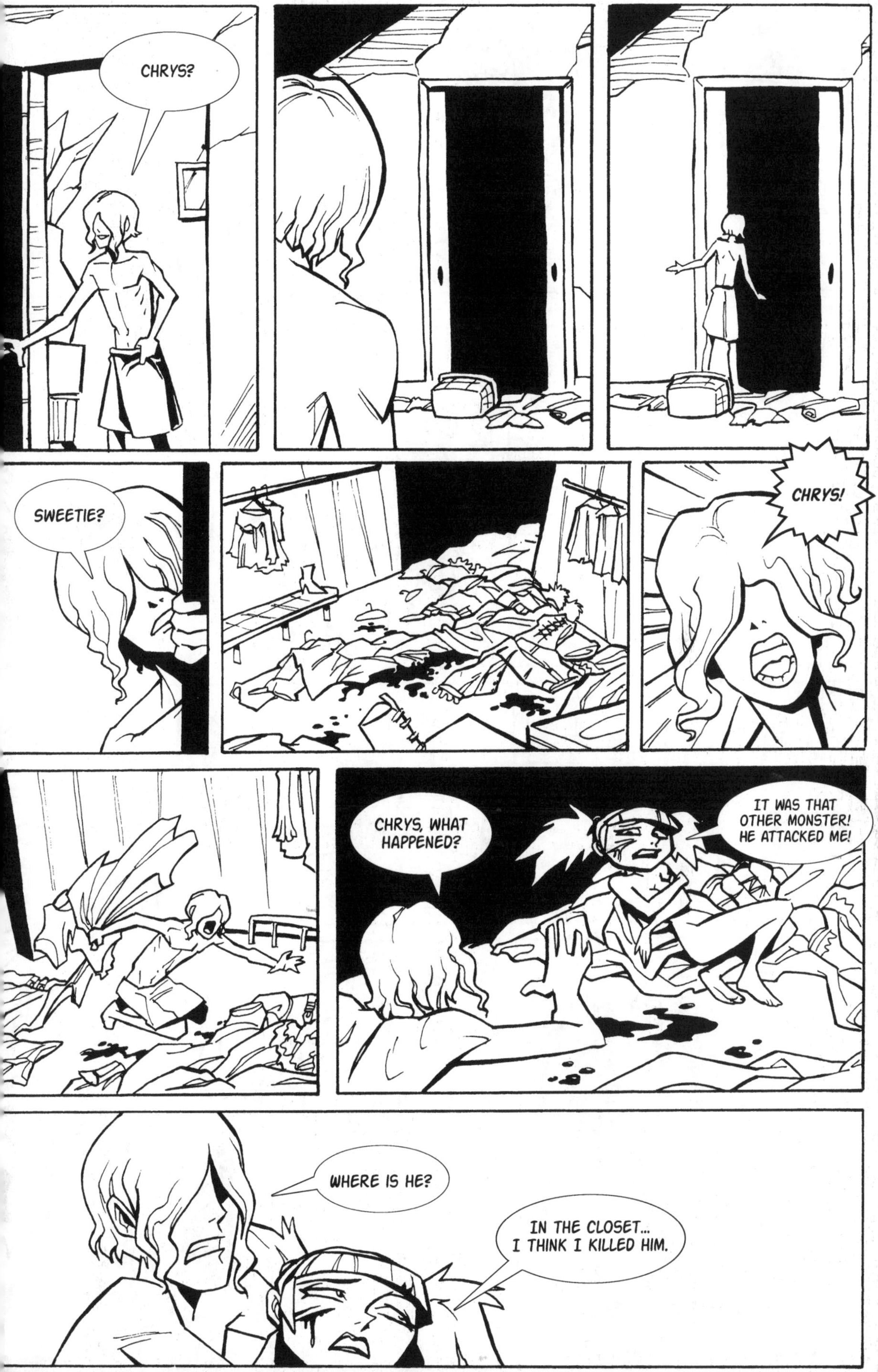
CHRYS?
SWEETIE?
CHRYS!
CHRYS, WHAT HAPPENED?
IT WAS THAT OTHER MONSTER! HE ATTACKED ME!
WHERE IS HE?
IN THE CLOSET... I THINK I KILLED HIM.

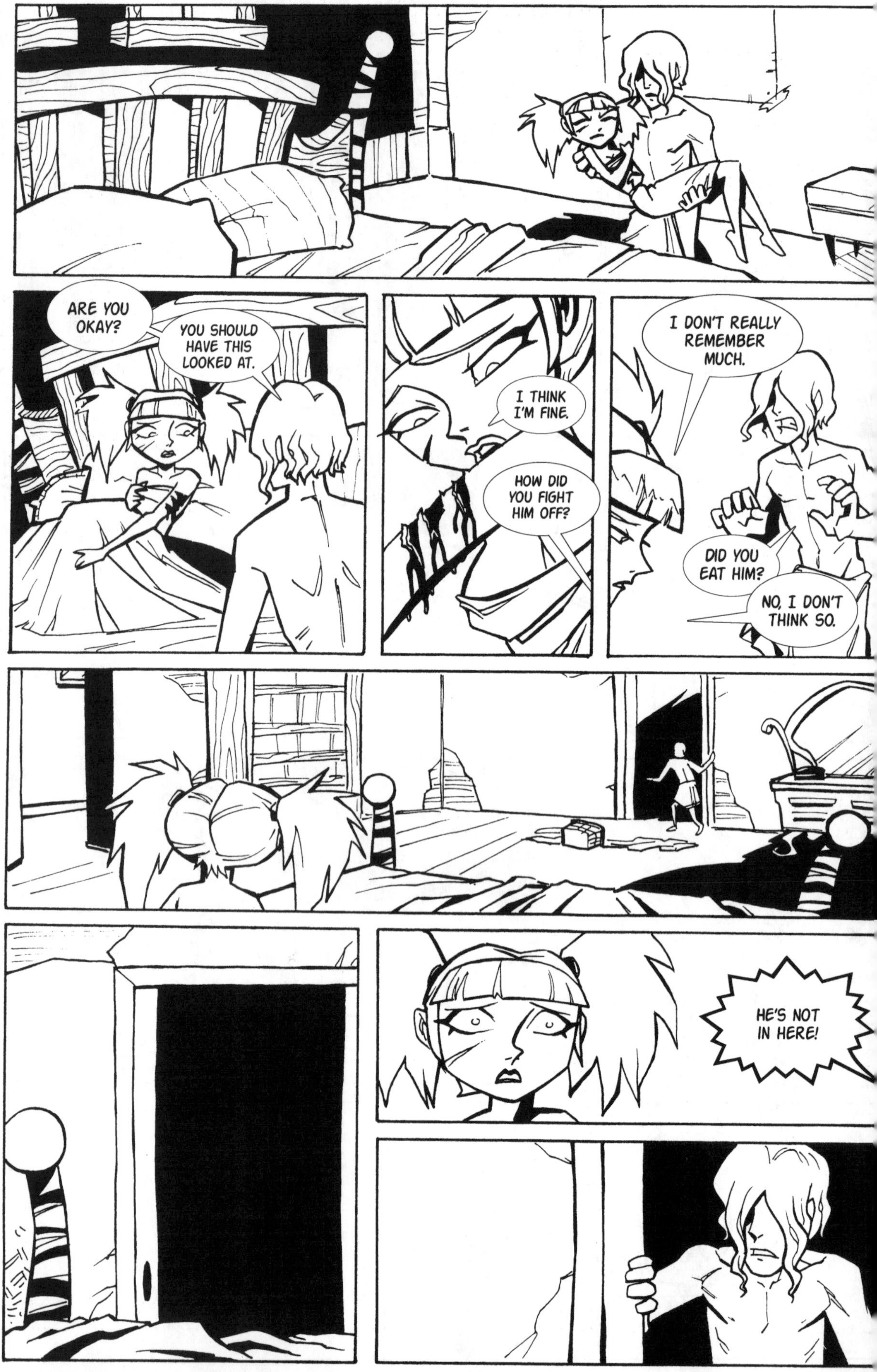
ARE YOU OKAY?
YOU SHOULD HAVE THIS LOOKED AT.
I THINK I'M FINE.
HOW DID YOU FIGHT HIM OFF?
I DON'T REALLY REMEMBER MUCH.
DID YOU EAT HIM?
NO, I DON'T THINK SO.
HE'S NOT IN HERE!

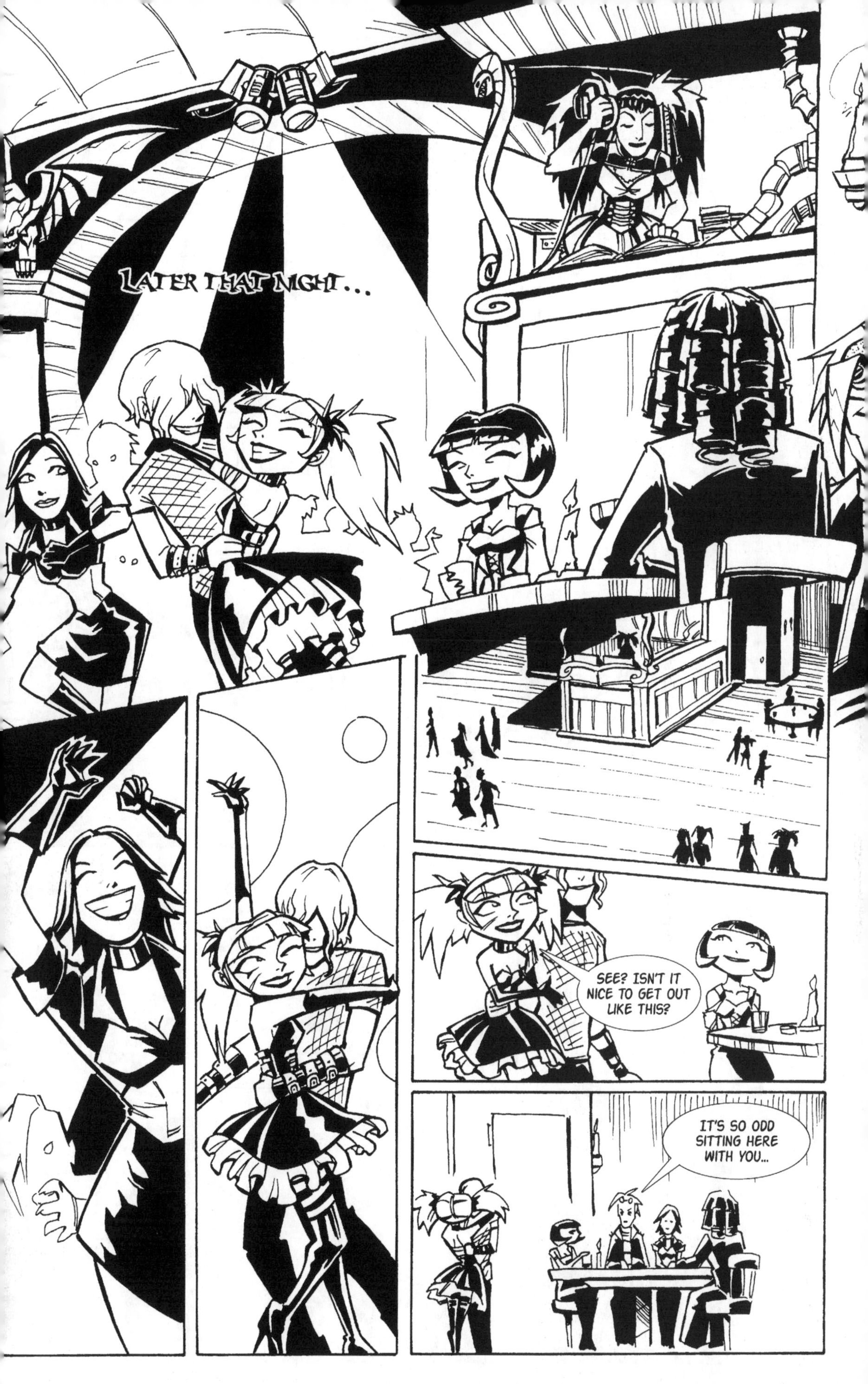
LATER THAT NIGHT...
SEE? ISN'T IT NICE TO GET OUT LIKE THIS?
IT'S SO ODD SITTING HERE WITH YOU...

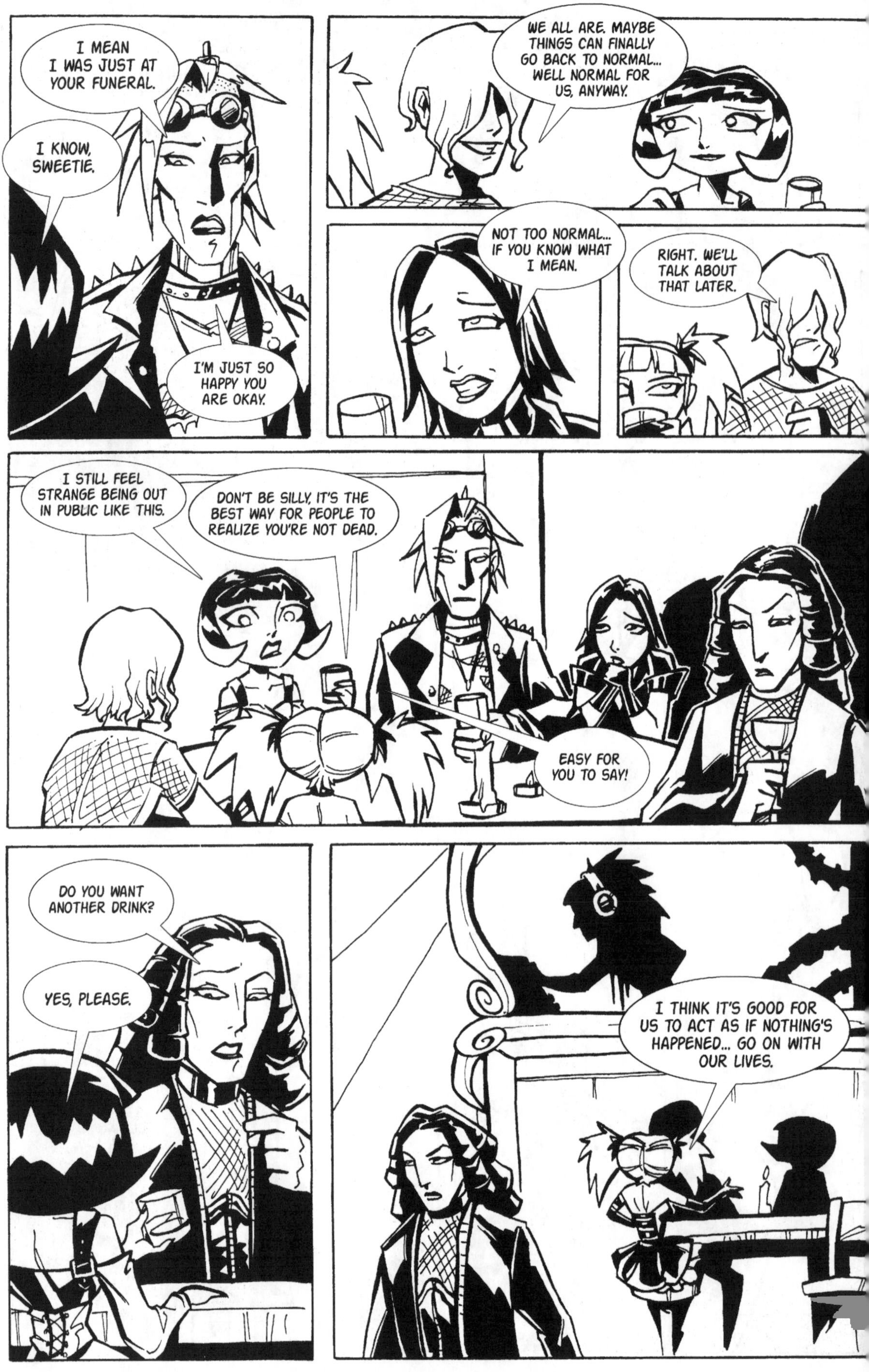

I MEAN I WAS JUST AT YOUR FUNERAL.
I KNOW, SWEETIE.
I'M JUST SO HAPPY YOU ARE OKAY.
WE ALL ARE. MAYBE THINGS CAN FINALLY GO BACK TO NORMAL... WELL NORMAL FOR US, ANYWAY.
NOT TOO NORMAL... IF YOU KNOW WHAT I MEAN.
RIGHT. WE'LL TALK ABOUT THAT LATER.
I STILL FEEL STRANGE BEING OUT IN PUBLIC LIKE THIS.
DON'T BE SILLY, IT'S THE BEST WAY FOR PEOPLE TO REALIZE YOU'RE NOT DEAD.
EASY FOR YOU TO SAY!
DO YOU WANT ANOTHER DRINK?
YES, PLEASE.
I THINK IT'S GOOD FOR US TO ACT AS IF NOTHING'S HAPPENED... GO ON WITH OUR LIVES.

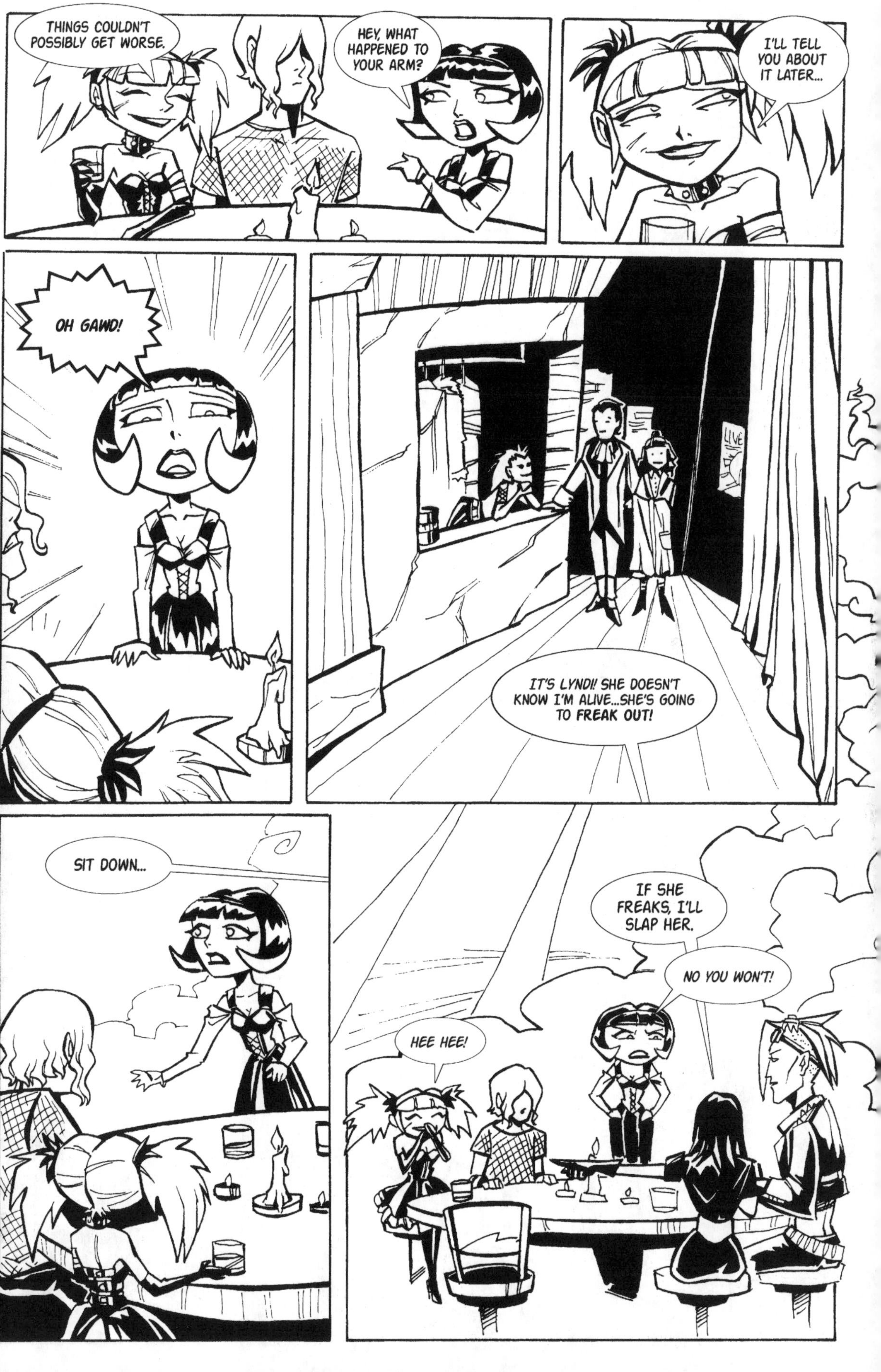
THINGS COULDN'T POSSIBLY GET WORSE.
HEY, WHAT HAPPENED TO YOUR ARM?
I'LL TELL YOU ABOUT IT LATER...
OH GAWD!
LIVE
IT'S LYNDI! SHE DOESN'T KNOW I'M ALIVE...SHE'S GOING TO FREAK OUT!
SIT DOWN...
IF SHE FREAKS, I'LL SLAP HER.
NO YOU WON'T!
HEE HEE!

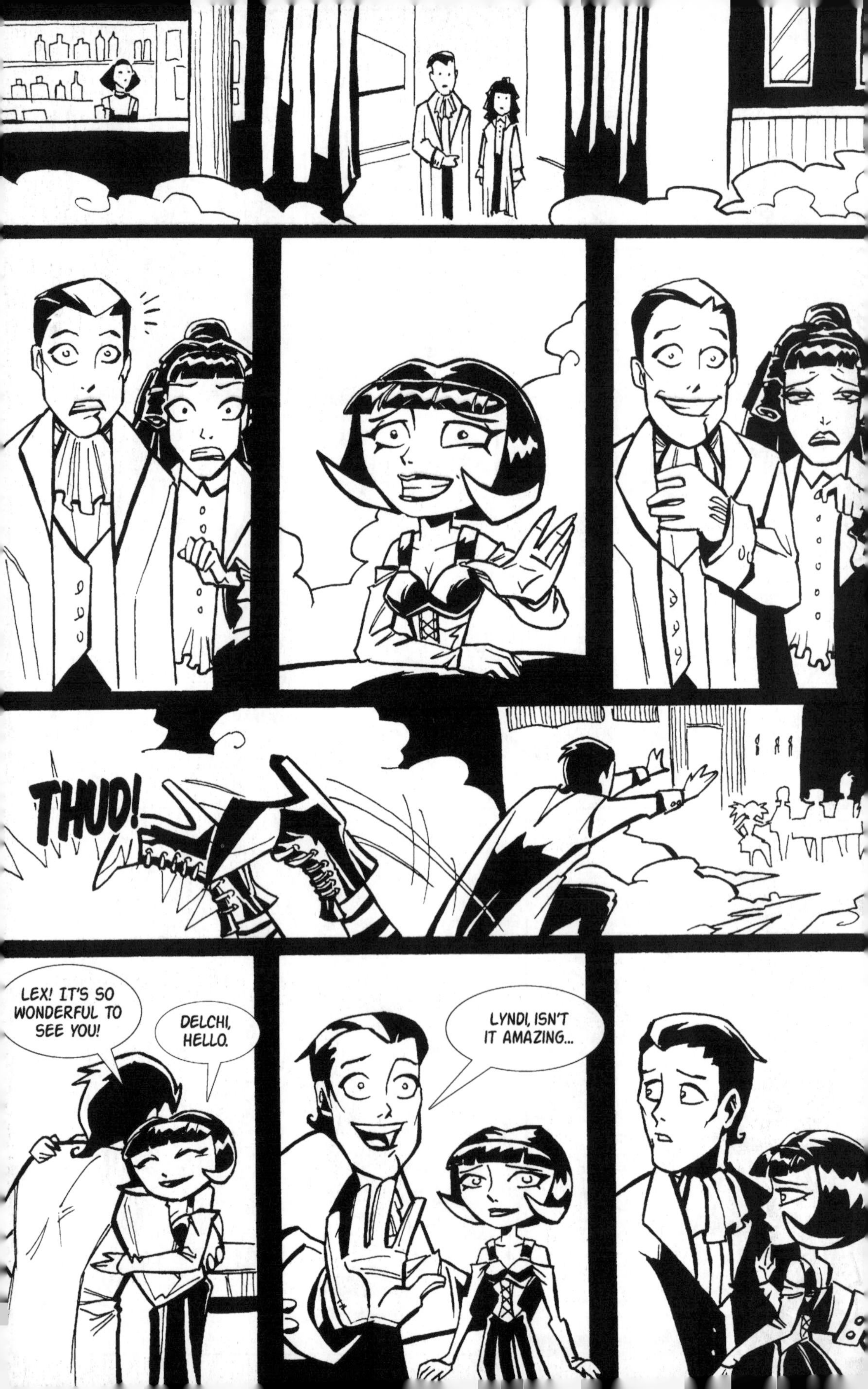
THUD!
LEX! IT'S SO WONDERFUL TO SEE YOU!
DELCHI, HELLO.
LYNDI, ISN'T IT AMAZING...

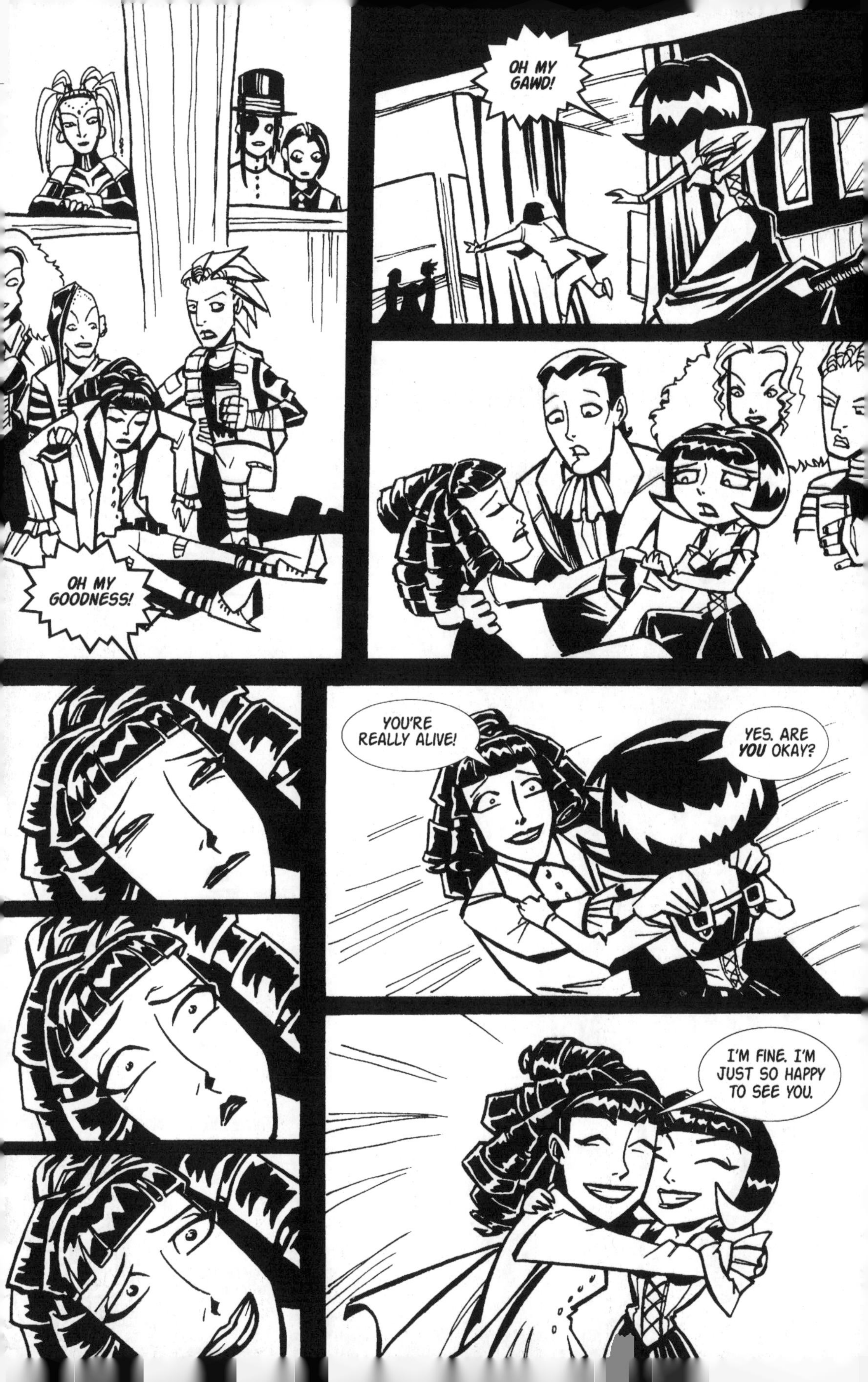
OH MY GOODNESS!
OH MY GAWD!
YOU'RE REALLY ALIVE!
YES. ARE *YOU* OKAY?
I'M FINE. I'M JUST SO HAPPY TO SEE YOU.

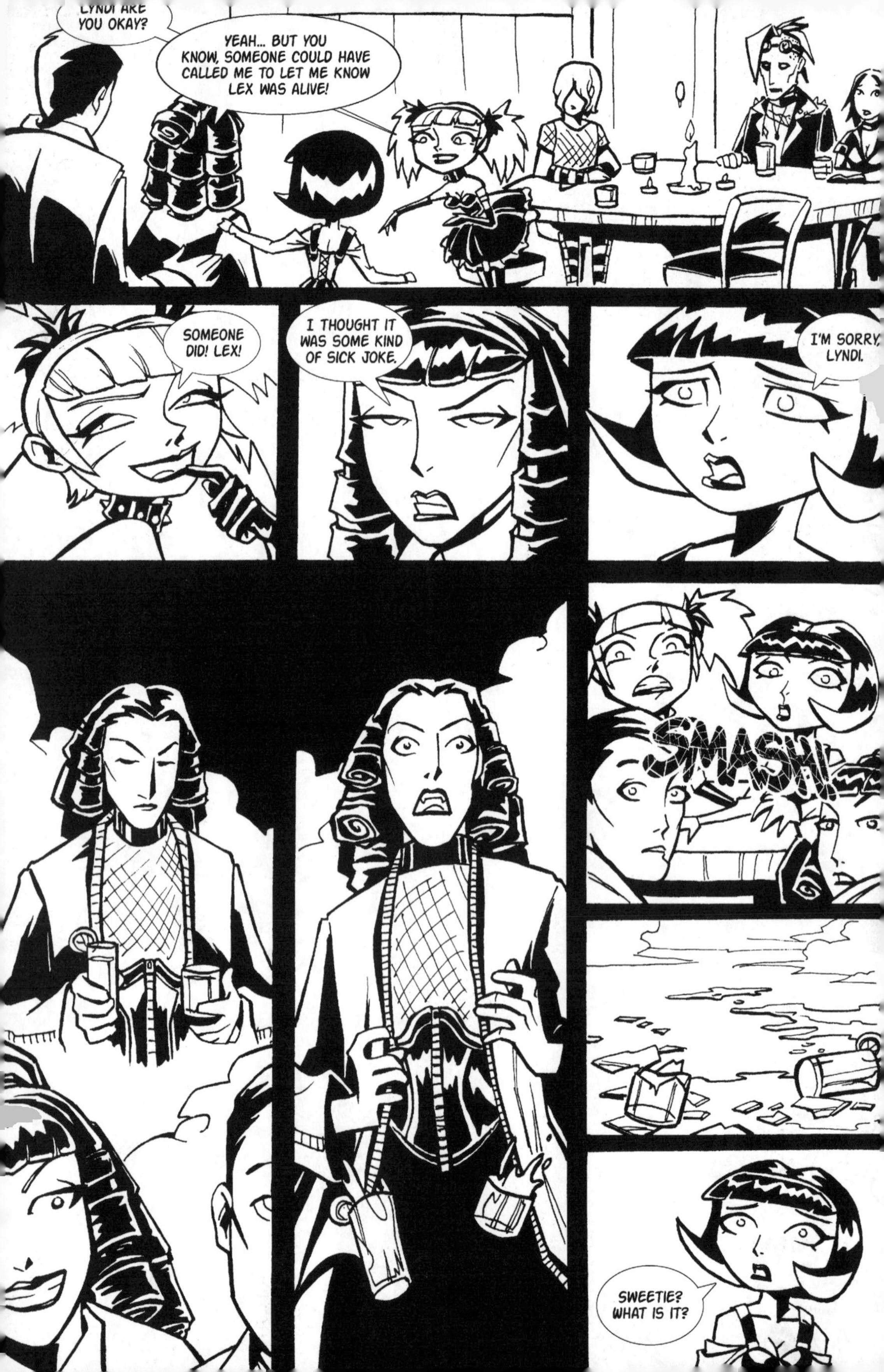
LYNDI ARE YOU OKAY?
YEAH... BUT YOU KNOW, SOMEONE COULD HAVE CALLED ME TO LET ME KNOW LEX WAS ALIVE!
SOMEONE DID! LEX!
I THOUGHT IT WAS SOME KIND OF SICK JOKE.
I'M SORRY, LYNDI.
SMASH!
SWEETIE? WHAT IS IT?

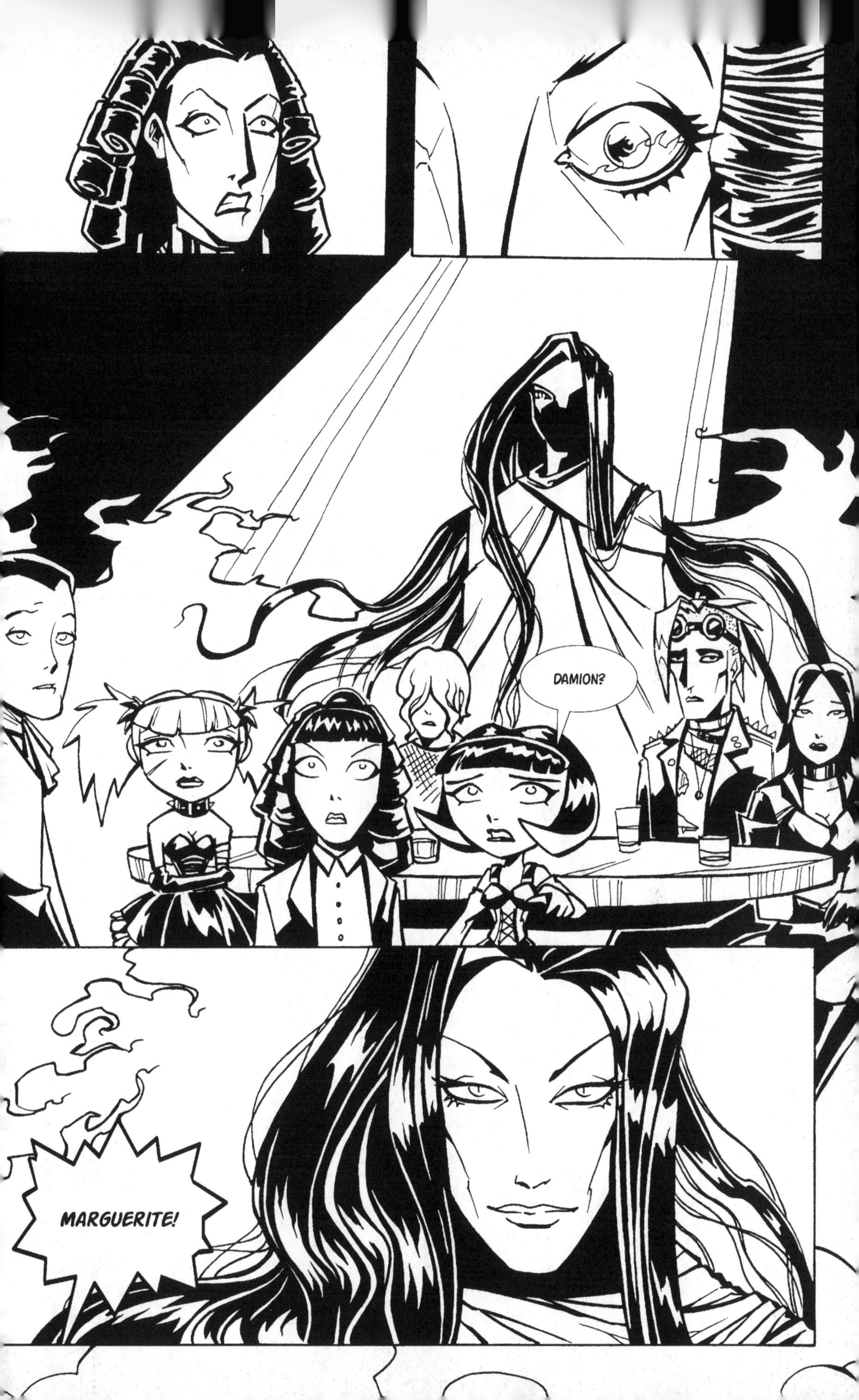
DAMION?
MARGUERITE!

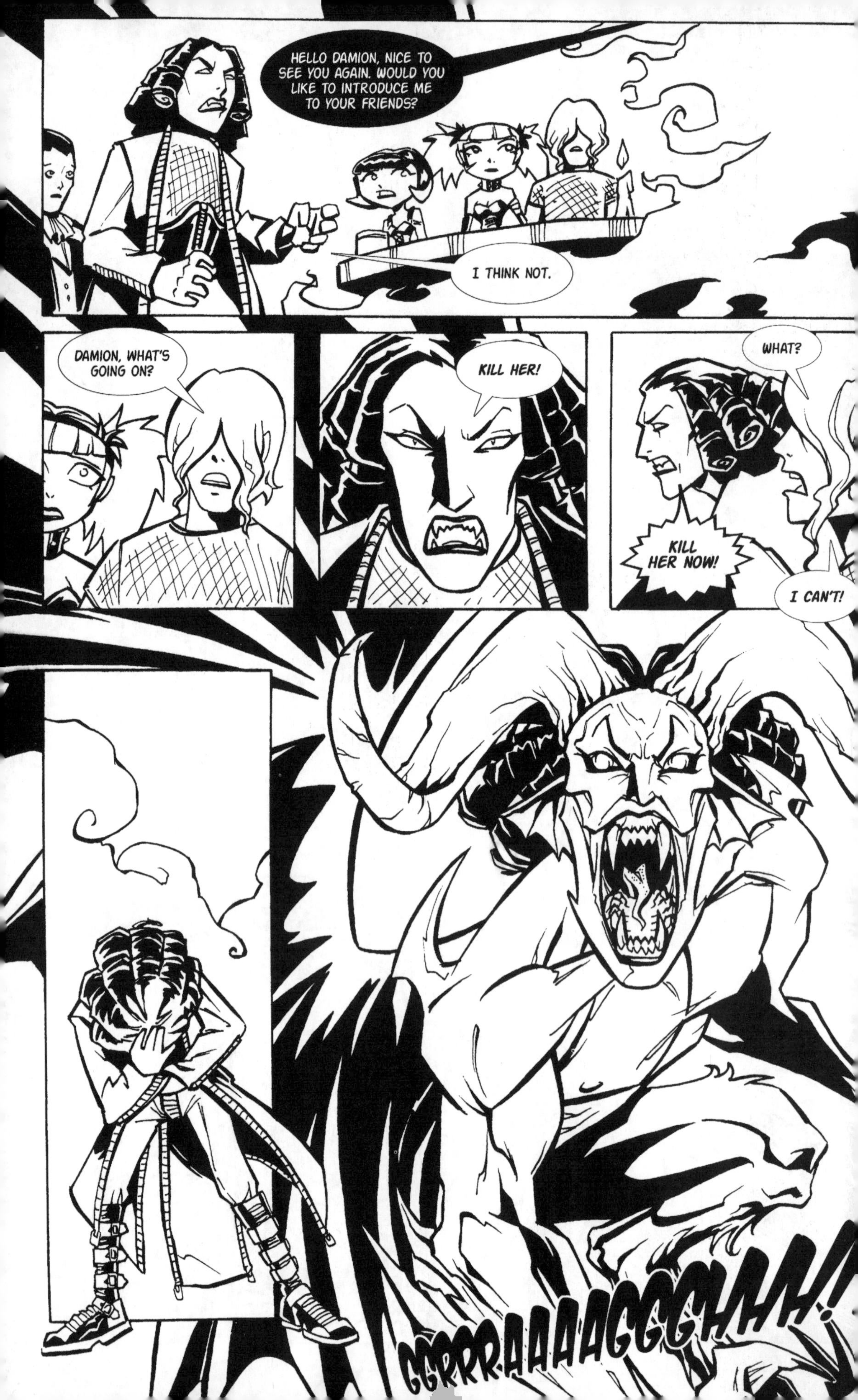
HELLO DAMION, NICE TO SEE YOU AGAIN. WOULD YOU LIKE TO INTRODUCE ME TO YOUR FRIENDS?
I THINK NOT.
DAMION, WHAT'S GOING ON?
KILL HER!
WHAT?
KILL HER NOW!
I CAN'T!
GGRRRAAAAAGGGHHH!

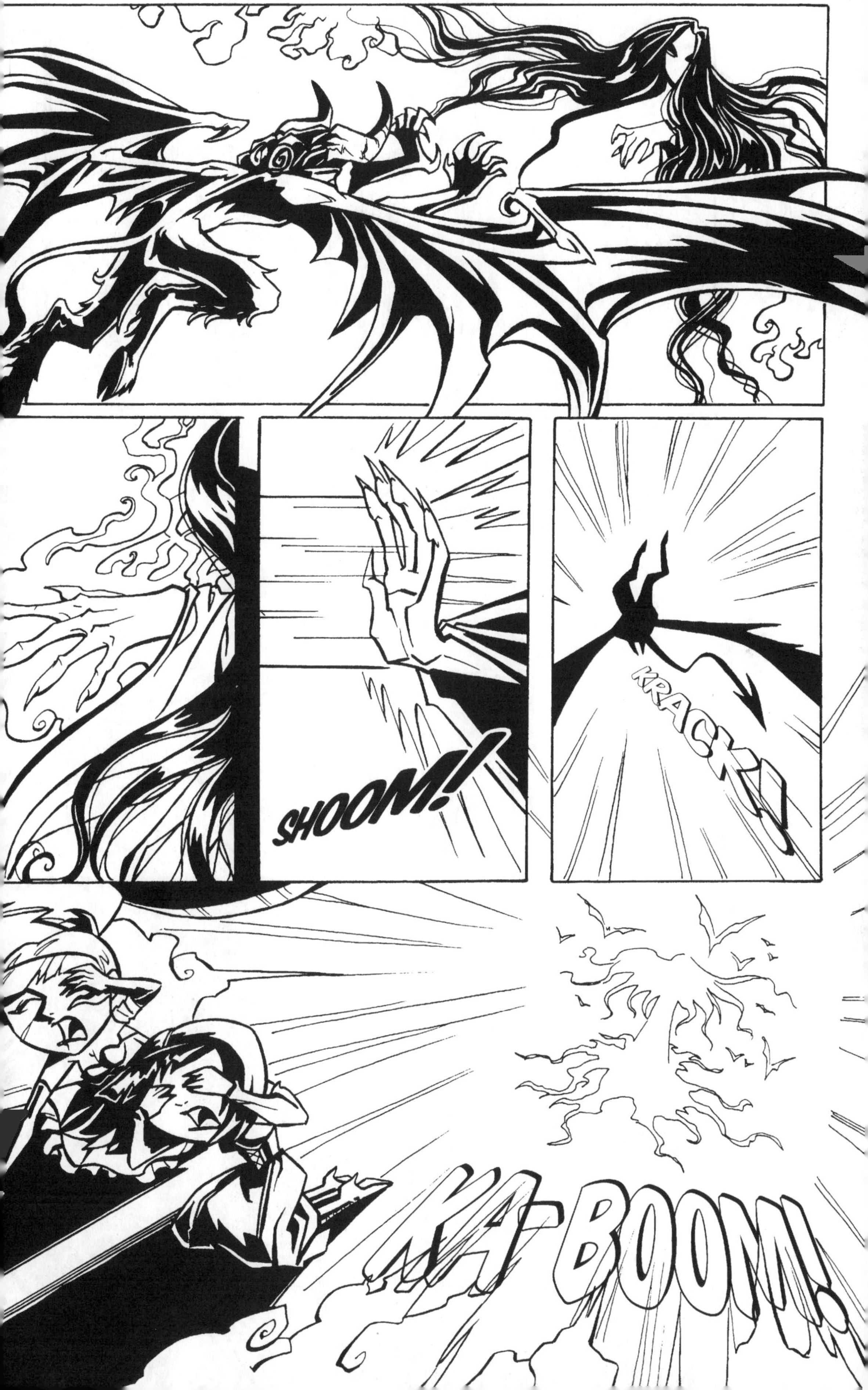
SHOOM!
KRACK!
KA-BOOM!

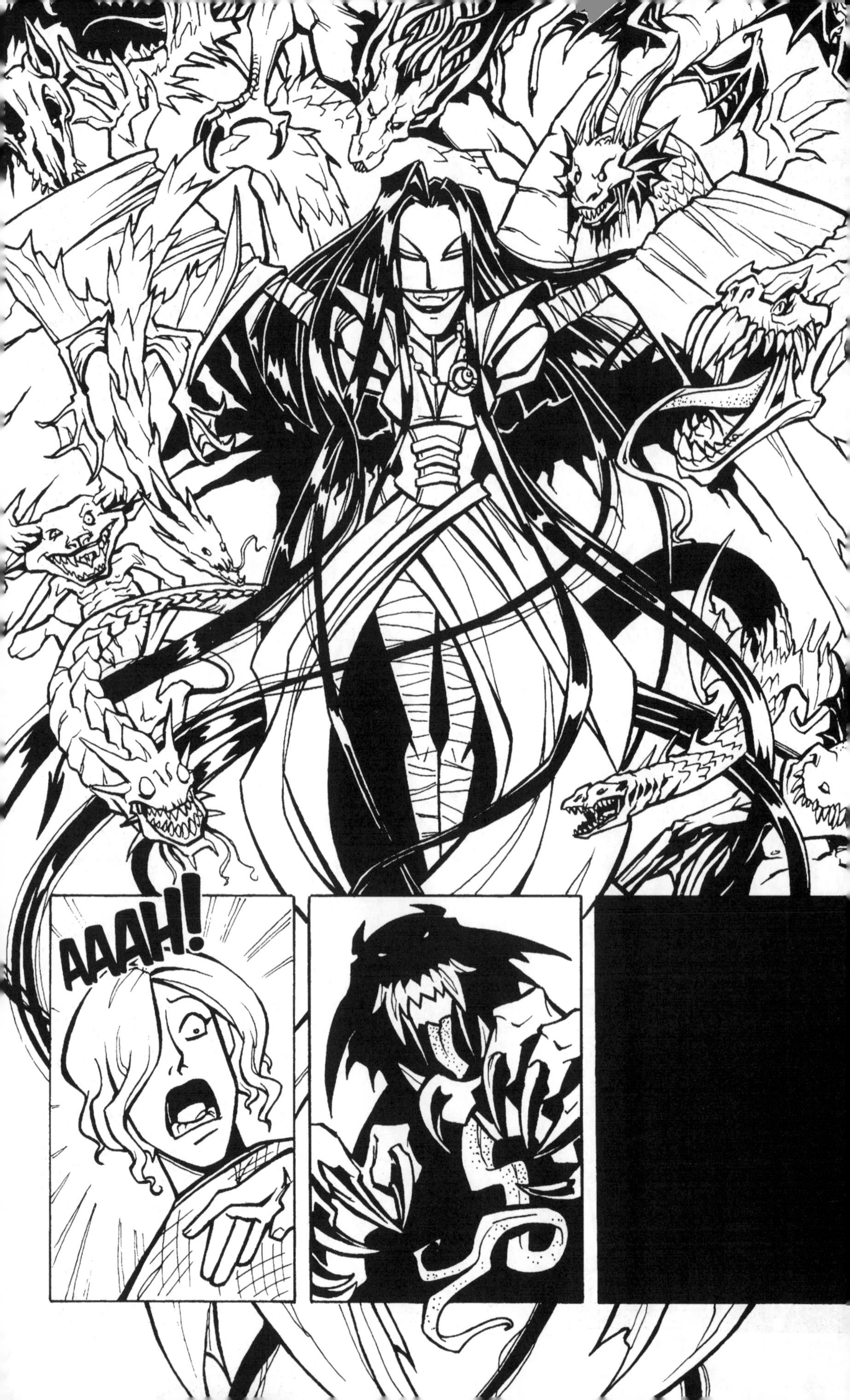
AAAH!

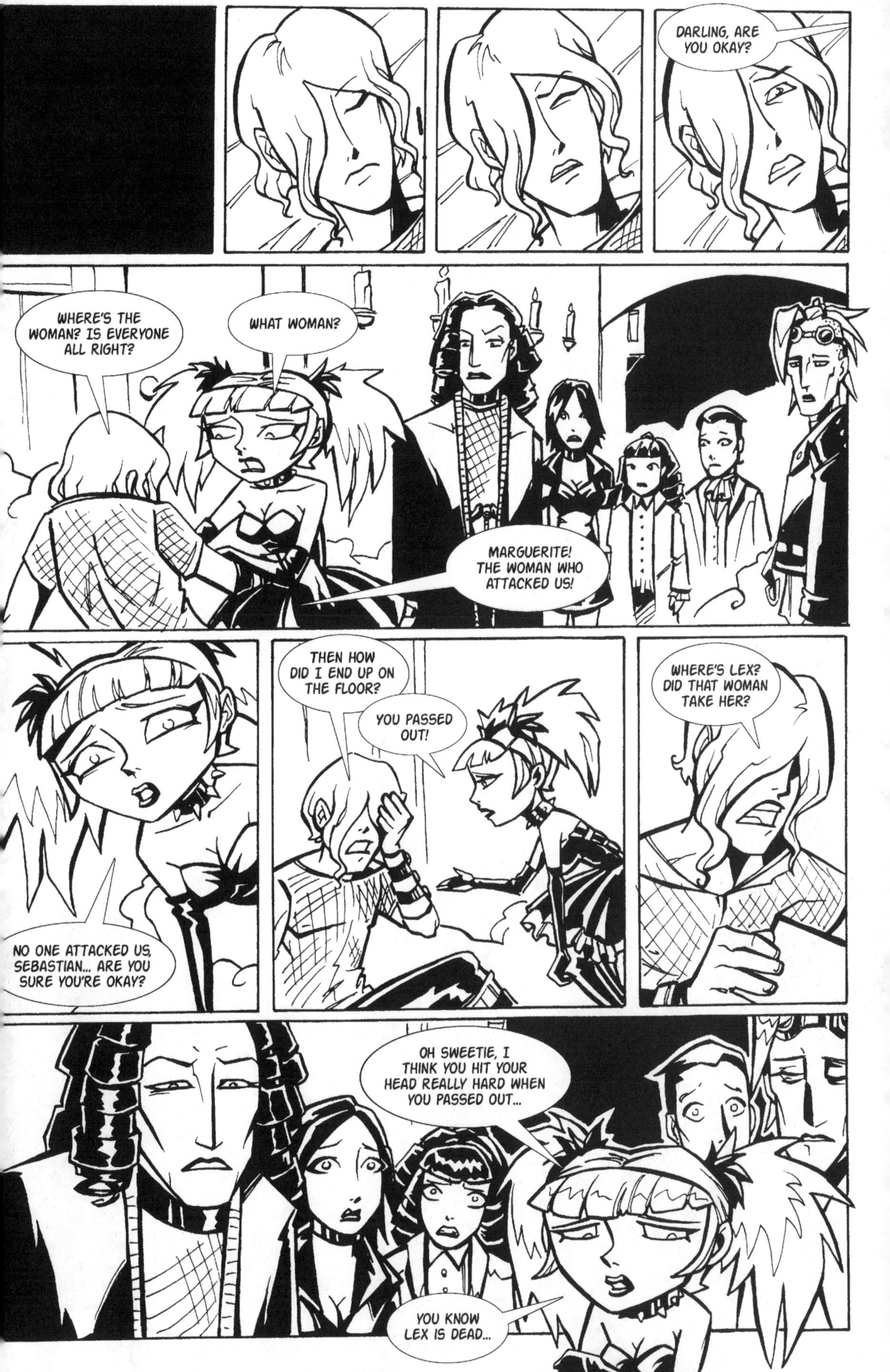
DARLING, ARE YOU OKAY?
WHERE'S THE WOMAN? IS EVERYONE ALL RIGHT?
WHAT WOMAN?
MARGUERITE! THE WOMAN WHO ATTACKED US!
NO ONE ATTACKED US, SEBASTIAN... ARE YOU SURE YOU'RE OKAY?
THEN HOW DID I END UP ON THE FLOOR?
YOU PASSED OUT!
WHERE'S LEX? DID THAT WOMAN TAKE HER?
OH SWEETIE, I THINK YOU HIT YOUR HEAD REALLY HARD WHEN YOU PASSED OUT...
YOU KNOW LEX IS DEAD...

Chapter 20

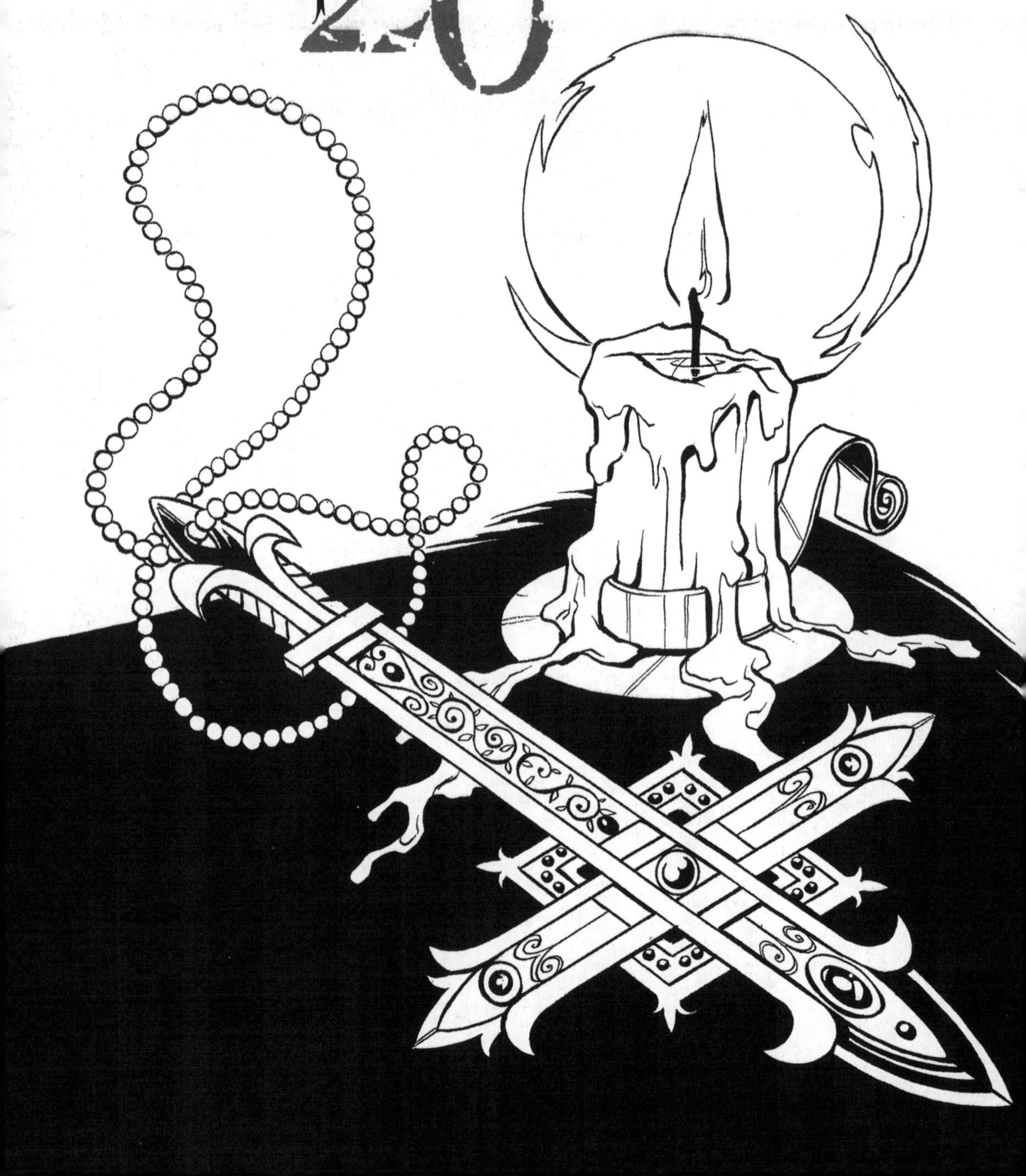

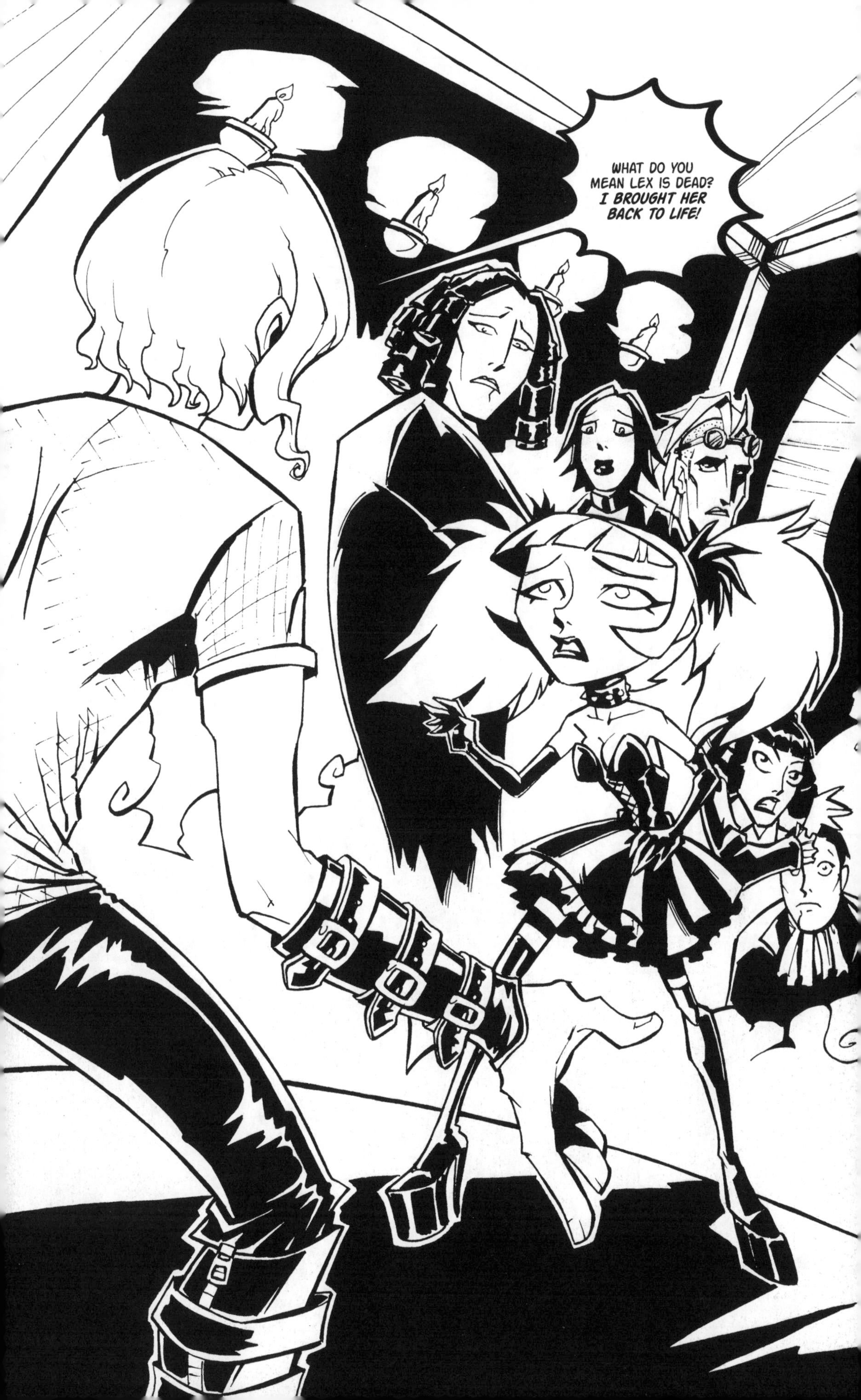
WHAT DO YOU MEAN LEX IS DEAD? *I BROUGHT HER BACK TO LIFE!*

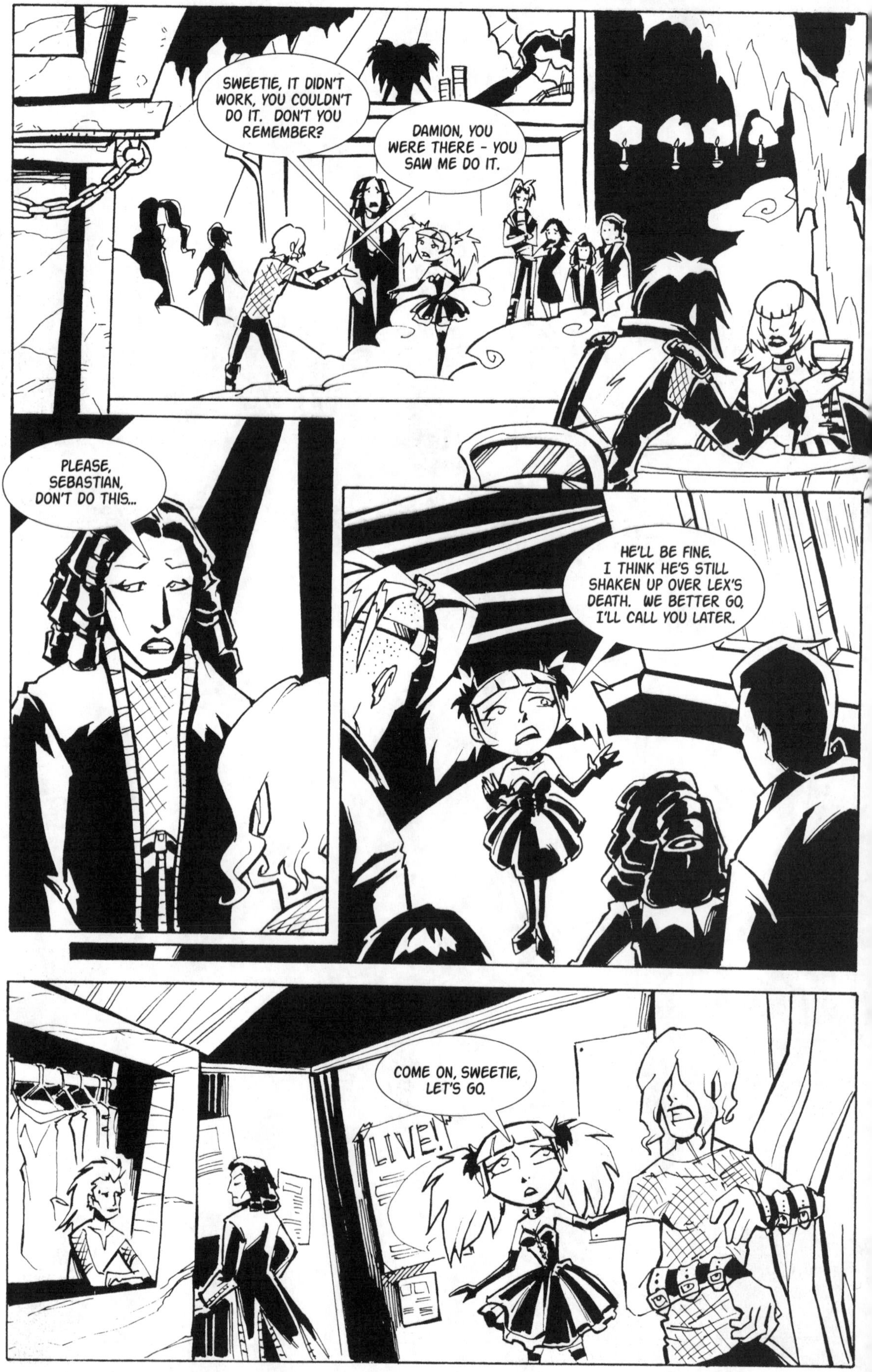
SWEETIE, IT DIDN'T WORK, YOU COULDN'T DO IT. DON'T YOU REMEMBER?
DAMION, YOU WERE THERE - YOU SAW ME DO IT.
PLEASE, SEBASTIAN, DON'T DO THIS...
HE'LL BE FINE. I THINK HE'S STILL SHAKEN UP OVER LEX'S DEATH. WE BETTER GO, I'LL CALL YOU LATER.
COME ON, SWEETIE, LET'S GO.
LIVE!

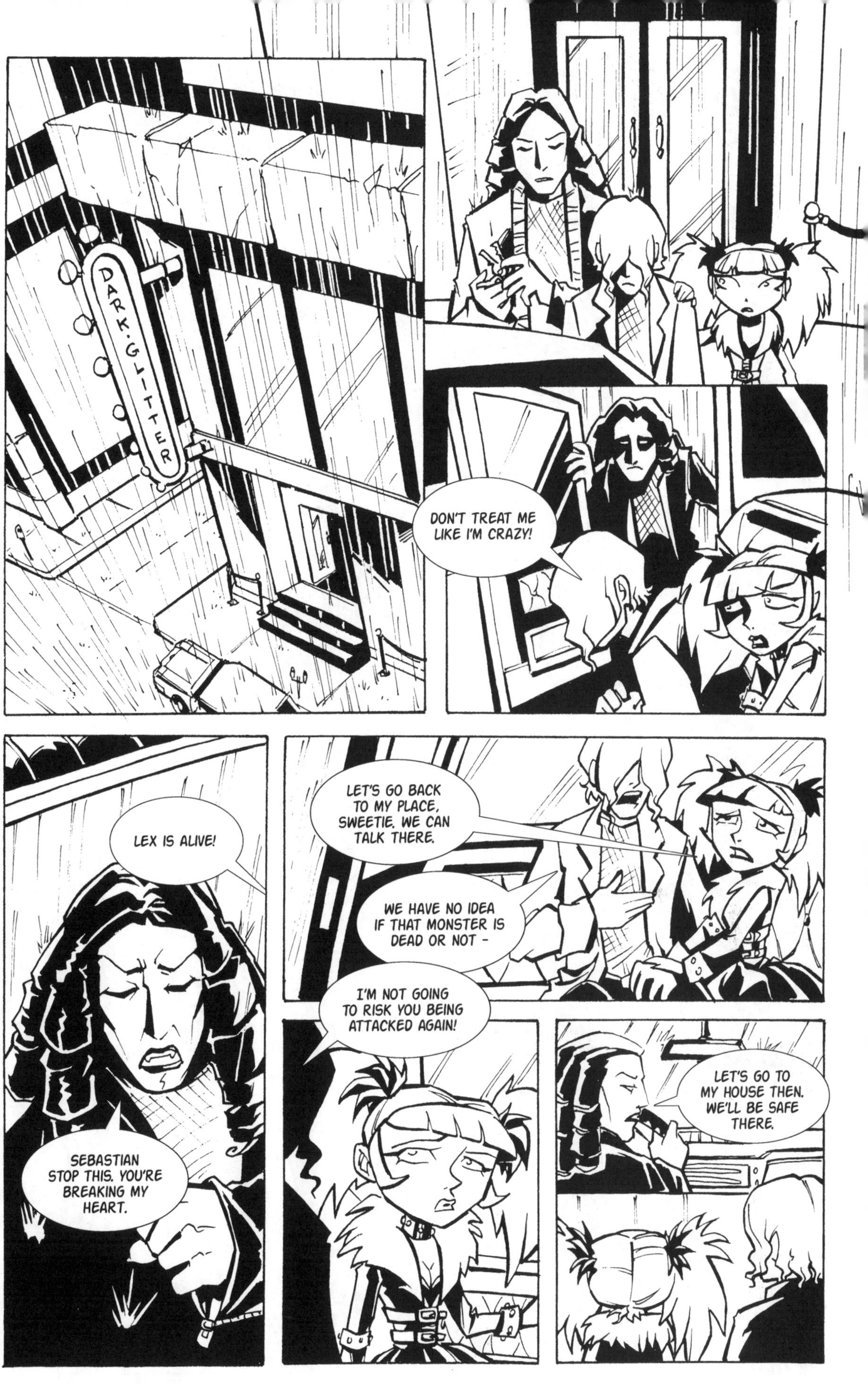
DARK·GLITTER
DON'T TREAT ME LIKE I'M CRAZY!
LEX IS ALIVE!
SEBASTIAN STOP THIS. YOU'RE BREAKING MY HEART.
LET'S GO BACK TO MY PLACE, SWEETIE. WE CAN TALK THERE.
WE HAVE NO IDEA IF THAT MONSTER IS DEAD OR NOT -
I'M NOT GOING TO RISK YOU BEING ATTACKED AGAIN!
LET'S GO TO MY HOUSE THEN. WE'LL BE SAFE THERE.

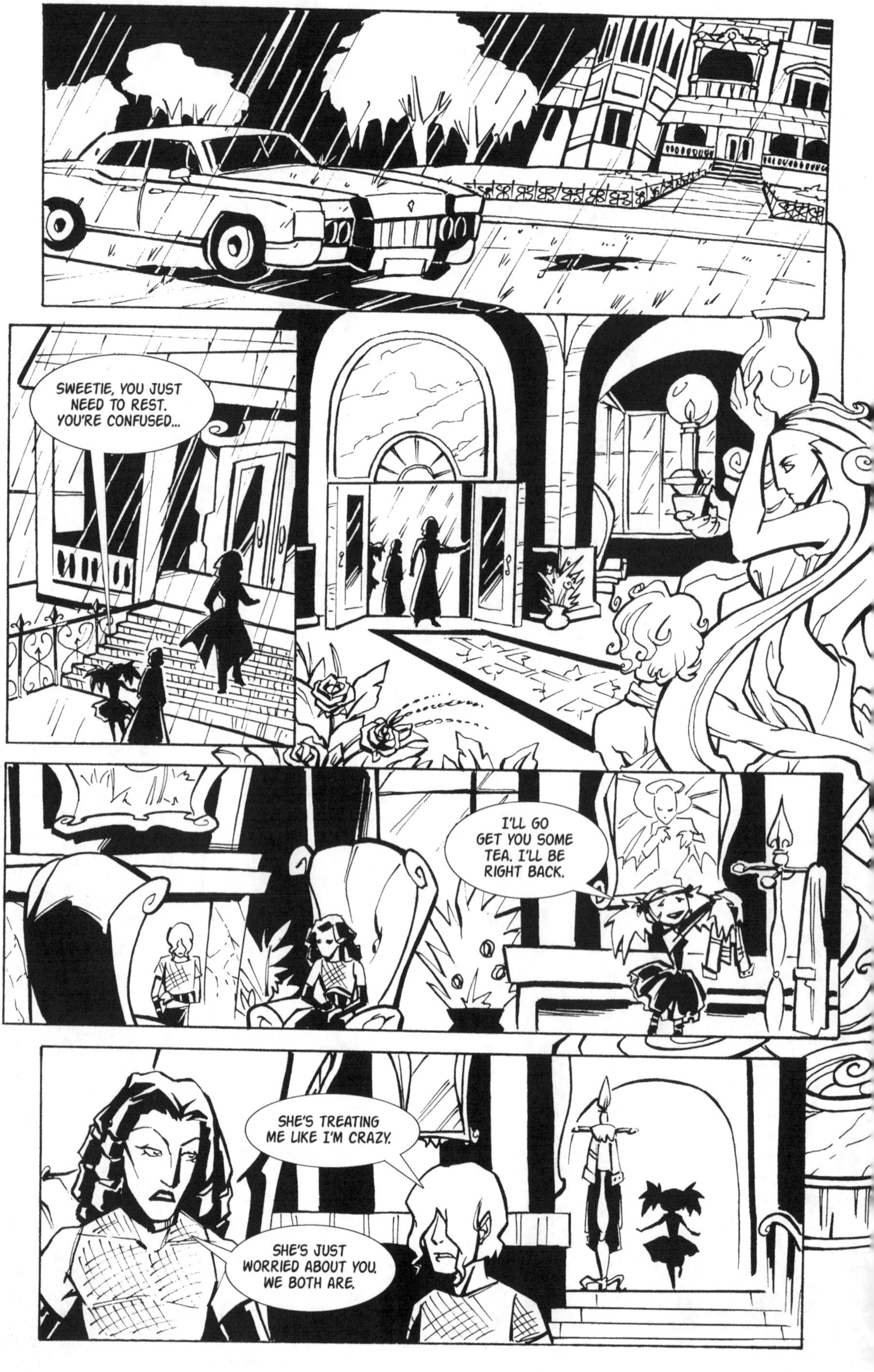
SWEETIE, YOU JUST NEED TO REST. YOU'RE CONFUSED...
I'LL GO GET YOU SOME TEA. I'LL BE RIGHT BACK.
SHE'S TREATING ME LIKE I'M CRAZY.
SHE'S JUST WORRIED ABOUT YOU. WE BOTH ARE.

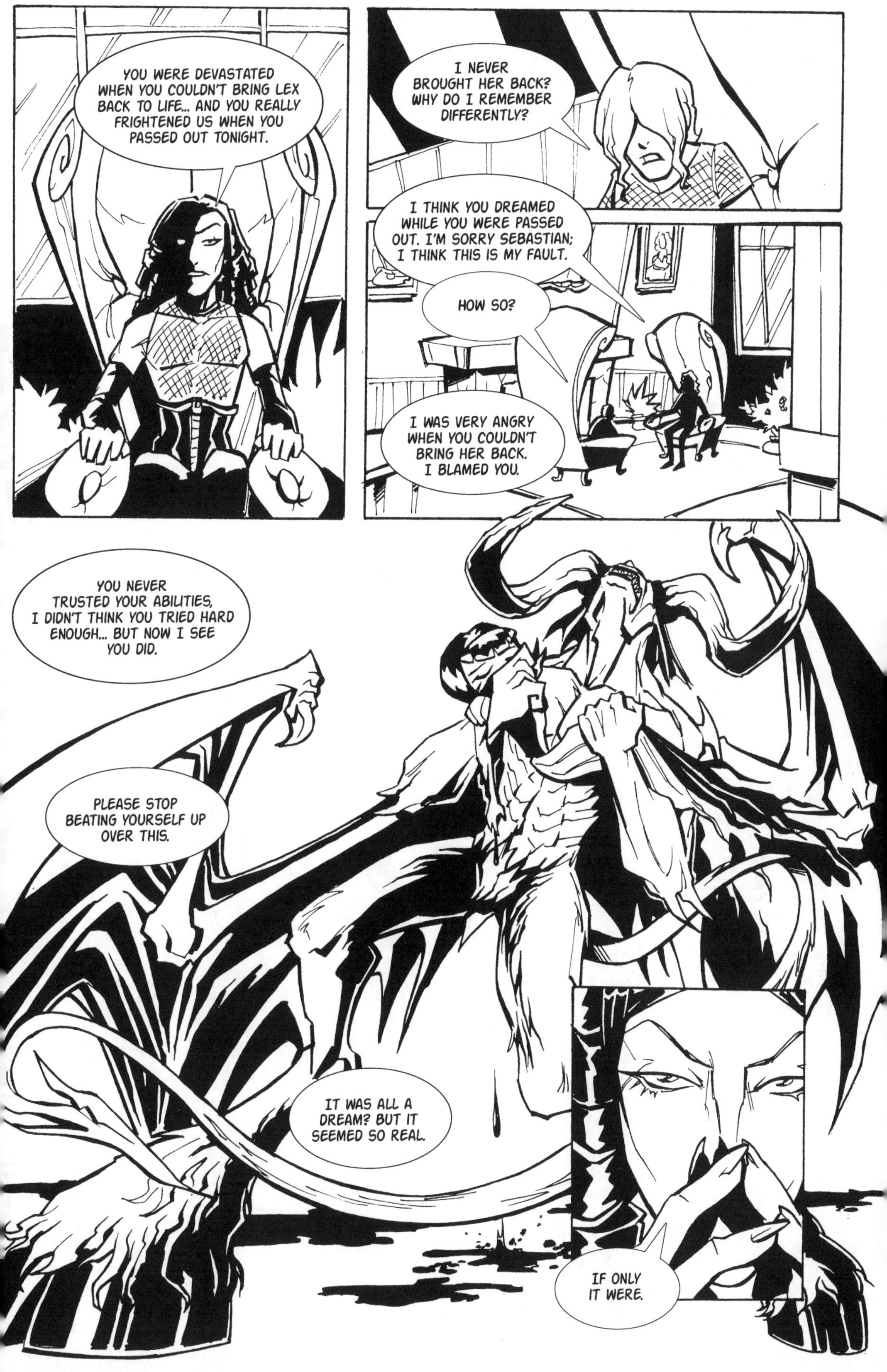
YOU WERE DEVASTATED WHEN YOU COULDN'T BRING LEX BACK TO LIFE... AND YOU REALLY FRIGHTENED US WHEN YOU PASSED OUT TONIGHT.
I NEVER BROUGHT HER BACK? WHY DO I REMEMBER DIFFERENTLY?
I THINK YOU DREAMED WHILE YOU WERE PASSED OUT. I'M SORRY SEBASTIAN; I THINK THIS IS MY FAULT.
HOW SO?
I WAS VERY ANGRY WHEN YOU COULDN'T BRING HER BACK. I BLAMED YOU.
YOU NEVER TRUSTED YOUR ABILITIES, I DIDN'T THINK YOU TRIED HARD ENOUGH... BUT NOW I SEE YOU DID.
PLEASE STOP BEATING YOURSELF UP OVER THIS.
IT WAS ALL A DREAM? BUT IT SEEMED SO REAL.
IF ONLY IT WERE.

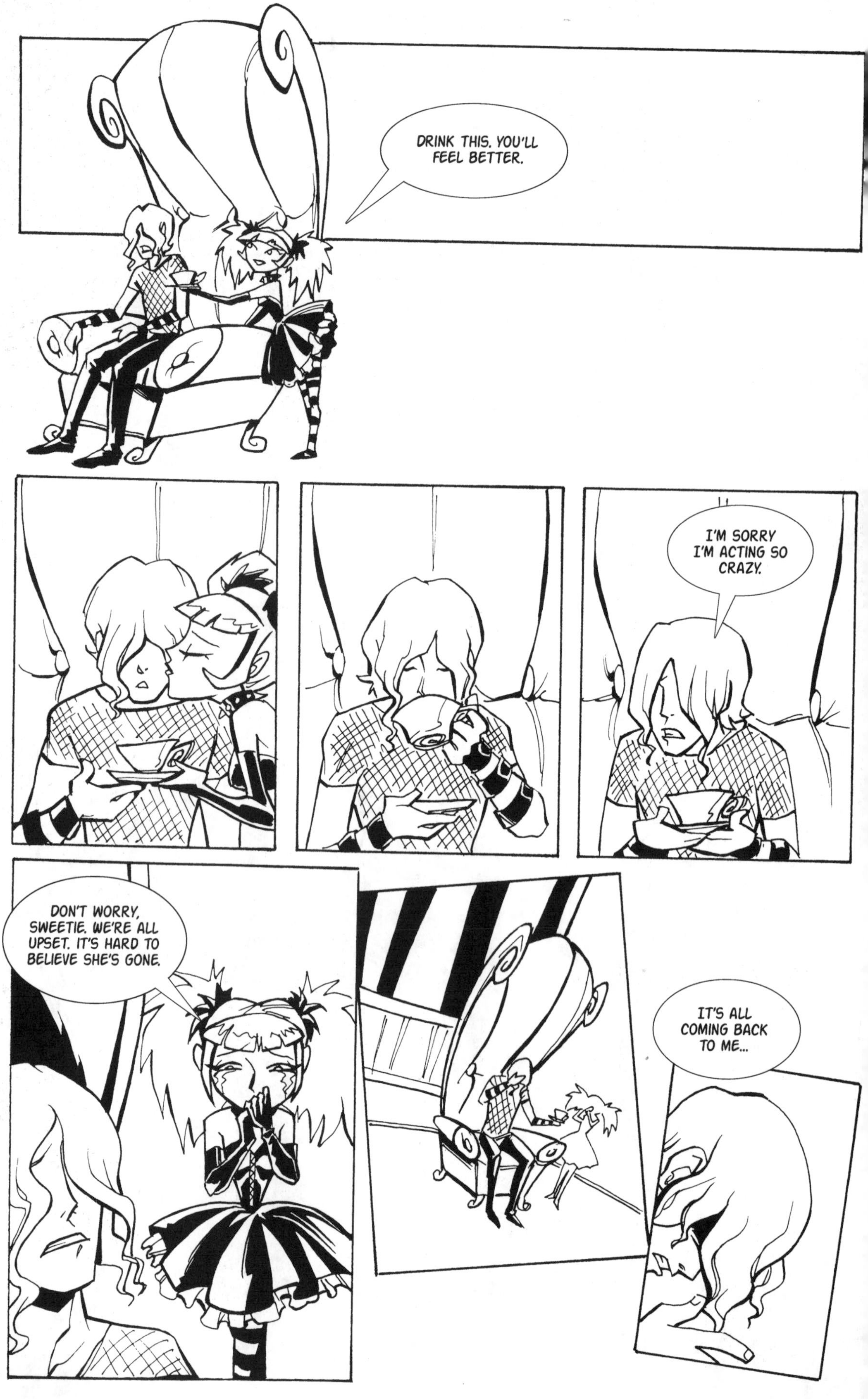
DRINK THIS. YOU'LL FEEL BETTER.
I'M SORRY I'M ACTING SO CRAZY.
DON'T WORRY, SWEETIE. WE'RE ALL UPSET. IT'S HARD TO BELIEVE SHE'S GONE.
IT'S ALL COMING BACK TO ME...

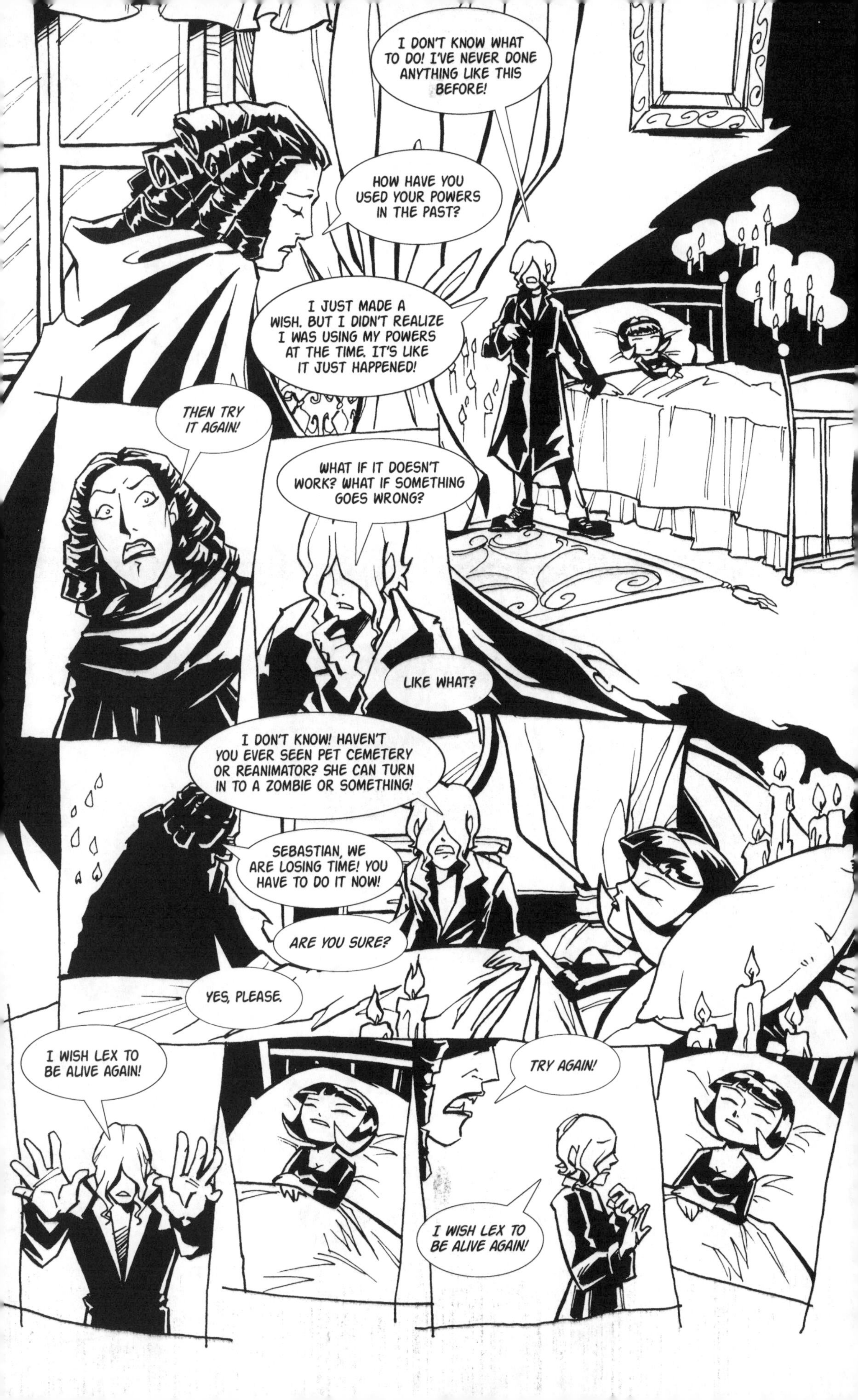
I DON'T KNOW WHAT TO DO! I'VE NEVER DONE ANYTHING LIKE THIS BEFORE!
HOW HAVE YOU USED YOUR POWERS IN THE PAST?
I JUST MADE A WISH. BUT I DIDN'T REALIZE I WAS USING MY POWERS AT THE TIME. IT'S LIKE IT JUST HAPPENED!
THEN TRY IT AGAIN!
WHAT IF IT DOESN'T WORK? WHAT IF SOMETHING GOES WRONG?
LIKE WHAT?
I DON'T KNOW! HAVEN'T YOU EVER SEEN PET CEMETERY OR REANIMATOR? SHE CAN TURN IN TO A ZOMBIE OR SOMETHING!
SEBASTIAN, WE ARE LOSING TIME! YOU HAVE TO DO IT NOW!
ARE YOU SURE?
YES, PLEASE.
I WISH LEX TO BE ALIVE AGAIN!
TRY AGAIN!
I WISH LEX TO BE ALIVE AGAIN!

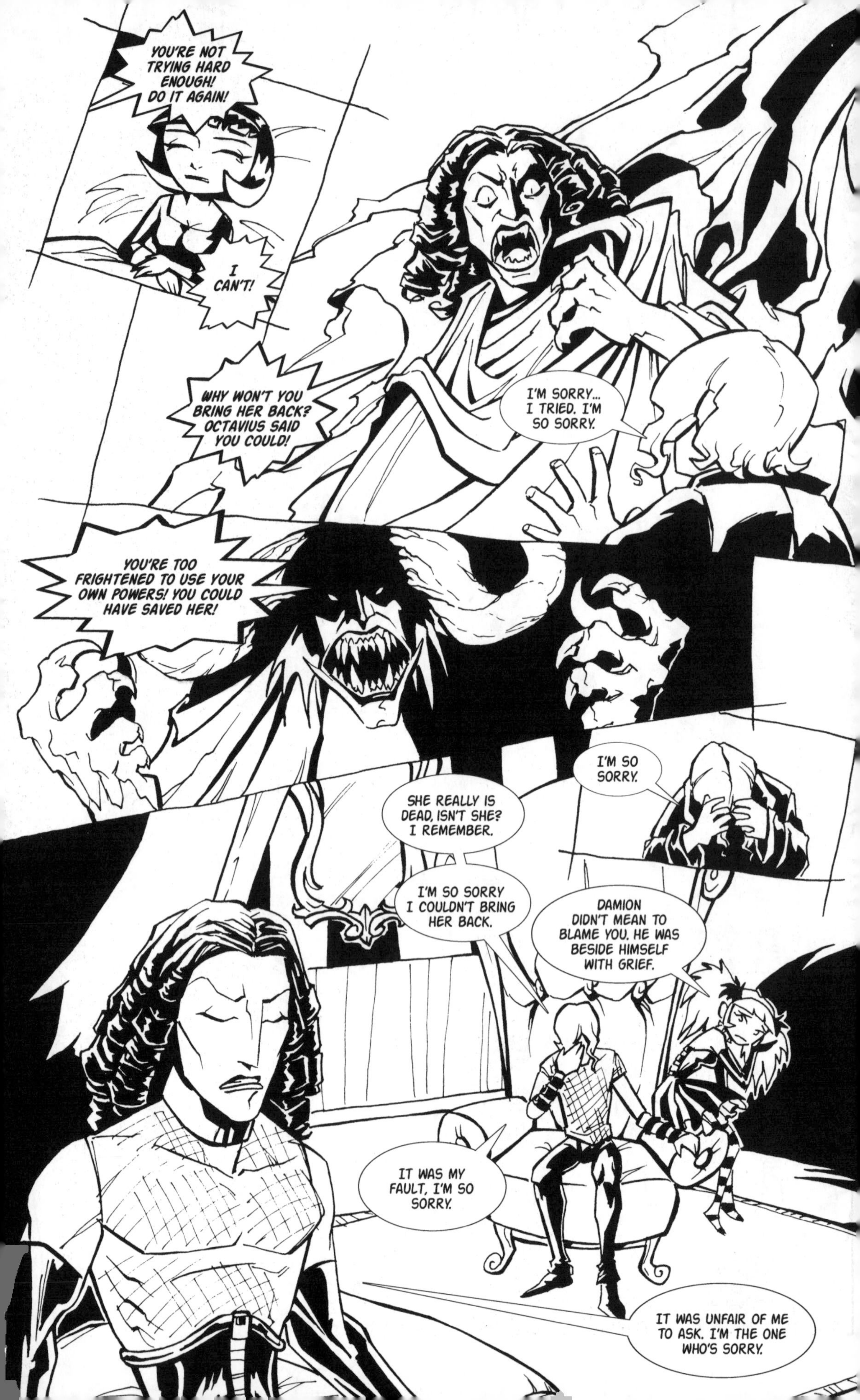
YOU'RE NOT TRYING HARD ENOUGH! DO IT AGAIN!
I CAN'T!
WHY WON'T YOU BRING HER BACK? OCTAVIUS SAID YOU COULD!
I'M SORRY... I TRIED. I'M SO SORRY.
YOU'RE TOO FRIGHTENED TO USE YOUR OWN POWERS! YOU COULD HAVE SAVED HER!
SHE REALLY IS DEAD, ISN'T SHE? I REMEMBER.
I'M SO SORRY.
I'M SO SORRY I COULDN'T BRING HER BACK.
DAMION DIDN'T MEAN TO BLAME YOU. HE WAS BESIDE HIMSELF WITH GRIEF.
IT WAS MY FAULT, I'M SO SORRY.
IT WAS UNFAIR OF ME TO ASK. I'M THE ONE WHO'S SORRY.

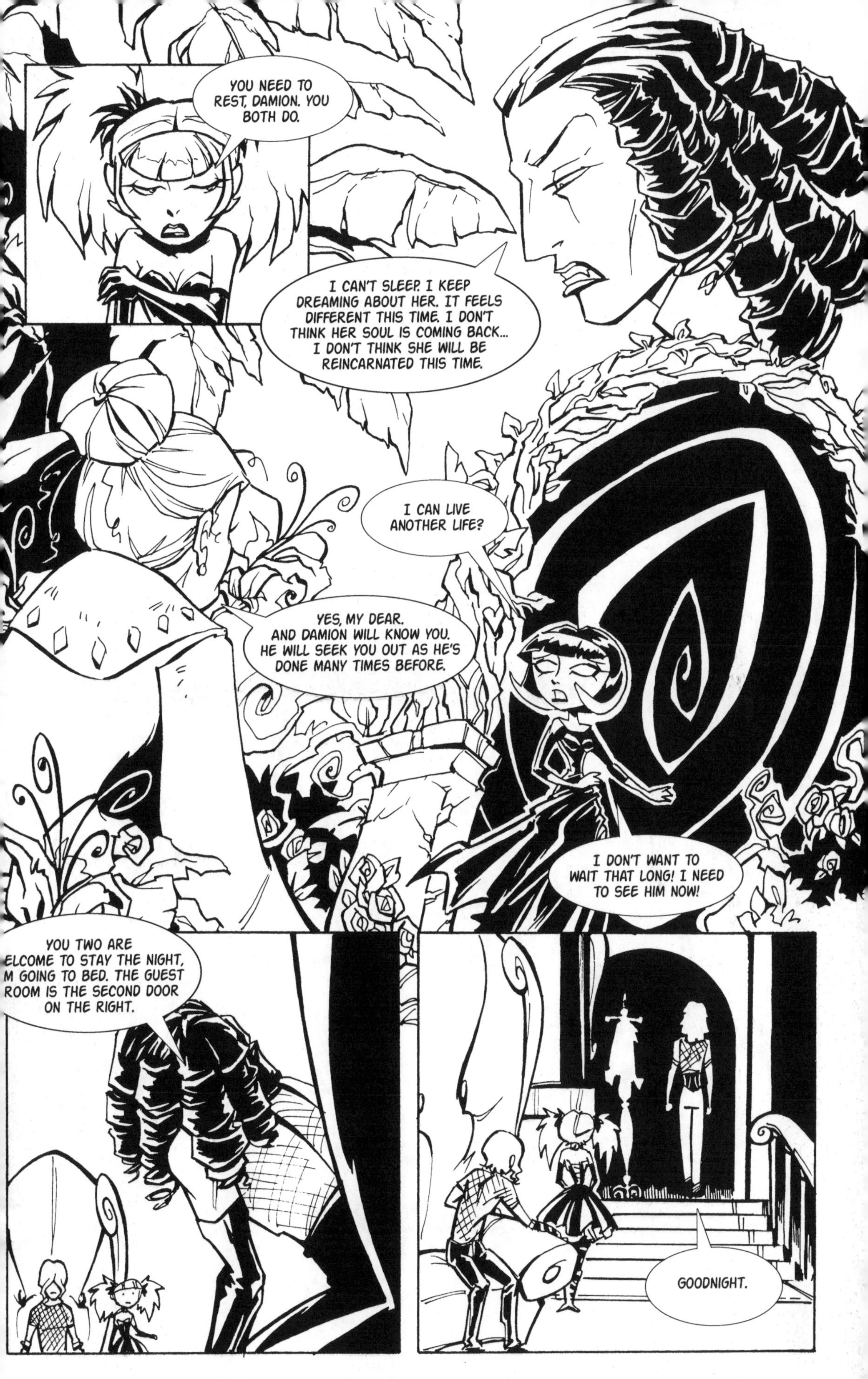
YOU NEED TO REST, DAMION. YOU BOTH DO.
I CAN'T SLEEP. I KEEP DREAMING ABOUT HER. IT FEELS DIFFERENT THIS TIME. I DON'T THINK HER SOUL IS COMING BACK... I DON'T THINK SHE WILL BE REINCARNATED THIS TIME.
I CAN LIVE ANOTHER LIFE?
YES, MY DEAR. AND DAMION WILL KNOW YOU. HE WILL SEEK YOU OUT AS HE'S DONE MANY TIMES BEFORE.
I DON'T WANT TO WAIT THAT LONG! I NEED TO SEE HIM NOW!
YOU TWO ARE ELCOME TO STAY THE NIGHT, M GOING TO BED. THE GUEST ROOM IS THE SECOND DOOR ON THE RIGHT.
GOODNIGHT.

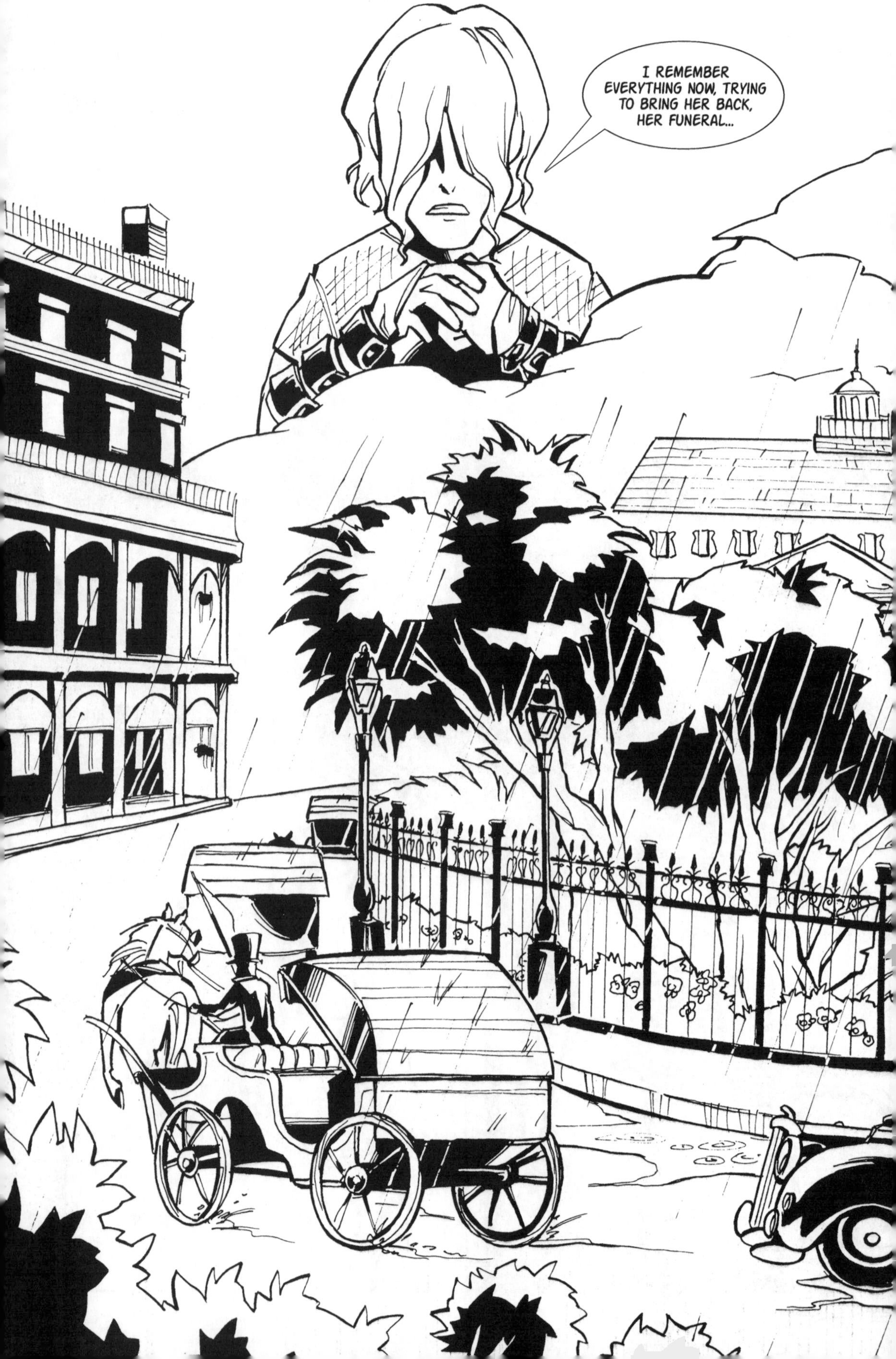
I REMEMBER EVERYTHING NOW, TRYING TO BRING HER BACK, HER FUNERAL...

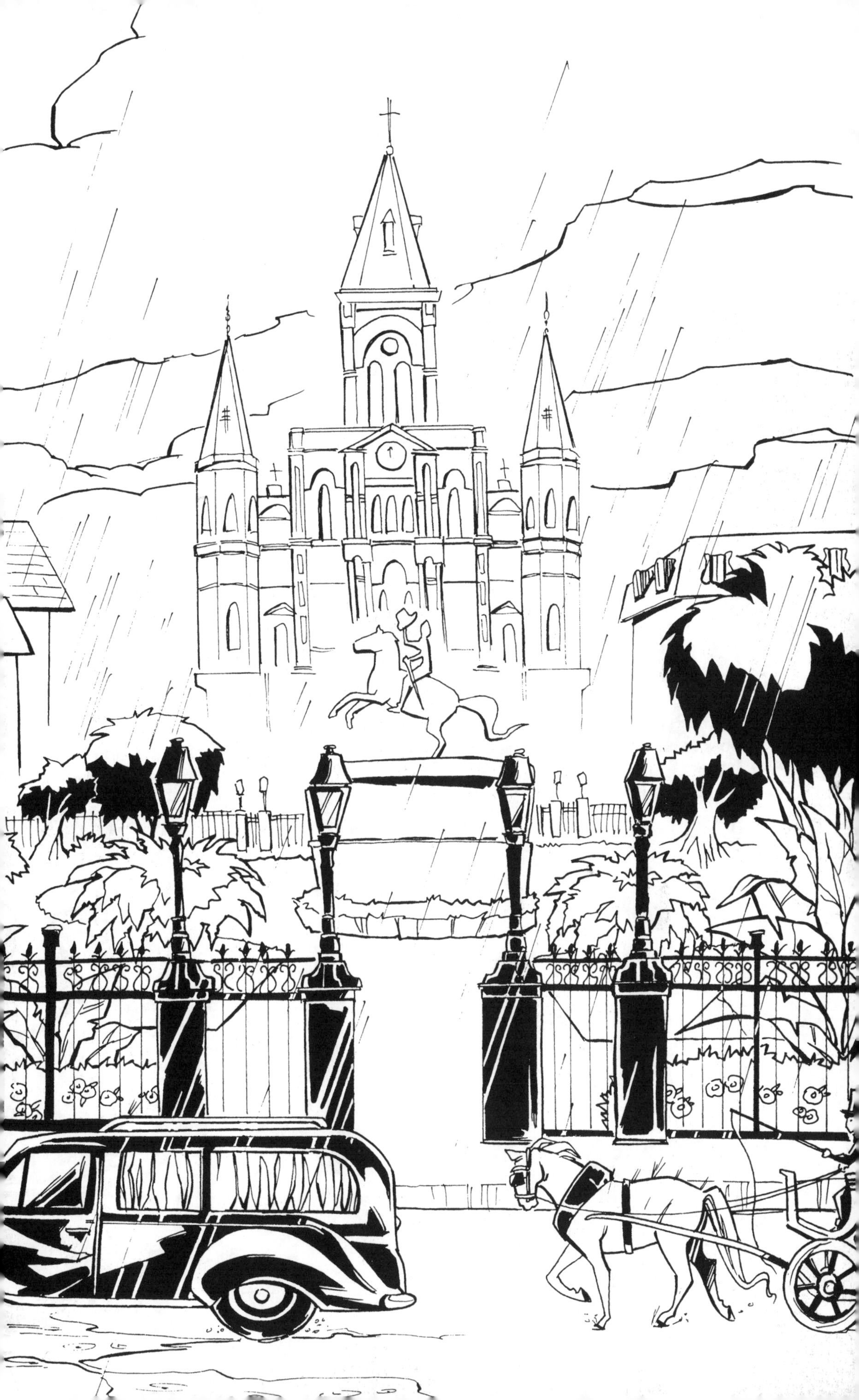

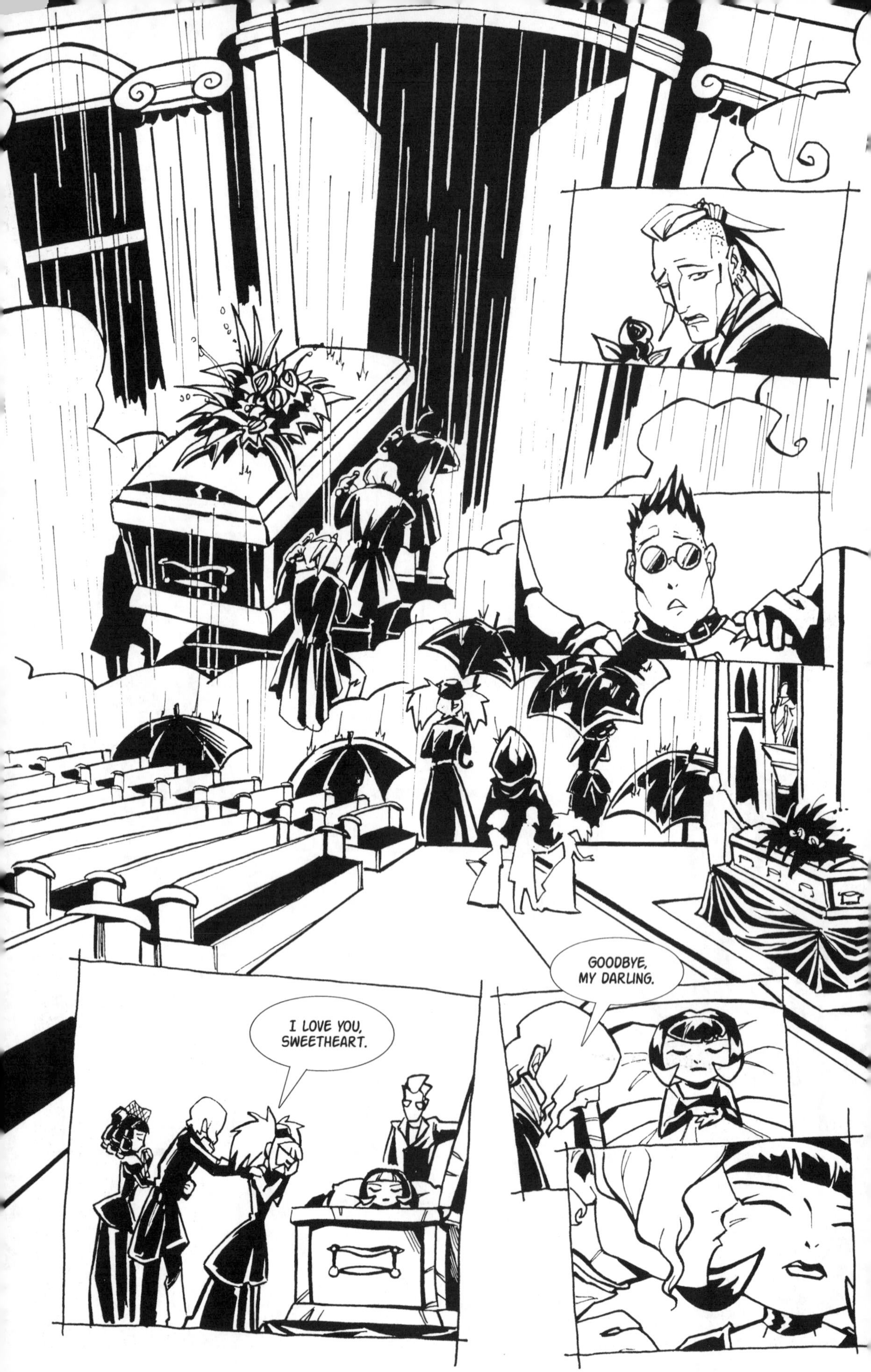
I LOVE YOU, SWEETHEART.
GOODBYE, MY DARLING.

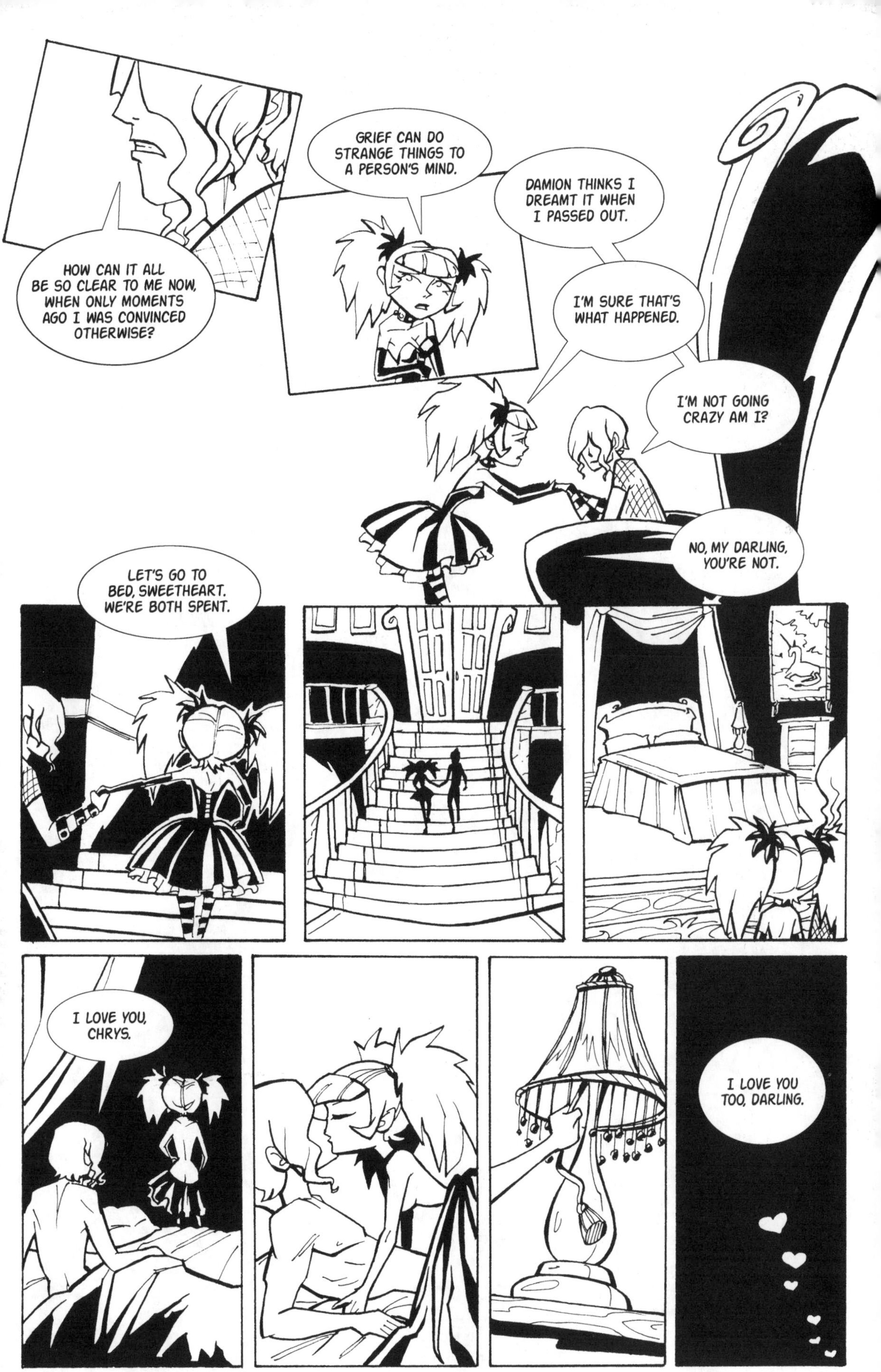
HOW CAN IT ALL BE SO CLEAR TO ME NOW, WHEN ONLY MOMENTS AGO I WAS CONVINCED OTHERWISE?
GRIEF CAN DO STRANGE THINGS TO A PERSON'S MIND.
DAMION THINKS I DREAMT IT WHEN I PASSED OUT.
I'M SURE THAT'S WHAT HAPPENED.
I'M NOT GOING CRAZY AM I?
NO, MY DARLING, YOU'RE NOT.
LET'S GO TO BED, SWEETHEART. WE'RE BOTH SPENT.
I LOVE YOU, CHRYS.
I LOVE YOU TOO, DARLING.

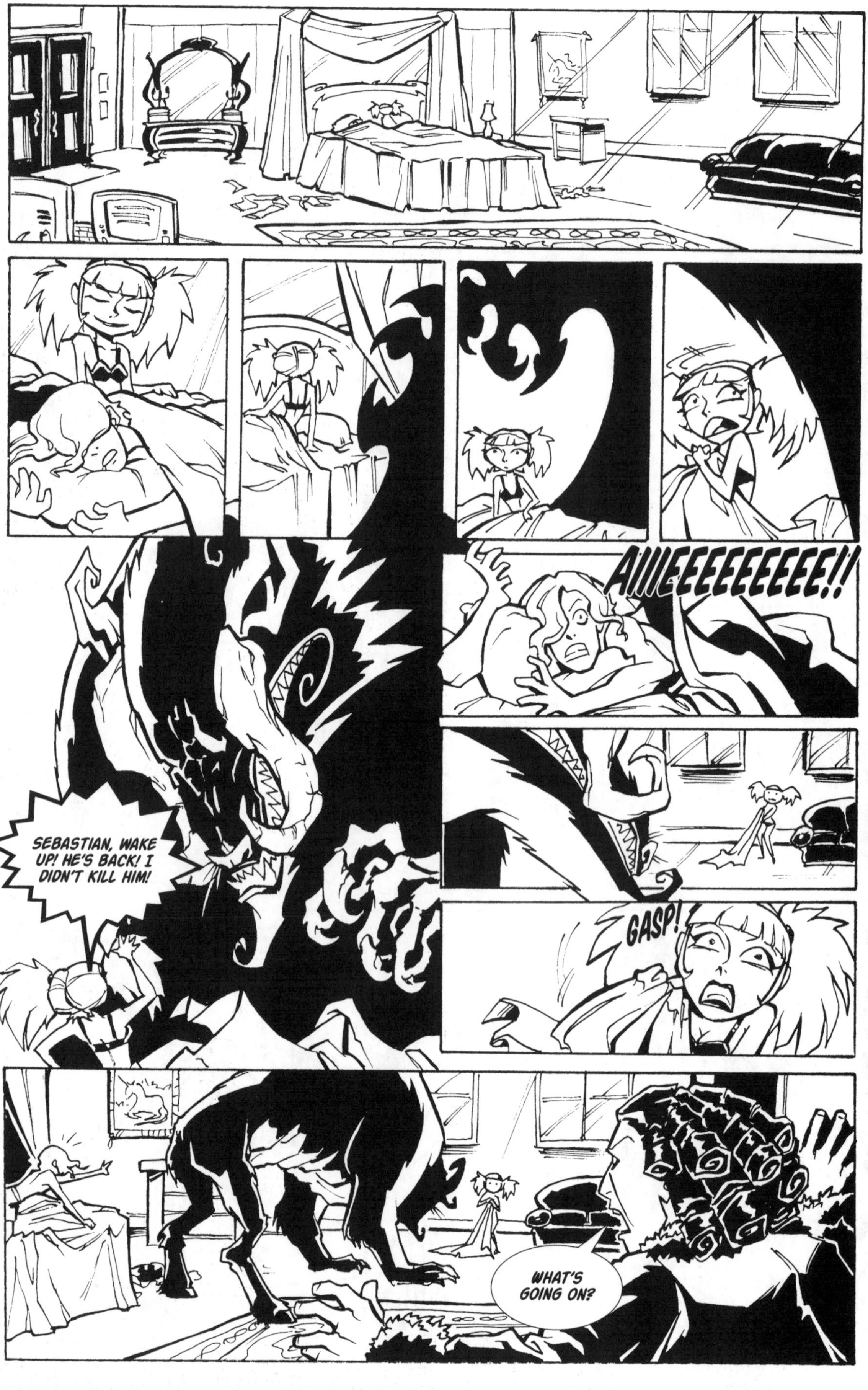
AIIIEEEEEEEEEE!!
SEBASTIAN, WAKE UP! HE'S BACK! I DIDN'T KILL HIM!
GASP!
WHAT'S GOING ON?

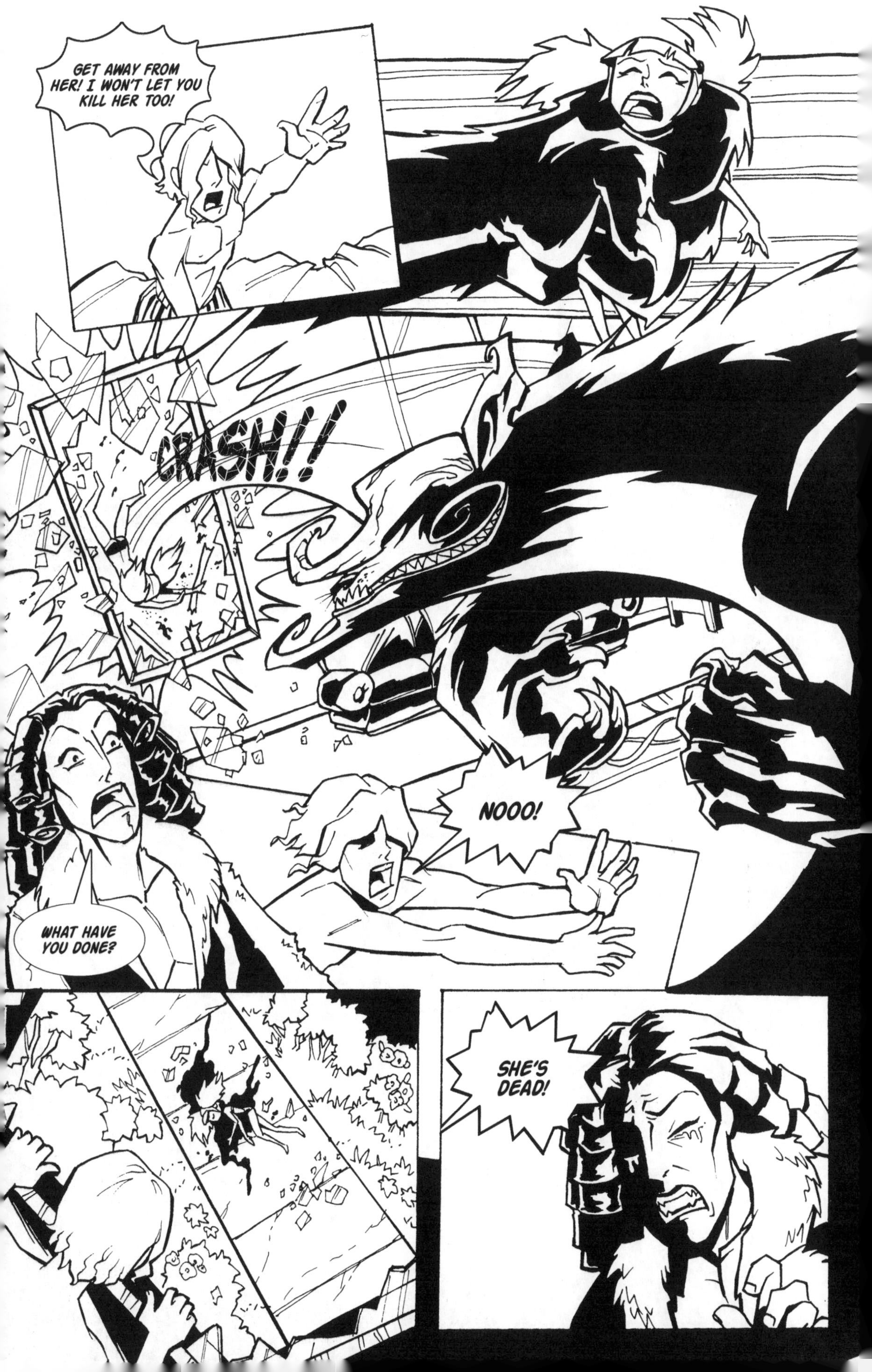
GET AWAY FROM HER! I WON'T LET YOU KILL HER TOO!
CRASH!!
NOOO!
WHAT HAVE YOU DONE?
SHE'S DEAD!

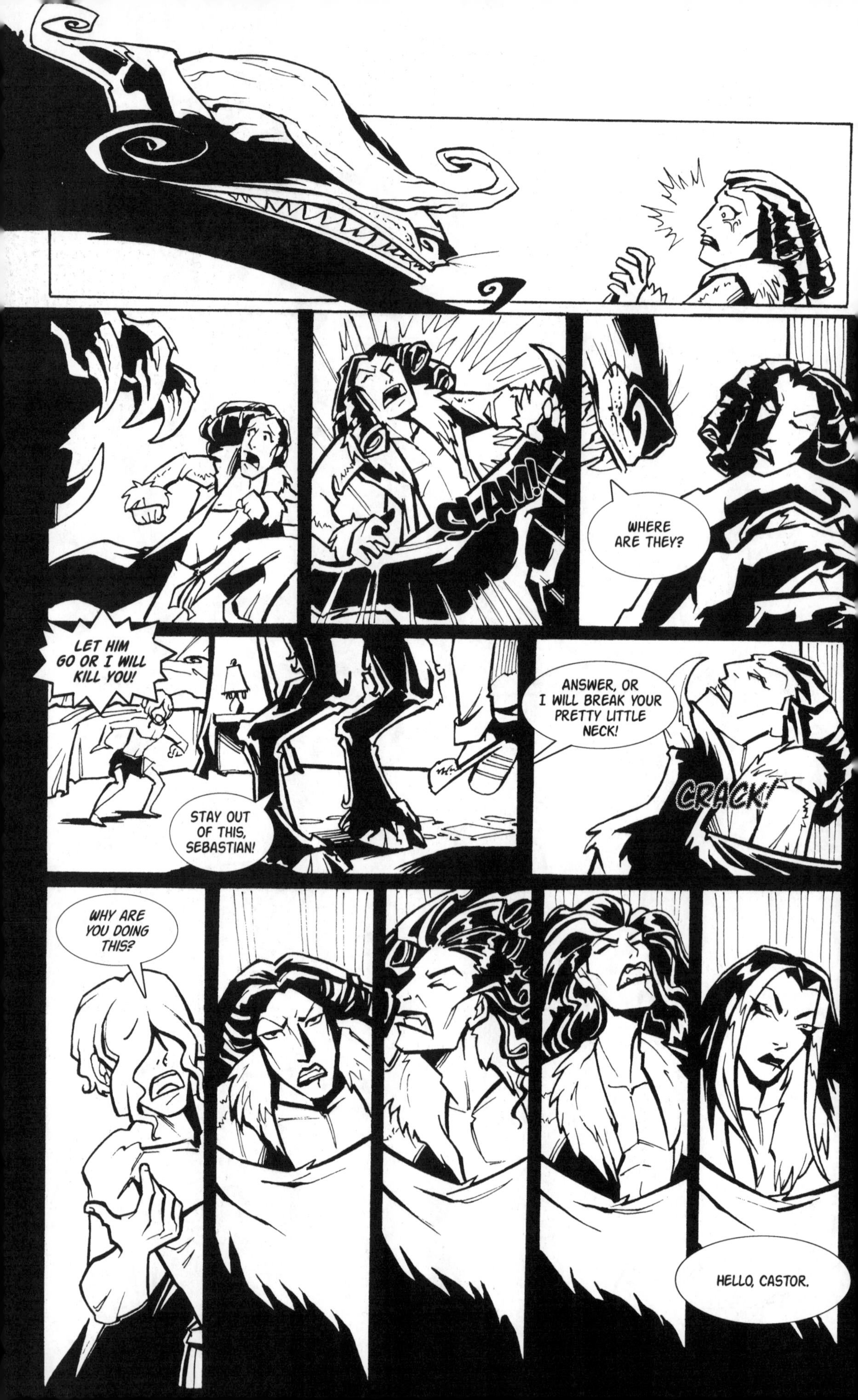
SLAM!
WHERE ARE THEY?
LET HIM GO OR I WILL KILL YOU!
STAY OUT OF THIS, SEBASTIAN!
ANSWER, OR I WILL BREAK YOUR PRETTY LITTLE NECK!
CRACK!
WHY ARE YOU DOING THIS?
HELLO, CASTOR.

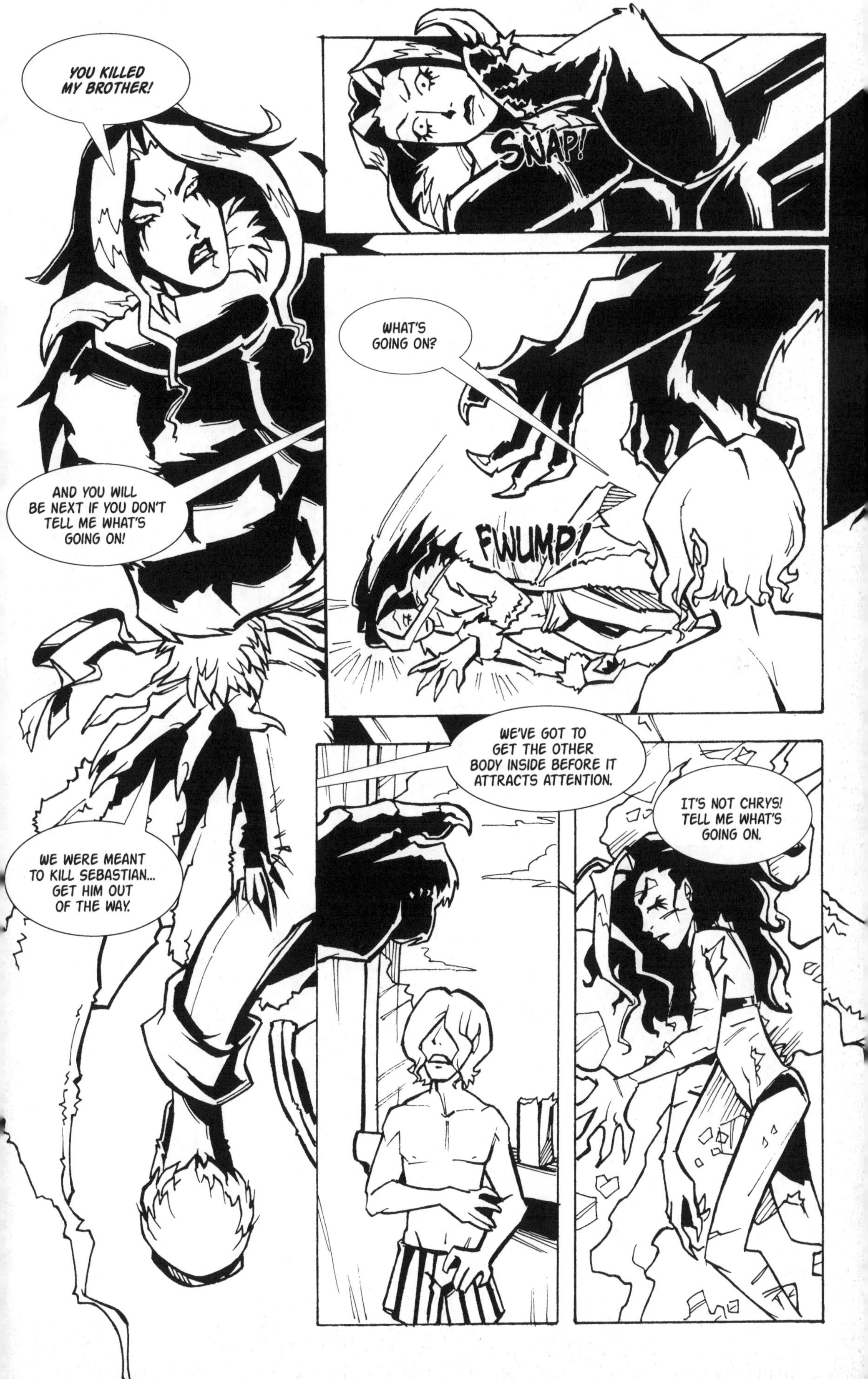
YOU KILLED MY BROTHER!
SNAP!
AND YOU WILL BE NEXT IF YOU DON'T TELL ME WHAT'S GOING ON!
WHAT'S GOING ON?
FWUMP!
WE WERE MEANT TO KILL SEBASTIAN... GET HIM OUT OF THE WAY.
WE'VE GOT TO GET THE OTHER BODY INSIDE BEFORE IT ATTRACTS ATTENTION.
IT'S NOT CHRYS! TELL ME WHAT'S GOING ON.

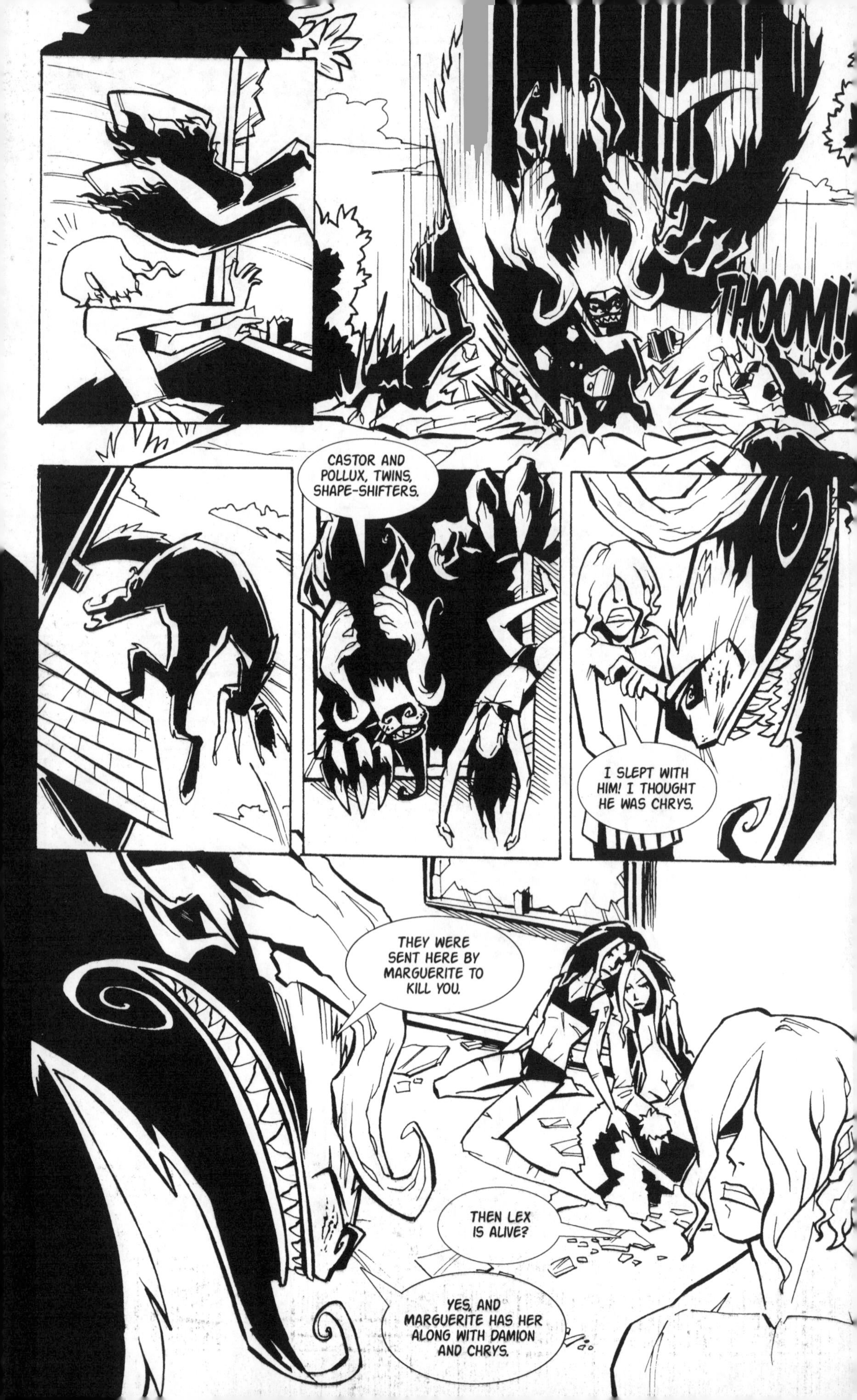
THOOM!!
CASTOR AND POLLUX, TWINS, SHAPE-SHIFTERS.
I SLEPT WITH HIM! I THOUGHT HE WAS CHRYS.
THEY WERE SENT HERE BY MARGUERITE TO KILL YOU.
THEN LEX IS ALIVE?
YES, AND MARGUERITE HAS HER ALONG WITH DAMION AND CHRYS.

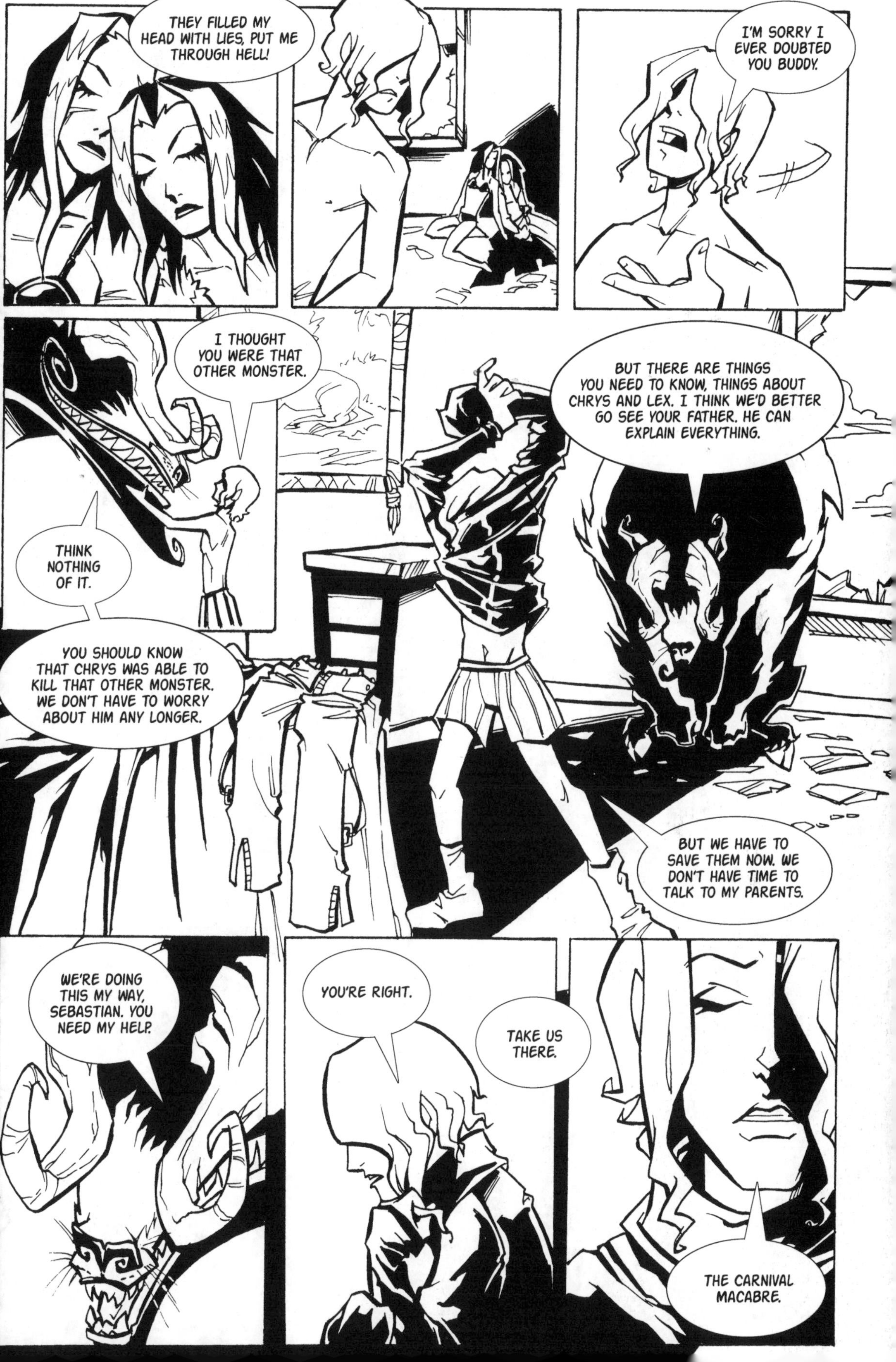
THEY FILLED MY HEAD WITH LIES, PUT ME THROUGH HELL!
I'M SORRY I EVER DOUBTED YOU BUDDY.
I THOUGHT YOU WERE THAT OTHER MONSTER.
THINK NOTHING OF IT.
BUT THERE ARE THINGS YOU NEED TO KNOW, THINGS ABOUT CHRYS AND LEX. I THINK WE'D BETTER GO SEE YOUR FATHER. HE CAN EXPLAIN EVERYTHING.
YOU SHOULD KNOW THAT CHRYS WAS ABLE TO KILL THAT OTHER MONSTER. WE DON'T HAVE TO WORRY ABOUT HIM ANY LONGER.
BUT WE HAVE TO SAVE THEM NOW. WE DON'T HAVE TIME TO TALK TO MY PARENTS.
WE'RE DOING THIS MY WAY, SEBASTIAN. YOU NEED MY HELP.
YOU'RE RIGHT.
TAKE US THERE.
THE CARNIVAL MACABRE.

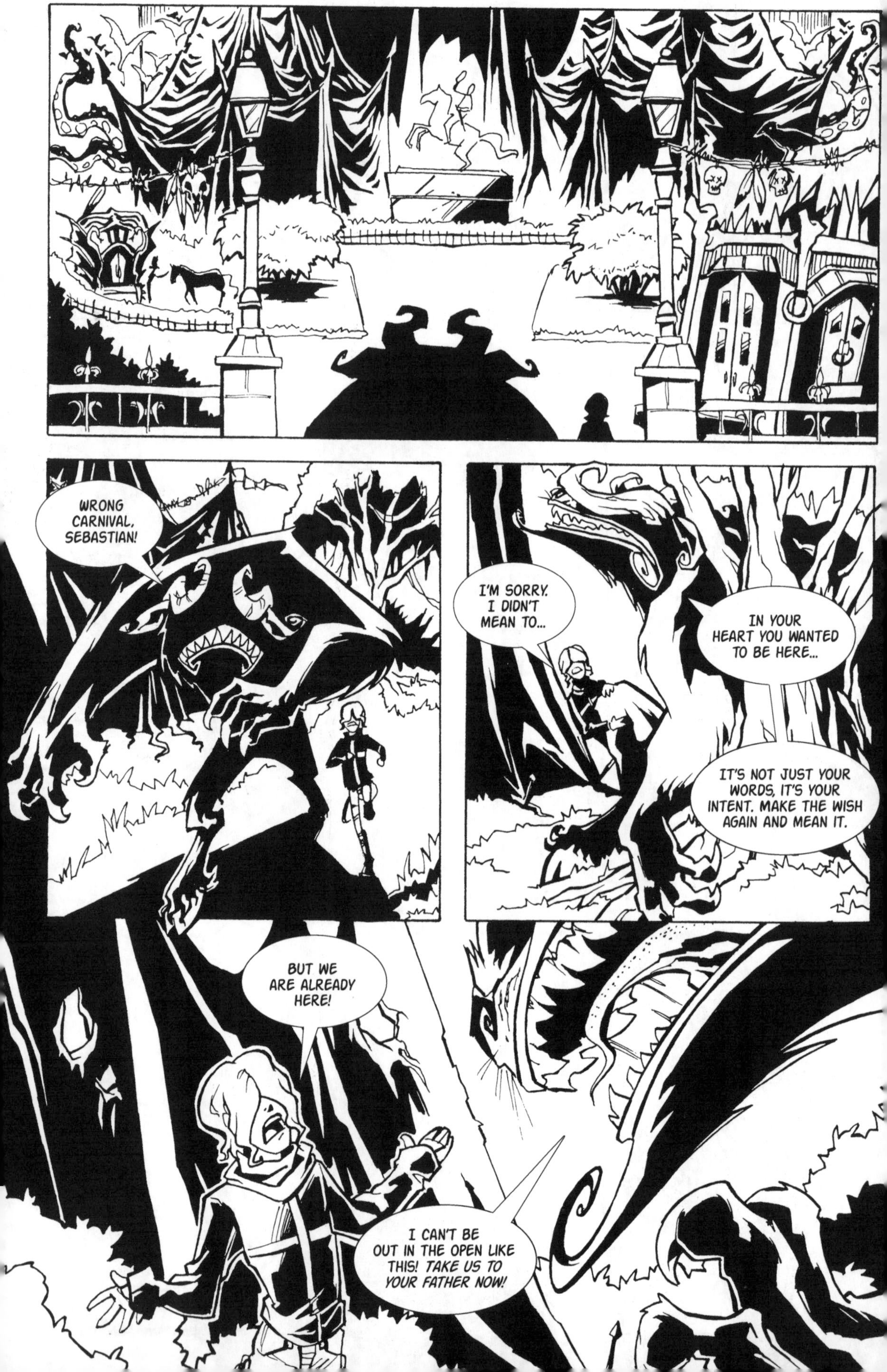
WRONG CARNIVAL, SEBASTIAN!
I'M SORRY. I DIDN'T MEAN TO...
IN YOUR HEART YOU WANTED TO BE HERE...
IT'S NOT JUST YOUR WORDS, IT'S YOUR INTENT. MAKE THE WISH AGAIN AND MEAN IT.
BUT WE ARE ALREADY HERE!
I CAN'T BE OUT IN THE OPEN LIKE THIS! *TAKE US TO YOUR FATHER NOW!*

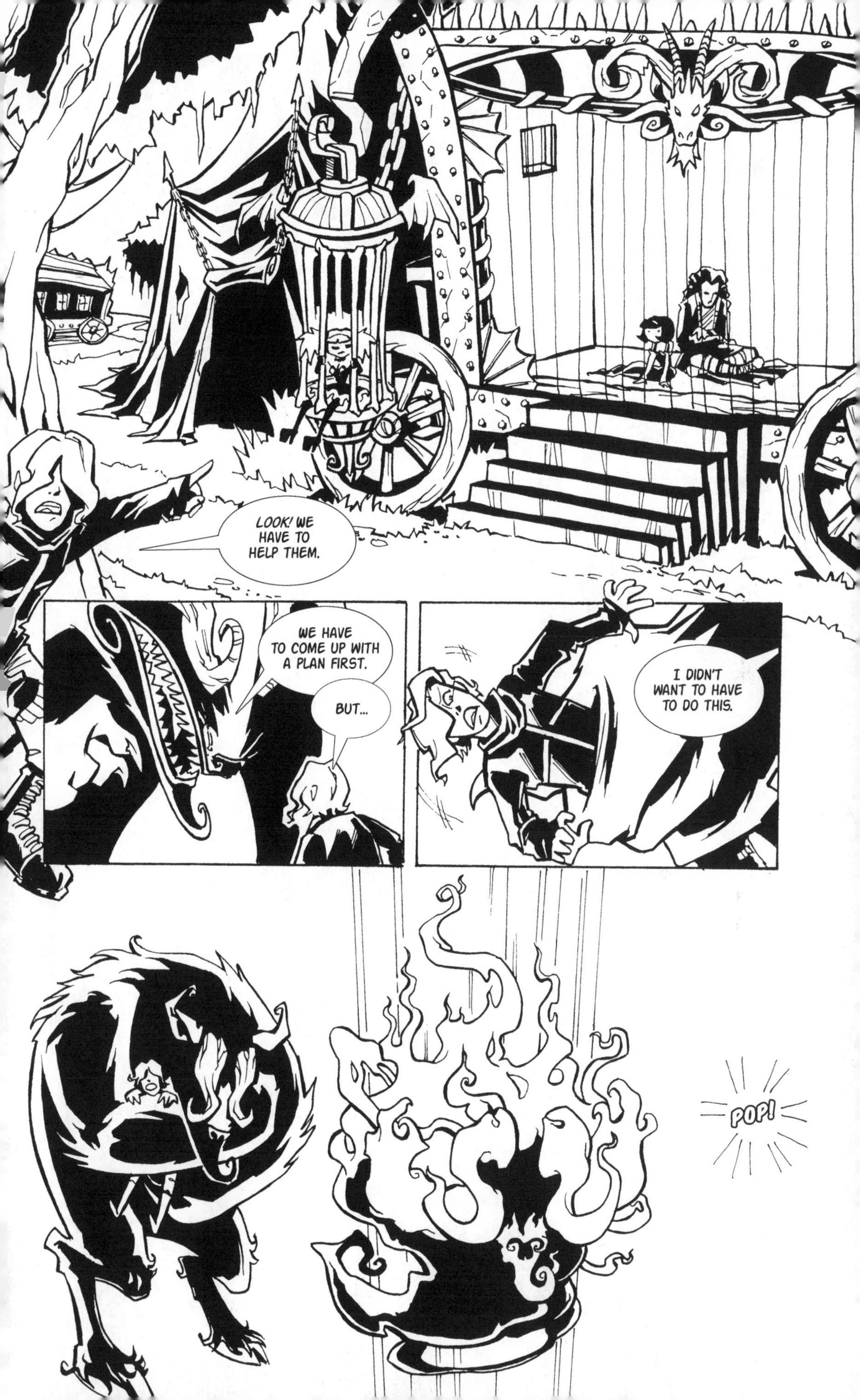
LOOK! WE HAVE TO HELP THEM.
WE HAVE TO COME UP WITH A PLAN FIRST.
BUT...
I DIDN'T WANT TO HAVE TO DO THIS.
POP!

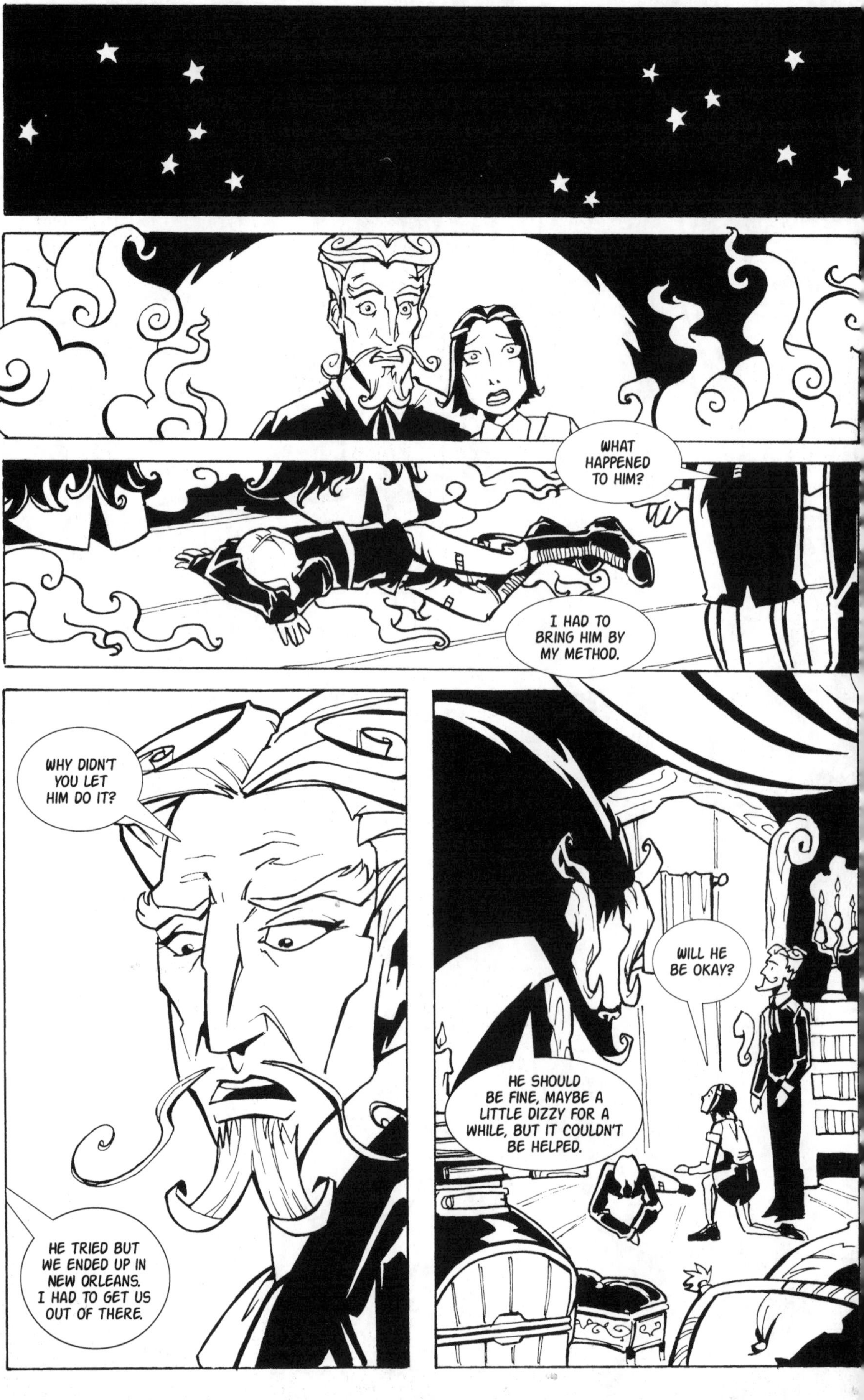
WHAT HAPPENED TO HIM?
I HAD TO BRING HIM BY MY METHOD.
WHY DIDN'T YOU LET HIM DO IT?
HE TRIED BUT WE ENDED UP IN NEW ORLEANS. I HAD TO GET US OUT OF THERE.
WILL HE BE OKAY?
HE SHOULD BE FINE, MAYBE A LITTLE DIZZY FOR A WHILE, BUT IT COULDN'T BE HELPED.

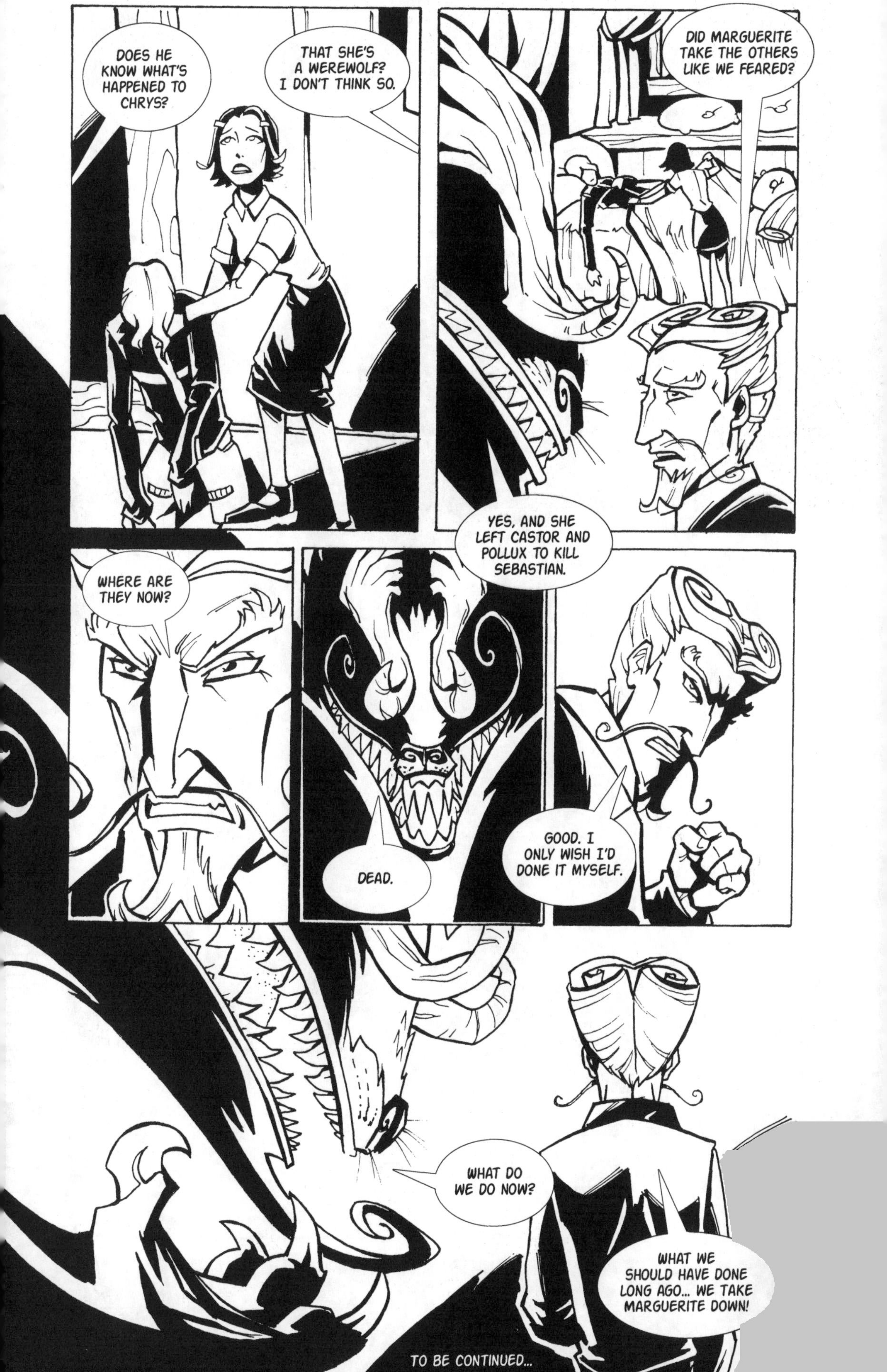
DOES HE KNOW WHAT'S HAPPENED TO CHRYS?
THAT SHE'S A WEREWOLF? I DON'T THINK SO.
DID MARGUERITE TAKE THE OTHERS LIKE WE FEARED?
YES, AND SHE LEFT CASTOR AND POLLUX TO KILL SEBASTIAN.
WHERE ARE THEY NOW?
DEAD.
GOOD. I ONLY WISH I'D DONE IT MYSELF.
WHAT DO WE DO NOW?
WHAT WE SHOULD HAVE DONE LONG AGO... WE TAKE MARGUERITE DOWN!
TO BE CONTINUED...

Chapter

21

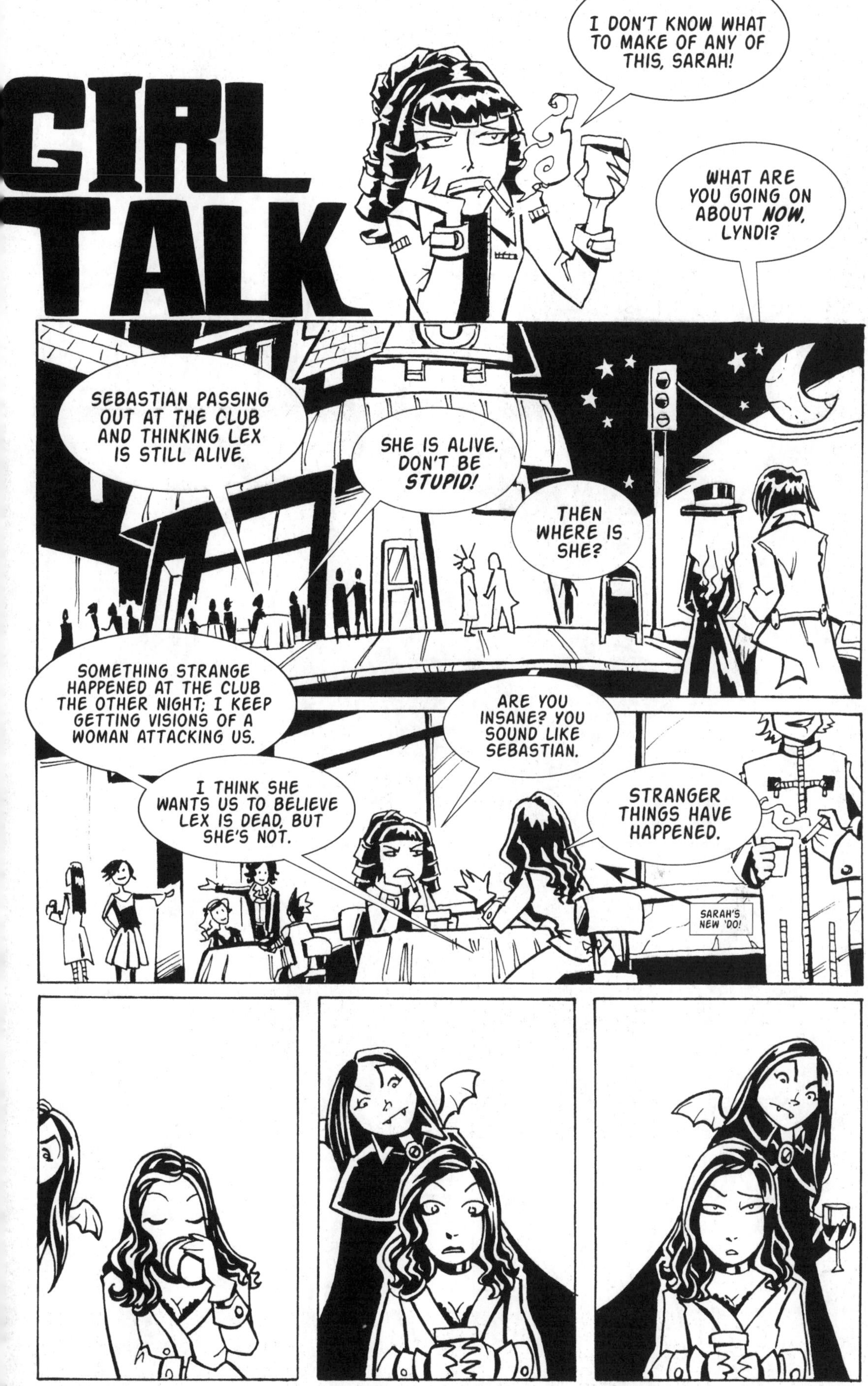
GIRL TALK
I DON'T KNOW WHAT TO MAKE OF ANY OF THIS, SARAH!
WHAT ARE YOU GOING ON ABOUT NOW, LYNDI?
SEBASTIAN PASSING OUT AT THE CLUB AND THINKING LEX IS STILL ALIVE.
SHE IS ALIVE. DON'T BE STUPID!
THEN WHERE IS SHE?
SOMETHING STRANGE HAPPENED AT THE CLUB THE OTHER NIGHT; I KEEP GETTING VISIONS OF A WOMAN ATTACKING US.
ARE YOU INSANE? YOU SOUND LIKE SEBASTIAN.
I THINK SHE WANTS US TO BELIEVE LEX IS DEAD, BUT SHE'S NOT.
STRANGER THINGS HAVE HAPPENED.
SARAH'S NEW 'DO!

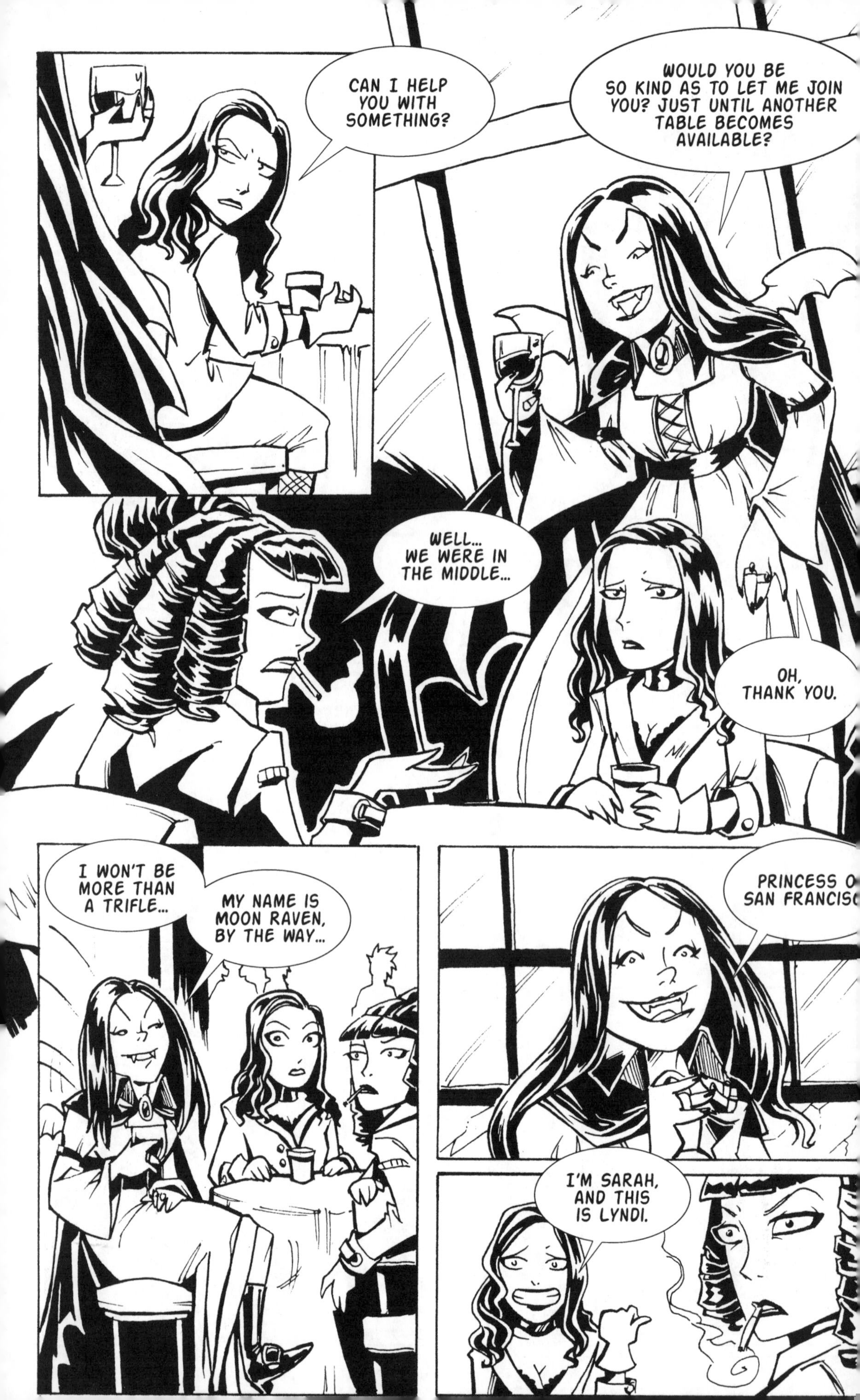

CAN I HELP YOU WITH SOMETHING?
WOULD YOU BE SO KIND AS TO LET ME JOIN YOU? JUST UNTIL ANOTHER TABLE BECOMES AVAILABLE?
WELL... WE WERE IN THE MIDDLE...
OH, THANK YOU.
I WON'T BE MORE THAN A TRIFLE...
MY NAME IS MOON RAVEN, BY THE WAY...
PRINCESS OF SAN FRANCISCO
I'M SARAH, AND THIS IS LYNDI.

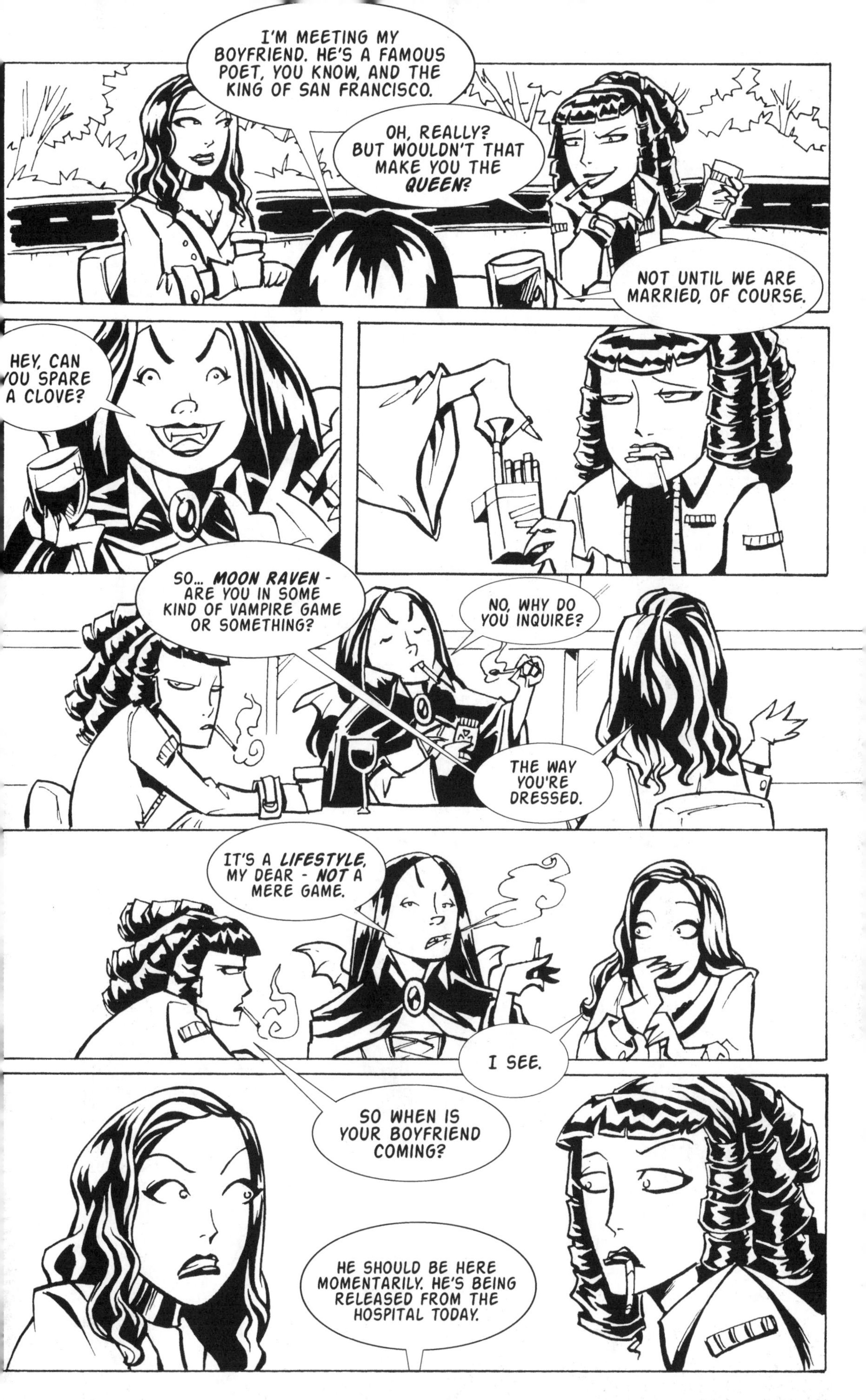
I'M MEETING MY BOYFRIEND. HE'S A FAMOUS POET, YOU KNOW, AND THE KING OF SAN FRANCISCO.
OH, REALLY? BUT WOULDN'T THAT MAKE YOU THE *QUEEN*?
NOT UNTIL WE ARE MARRIED, OF COURSE.
HEY, CAN YOU SPARE A CLOVE?
SO... *MOON RAVEN* - ARE YOU IN SOME KIND OF VAMPIRE GAME OR SOMETHING?
NO, WHY DO YOU INQUIRE?
THE WAY YOU'RE DRESSED.
IT'S A *LIFESTYLE*, MY DEAR - *NOT* A MERE GAME.
I SEE.
SO WHEN IS YOUR BOYFRIEND COMING?
HE SHOULD BE HERE MOMENTARILY. HE'S BEING RELEASED FROM THE HOSPITAL TODAY.

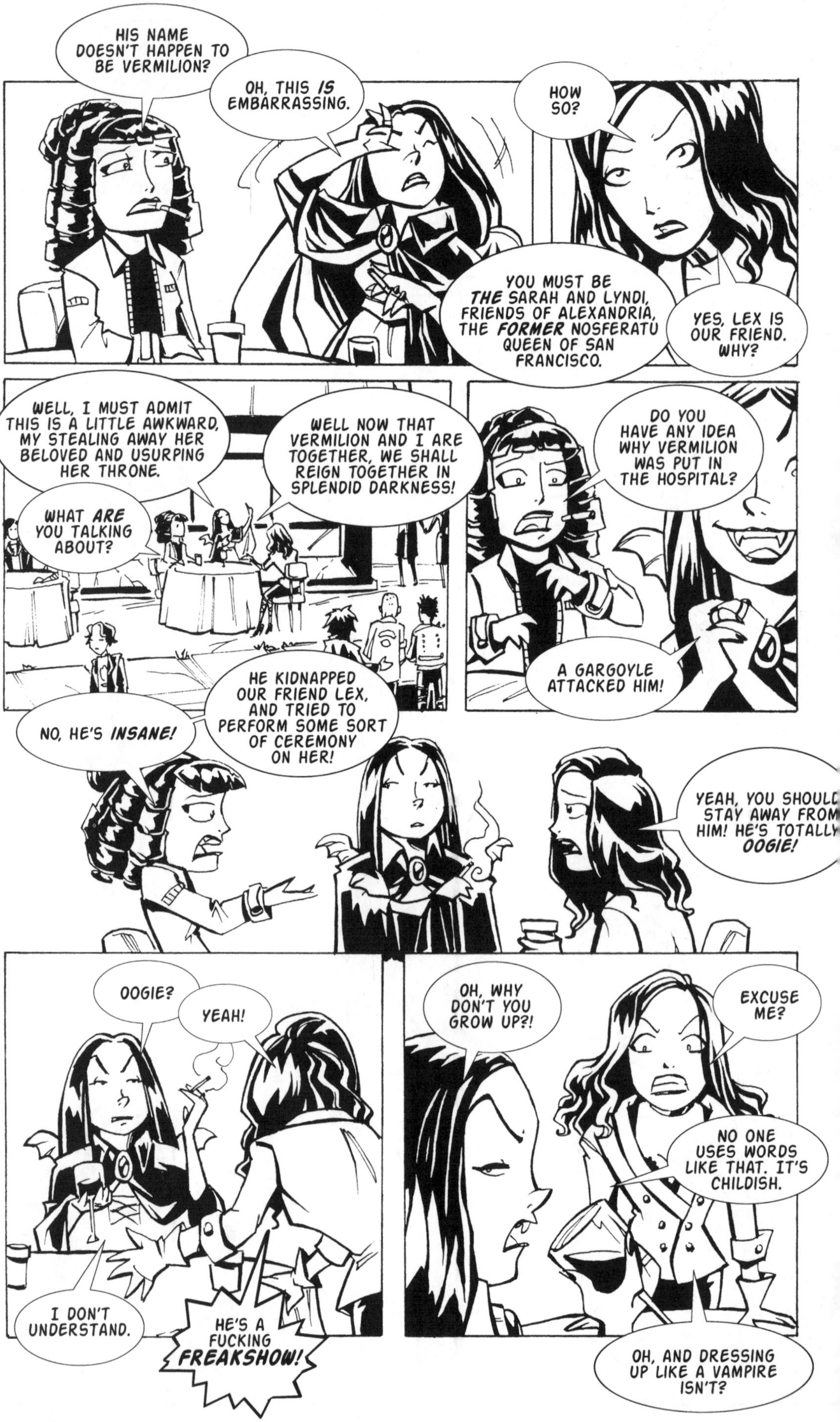
HIS NAME DOESN'T HAPPEN TO BE VERMILION?
OH, THIS IS EMBARRASSING.
HOW SO?
YOU MUST BE THE SARAH AND LYNDI, FRIENDS OF ALEXANDRIA, THE FORMER NOSFERATU QUEEN OF SAN FRANCISCO.
YES, LEX IS OUR FRIEND. WHY?
WELL, I MUST ADMIT THIS IS A LITTLE AWKWARD, MY STEALING AWAY HER BELOVED AND USURPING HER THRONE.
WHAT ARE YOU TALKING ABOUT?
WELL NOW THAT VERMILION AND I ARE TOGETHER, WE SHALL REIGN TOGETHER IN SPLENDID DARKNESS!
DO YOU HAVE ANY IDEA WHY VERMILION WAS PUT IN THE HOSPITAL?
A GARGOYLE ATTACKED HIM!
NO, HE'S INSANE!
HE KIDNAPPED OUR FRIEND LEX, AND TRIED TO PERFORM SOME SORT OF CEREMONY ON HER!
YEAH, YOU SHOULD STAY AWAY FROM HIM! HE'S TOTALLY OOGIE!
OOGIE?
YEAH!
I DON'T UNDERSTAND.
HE'S A FUCKING FREAKSHOW!
OH, WHY DON'T YOU GROW UP?!
EXCUSE ME?
NO ONE USES WORDS LIKE THAT. IT'S CHILDISH.
OH, AND DRESSING UP LIKE A VAMPIRE ISN'T?

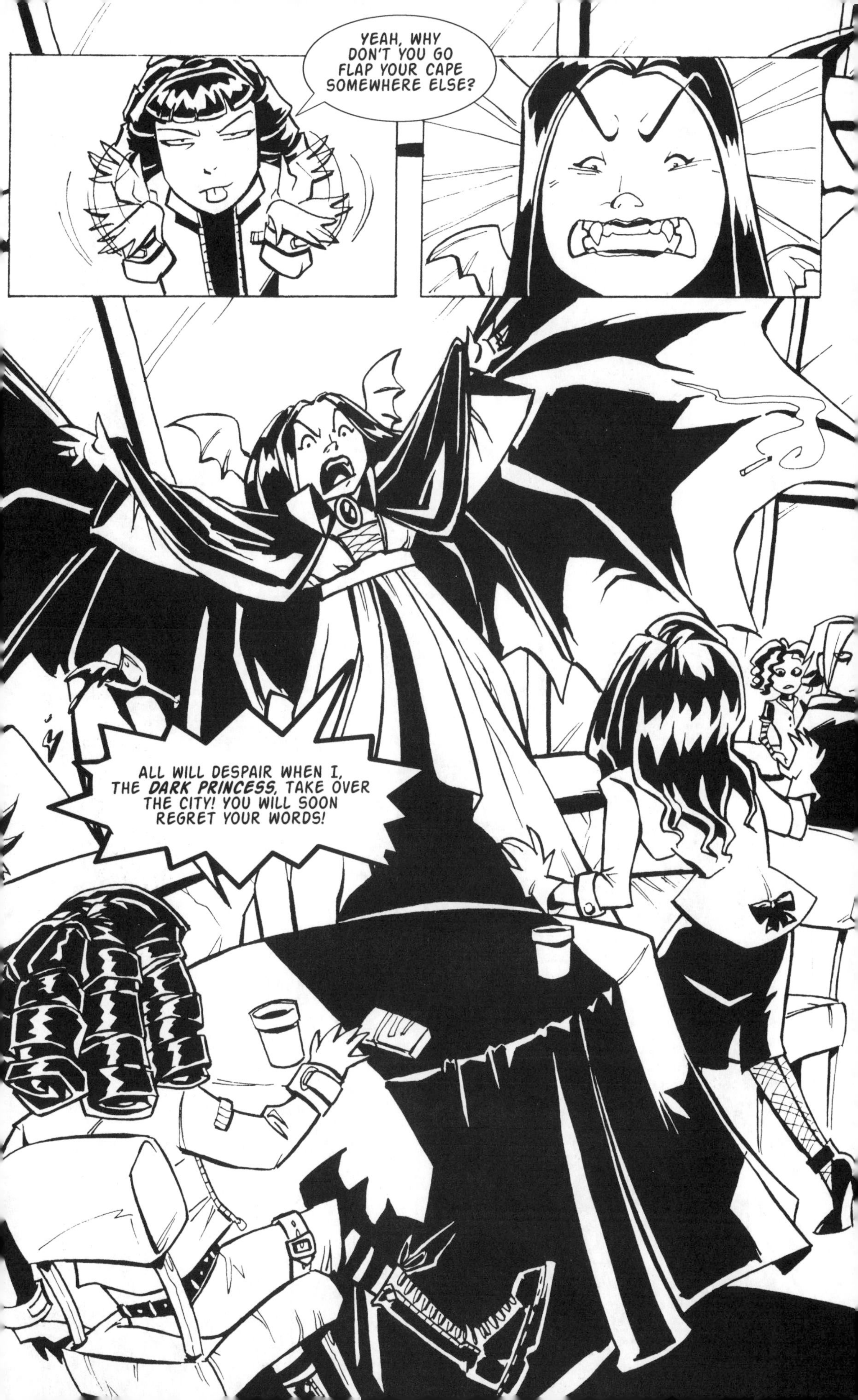
YEAH, WHY DON'T YOU GO FLAP YOUR CAPE SOMEWHERE ELSE?
ALL WILL DESPAIR WHEN I, THE *DARK PRINCESS*, TAKE OVER THE CITY! YOU WILL SOON REGRET YOUR WORDS!

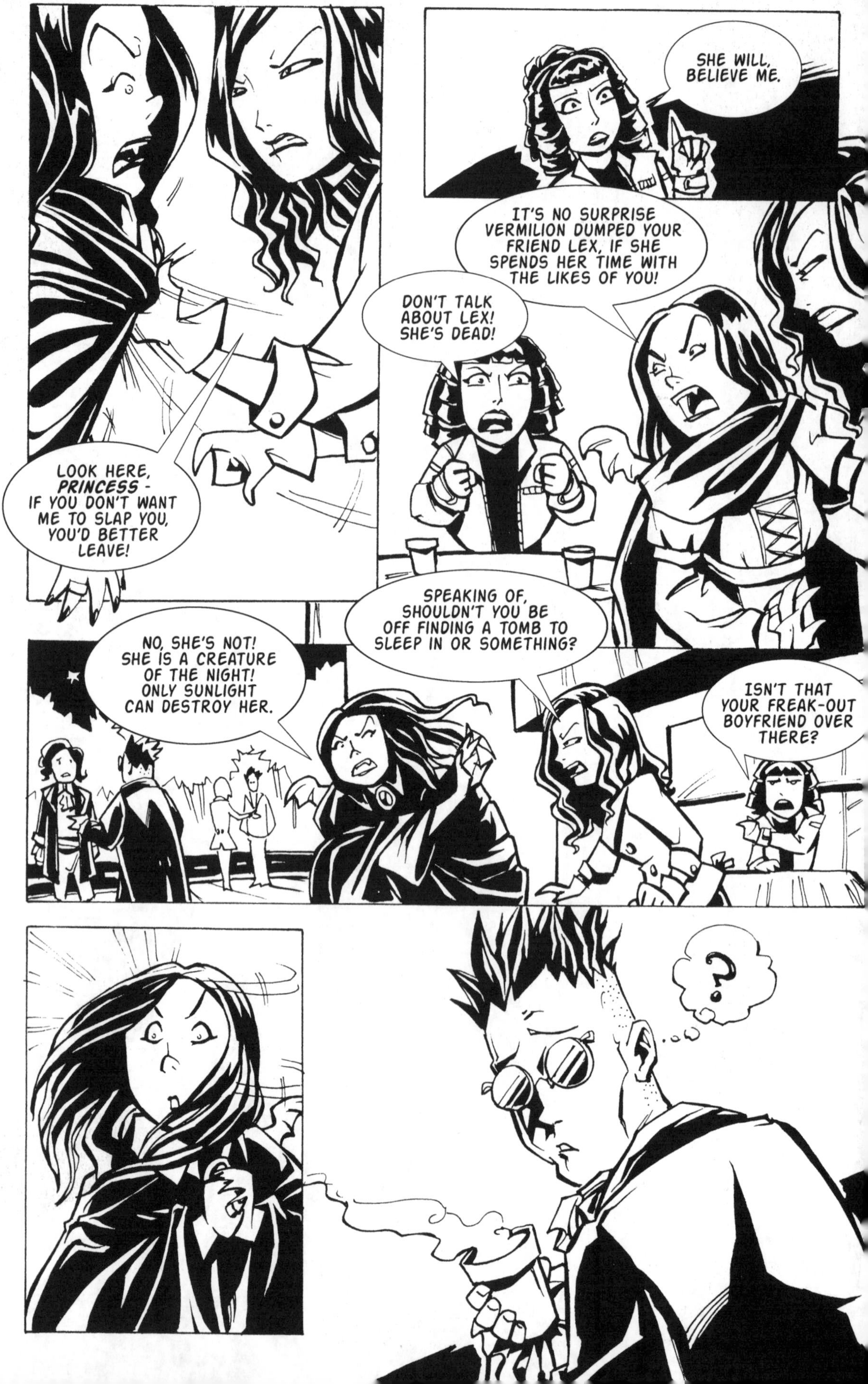

LOOK HERE, **PRINCESS** - IF YOU DON'T WANT ME TO SLAP YOU, YOU'D BETTER LEAVE!
SHE WILL, BELIEVE ME.
IT'S NO SURPRISE VERMILION DUMPED YOUR FRIEND LEX, IF SHE SPENDS HER TIME WITH THE LIKES OF YOU!
DON'T TALK ABOUT LEX! SHE'S DEAD!
NO, SHE'S NOT! SHE IS A CREATURE OF THE NIGHT! ONLY SUNLIGHT CAN DESTROY HER.
SPEAKING OF, SHOULDN'T YOU BE OFF FINDING A TOMB TO SLEEP IN OR SOMETHING?
ISN'T THAT YOUR FREAK-OUT BOYFRIEND OVER THERE?
?

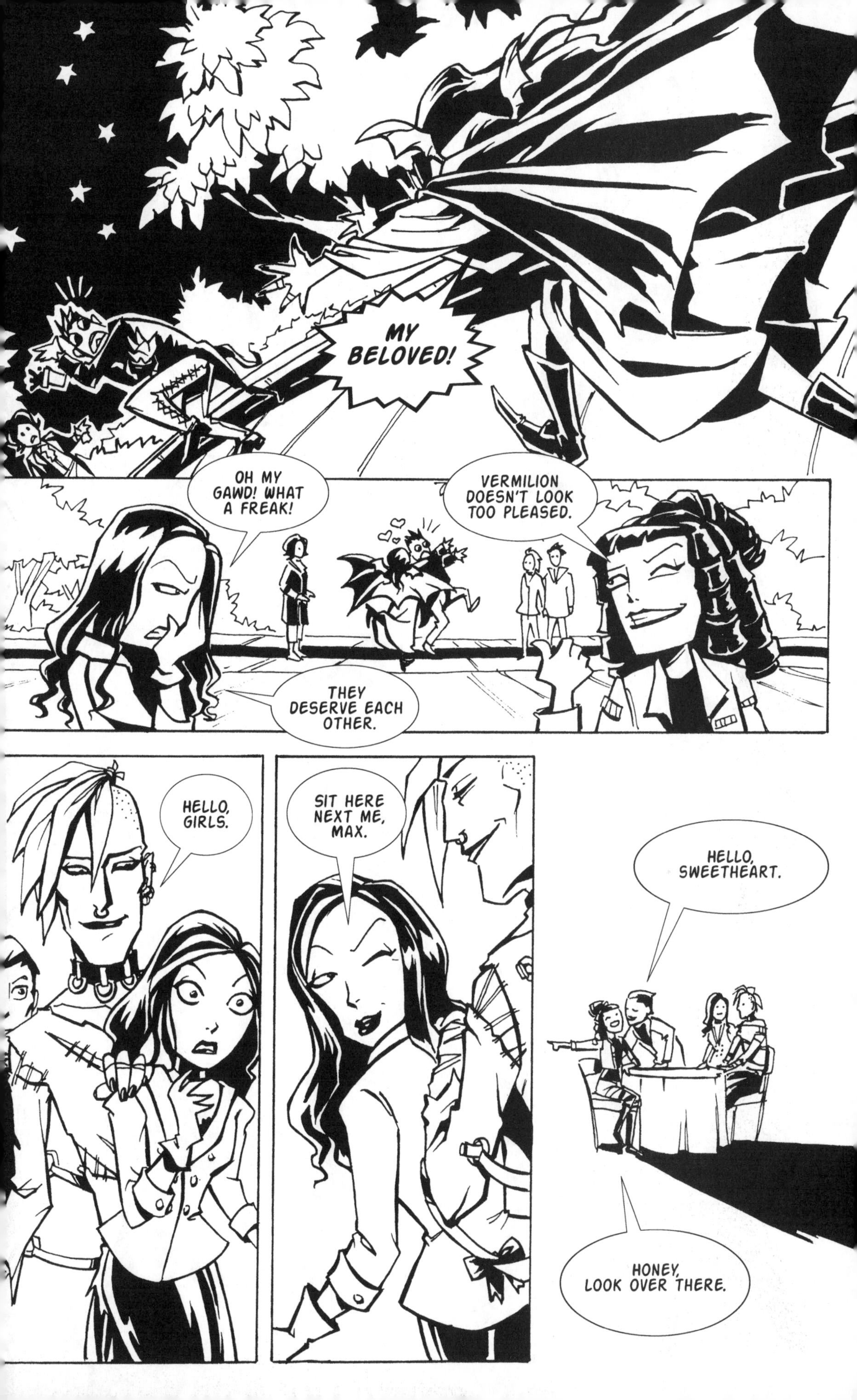
MY BELOVED!
OH MY GAWD! WHAT A FREAK!
VERMILION DOESN'T LOOK TOO PLEASED.
THEY DESERVE EACH OTHER.
HELLO, GIRLS.
SIT HERE NEXT ME, MAX.
HELLO, SWEETHEART.
HONEY, LOOK OVER THERE.

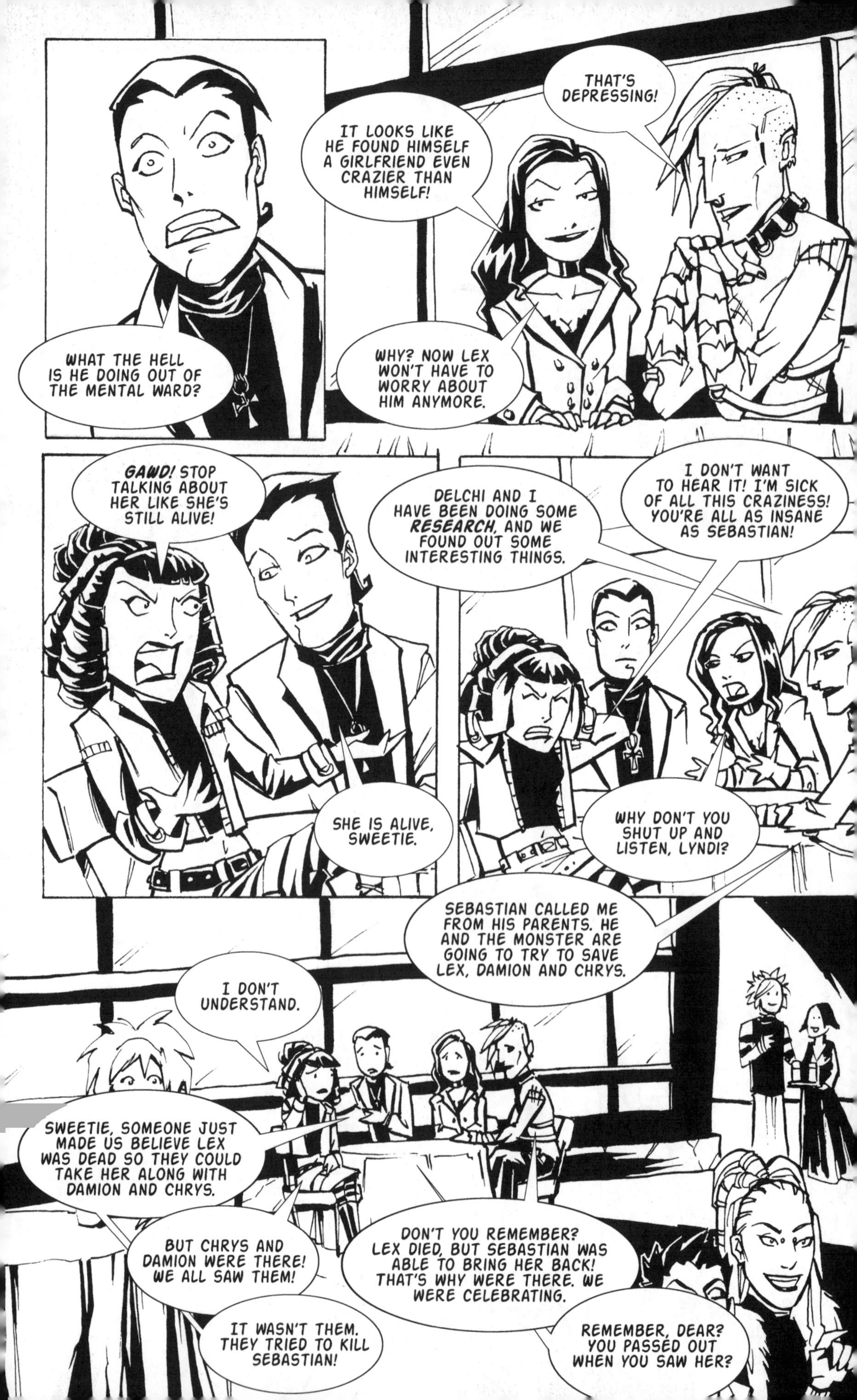
WHAT THE HELL IS HE DOING OUT OF THE MENTAL WARD?
IT LOOKS LIKE HE FOUND HIMSELF A GIRLFRIEND EVEN CRAZIER THAN HIMSELF!
THAT'S DEPRESSING!
WHY? NOW LEX WON'T HAVE TO WORRY ABOUT HIM ANYMORE.
GAWD! STOP TALKING ABOUT HER LIKE SHE'S STILL ALIVE!
SHE IS ALIVE, SWEETIE.
DELCHI AND I HAVE BEEN DOING SOME RESEARCH, AND WE FOUND OUT SOME INTERESTING THINGS.
I DON'T WANT TO HEAR IT! I'M SICK OF ALL THIS CRAZINESS! YOU'RE ALL AS INSANE AS SEBASTIAN!
WHY DON'T YOU SHUT UP AND LISTEN, LYNDI?
SEBASTIAN CALLED ME FROM HIS PARENTS. HE AND THE MONSTER ARE GOING TO TRY TO SAVE LEX, DAMION AND CHRYS.
I DON'T UNDERSTAND.
SWEETIE, SOMEONE JUST MADE US BELIEVE LEX WAS DEAD SO THEY COULD TAKE HER ALONG WITH DAMION AND CHRYS.
BUT CHRYS AND DAMION WERE THERE! WE ALL SAW THEM!
IT WASN'T THEM. THEY TRIED TO KILL SEBASTIAN!
DON'T YOU REMEMBER? LEX DIED, BUT SEBASTIAN WAS ABLE TO BRING HER BACK! THAT'S WHY WERE THERE. WE WERE CELEBRATING.
REMEMBER, DEAR? YOU PASSED OUT WHEN YOU SAW HER?

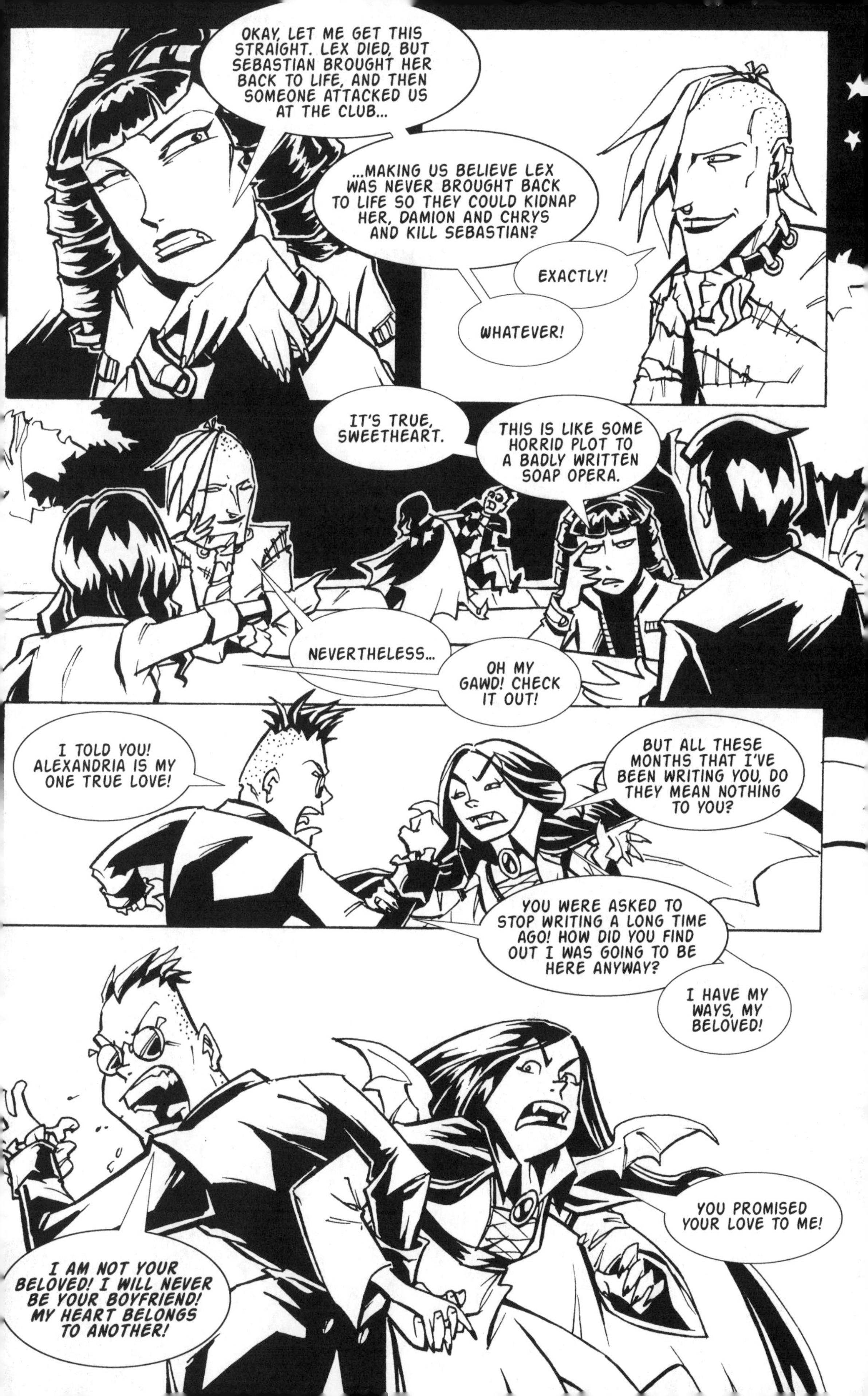

OKAY, LET ME GET THIS STRAIGHT. LEX DIED, BUT SEBASTIAN BROUGHT HER BACK TO LIFE, AND THEN SOMEONE ATTACKED US AT THE CLUB...
...MAKING US BELIEVE LEX WAS NEVER BROUGHT BACK TO LIFE SO THEY COULD KIDNAP HER, DAMION AND CHRYS AND KILL SEBASTIAN?
EXACTLY!
WHATEVER!
IT'S TRUE, SWEETHEART.
THIS IS LIKE SOME HORRID PLOT TO A BADLY WRITTEN SOAP OPERA.
NEVERTHELESS...
OH MY GAWD! CHECK IT OUT!
I TOLD YOU! ALEXANDRIA IS MY ONE TRUE LOVE!
BUT ALL THESE MONTHS THAT I'VE BEEN WRITING YOU, DO THEY MEAN NOTHING TO YOU?
YOU WERE ASKED TO STOP WRITING A LONG TIME AGO! HOW DID YOU FIND OUT I WAS GOING TO BE HERE ANYWAY?
I HAVE MY WAYS, MY BELOVED!
YOU PROMISED YOUR LOVE TO ME!
I AM NOT YOUR BELOVED! I WILL NEVER BE YOUR BOYFRIEND! MY HEART BELONGS TO ANOTHER!

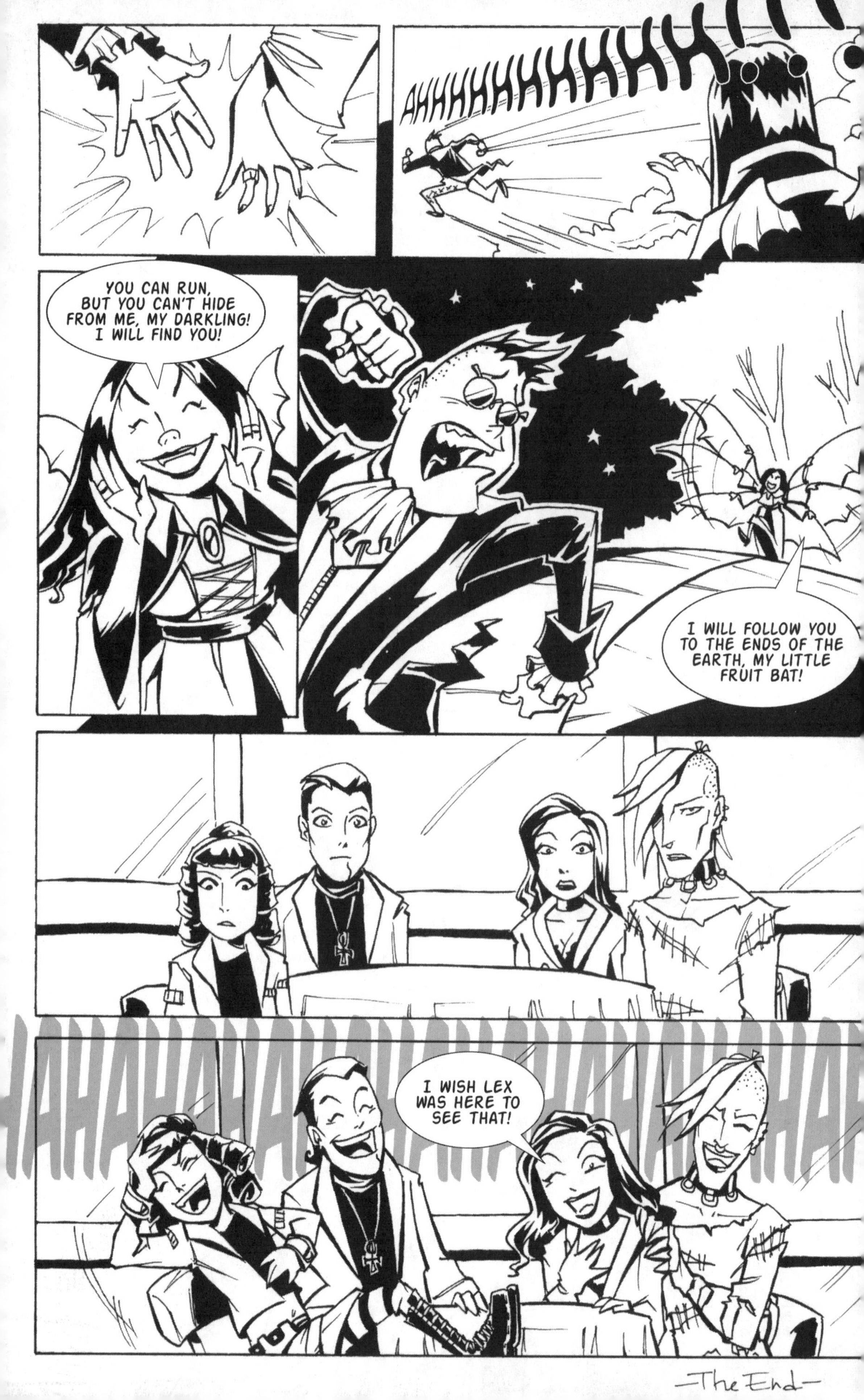
AHHHHHHHHHHHK!!!
YOU CAN RUN, BUT YOU CAN'T HIDE FROM ME, MY DARKLING! I WILL FIND YOU!
I WILL FOLLOW YOU TO THE ENDS OF THE EARTH, MY LITTLE FRUIT BAT!
HAHAHAHAHAHAHAHAHAHA
I WISH LEX WAS HERE TO SEE THAT!
—The End—

The Carnival Wars

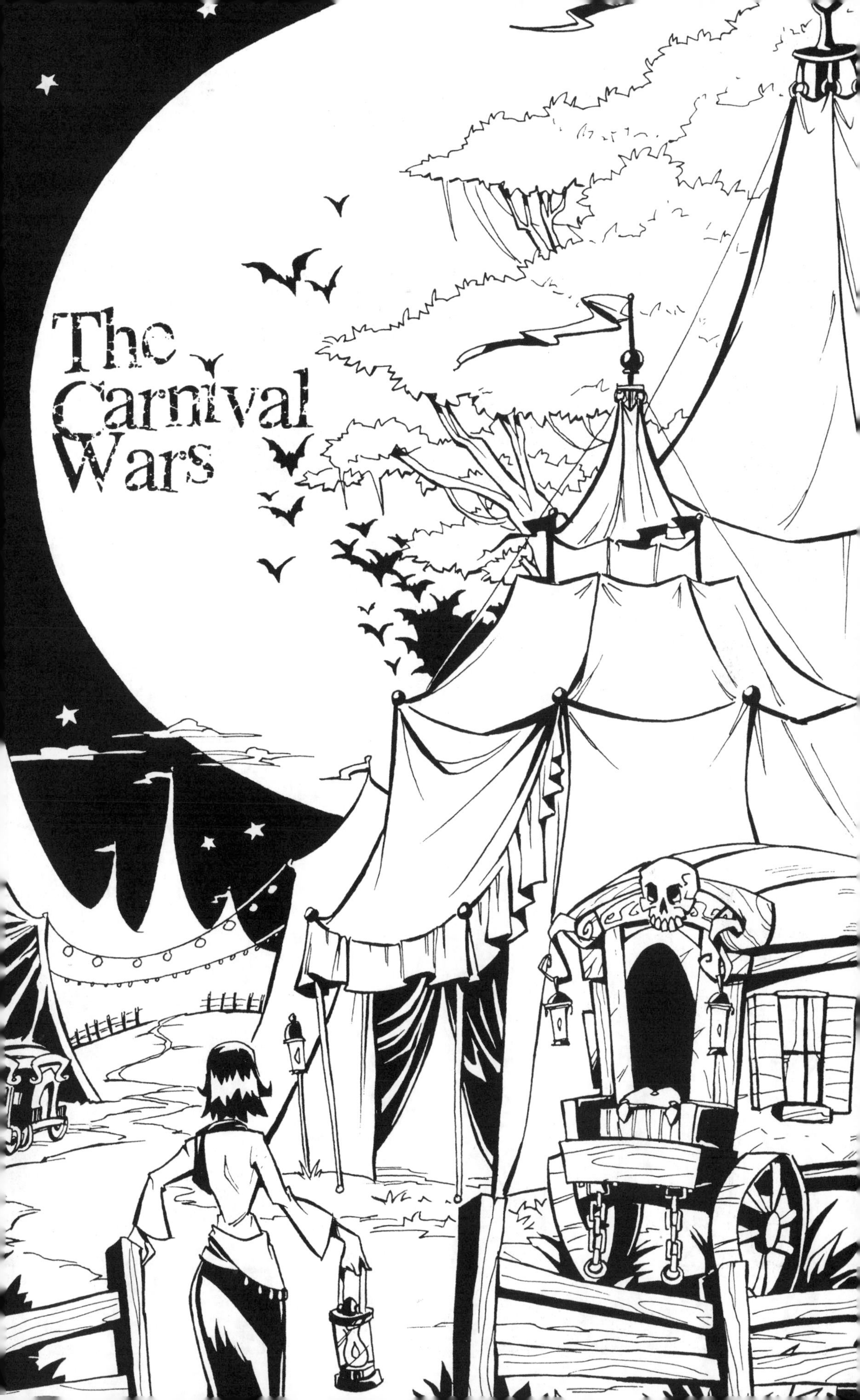

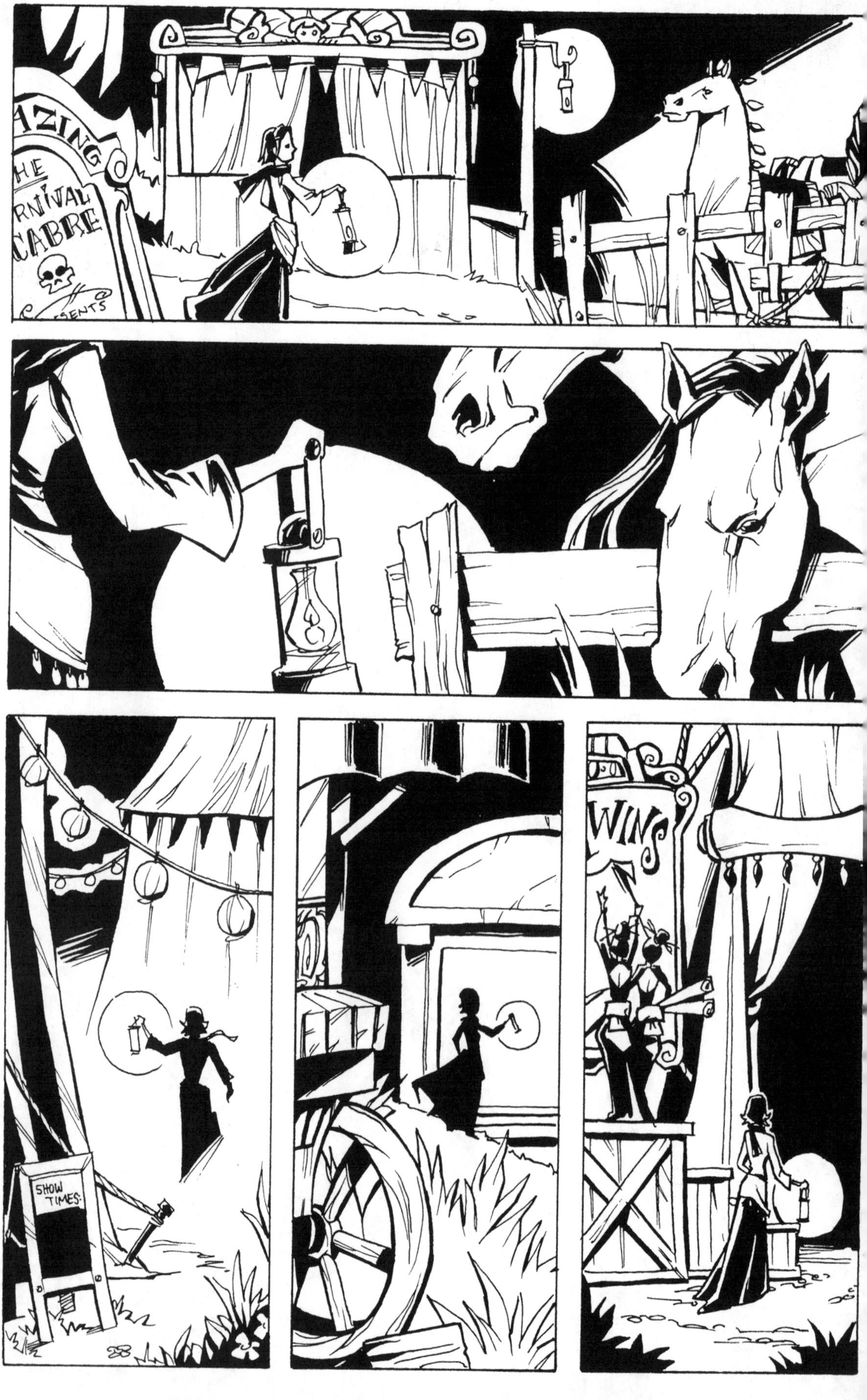
SHOW TIMES:

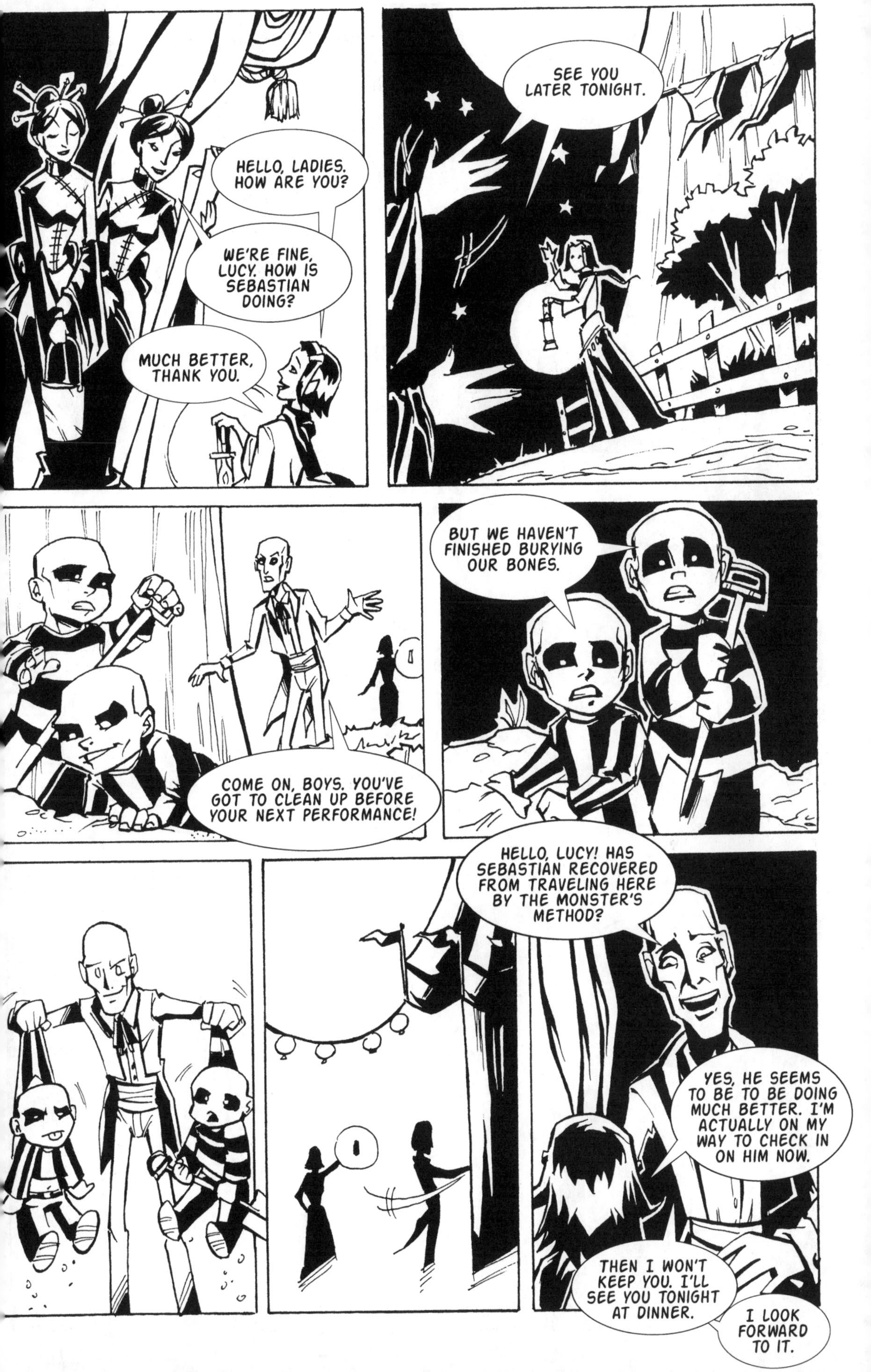

HELLO, LADIES. HOW ARE YOU?
WE'RE FINE, LUCY. HOW IS SEBASTIAN DOING?
MUCH BETTER, THANK YOU.
SEE YOU LATER TONIGHT.
COME ON, BOYS. YOU'VE GOT TO CLEAN UP BEFORE YOUR NEXT PERFORMANCE!
BUT WE HAVEN'T FINISHED BURYING OUR BONES.
HELLO, LUCY! HAS SEBASTIAN RECOVERED FROM TRAVELING HERE BY THE MONSTER'S METHOD?
YES, HE SEEMS TO BE TO BE DOING MUCH BETTER. I'M ACTUALLY ON MY WAY TO CHECK IN ON HIM NOW.
THEN I WON'T KEEP YOU. I'LL SEE YOU TONIGHT AT DINNER.
I LOOK FORWARD TO IT.

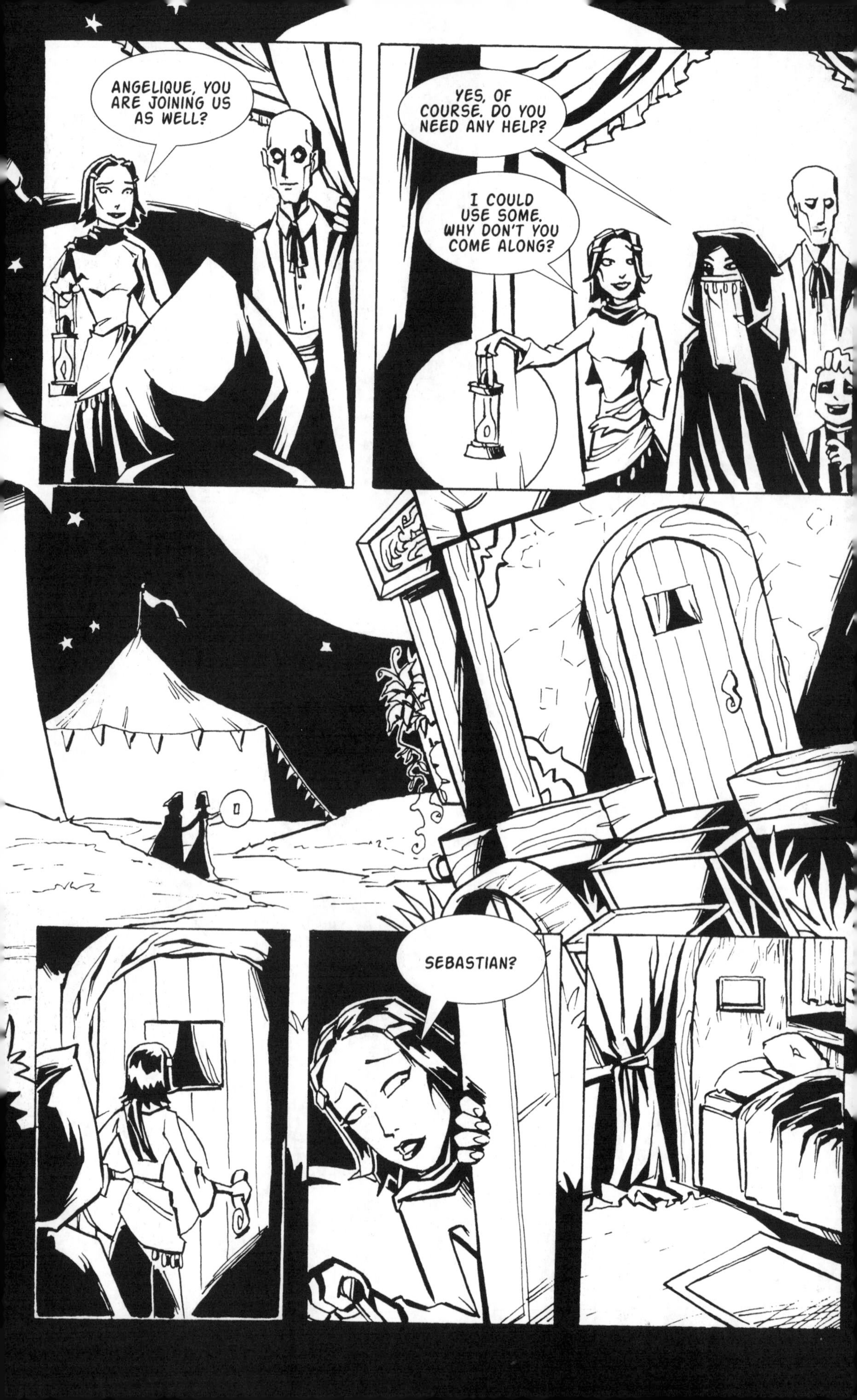
ANGELIQUE, YOU ARE JOINING US AS WELL?
YES, OF COURSE. DO YOU NEED ANY HELP?
I COULD USE SOME. WHY DON'T YOU COME ALONG?
SEBASTIAN?

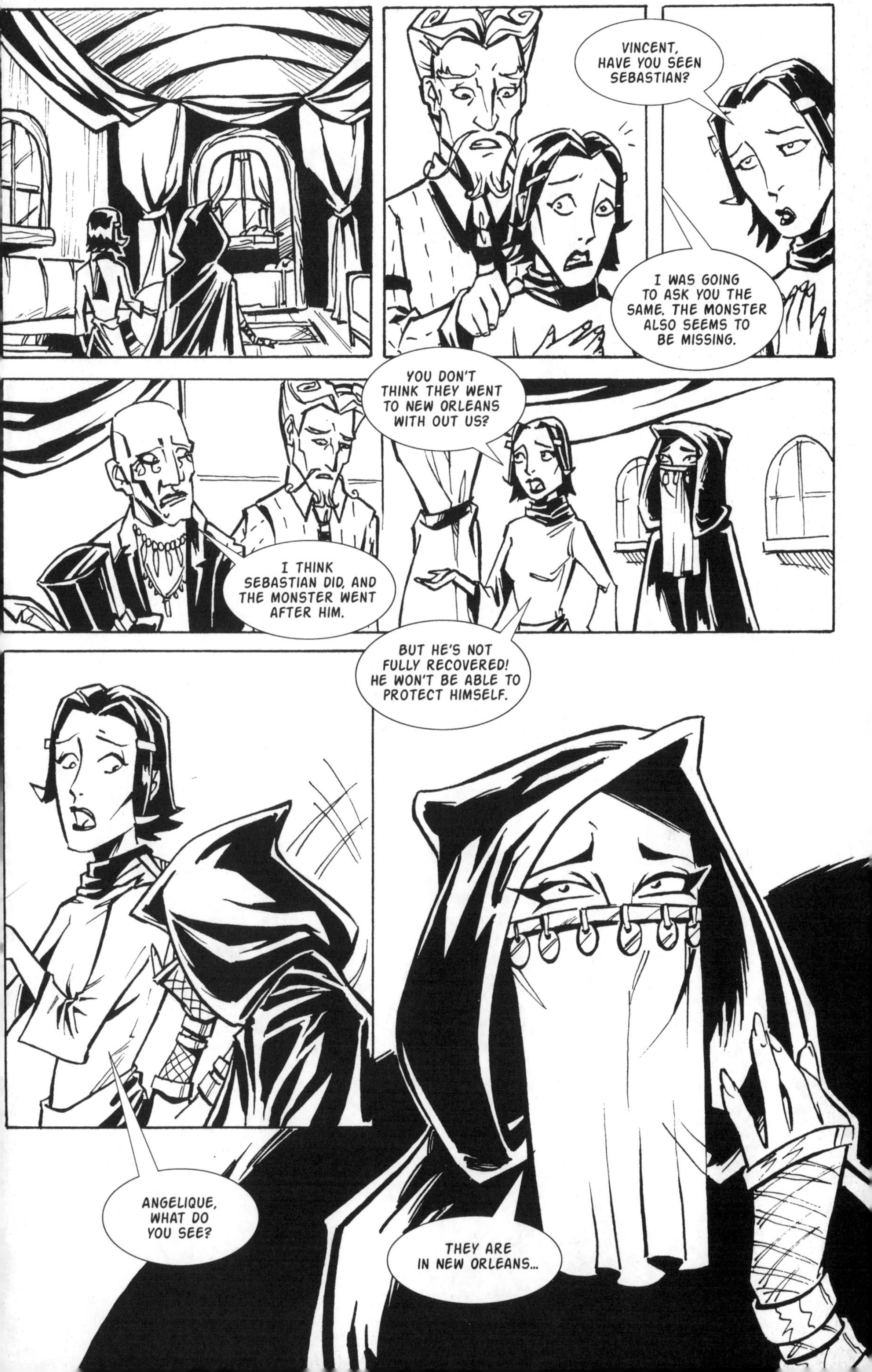
VINCENT, HAVE YOU SEEN SEBASTIAN?
I WAS GOING TO ASK YOU THE SAME. THE MONSTER ALSO SEEMS TO BE MISSING.
YOU DON'T THINK THEY WENT TO NEW ORLEANS WITH OUT US?
I THINK SEBASTIAN DID, AND THE MONSTER WENT AFTER HIM.
BUT HE'S NOT FULLY RECOVERED! HE WON'T BE ABLE TO PROTECT HIMSELF.
ANGELIQUE, WHAT DO YOU SEE?
THEY ARE IN NEW ORLEANS...

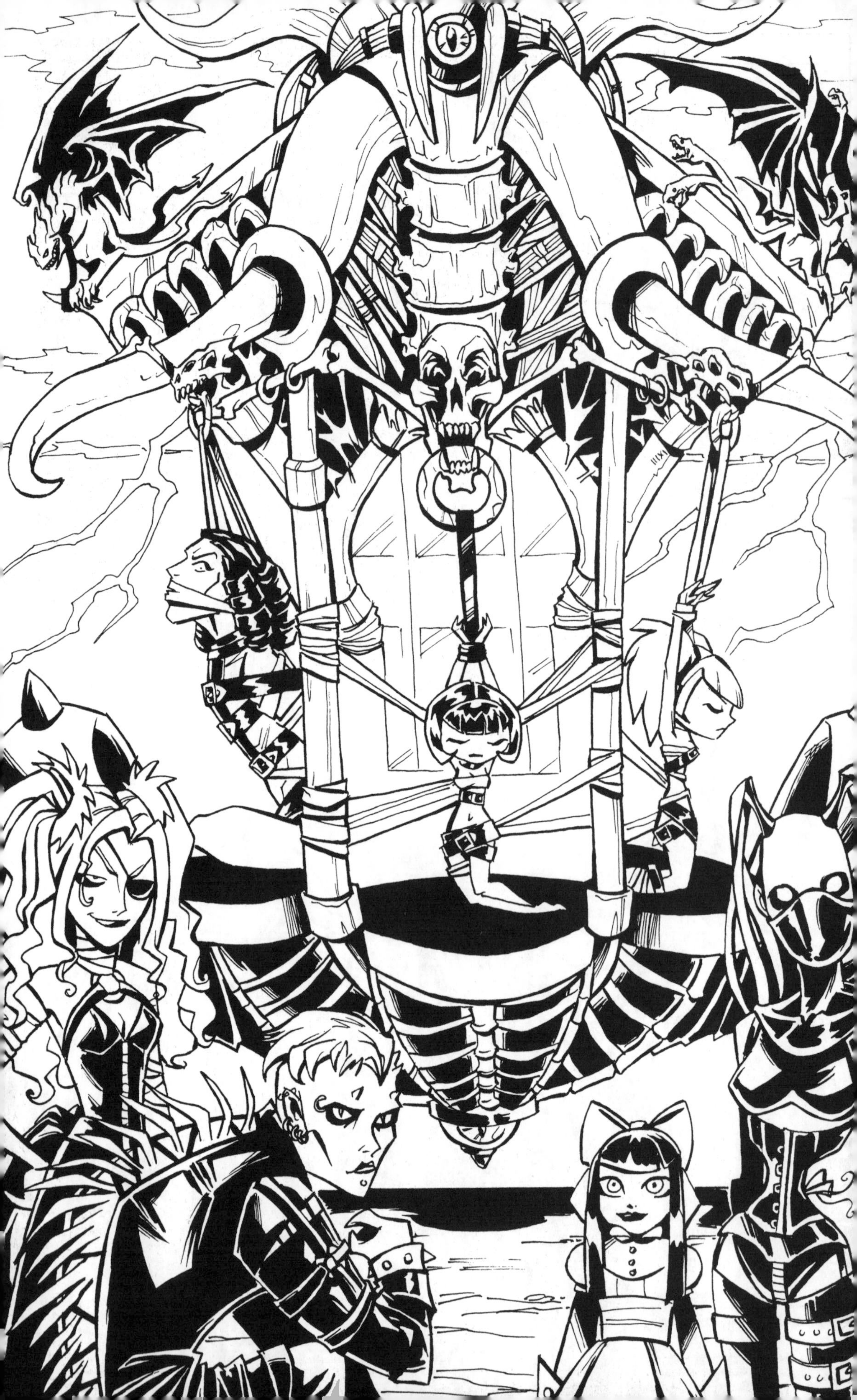

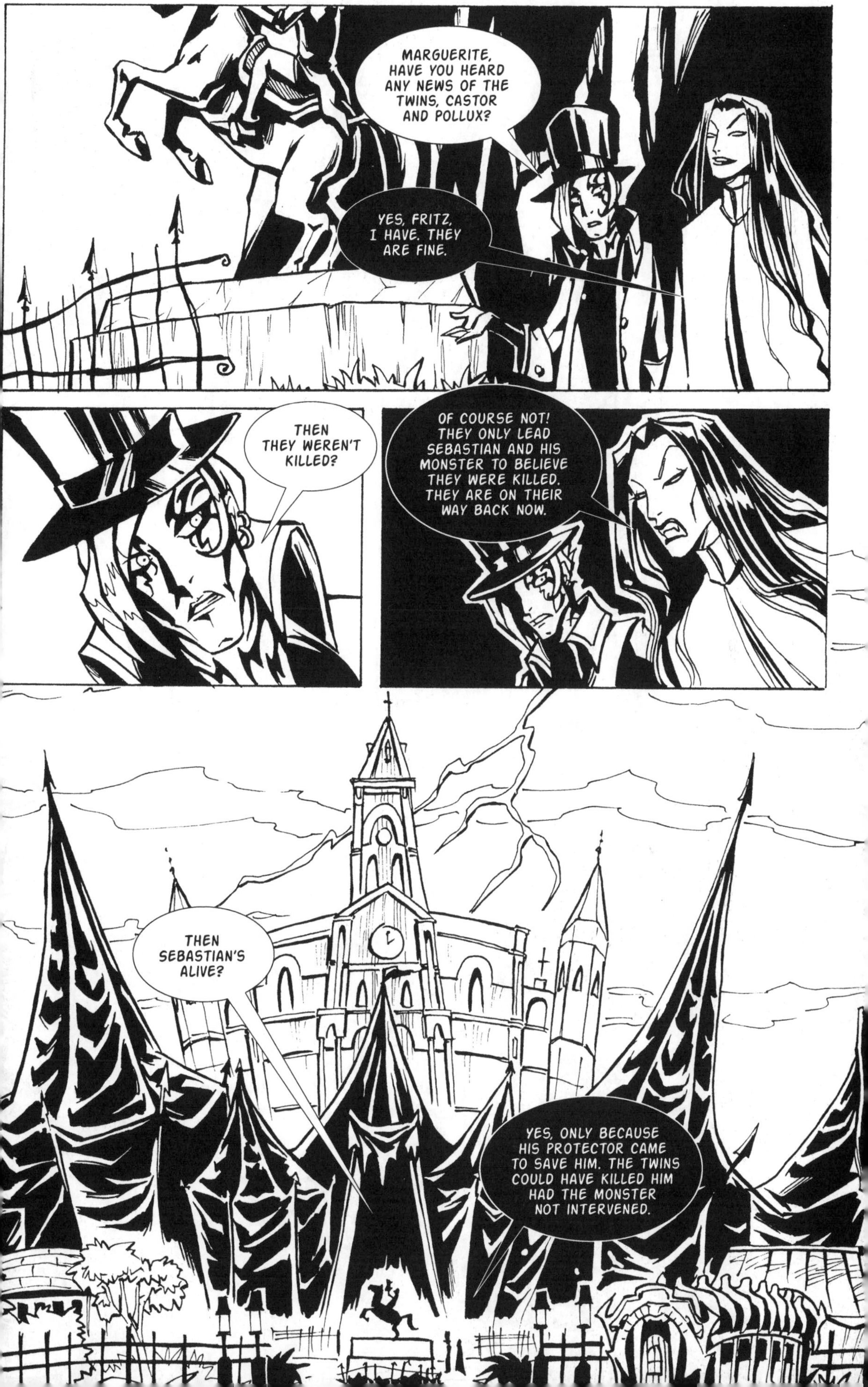
MARGUERITE, HAVE YOU HEARD ANY NEWS OF THE TWINS, CASTOR AND POLLUX?
YES, FRITZ, I HAVE. THEY ARE FINE.
THEN THEY WEREN'T KILLED?
OF COURSE NOT! THEY ONLY LEAD SEBASTIAN AND HIS MONSTER TO BELIEVE THEY WERE KILLED. THEY ARE ON THEIR WAY BACK NOW.
THEN SEBASTIAN'S ALIVE?
YES, ONLY BECAUSE HIS PROTECTOR CAME TO SAVE HIM. THE TWINS COULD HAVE KILLED HIM HAD THE MONSTER NOT INTERVENED.

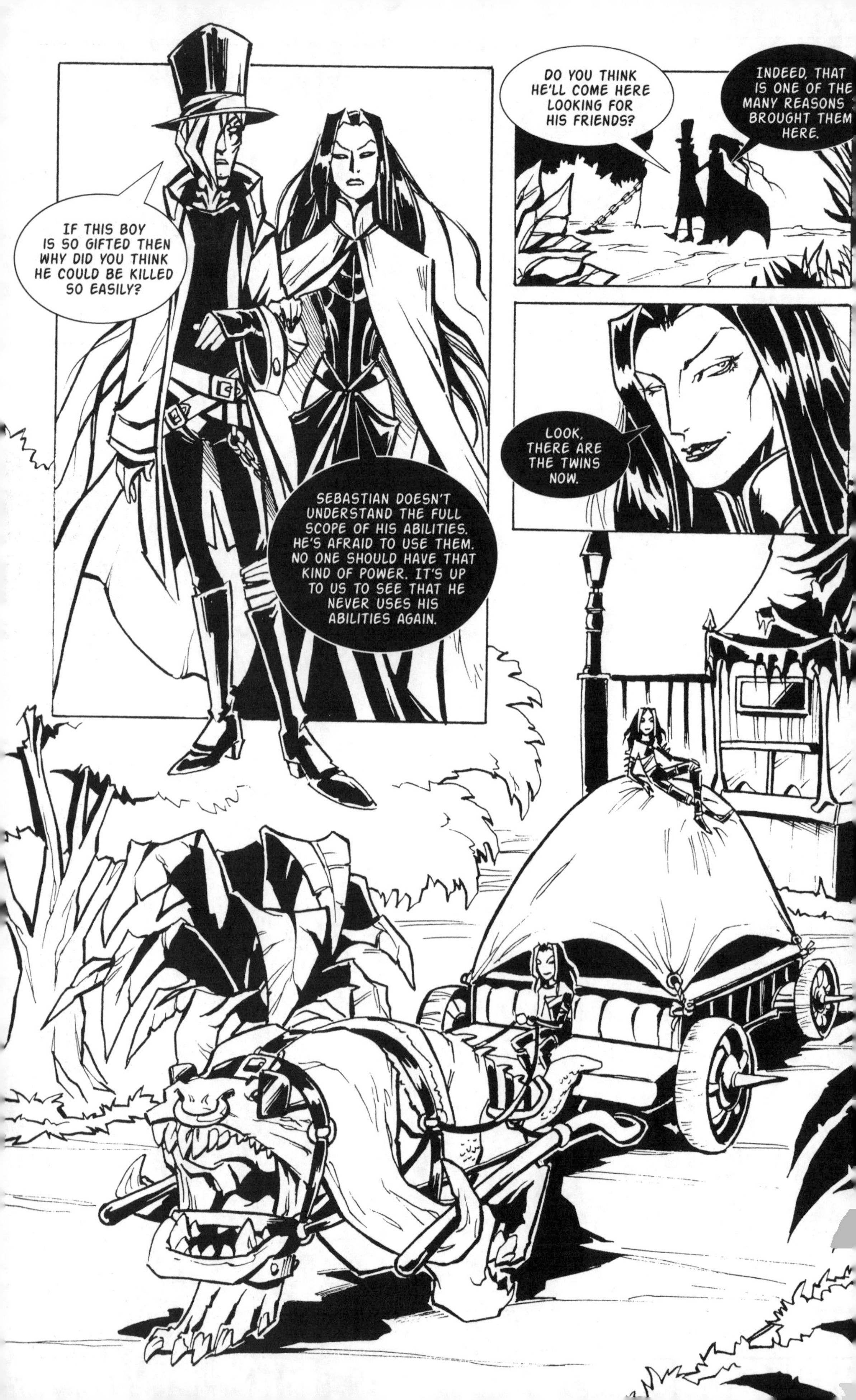
IF THIS BOY IS SO GIFTED THEN WHY DID YOU THINK HE COULD BE KILLED SO EASILY?
SEBASTIAN DOESN'T UNDERSTAND THE FULL SCOPE OF HIS ABILITIES. HE'S AFRAID TO USE THEM. NO ONE SHOULD HAVE THAT KIND OF POWER. IT'S UP TO US TO SEE THAT HE NEVER USES HIS ABILITIES AGAIN.
DO YOU THINK HE'LL COME HERE LOOKING FOR HIS FRIENDS?
INDEED, THAT IS ONE OF THE MANY REASONS I BROUGHT THEM HERE.
LOOK, THERE ARE THE TWINS NOW.

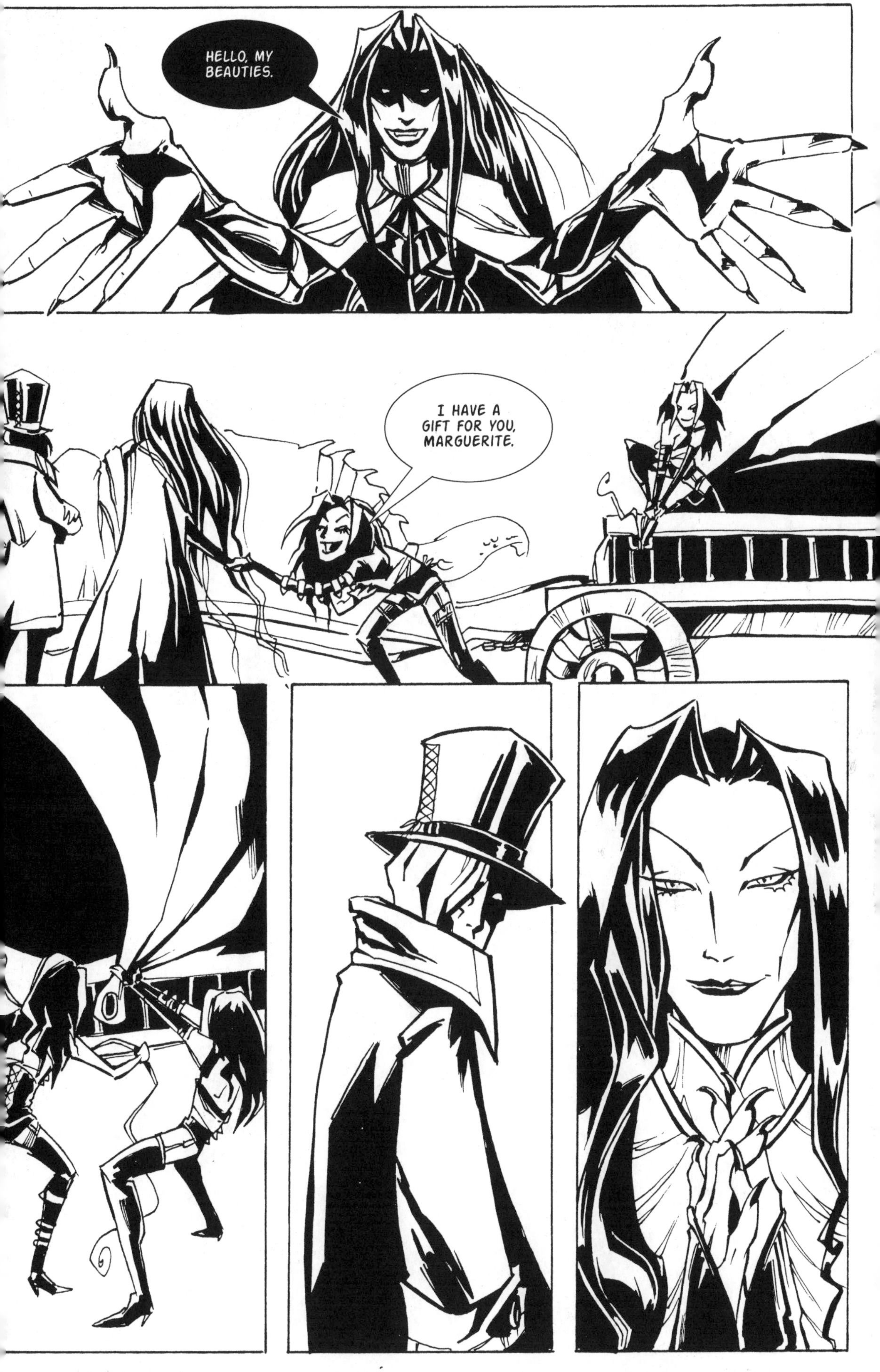
HELLO, MY BEAUTIES.
I HAVE A GIFT FOR YOU, MARGUERITE.

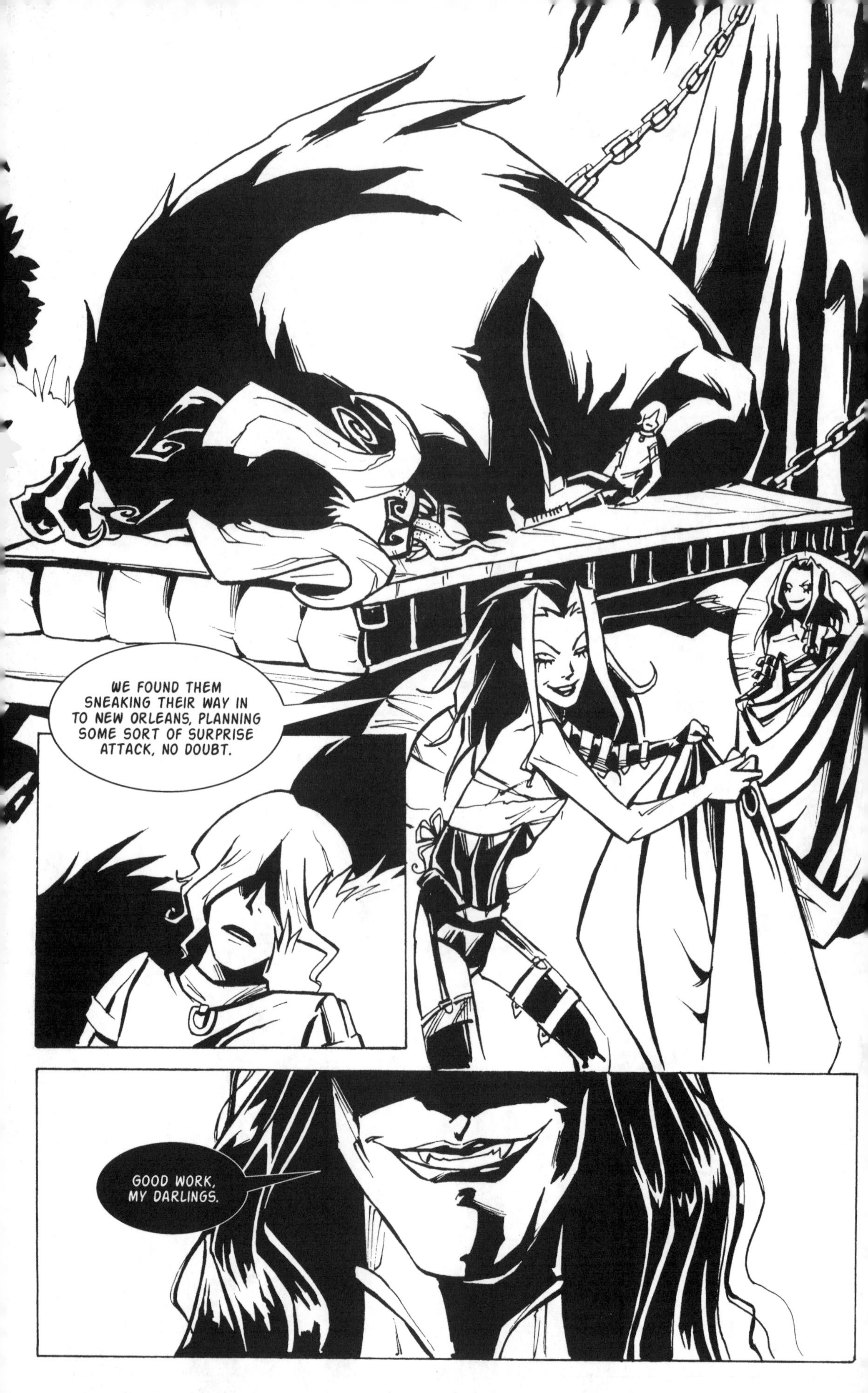
WE FOUND THEM SNEAKING THEIR WAY IN TO NEW ORLEANS, PLANNING SOME SORT OF SURPRISE ATTACK, NO DOUBT.
GOOD WORK, MY DARLINGS.

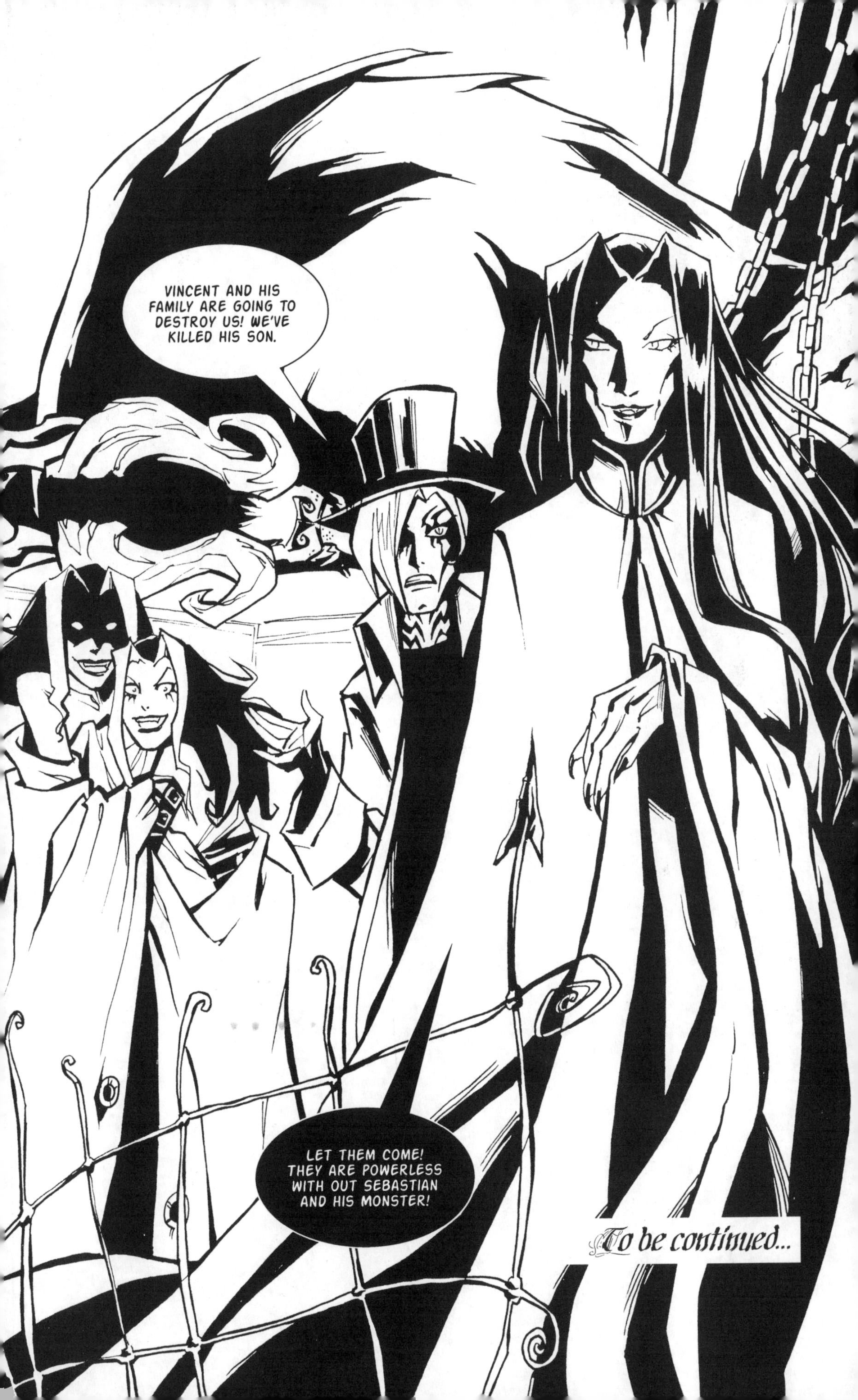
VINCENT AND HIS FAMILY ARE GOING TO DESTROY US! WE'VE KILLED HIS SON.
LET THEM COME! THEY ARE POWERLESS WITH OUT SEBASTIAN AND HIS MONSTER!
To be continued...

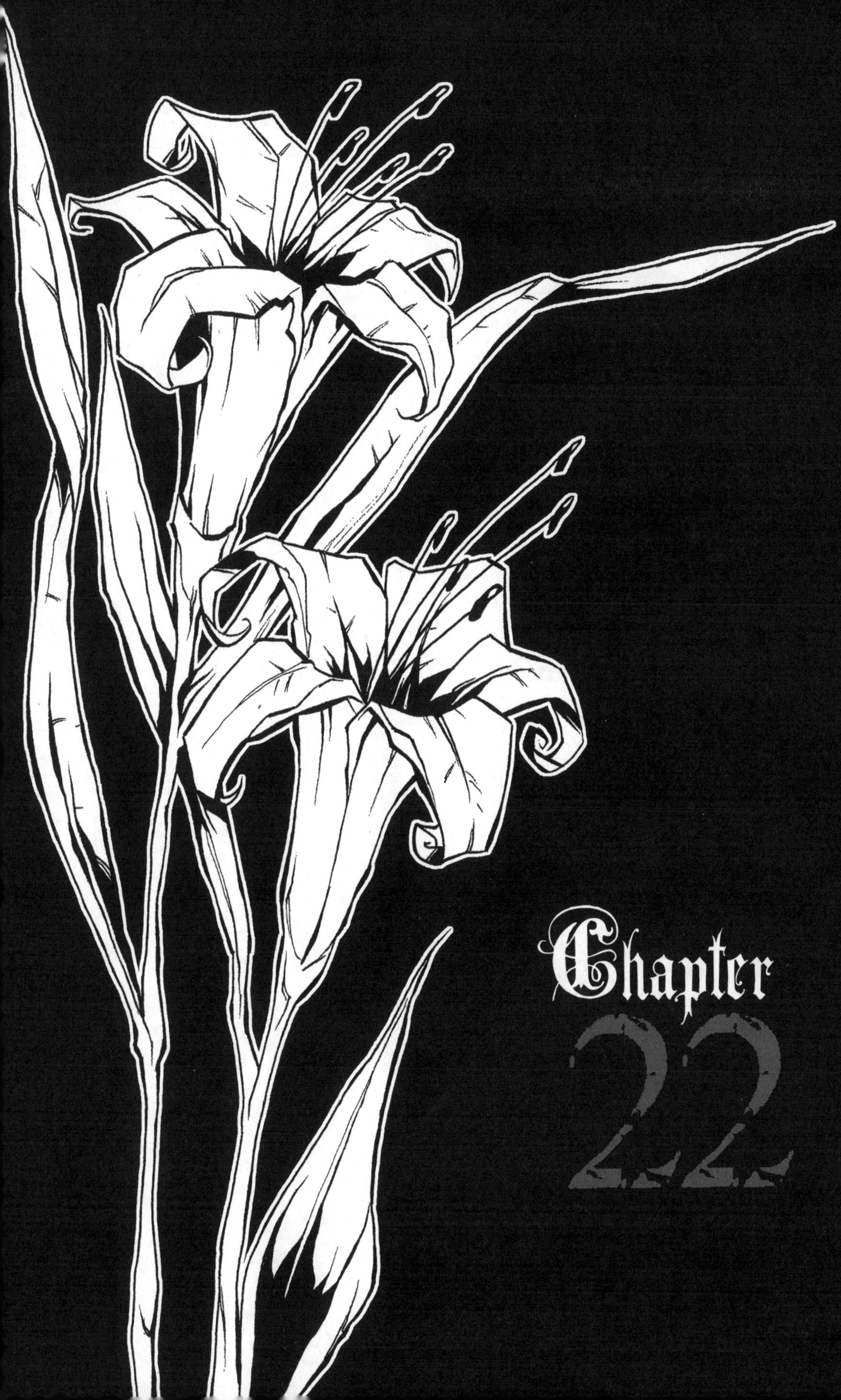

Chapter 22

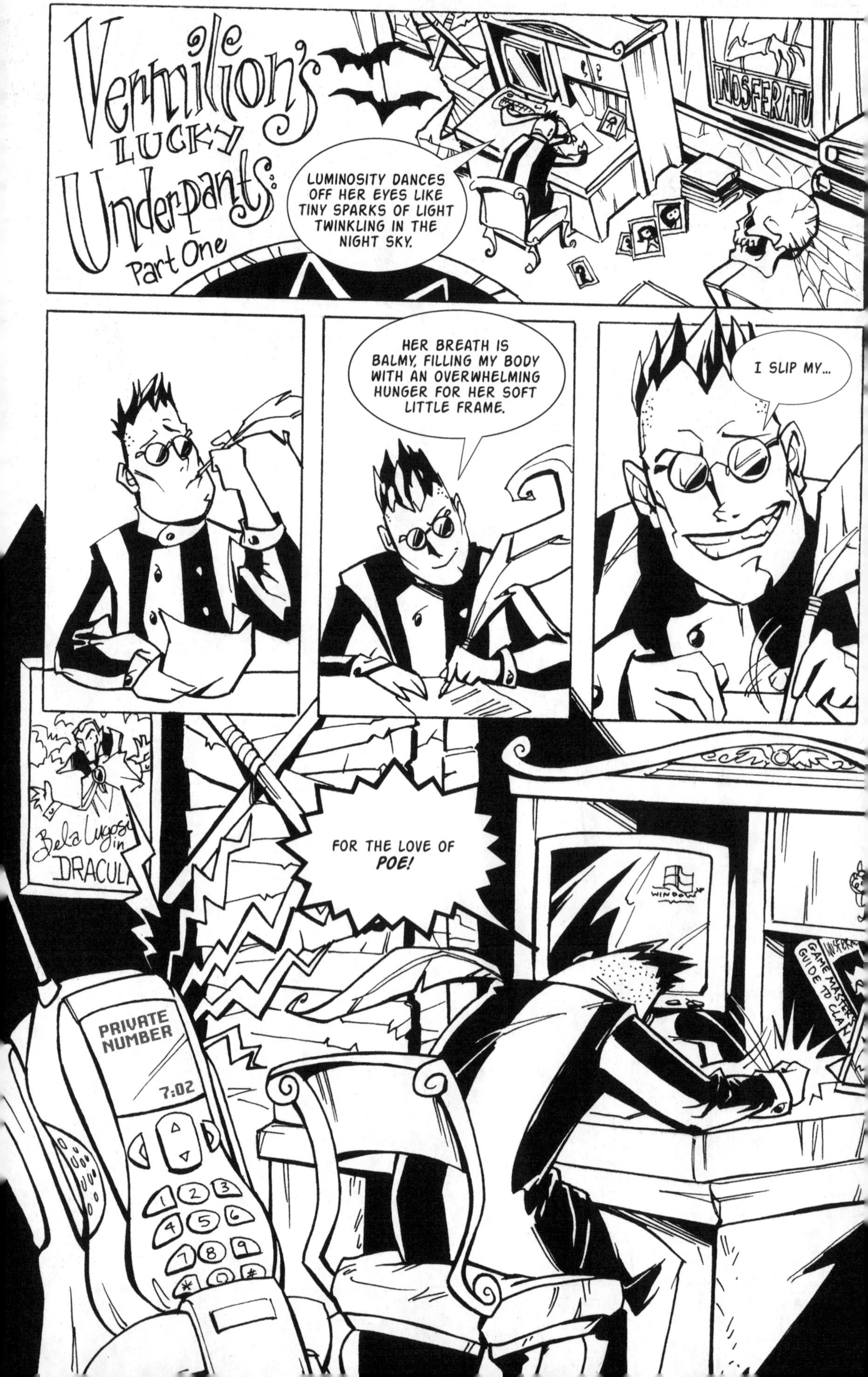
Vermilion's
LUCKY
Underpants...
Part One
INOSFERATU
LUMINOSITY DANCES OFF HER EYES LIKE TINY SPARKS OF LIGHT TWINKLING IN THE NIGHT SKY.
HER BREATH IS BALMY, FILLING MY BODY WITH AN OVERWHELMING HUNGER FOR HER SOFT LITTLE FRAME.
I SLIP MY...
Bela Lugosi in DRACULA
FOR THE LOVE OF POE!
PRIVATE NUMBER
7:02
GAME MASTER'S GUIDE TO CLAN

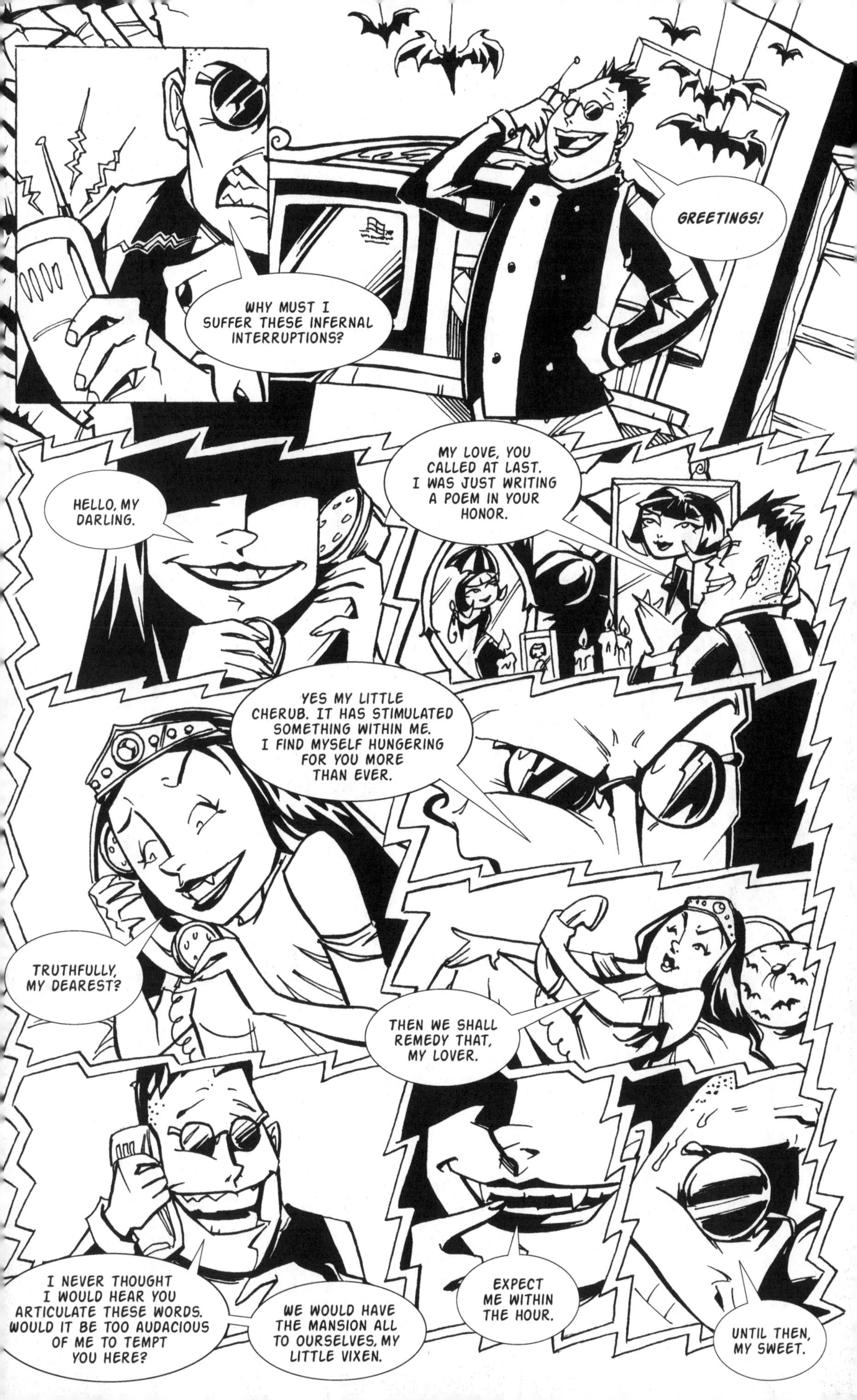
GREETINGS!
WHY MUST I SUFFER THESE INFERNAL INTERRUPTIONS?
HELLO, MY DARLING.
MY LOVE, YOU CALLED AT LAST. I WAS JUST WRITING A POEM IN YOUR HONOR.
YES MY LITTLE CHERUB. IT HAS STIMULATED SOMETHING WITHIN ME. I FIND MYSELF HUNGERING FOR YOU MORE THAN EVER.
TRUTHFULLY, MY DEAREST?
THEN WE SHALL REMEDY THAT, MY LOVER.
I NEVER THOUGHT I WOULD HEAR YOU ARTICULATE THESE WORDS. WOULD IT BE TOO AUDACIOUS OF ME TO TEMPT YOU HERE?
WE WOULD HAVE THE MANSION ALL TO OURSELVES, MY LITTLE VIXEN.
EXPECT ME WITHIN THE HOUR.
UNTIL THEN, MY SWEET.

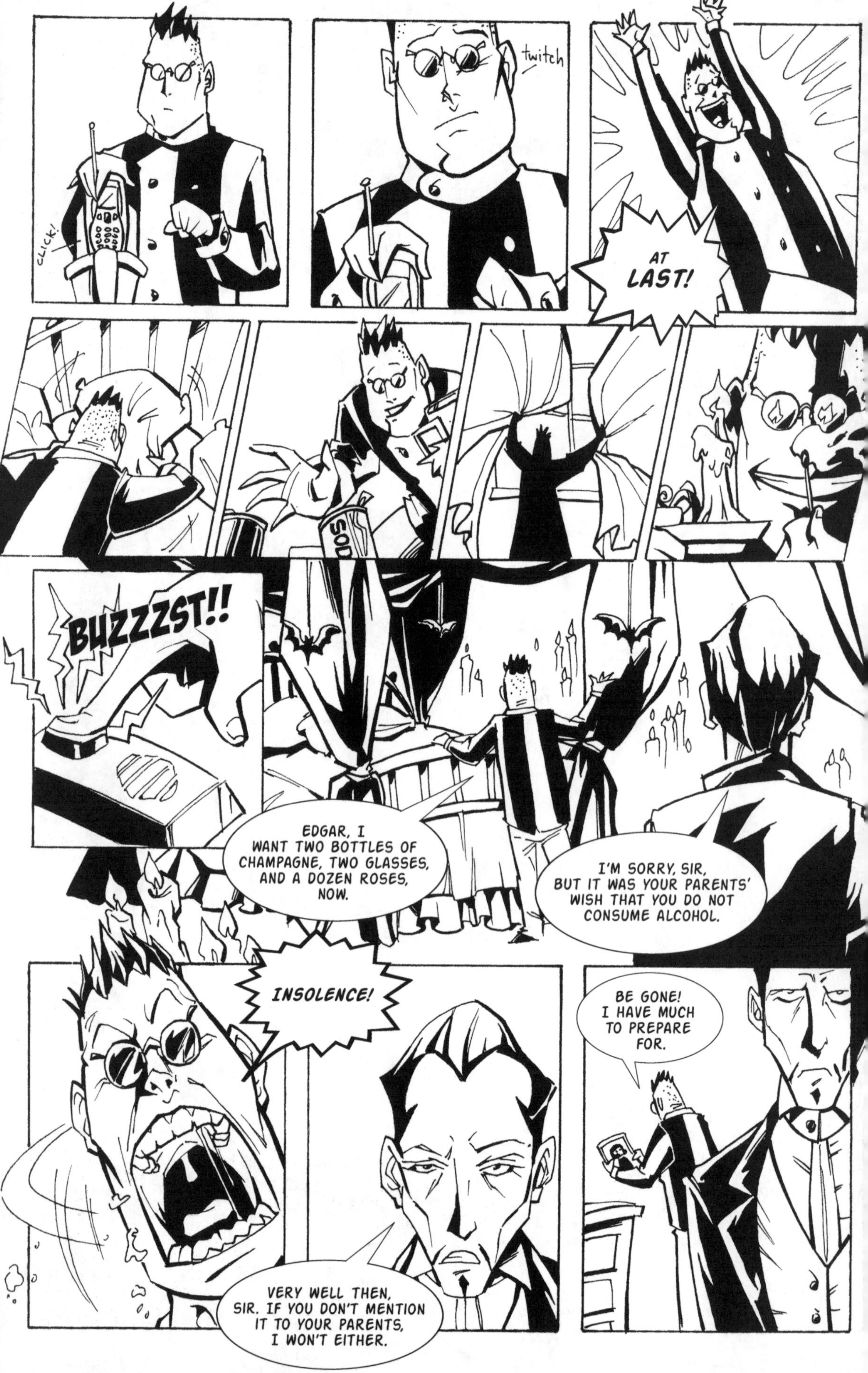

CLICK!
twitch
AT LAST!
BUZZZST!!
EDGAR, I WANT TWO BOTTLES OF CHAMPAGNE, TWO GLASSES, AND A DOZEN ROSES, NOW.
I'M SORRY, SIR, BUT IT WAS YOUR PARENTS' WISH THAT YOU DO NOT CONSUME ALCOHOL.
INSOLENCE!
VERY WELL THEN, SIR. IF YOU DON'T MENTION IT TO YOUR PARENTS, I WON'T EITHER.
BE GONE! I HAVE MUCH TO PREPARE FOR.

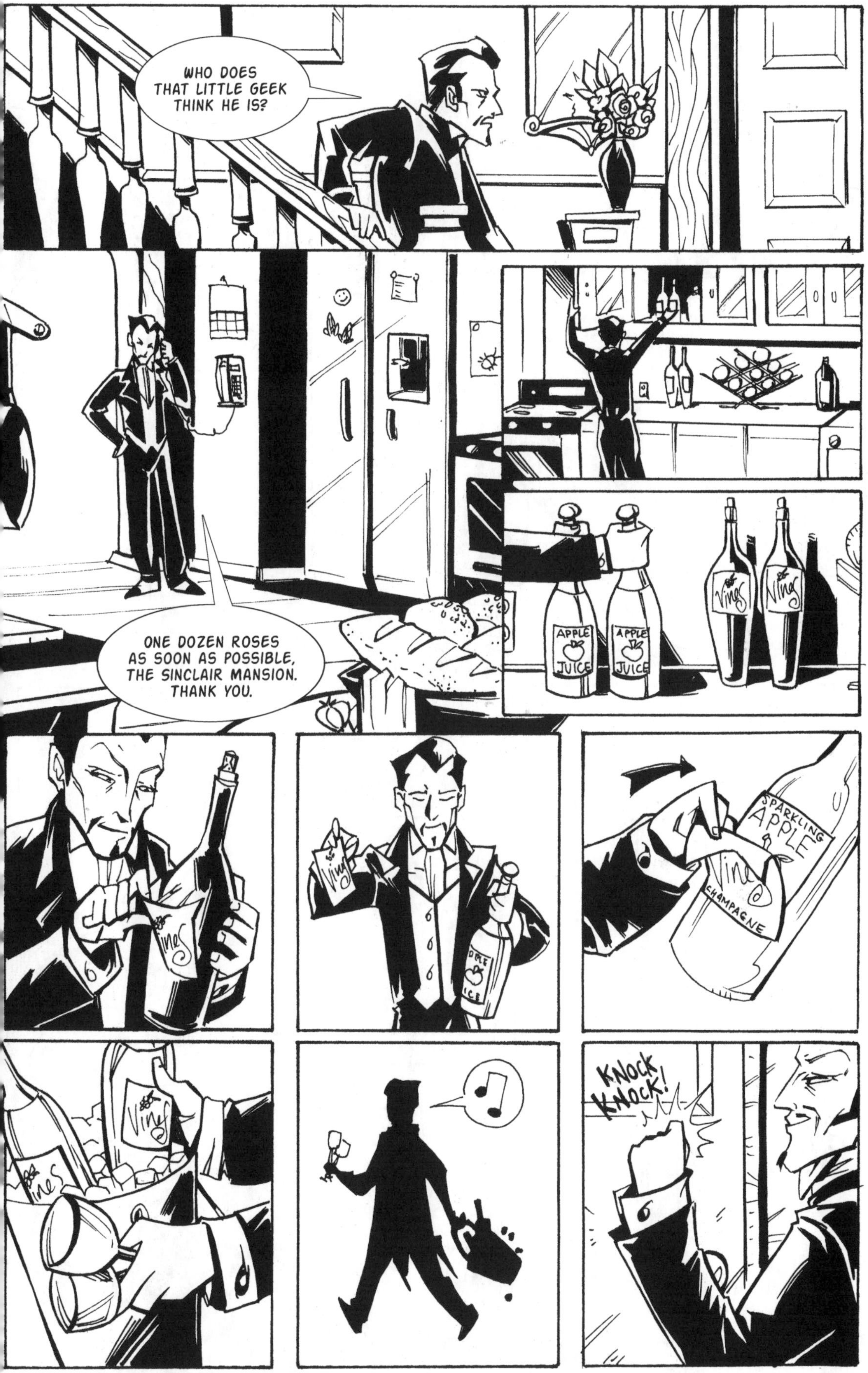
WHO DOES THAT LITTLE GEEK THINK HE IS?
ONE DOZEN ROSES AS SOON AS POSSIBLE, THE SINCLAIR MANSION. THANK YOU.
APPLE JUICE
APPLE JUICE
Vines
Vines
SPARKLING APPLE CHAMPAGNE
KNOCK KNOCK!

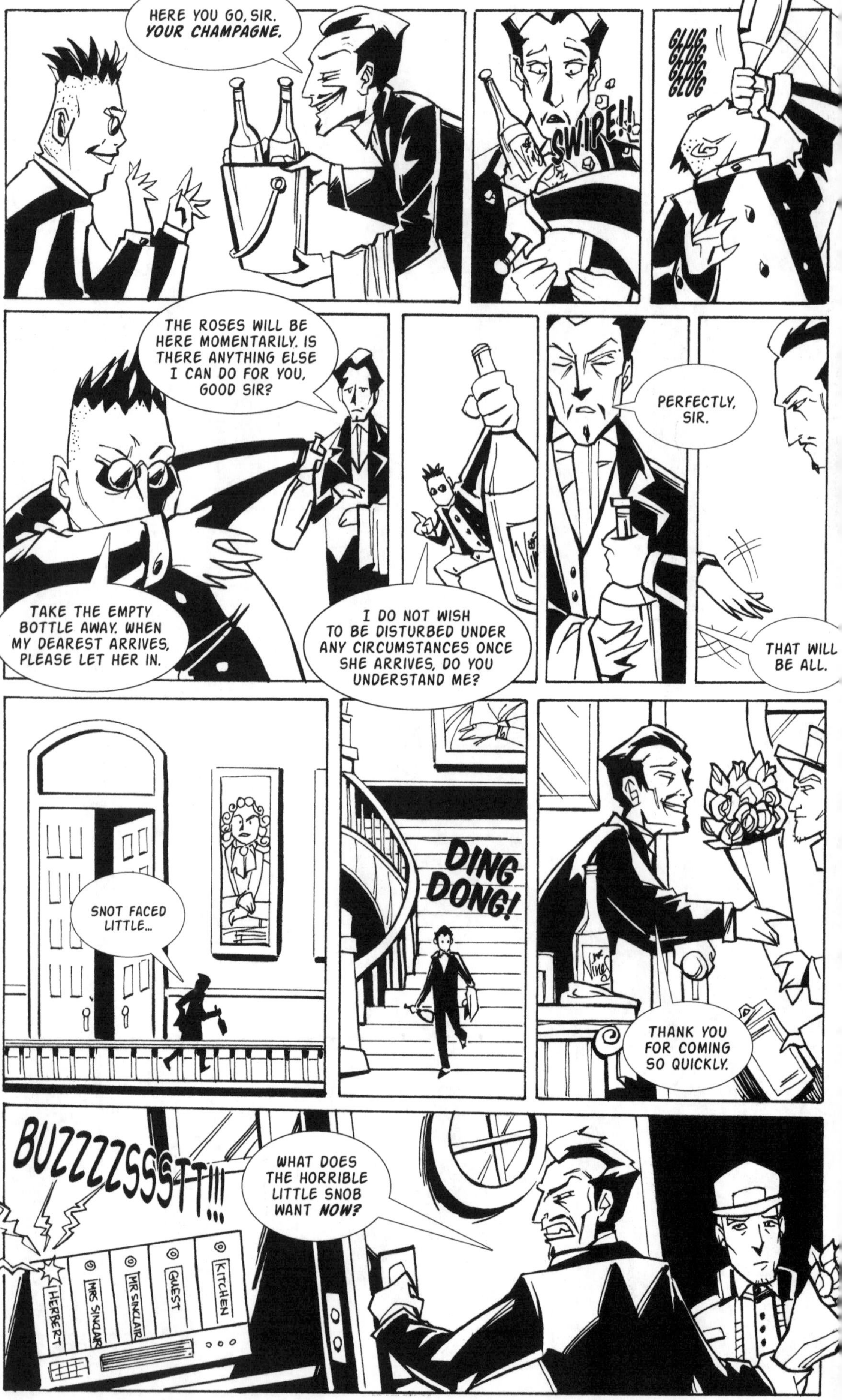
HERE YOU GO, SIR. *YOUR CHAMPAGNE.*
SWIPE!!
GLUG GLUG GLUG GLUG
THE ROSES WILL BE HERE MOMENTARILY. IS THERE ANYTHING ELSE I CAN DO FOR YOU, GOOD SIR?
TAKE THE EMPTY BOTTLE AWAY. WHEN MY DEAREST ARRIVES, PLEASE LET HER IN.
I DO NOT WISH TO BE DISTURBED UNDER ANY CIRCUMSTANCES ONCE SHE ARRIVES, DO YOU UNDERSTAND ME?
PERFECTLY, SIR.
THAT WILL BE ALL.
SNOT FACED LITTLE...
DING DONG!
THANK YOU FOR COMING SO QUICKLY.
BUZZZZZSSSTT!!!
WHAT DOES THE HORRIBLE LITTLE SNOB WANT *NOW?*
HERBERT
MRS SINCLAIR
MR SINCLAIR
GUEST
KITCHEN

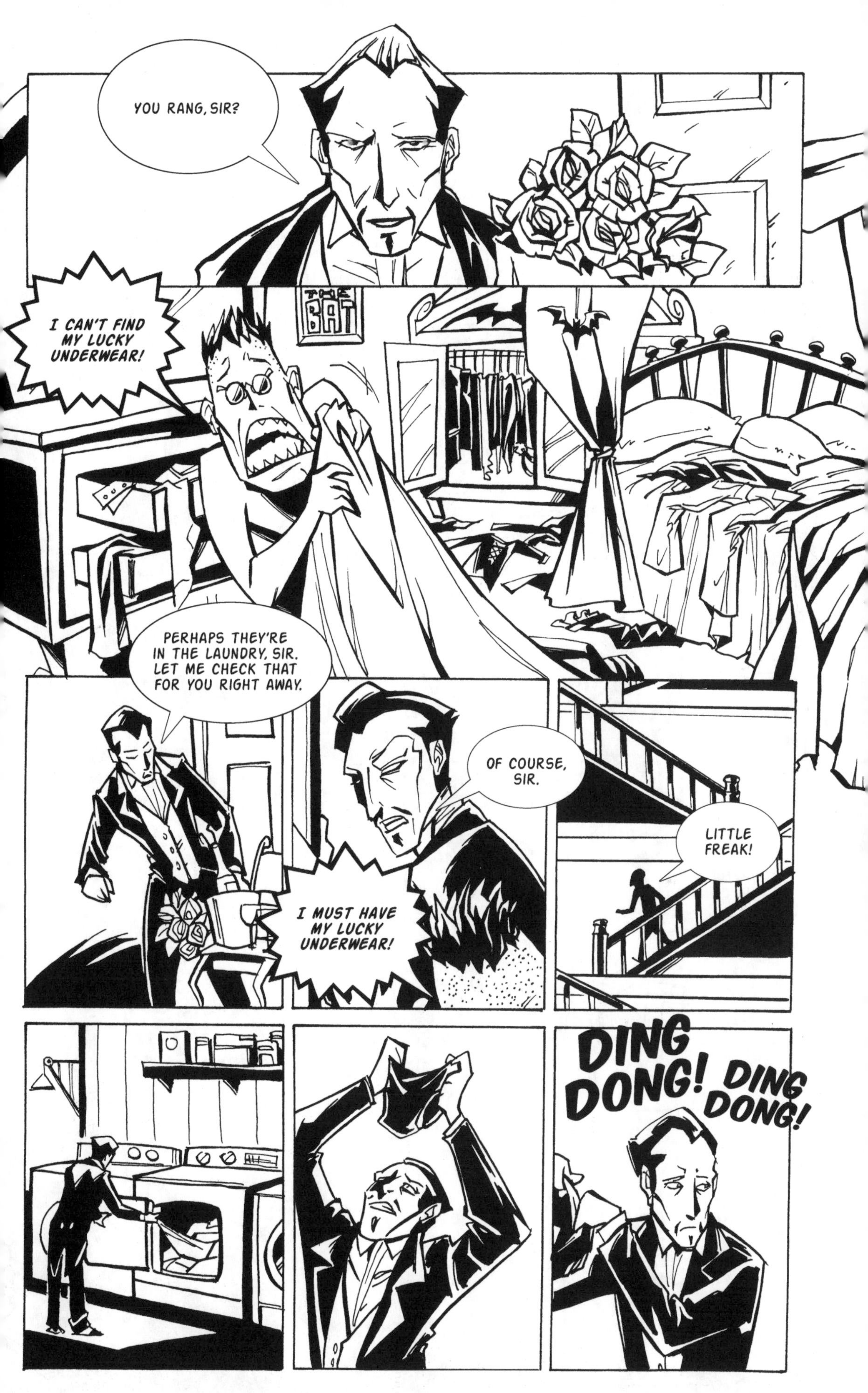
YOU RANG, SIR?
I CAN'T FIND MY LUCKY UNDERWEAR!
THE BAT
PERHAPS THEY'RE IN THE LAUNDRY, SIR. LET ME CHECK THAT FOR YOU RIGHT AWAY.
OF COURSE, SIR.
I MUST HAVE MY LUCKY UNDERWEAR!
LITTLE FREAK!
DING DONG! DING DONG!

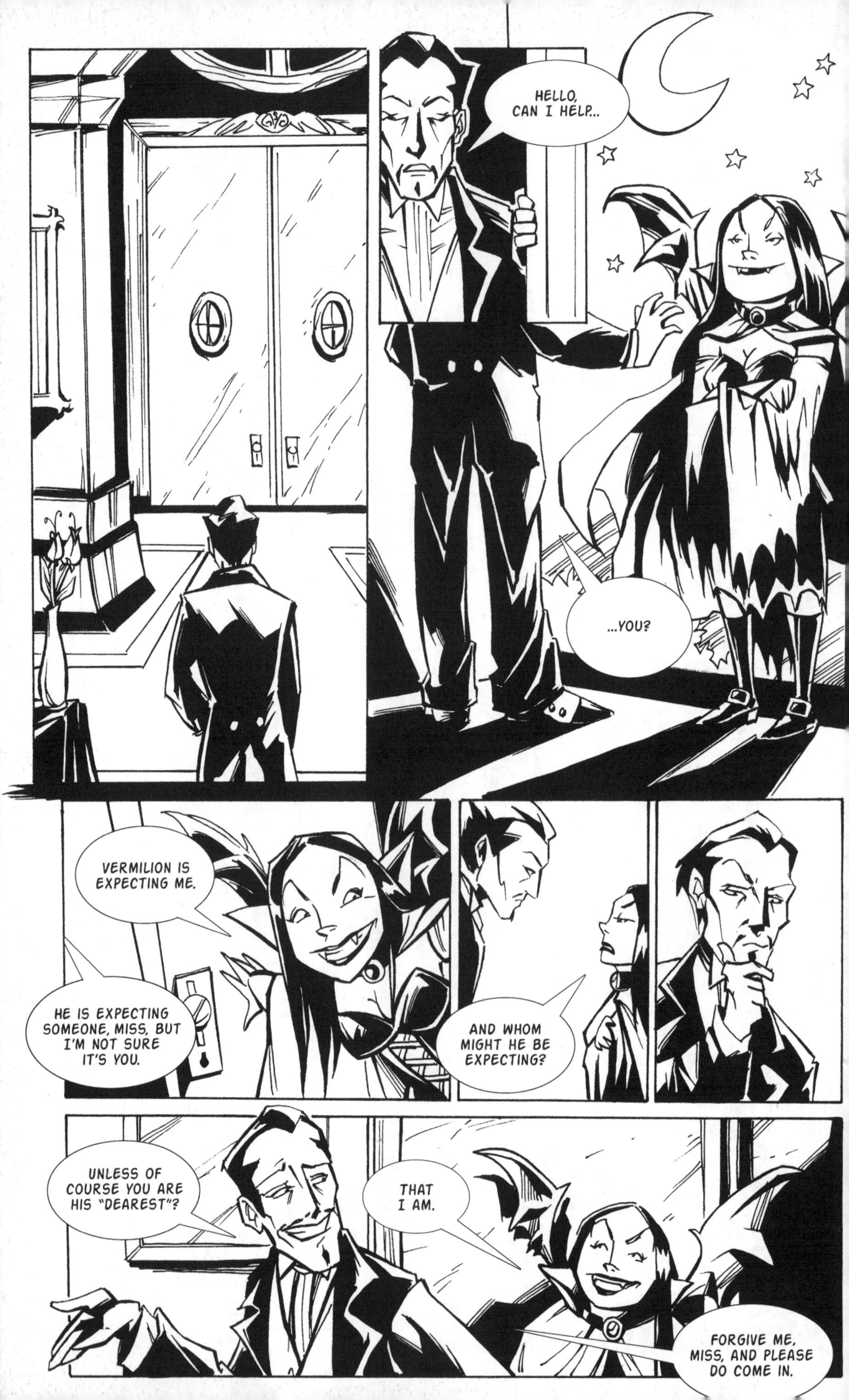
HELLO, CAN I HELP...
...YOU?
VERMILION IS EXPECTING ME.
HE IS EXPECTING SOMEONE, MISS, BUT I'M NOT SURE IT'S YOU.
AND WHOM MIGHT HE BE EXPECTING?
UNLESS OF COURSE YOU ARE HIS "DEAREST"?
THAT I AM.
FORGIVE ME, MISS, AND PLEASE DO COME IN.

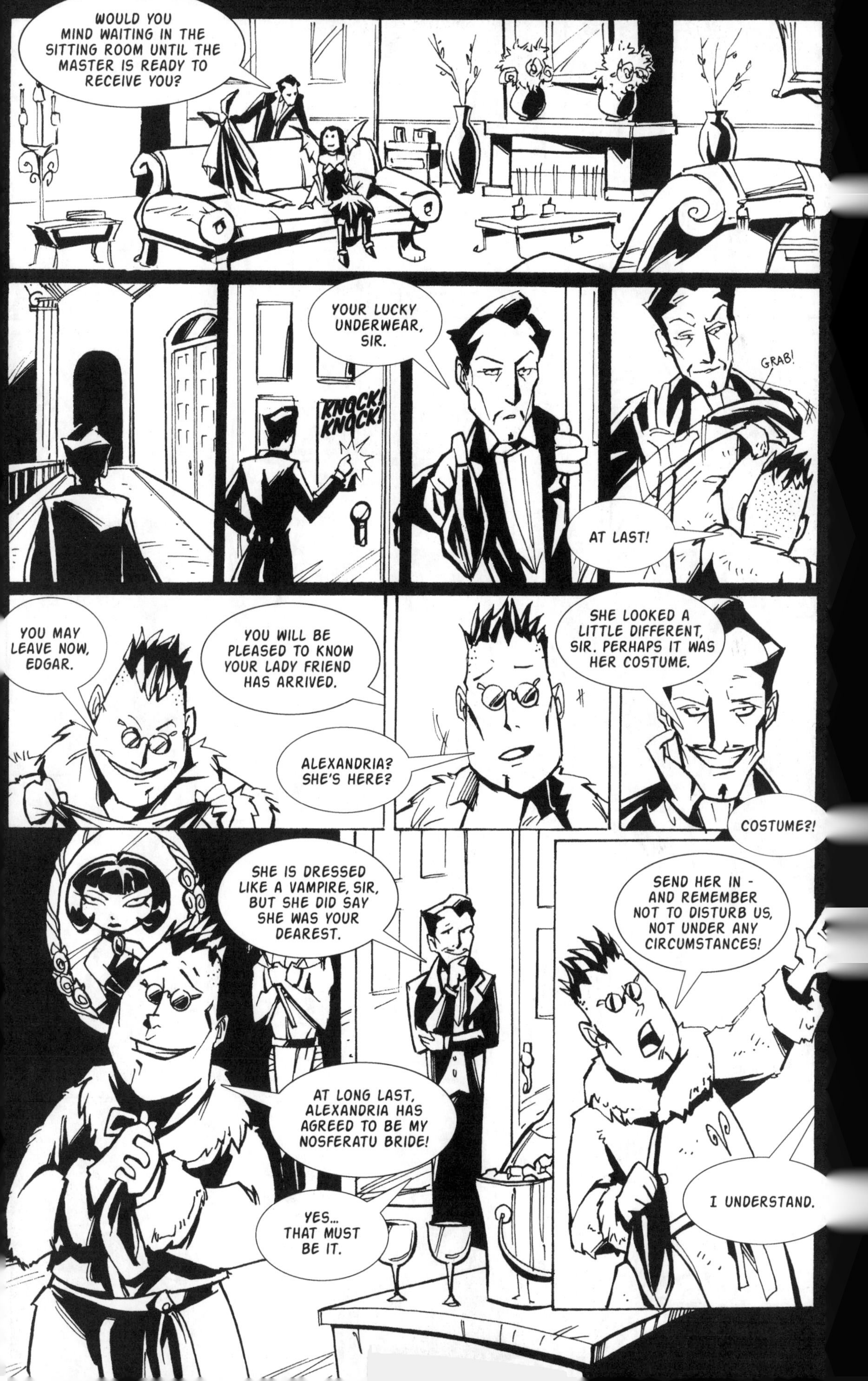
WOULD YOU MIND WAITING IN THE SITTING ROOM UNTIL THE MASTER IS READY TO RECEIVE YOU?
KNOCK! KNOCK!
YOUR LUCKY UNDERWEAR, SIR.
GRAB!
AT LAST!
YOU MAY LEAVE NOW, EDGAR.
YOU WILL BE PLEASED TO KNOW YOUR LADY FRIEND HAS ARRIVED.
ALEXANDRIA? SHE'S HERE?
SHE LOOKED A LITTLE DIFFERENT, SIR. PERHAPS IT WAS HER COSTUME.
COSTUME?!
SHE IS DRESSED LIKE A VAMPIRE, SIR, BUT SHE DID SAY SHE WAS YOUR DEAREST.
AT LONG LAST, ALEXANDRIA HAS AGREED TO BE MY NOSFERATU BRIDE!
YES... THAT MUST BE IT.
SEND HER IN - AND REMEMBER NOT TO DISTURB US, NOT UNDER ANY CIRCUMSTANCES!
I UNDERSTAND.

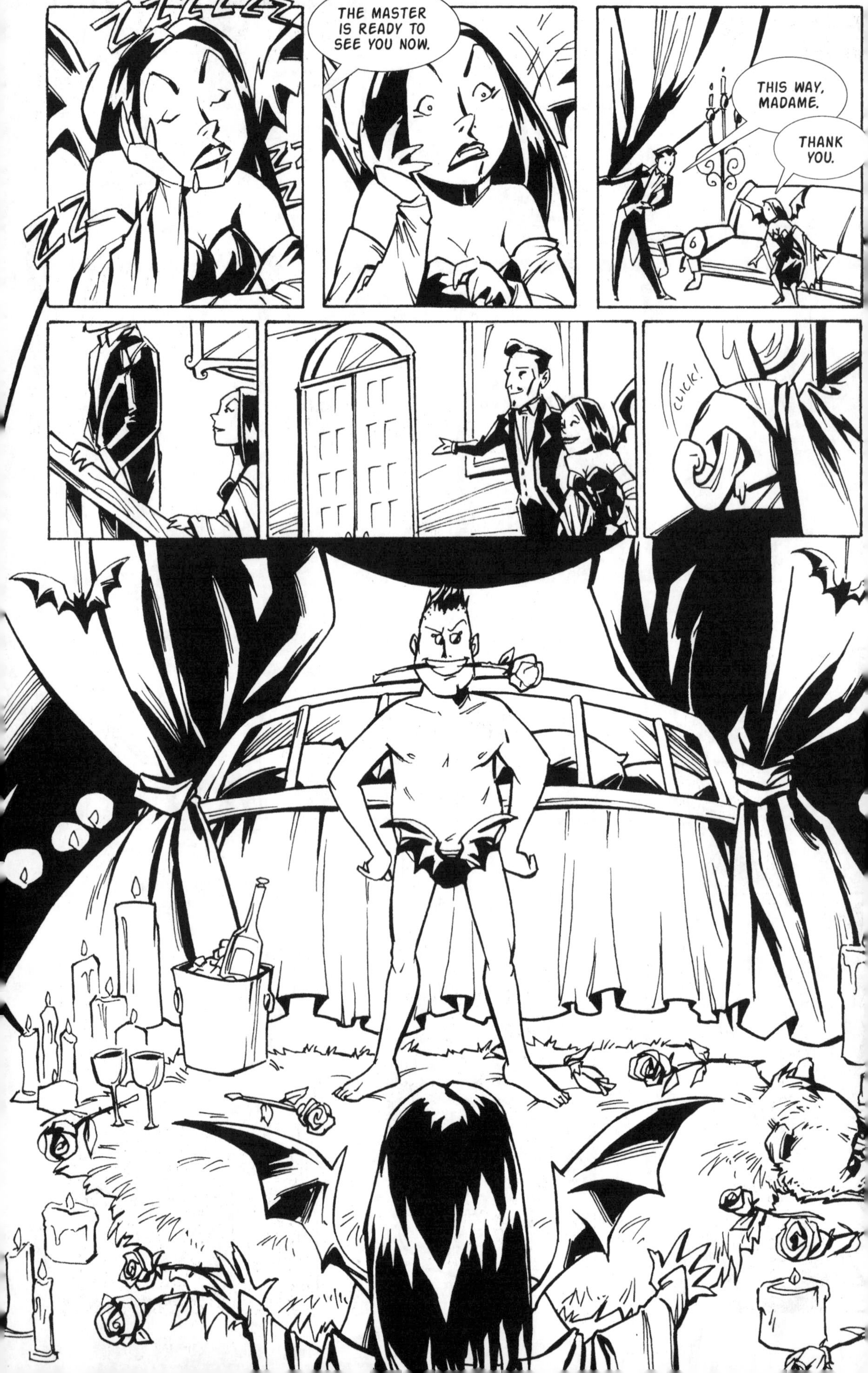
ZZZZZZZ
ZZ
ZZ
THE MASTER IS READY TO SEE YOU NOW.
THIS WAY, MADAME.
THANK YOU.
CLICK!

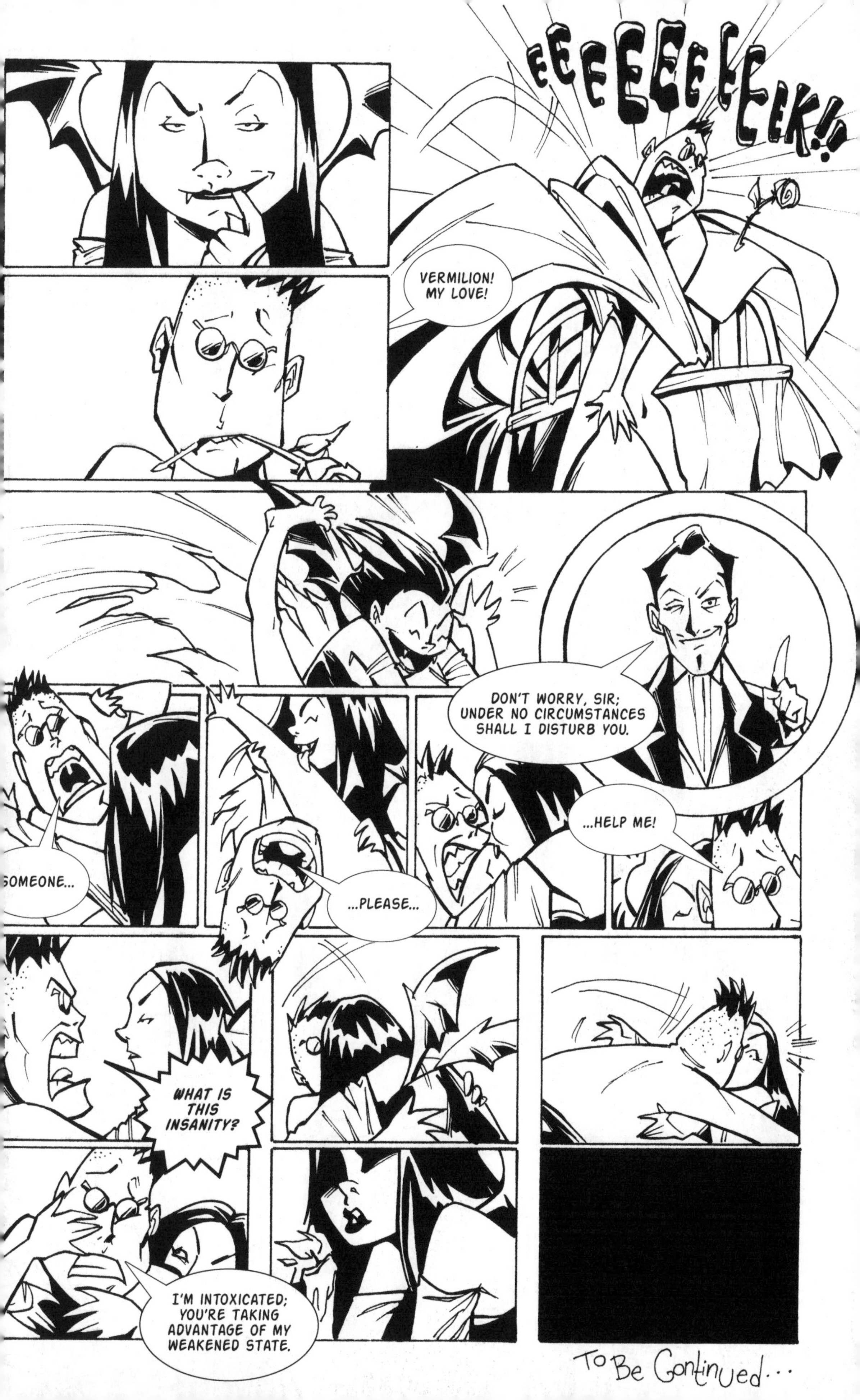
EEEEEEEEEEEK!!
VERMILION! MY LOVE!
DON'T WORRY, SIR; UNDER NO CIRCUMSTANCES SHALL I DISTURB YOU.
SOMEONE...
...PLEASE...
...HELP ME!
WHAT IS THIS INSANITY?
I'M INTOXICATED; YOU'RE TAKING ADVANTAGE OF MY WEAKENED STATE.
To Be Continued...

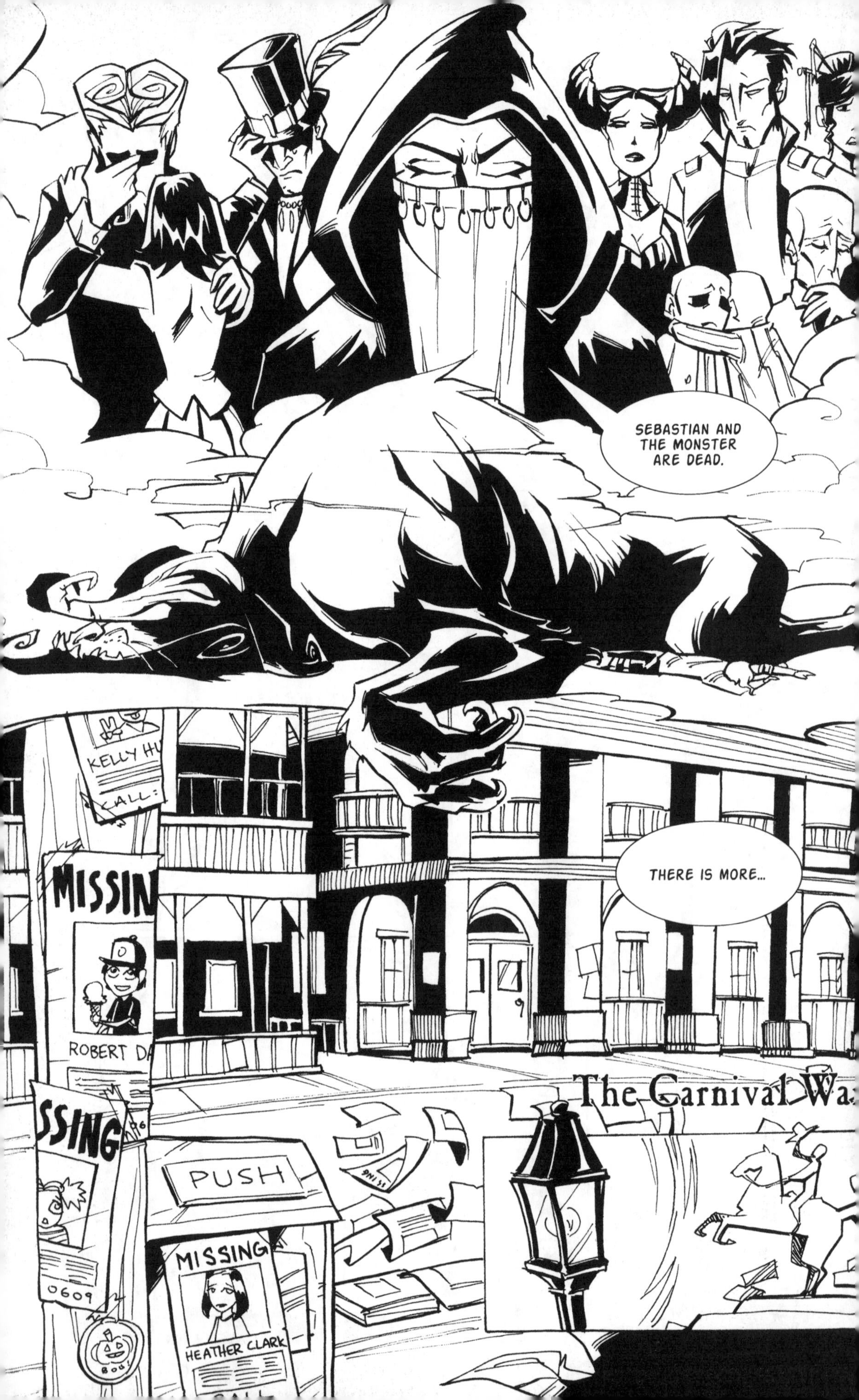
SEBASTIAN AND THE MONSTER ARE DEAD.
THERE IS MORE...
KELLY HU
CALL:
MISSIN
ROBERT DA
The Carnival Wa
SSING
PUSH
MISSING
HEATHER CLARK
0609

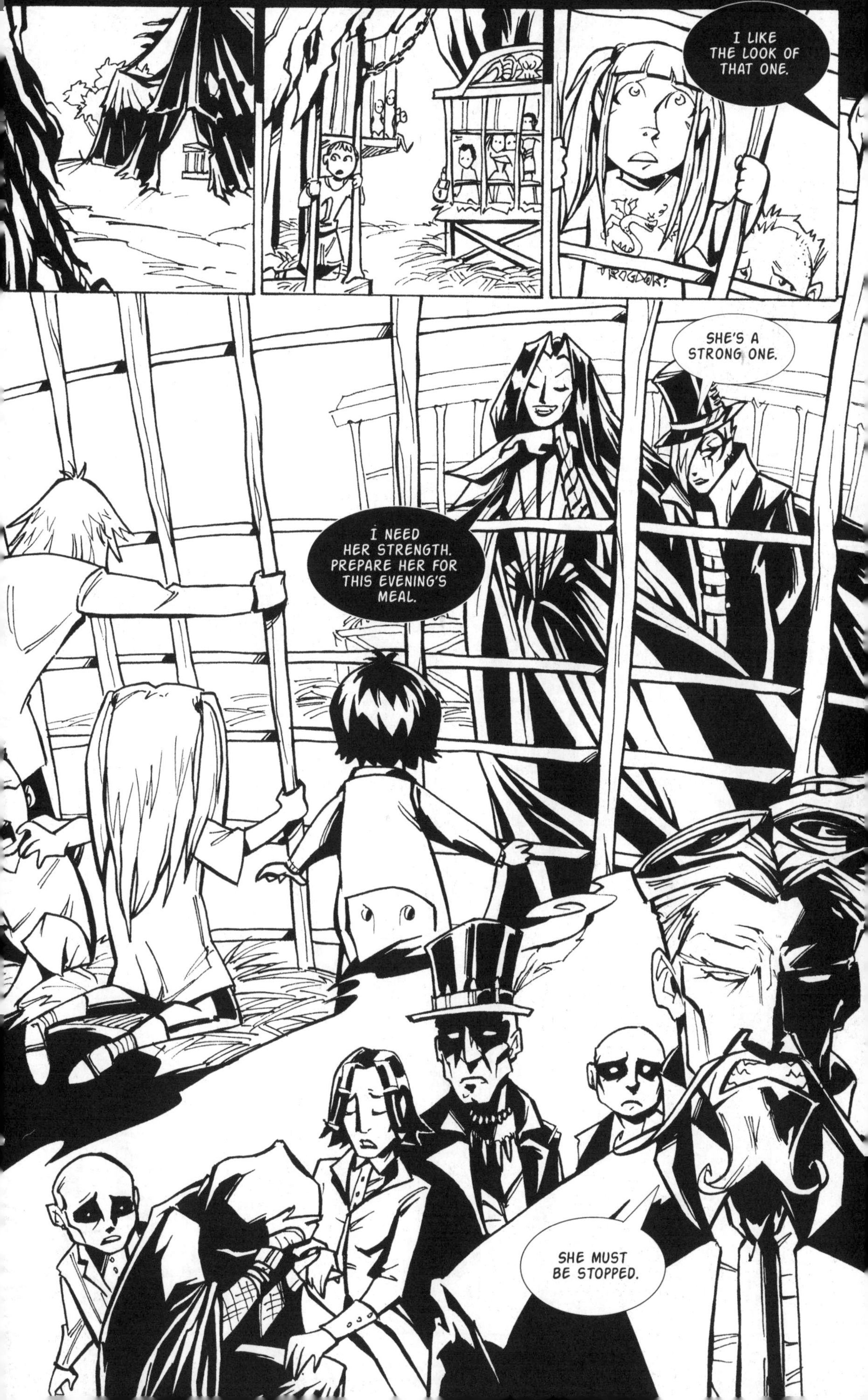
I LIKE THE LOOK OF THAT ONE.
TROGDOR!
SHE'S A STRONG ONE.
I NEED HER STRENGTH. PREPARE HER FOR THIS EVENING'S MEAL.
SHE MUST BE STOPPED.

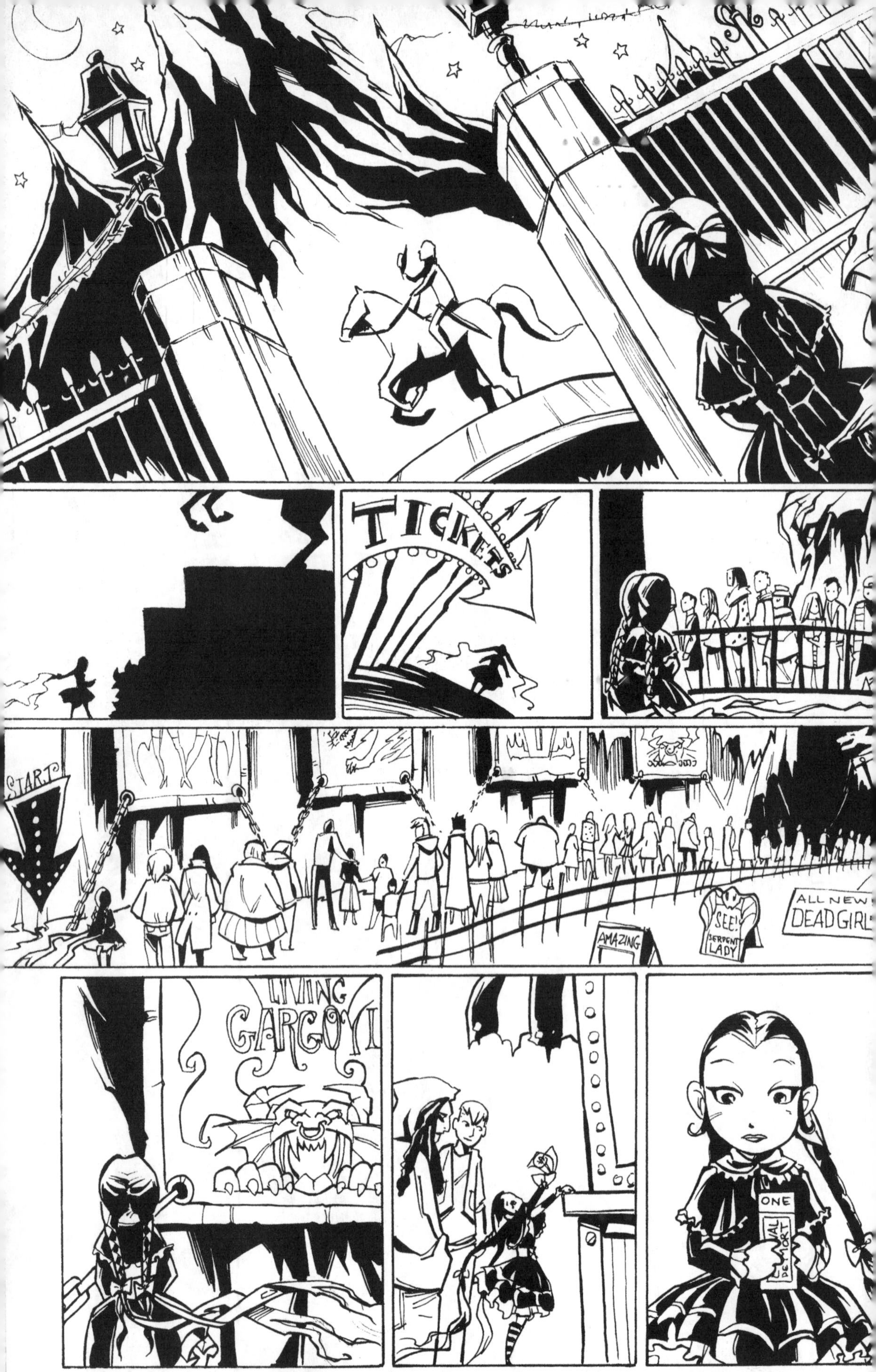
TICKETS
START
SEE! SERPENT LADY
ALL NEW DEADGIRL
AMAZING
LIVING
ONE

New Orleans Carnival

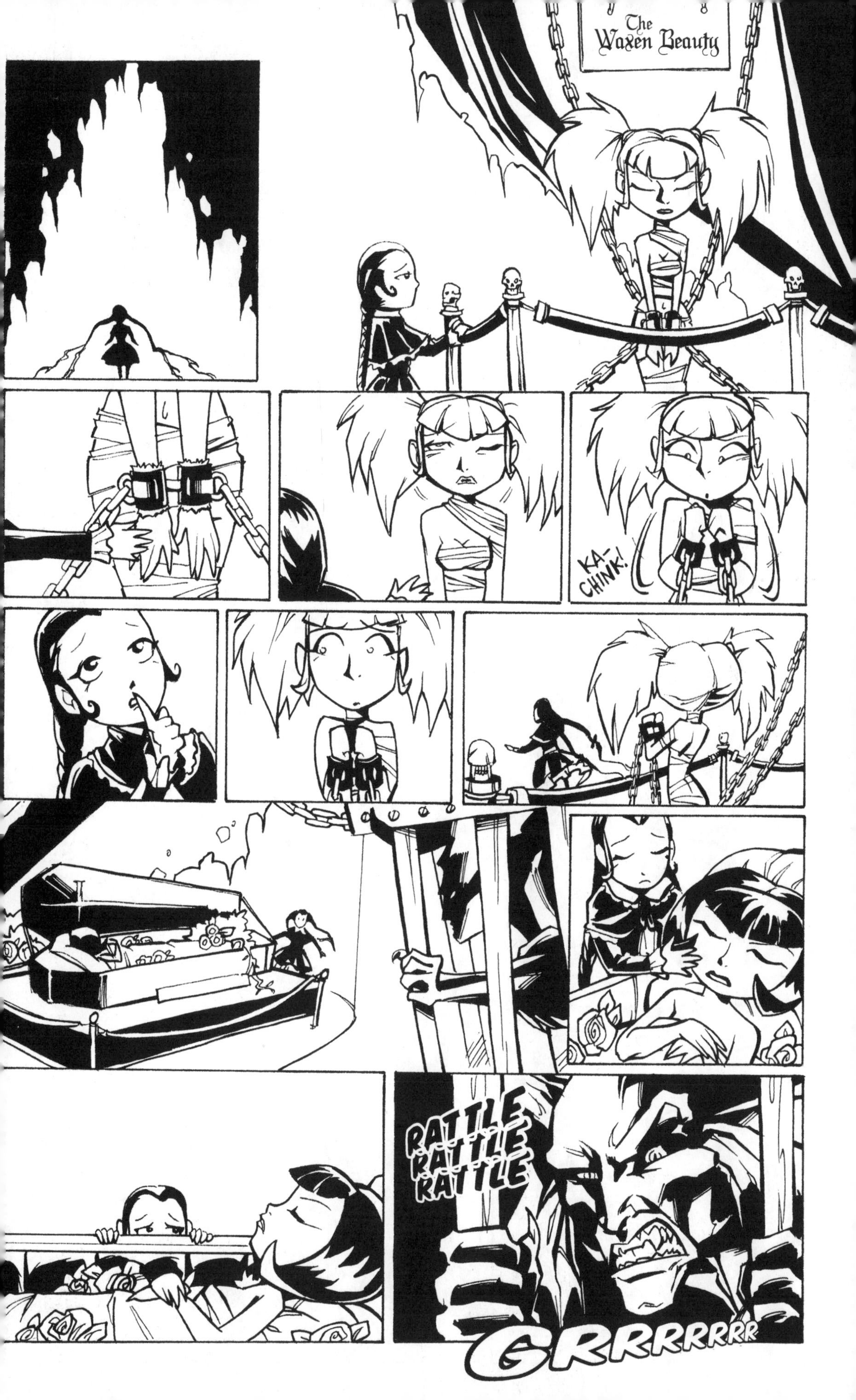
The Waxen Beauty
KA-CHINK!
RATTLE RATTLE RATTLE
GRRRRRRR

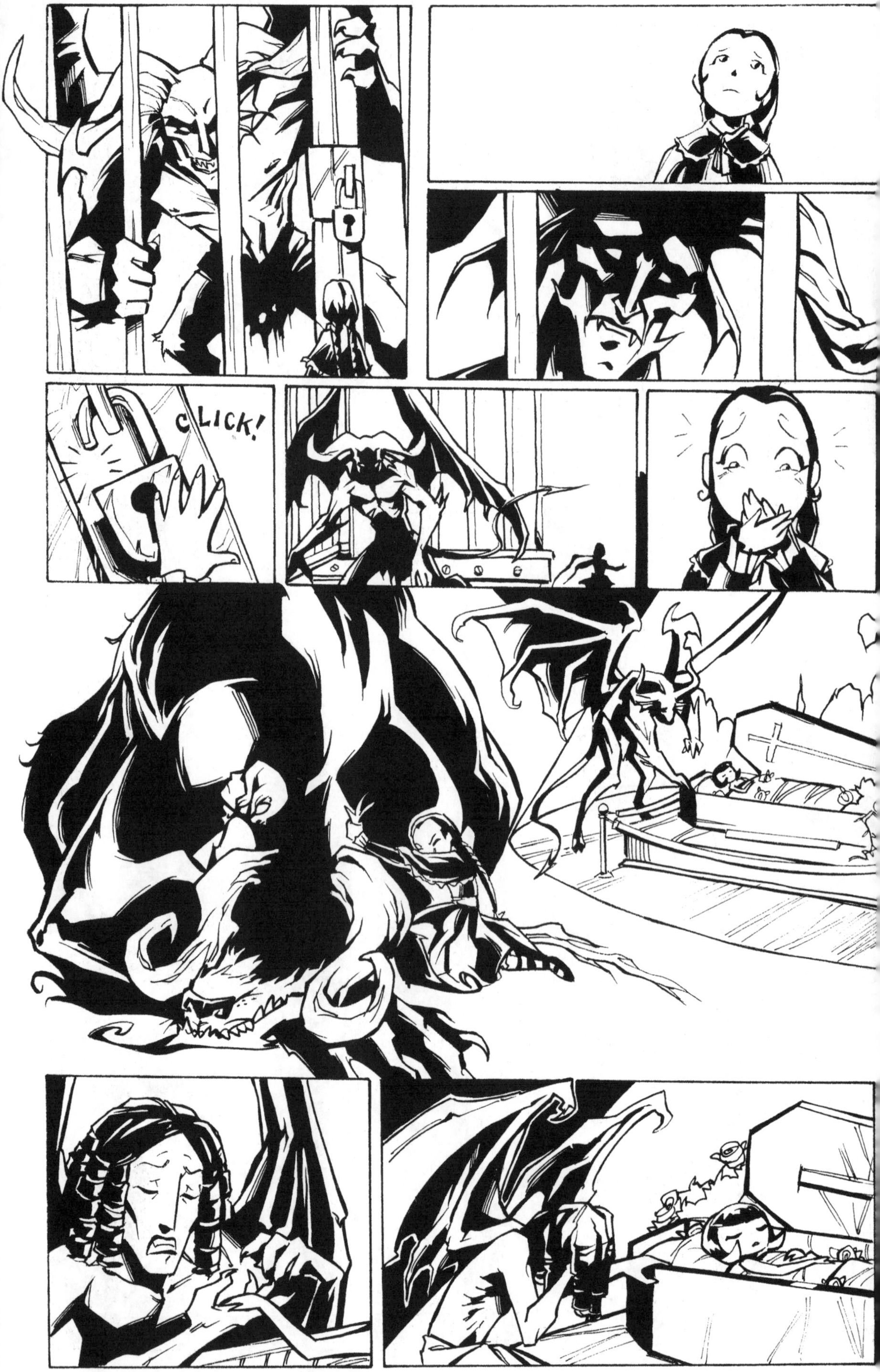
CLICK!

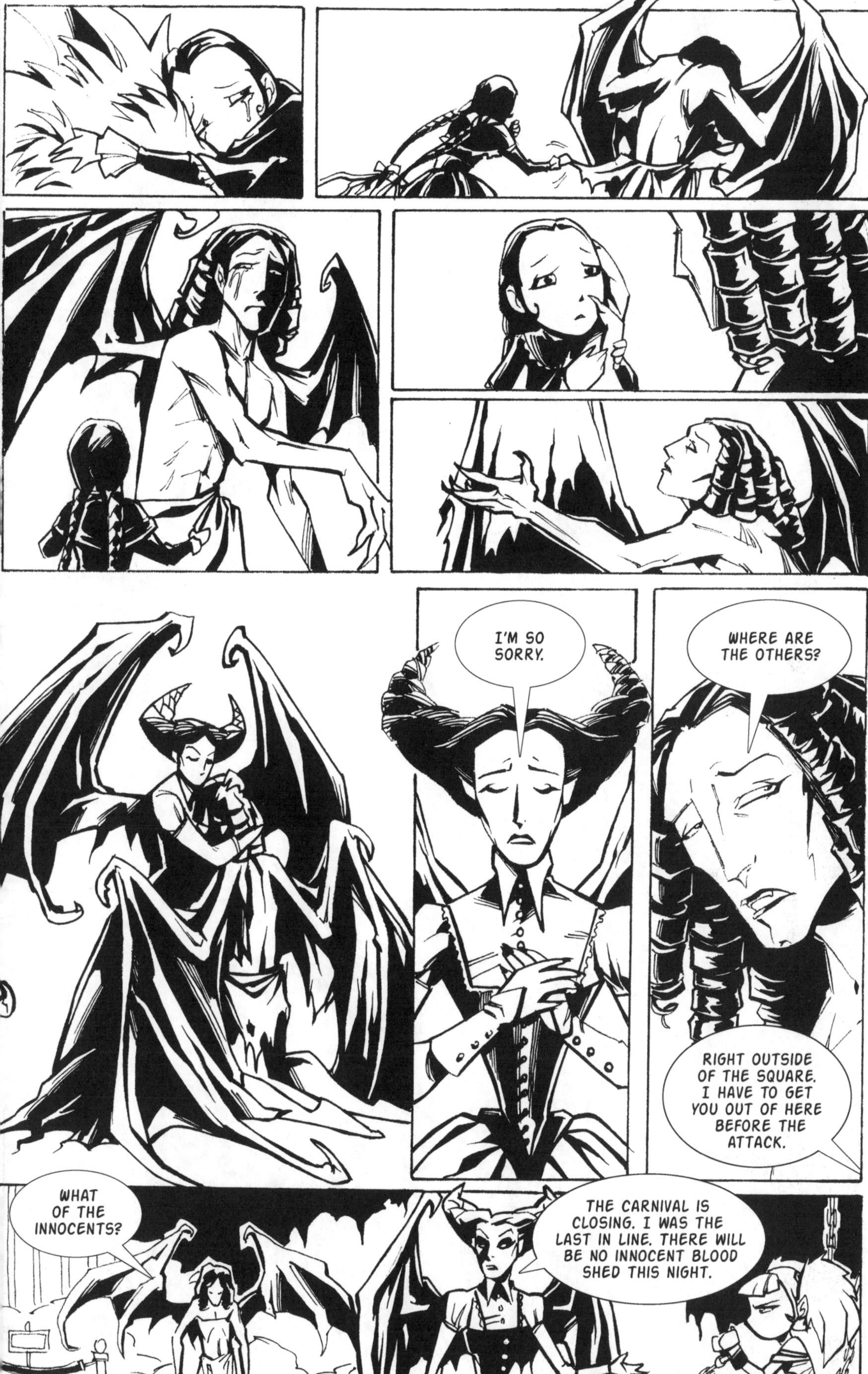
I'M SO SORRY.
WHERE ARE THE OTHERS?
RIGHT OUTSIDE OF THE SQUARE. I HAVE TO GET YOU OUT OF HERE BEFORE THE ATTACK.
WHAT OF THE INNOCENTS?
THE CARNIVAL IS CLOSING. I WAS THE LAST IN LINE. THERE WILL BE NO INNOCENT BLOOD SHED THIS NIGHT.

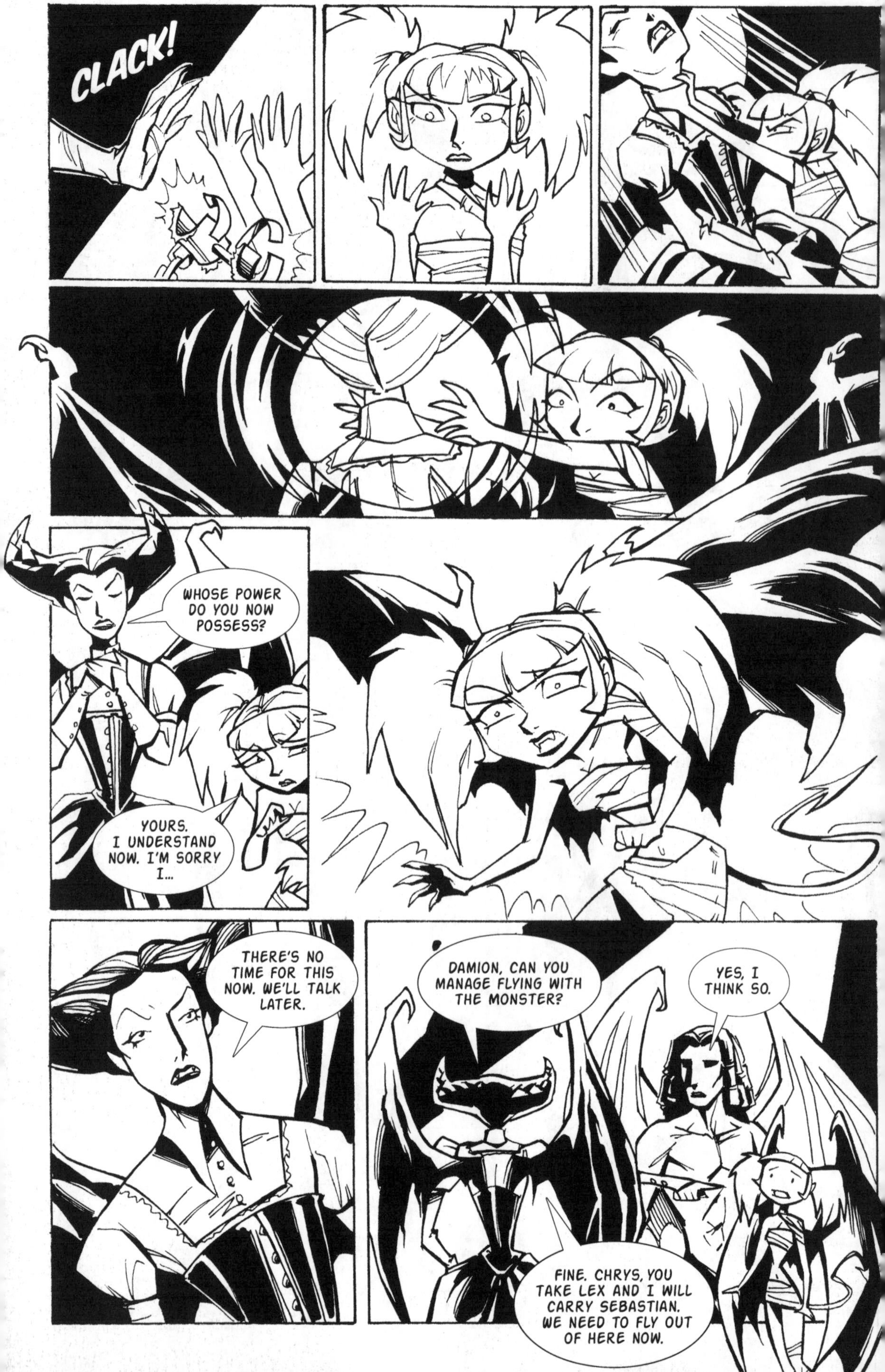
CLACK!
WHOSE POWER DO YOU NOW POSSESS?
YOURS. I UNDERSTAND NOW. I'M SORRY I...
THERE'S NO TIME FOR THIS NOW. WE'LL TALK LATER.
DAMION, CAN YOU MANAGE FLYING WITH THE MONSTER?
YES, I THINK SO.
FINE. CHRYS, YOU TAKE LEX AND I WILL CARRY SEBASTIAN. WE NEED TO FLY OUT OF HERE NOW.

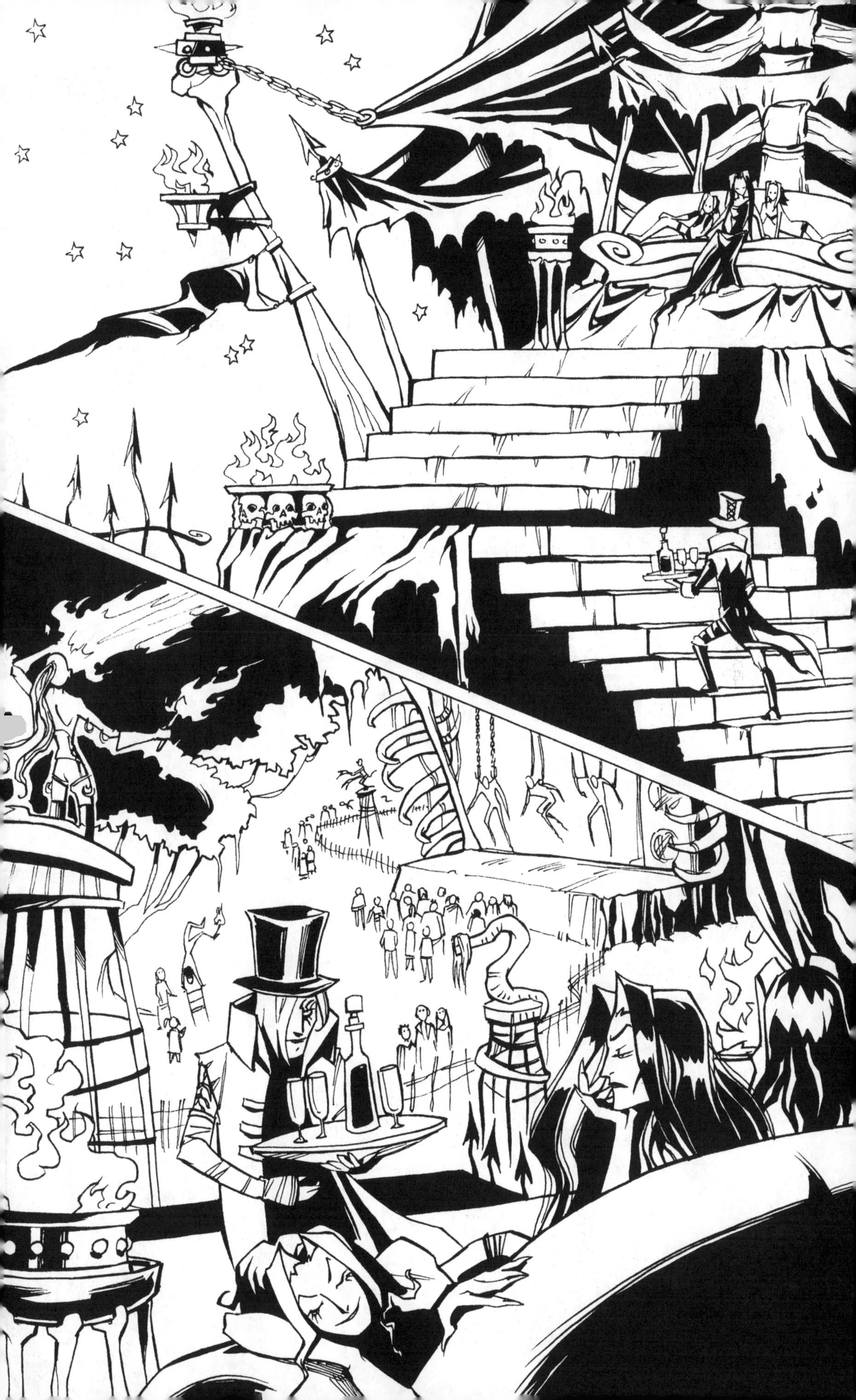

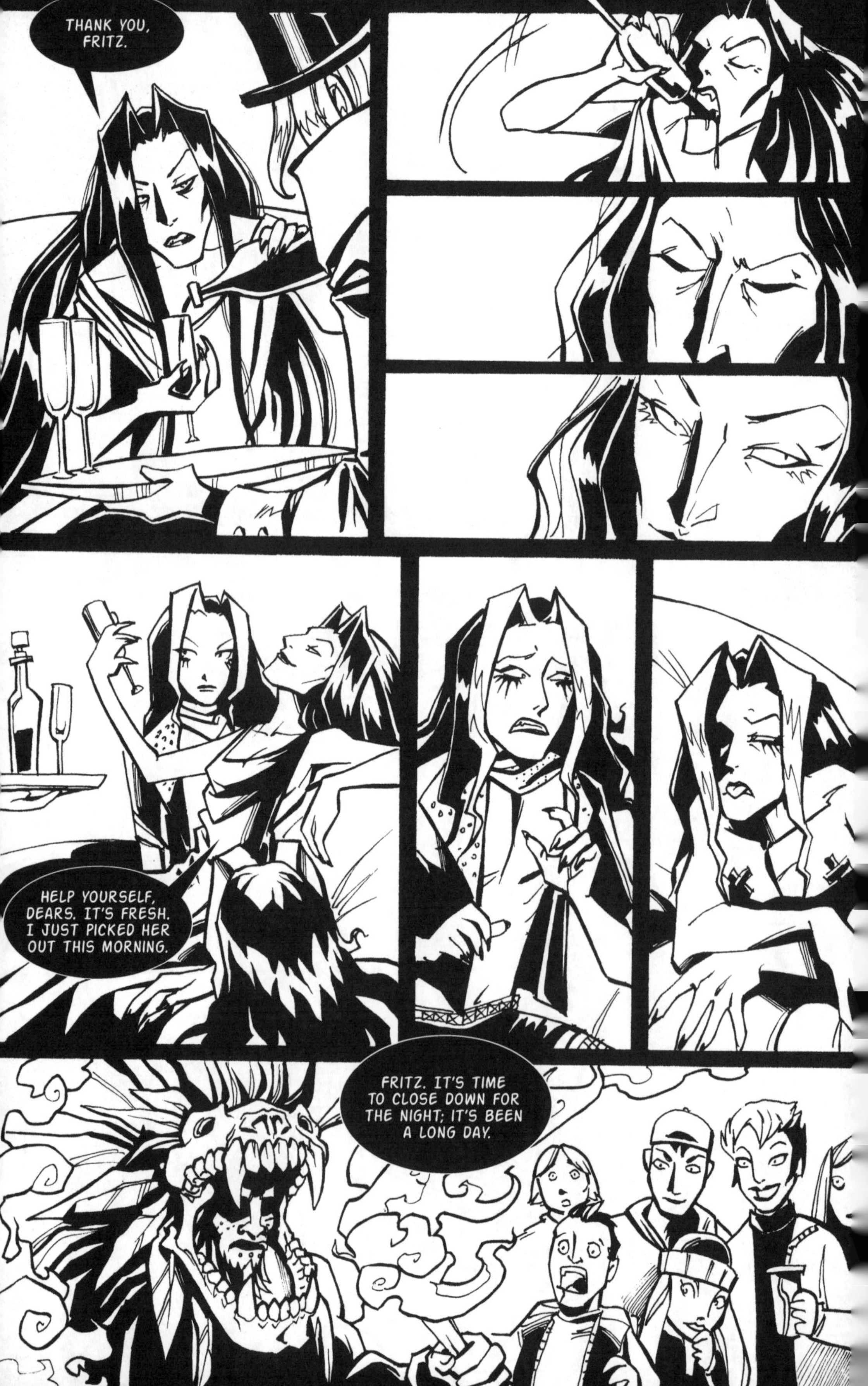
THANK YOU, FRITZ.
HELP YOURSELF, DEARS. IT'S FRESH. I JUST PICKED HER OUT THIS MORNING.
FRITZ. IT'S TIME TO CLOSE DOWN FOR THE NIGHT; IT'S BEEN A LONG DAY.

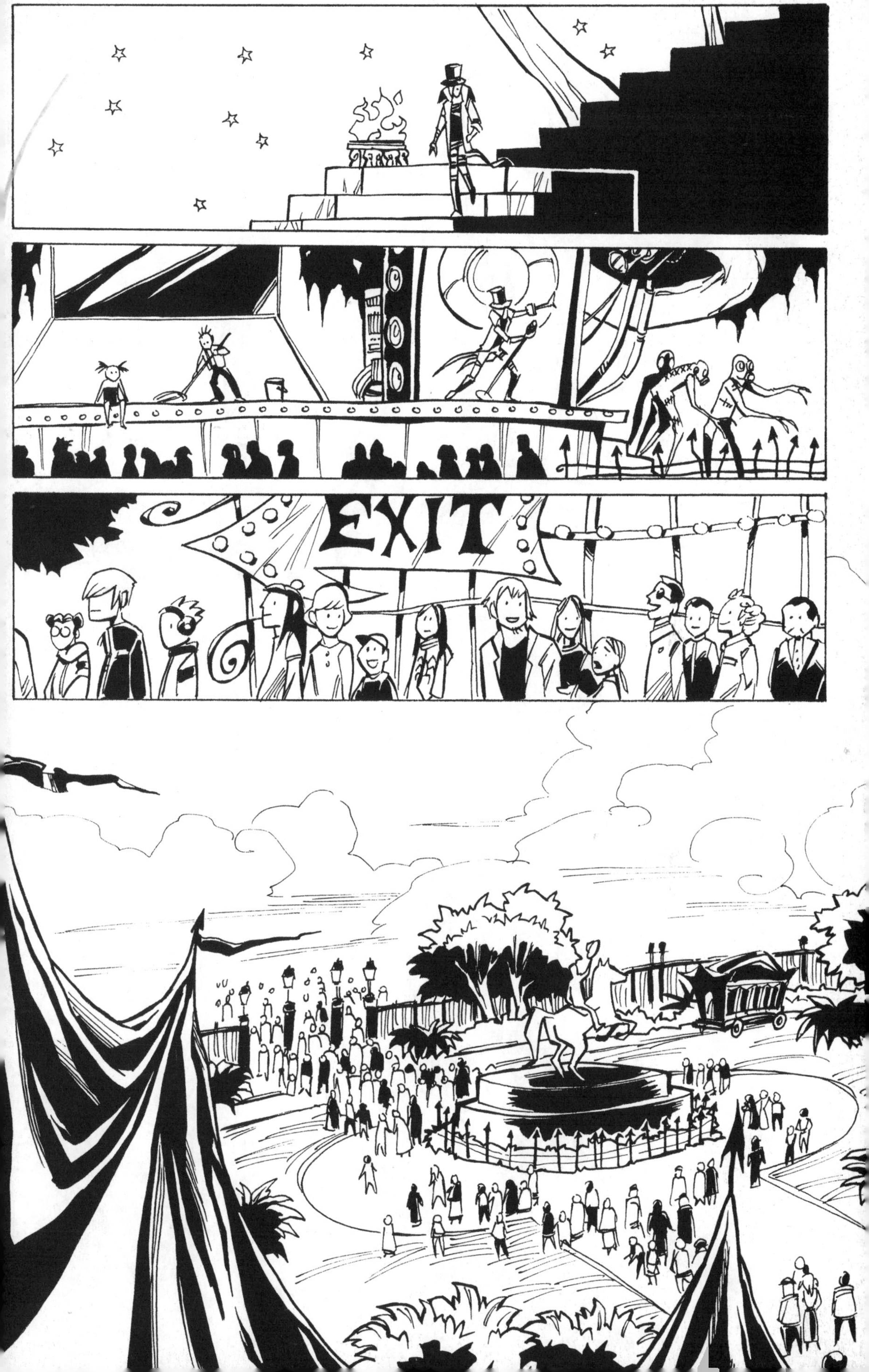
EXIT

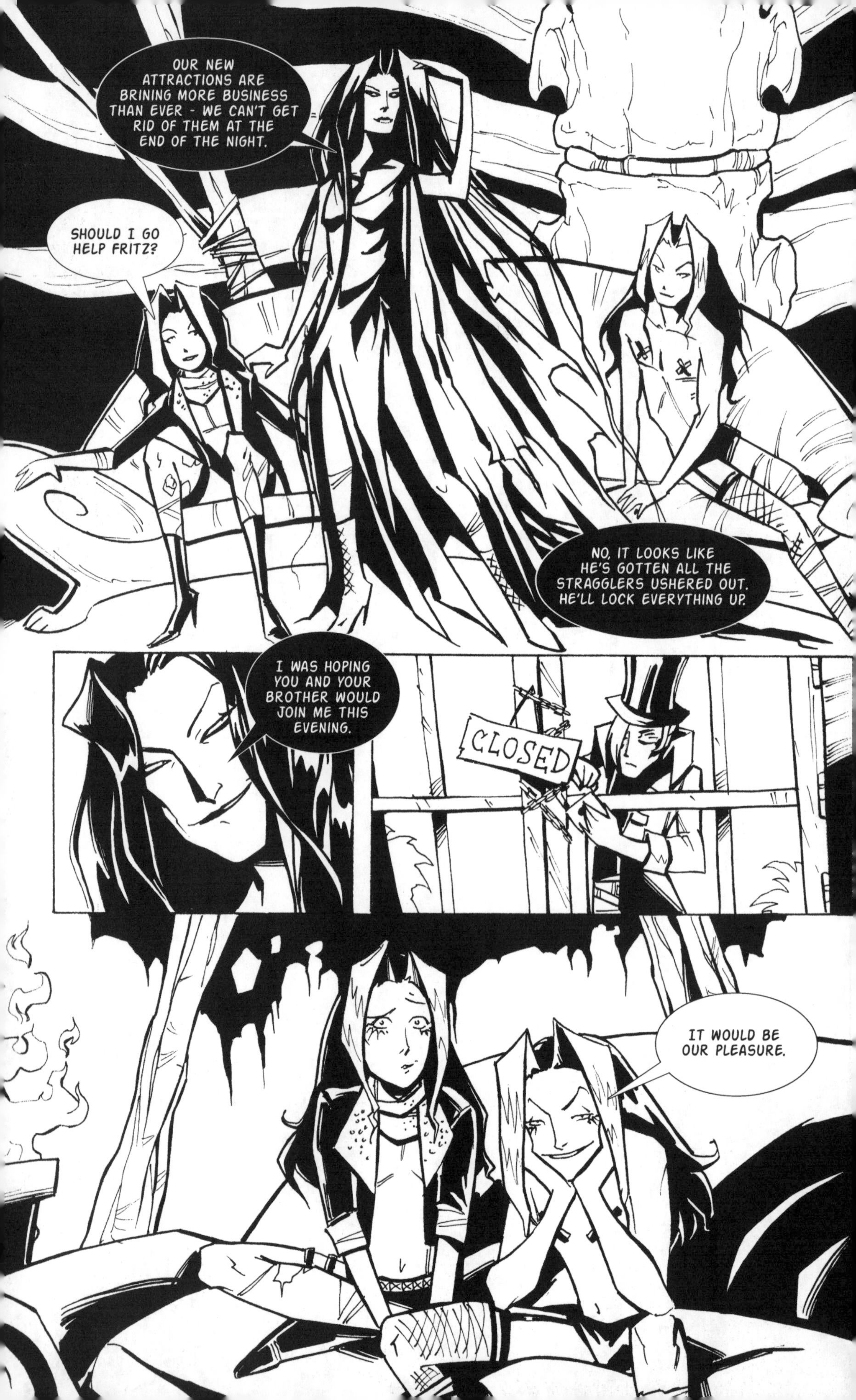
OUR NEW ATTRACTIONS ARE BRINING MORE BUSINESS THAN EVER - WE CAN'T GET RID OF THEM AT THE END OF THE NIGHT.
SHOULD I GO HELP FRITZ?
NO, IT LOOKS LIKE HE'S GOTTEN ALL THE STRAGGLERS USHERED OUT. HE'LL LOCK EVERYTHING UP.
I WAS HOPING YOU AND YOUR BROTHER WOULD JOIN ME THIS EVENING.
CLOSED
IT WOULD BE OUR PLEASURE.

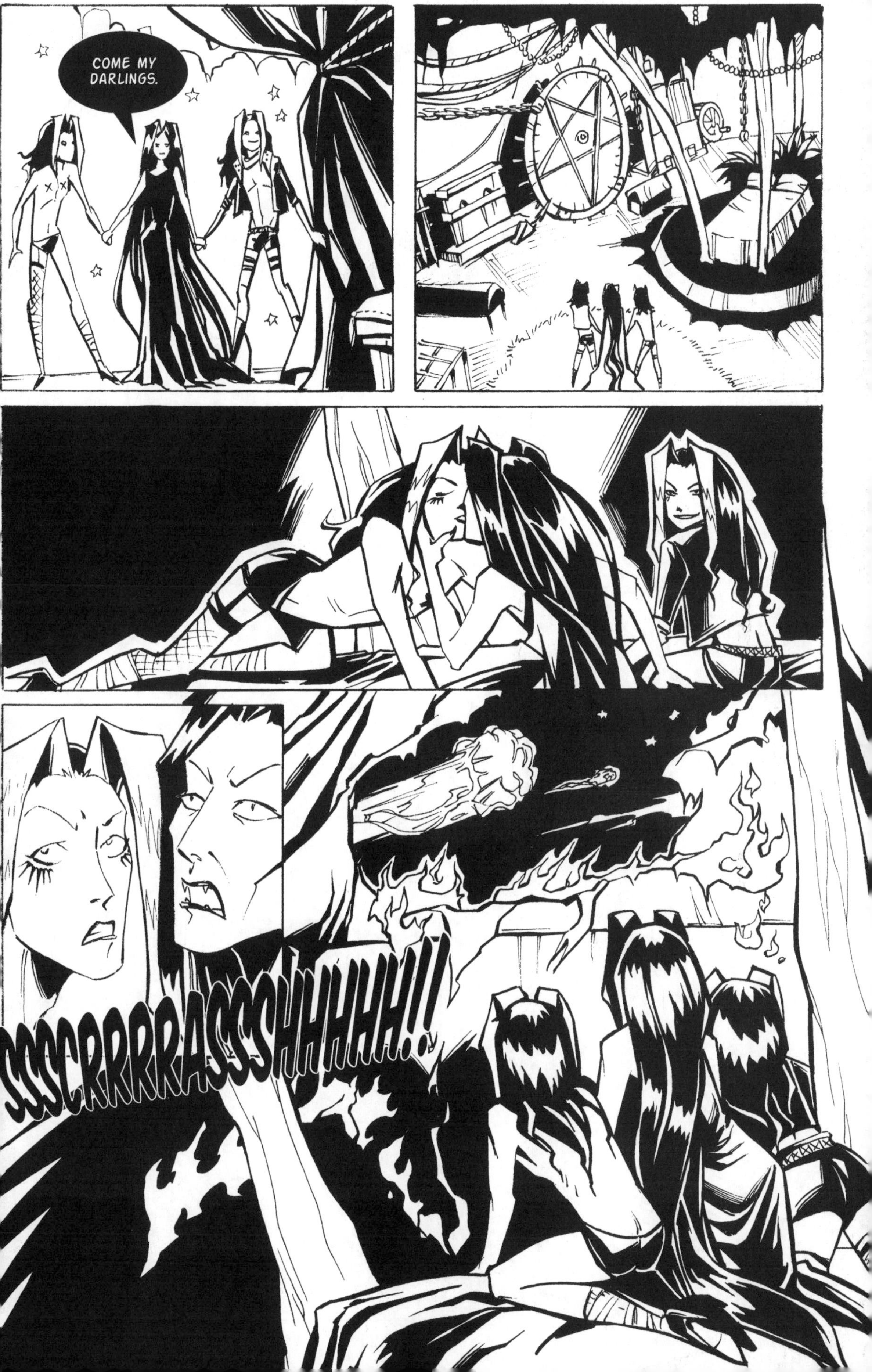
COME MY DARLINGS.
SSSCRRRRASSSHHHHH!!

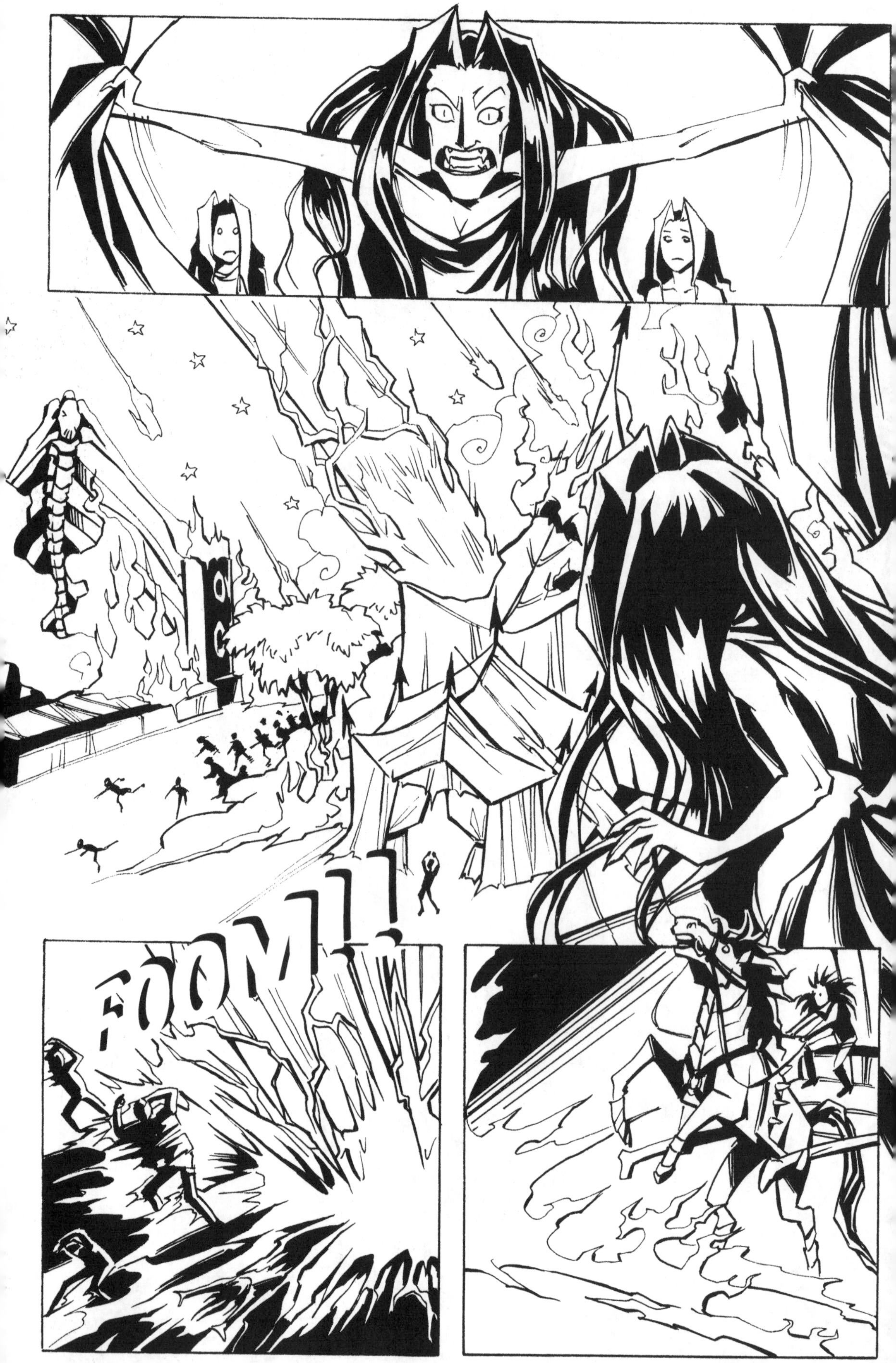
FOOM!!!

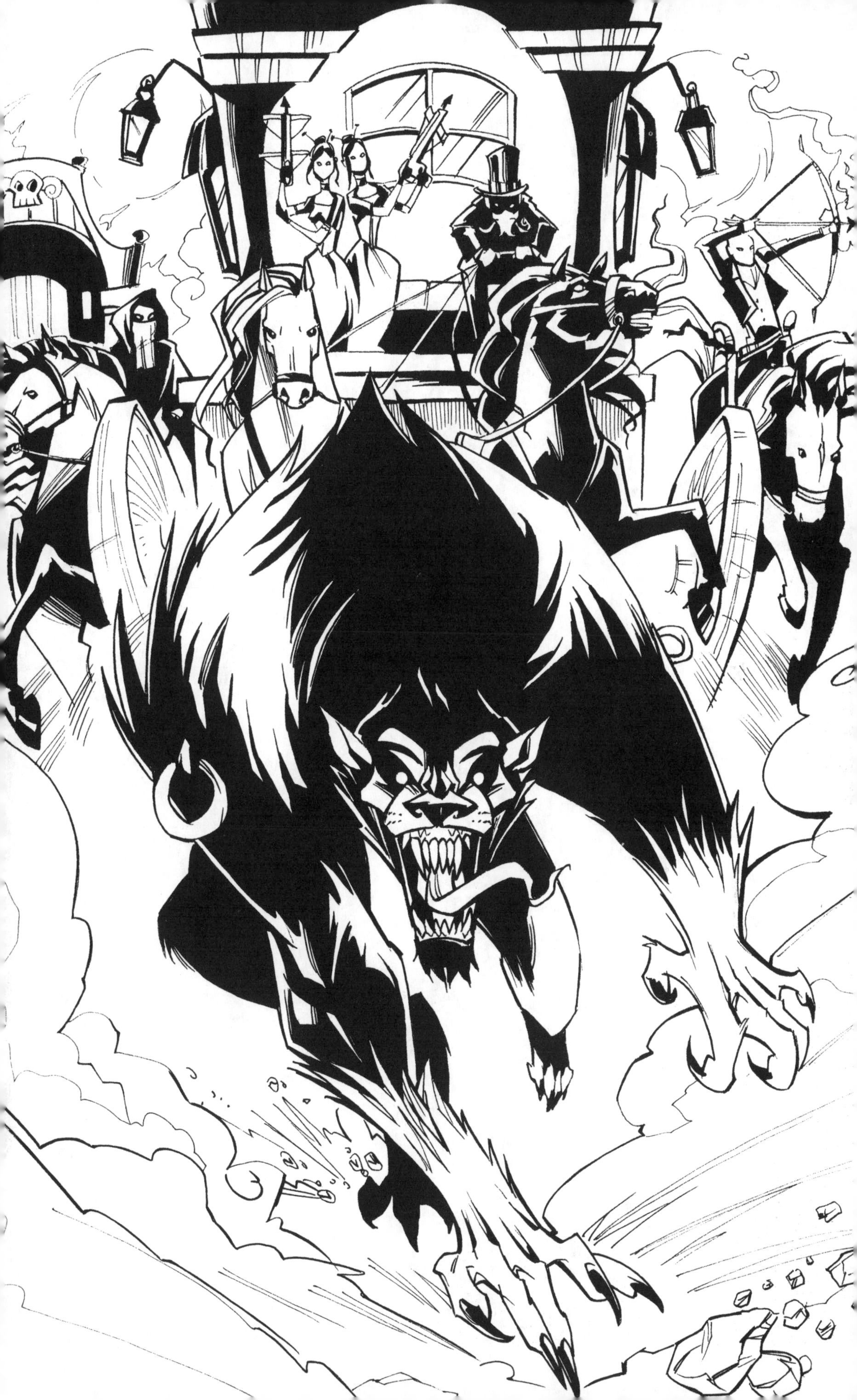

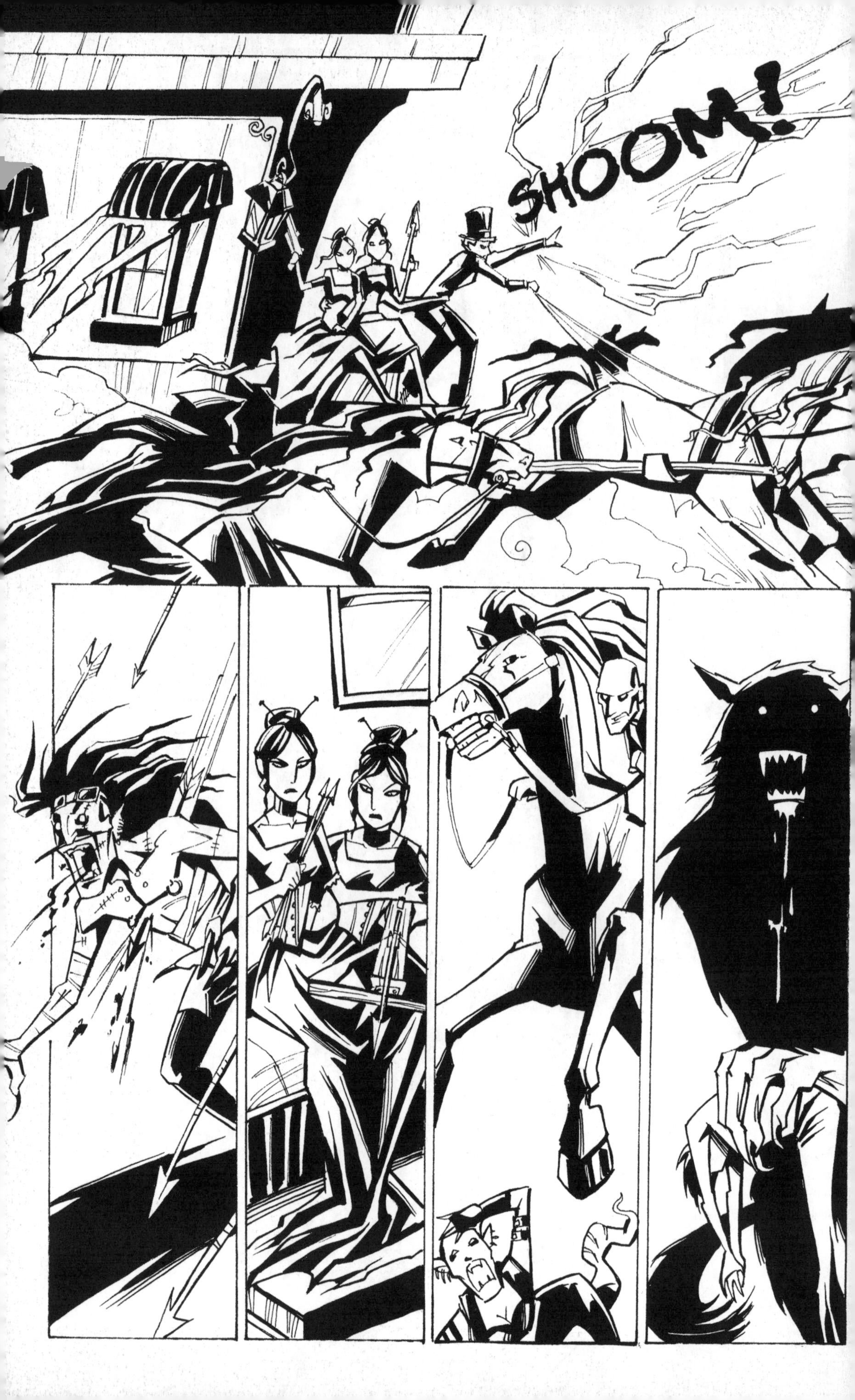
SHOOM!

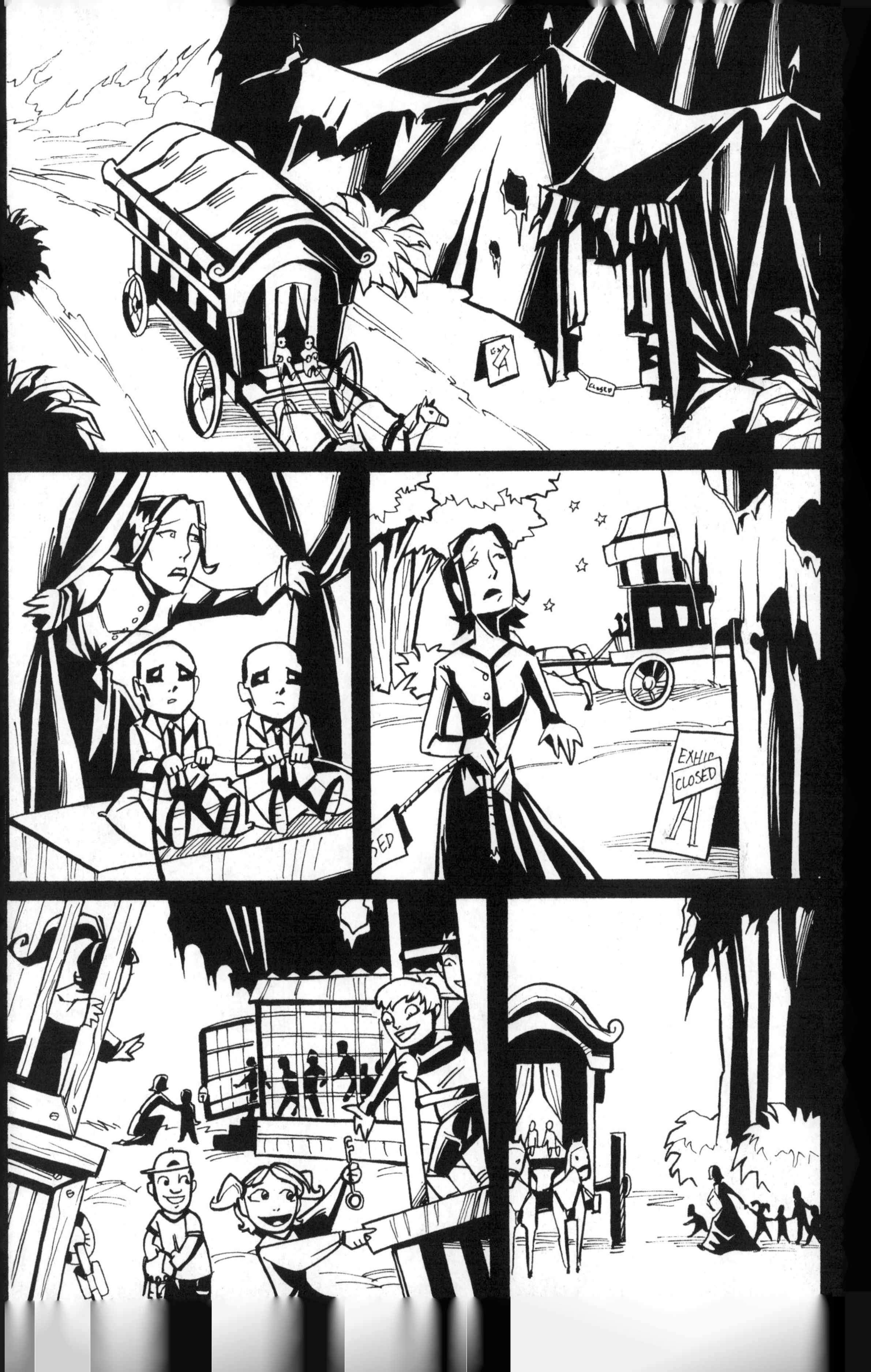
CLOSED
CLOSED

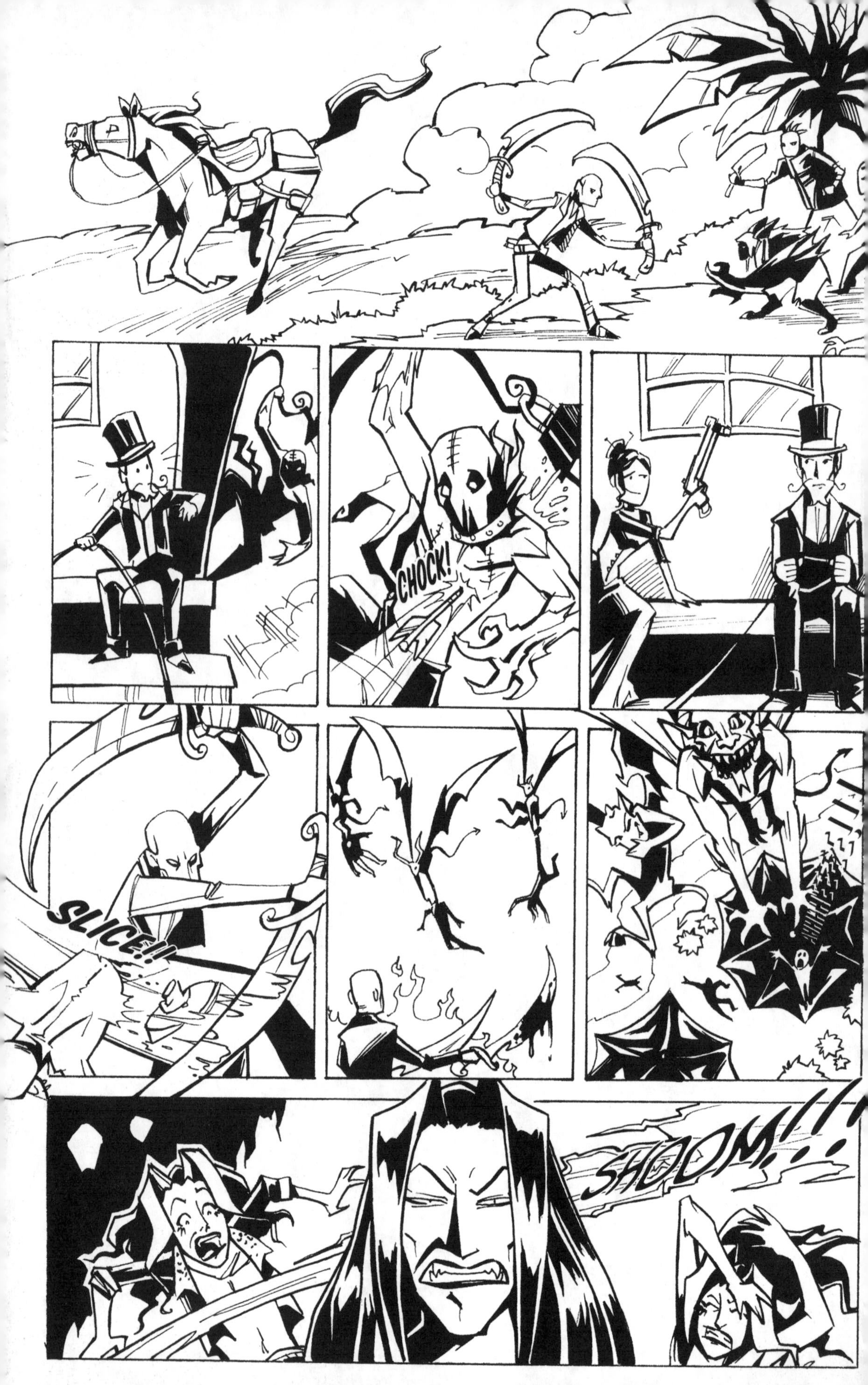
CHOCK!
SLICE!!!
SHOOM!!!

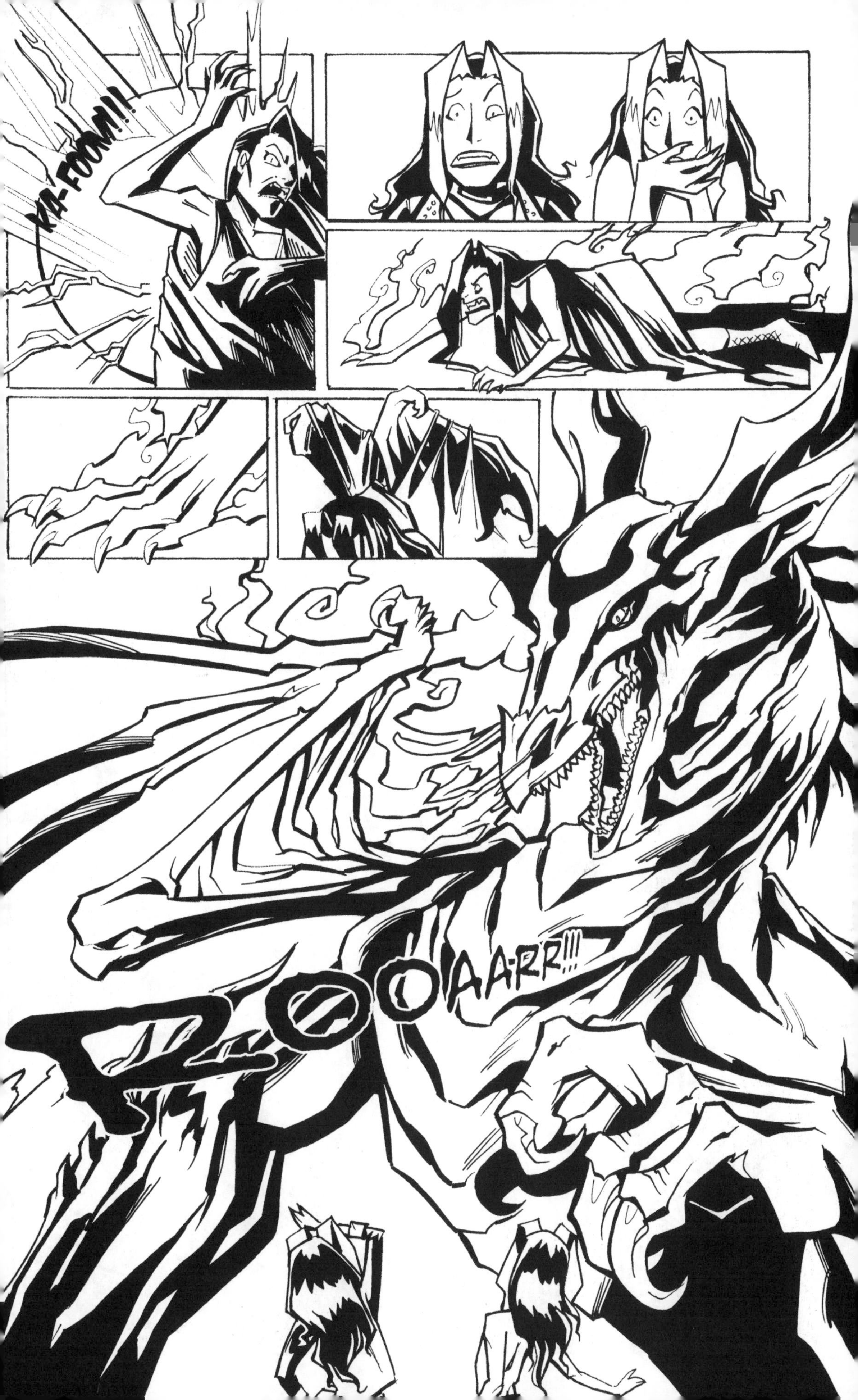
KA-FOOM!!
ROOOAARR!!!

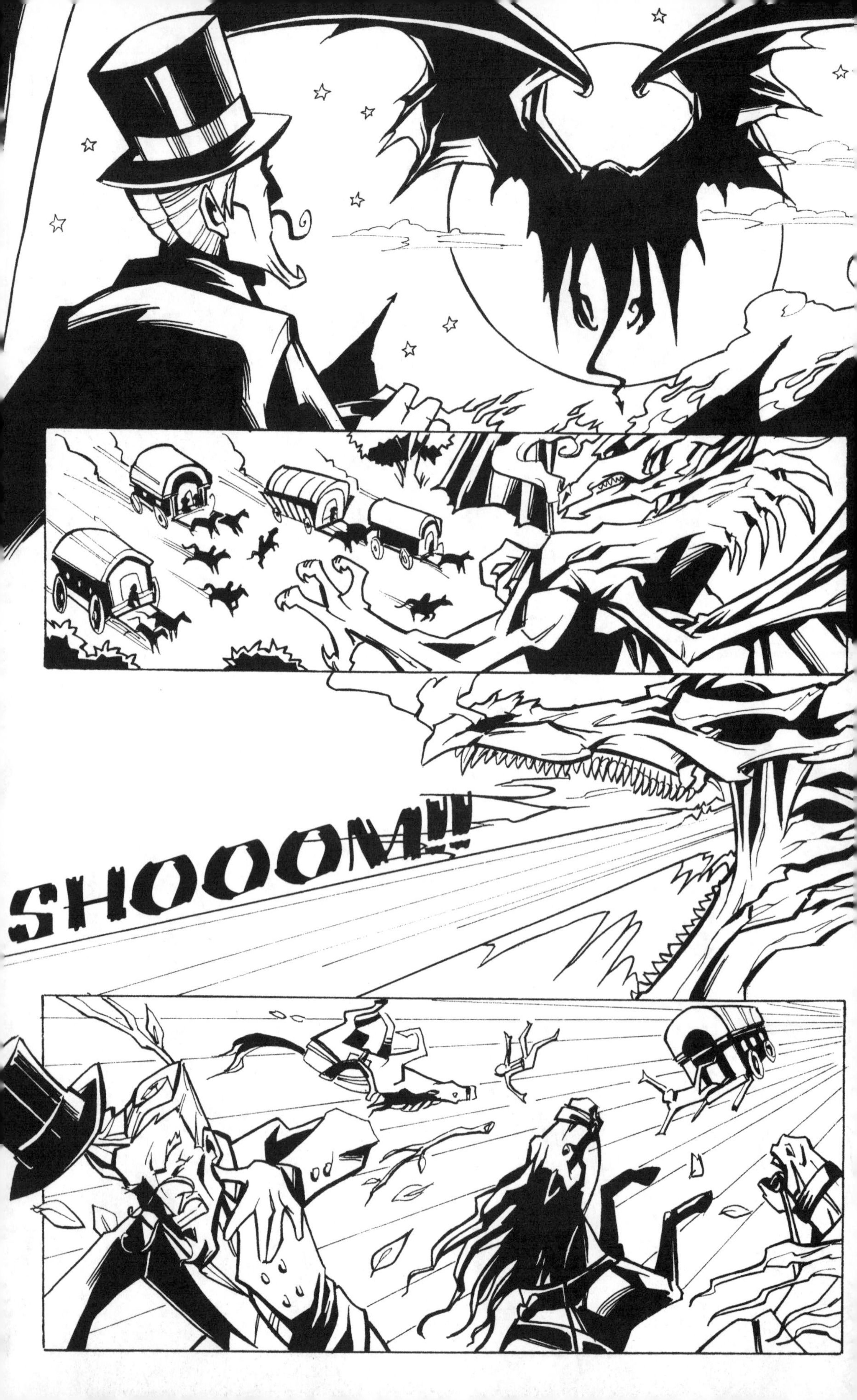
SHOOOM!!

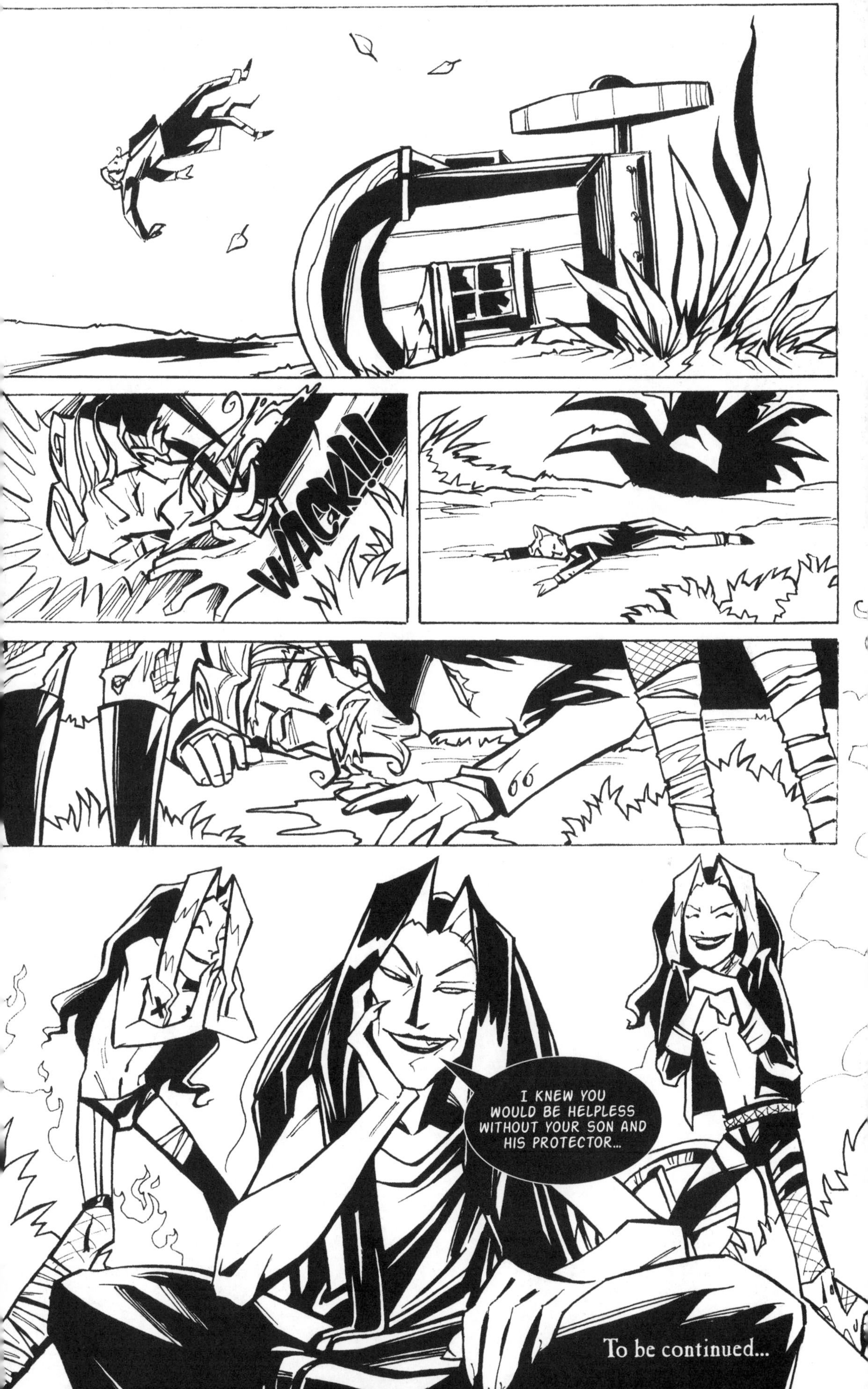
WACK!!!
I KNEW YOU WOULD BE HELPLESS WITHOUT YOUR SON AND HIS PROTECTOR...
To be continued...

Chapter 23

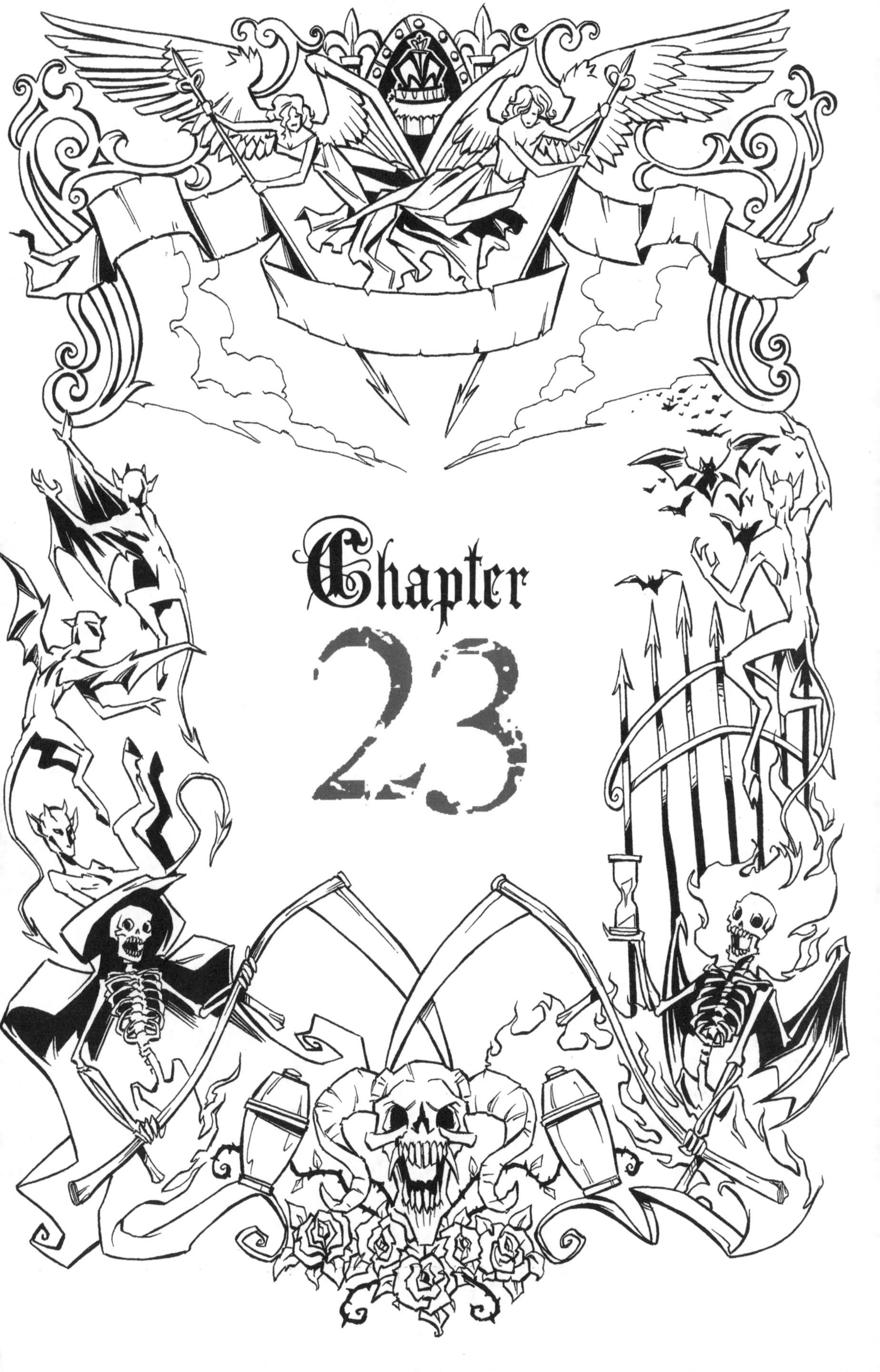

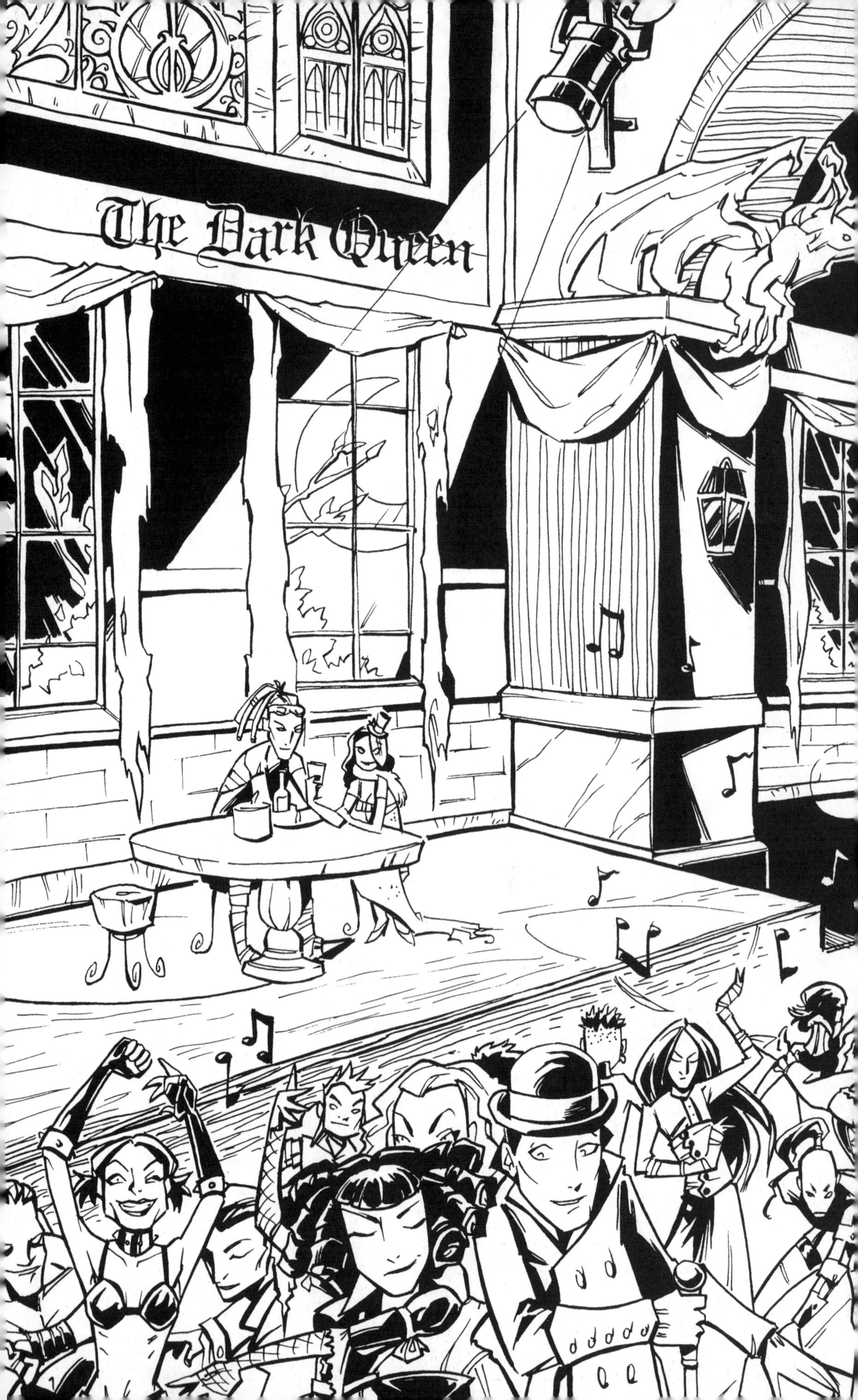
The Dark Queen

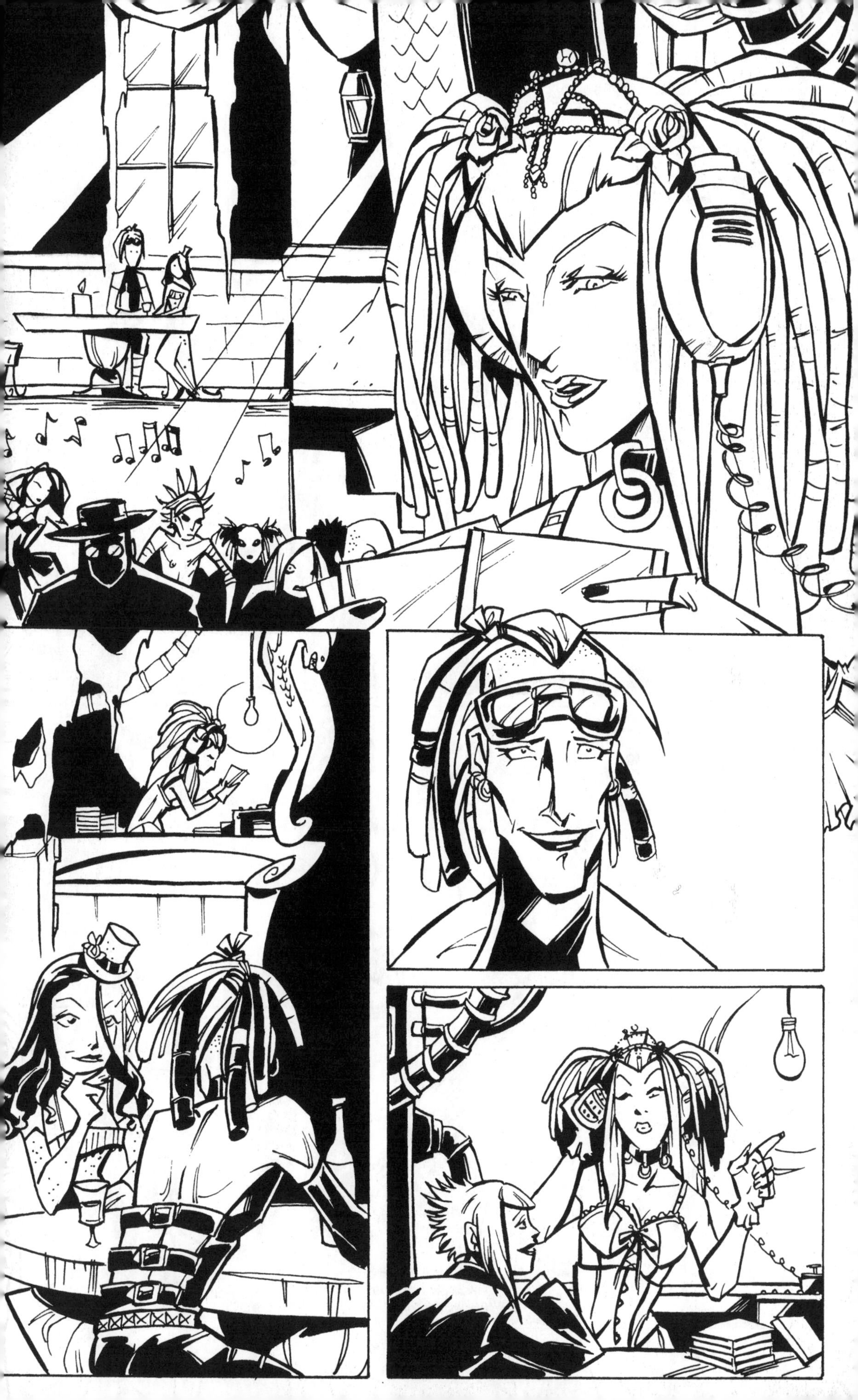

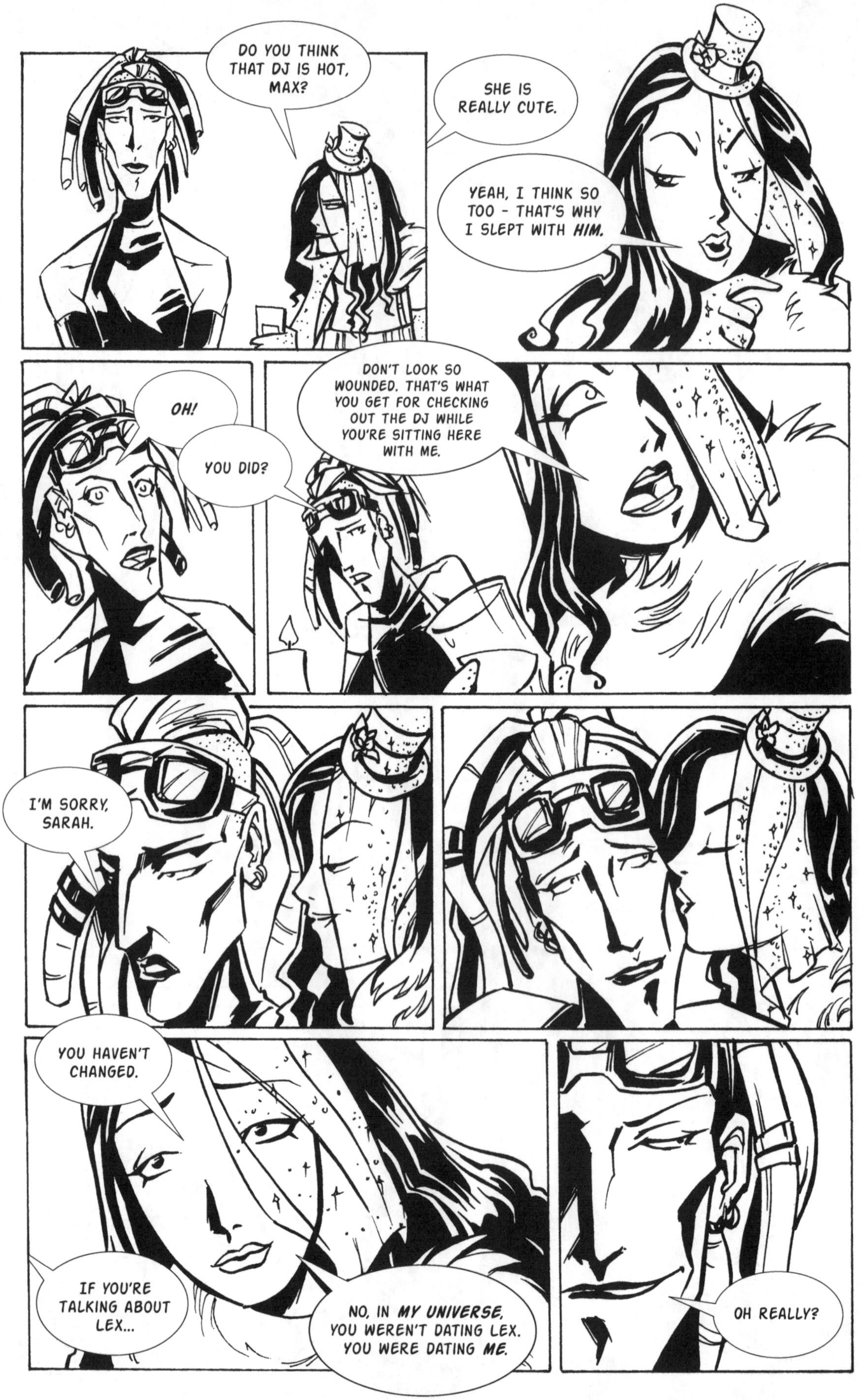
DO YOU THINK THAT DJ IS HOT, MAX?
SHE IS REALLY CUTE.
YEAH, I THINK SO TOO - THAT'S WHY I SLEPT WITH *HIM.*
OH!
YOU DID?
DON'T LOOK SO WOUNDED. THAT'S WHAT YOU GET FOR CHECKING OUT THE DJ WHILE YOU'RE SITTING HERE WITH ME.
I'M SORRY, SARAH.
YOU HAVEN'T CHANGED.
IF YOU'RE TALKING ABOUT LEX...
NO, IN *MY UNIVERSE*, YOU WEREN'T DATING LEX. YOU WERE DATING *ME*.
OH REALLY?

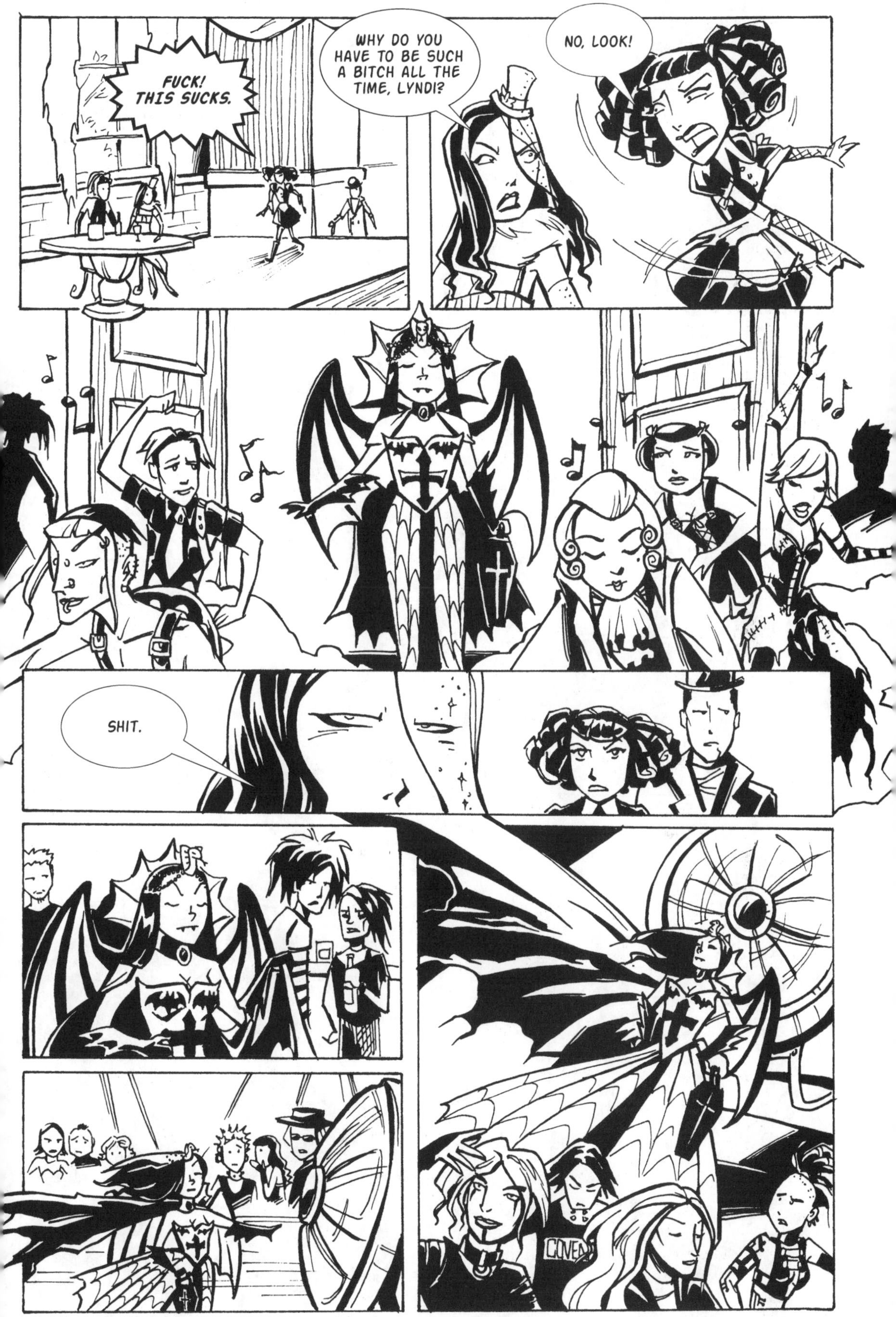
FUCK! THIS SUCKS.
WHY DO YOU HAVE TO BE SUCH A BITCH ALL THE TIME, LYNDI?
NO, LOOK!
SHIT.
COVEN

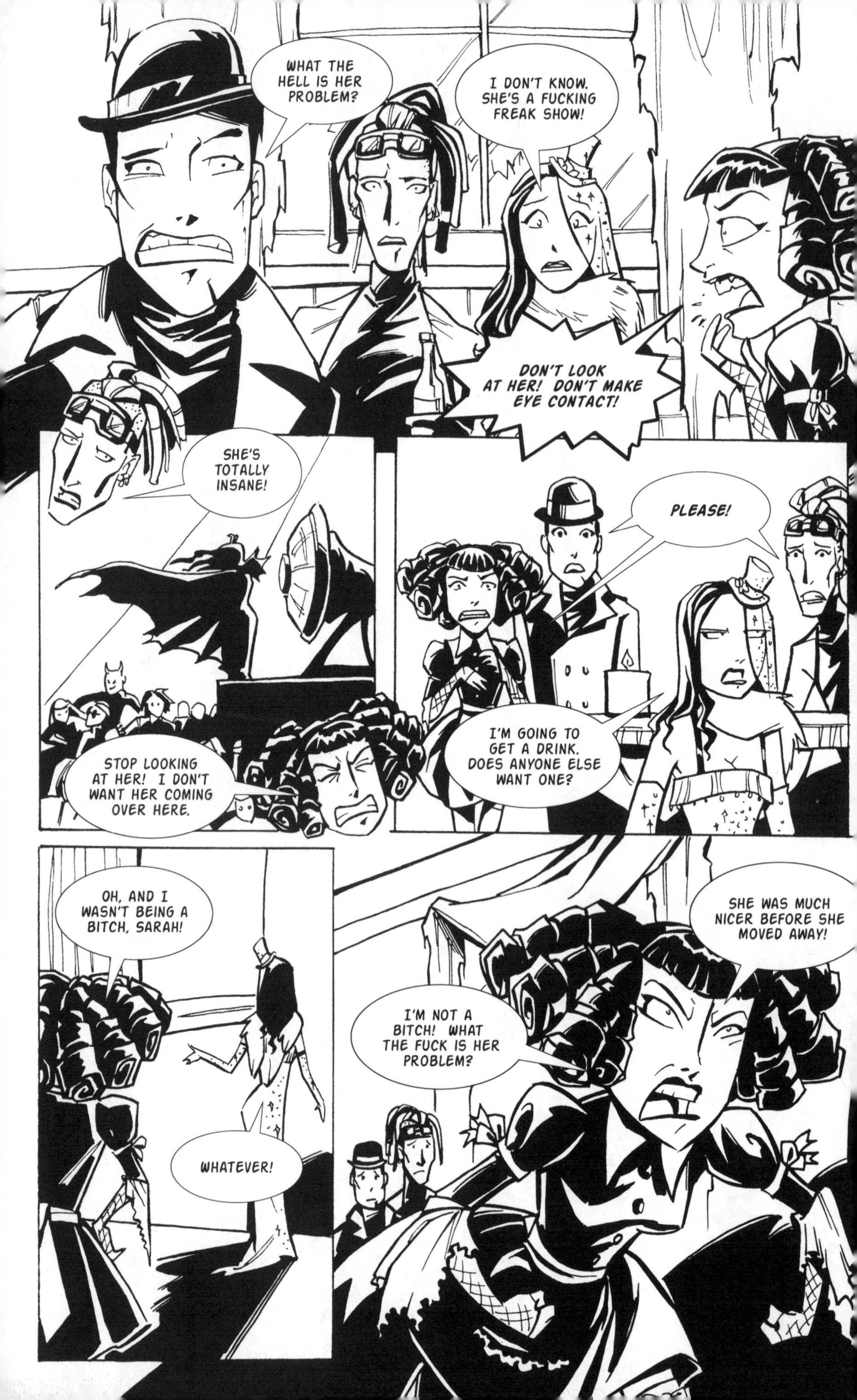
WHAT THE HELL IS HER PROBLEM?
I DON'T KNOW. SHE'S A FUCKING FREAK SHOW!
DON'T LOOK AT HER! DON'T MAKE EYE CONTACT!
SHE'S TOTALLY INSANE!
STOP LOOKING AT HER! I DON'T WANT HER COMING OVER HERE.
PLEASE!
I'M GOING TO GET A DRINK. DOES ANYONE ELSE WANT ONE?
OH, AND I WASN'T BEING A BITCH, SARAH!
WHATEVER!
SHE WAS MUCH NICER BEFORE SHE MOVED AWAY!
I'M NOT A BITCH! WHAT THE FUCK IS HER PROBLEM?

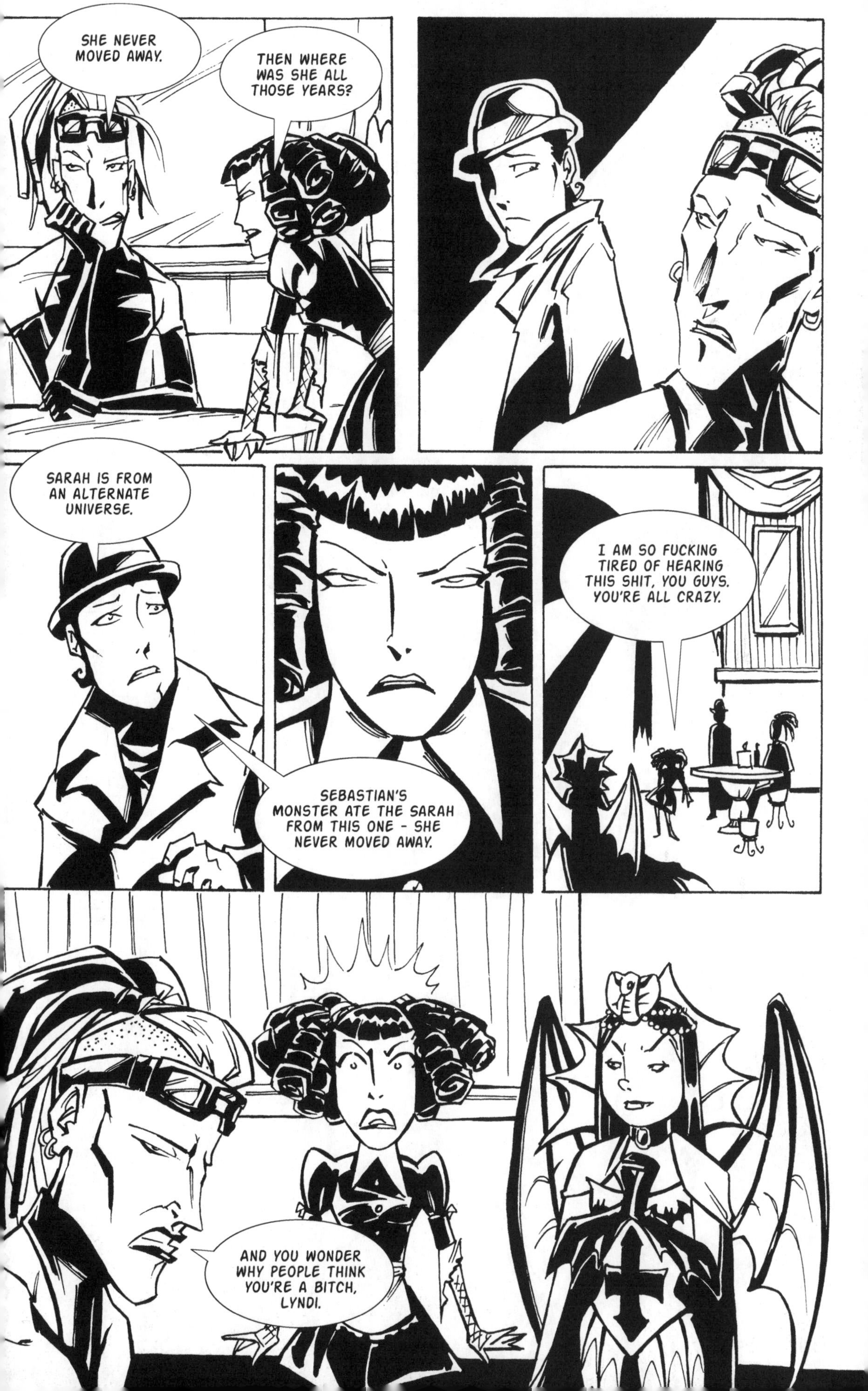
SHE NEVER MOVED AWAY.
THEN WHERE WAS SHE ALL THOSE YEARS?
SARAH IS FROM AN ALTERNATE UNIVERSE.
SEBASTIAN'S MONSTER ATE THE SARAH FROM THIS ONE - SHE NEVER MOVED AWAY.
I AM SO FUCKING TIRED OF HEARING THIS SHIT, YOU GUYS. YOU'RE ALL CRAZY.
AND YOU WONDER WHY PEOPLE THINK YOU'RE A BITCH, LYNDI.

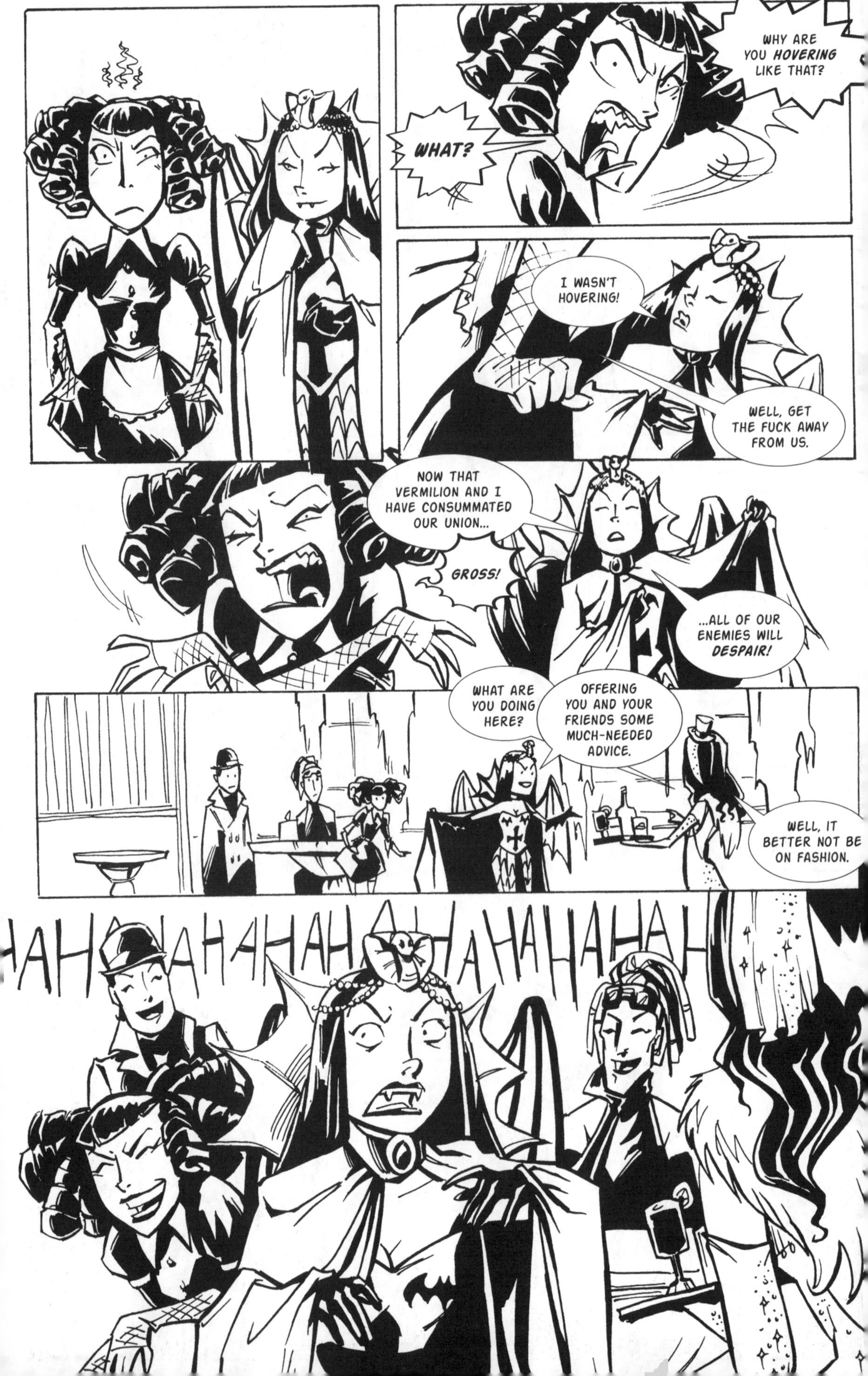

WHAT?
WHY ARE YOU HOVERING LIKE THAT?
I WASN'T HOVERING!
WELL, GET THE FUCK AWAY FROM US.
NOW THAT VERMILION AND I HAVE CONSUMMATED OUR UNION...
GROSS!
...ALL OF OUR ENEMIES WILL DESPAIR!
WHAT ARE YOU DOING HERE?
OFFERING YOU AND YOUR FRIENDS SOME MUCH-NEEDED ADVICE.
WELL, IT BETTER NOT BE ON FASHION.
HAHAHAHAHAHAHAHAHAHAHAH

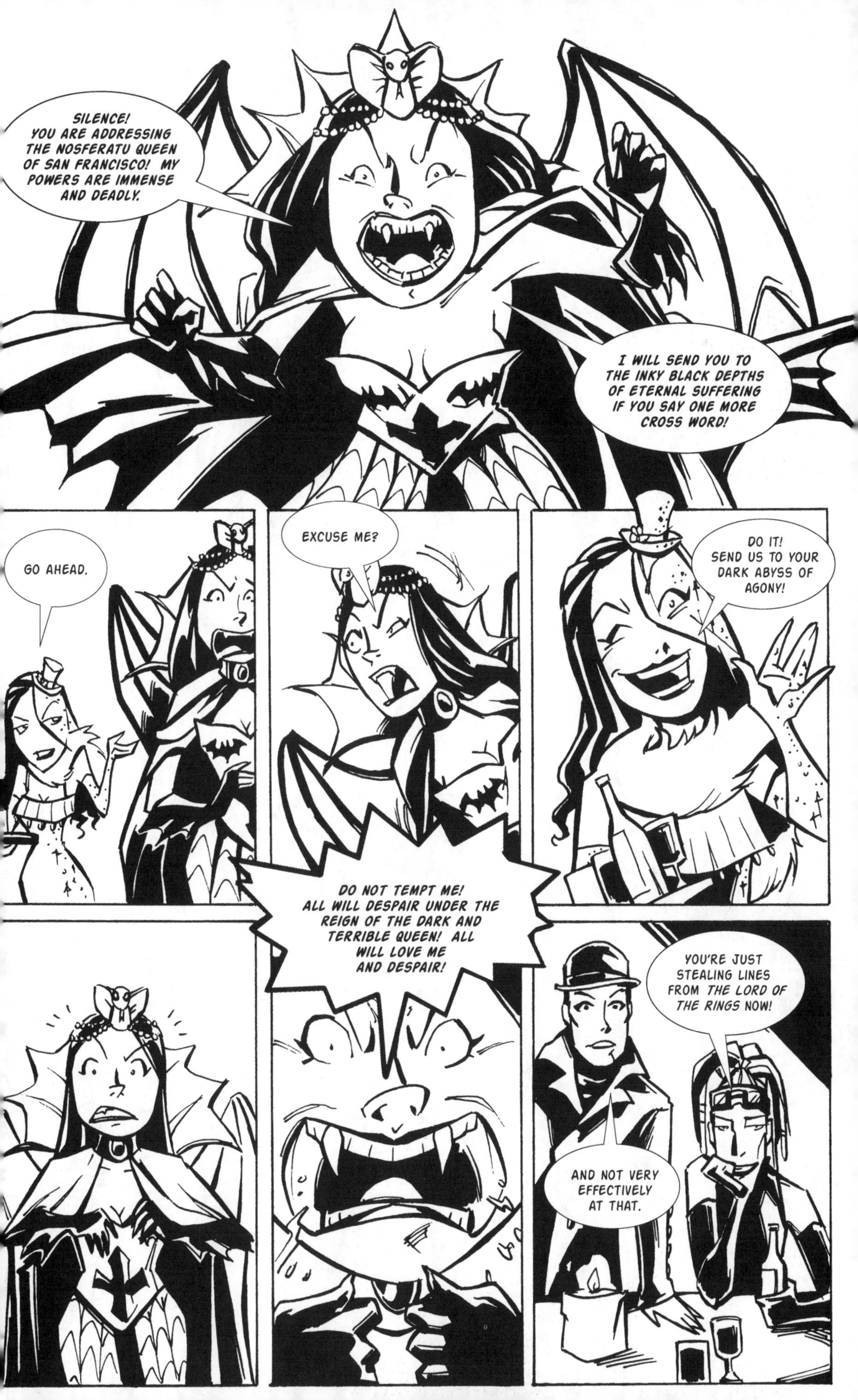
SILENCE! YOU ARE ADDRESSING THE NOSFERATU QUEEN OF SAN FRANCISCO! MY POWERS ARE IMMENSE AND DEADLY.
I WILL SEND YOU TO THE INKY BLACK DEPTHS OF ETERNAL SUFFERING IF YOU SAY ONE MORE CROSS WORD!
GO AHEAD.
EXCUSE ME?
DO IT! SEND US TO YOUR DARK ABYSS OF AGONY!
DO NOT TEMPT ME! ALL WILL DESPAIR UNDER THE REIGN OF THE DARK AND TERRIBLE QUEEN! ALL WILL LOVE ME AND DESPAIR!
YOU'RE JUST STEALING LINES FROM THE LORD OF THE RINGS NOW!
AND NOT VERY EFFECTIVELY AT THAT.

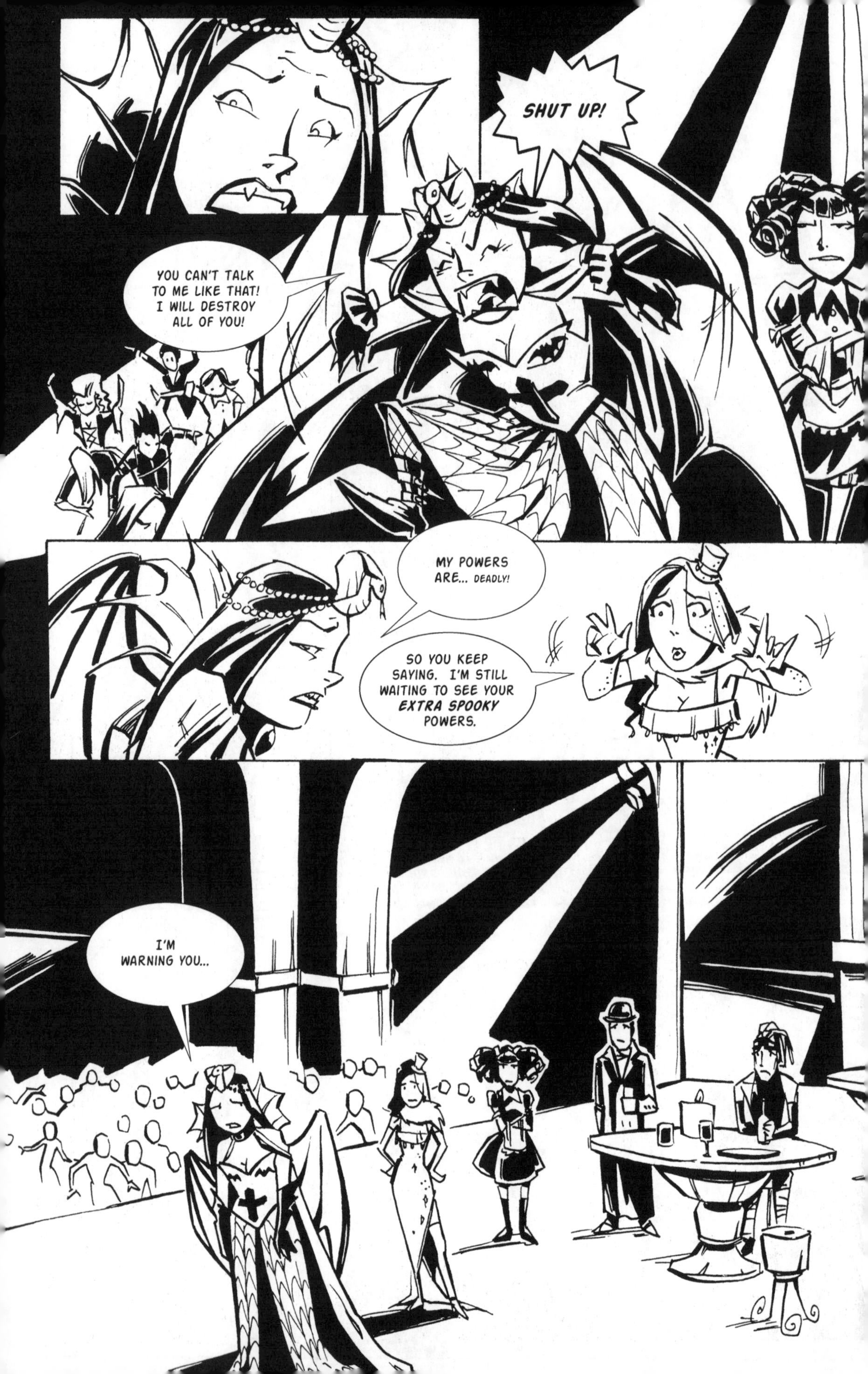
SHUT UP!
YOU CAN'T TALK TO ME LIKE THAT! I WILL DESTROY ALL OF YOU!
MY POWERS ARE... DEADLY!
SO YOU KEEP SAYING. I'M STILL WAITING TO SEE YOUR EXTRA SPOOKY POWERS.
I'M WARNING YOU...

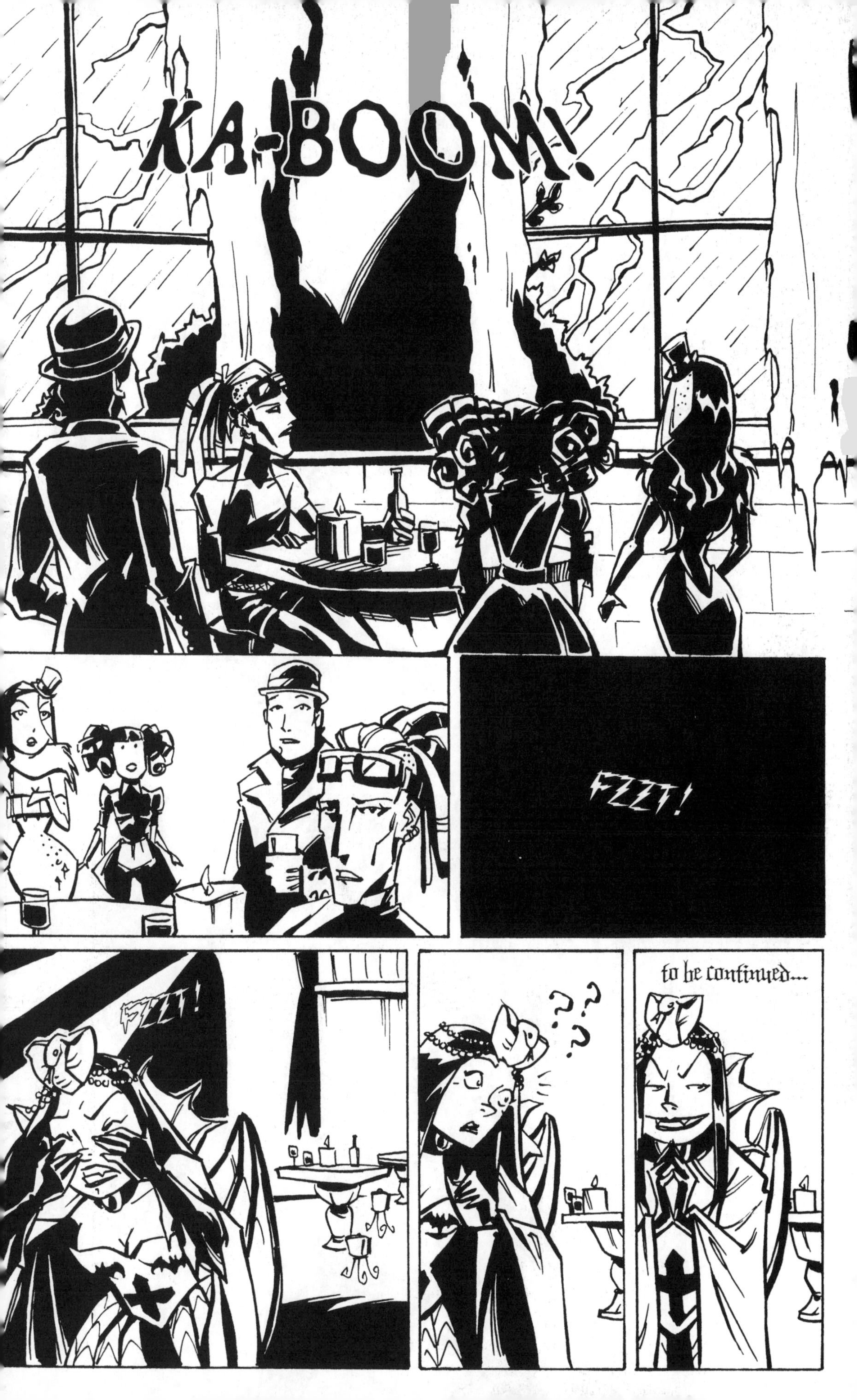

KA-BOOM!
FZZT!
FZZT!
? ? ?
to be continued...

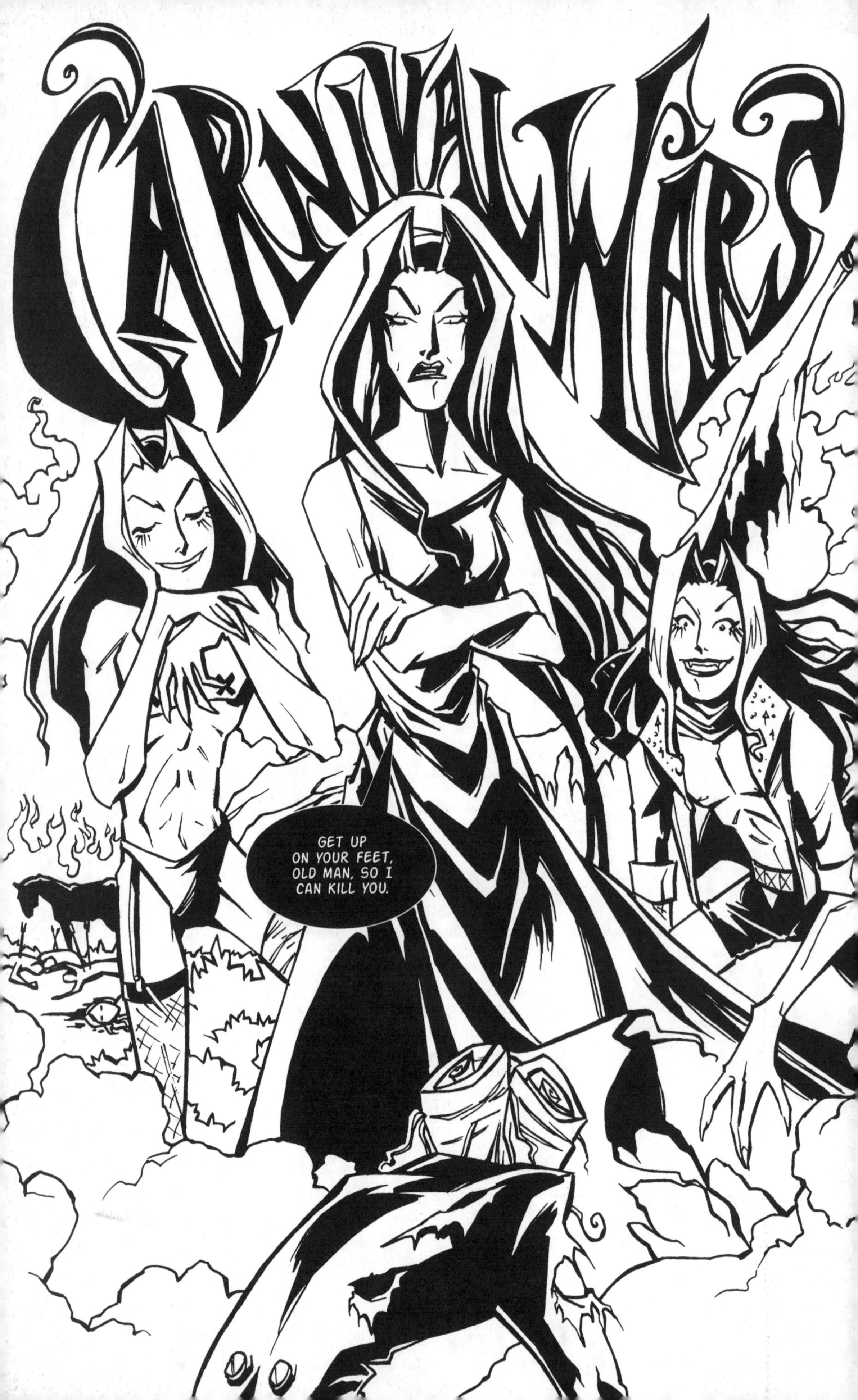
CARNIVAL WARS
GET UP ON YOUR FEET, OLD MAN, SO I CAN KILL YOU.

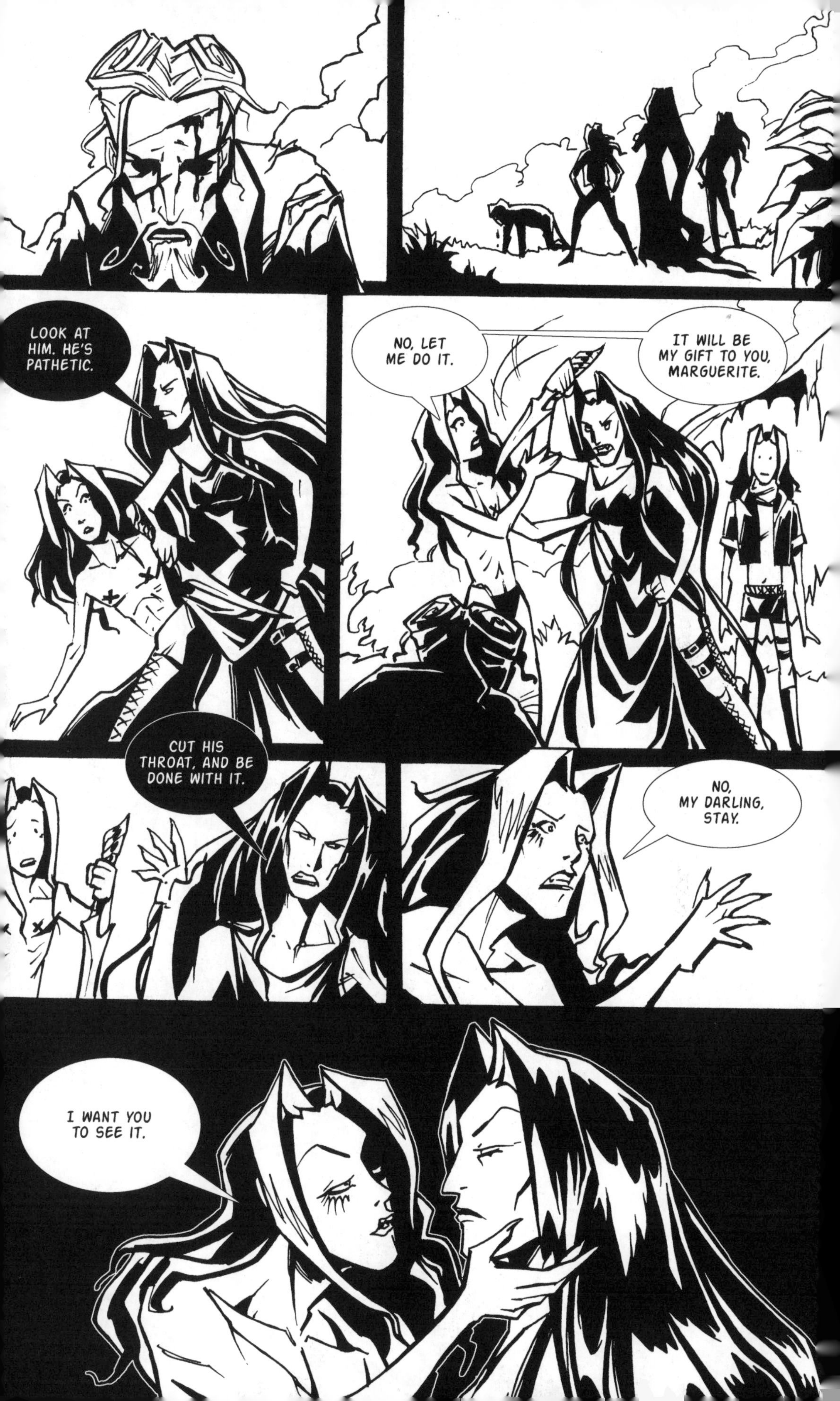
LOOK AT HIM. HE'S PATHETIC.
NO, LET ME DO IT.
IT WILL BE MY GIFT TO YOU, MARGUERITE.
CUT HIS THROAT, AND BE DONE WITH IT.
NO, MY DARLING, STAY.
I WANT YOU TO SEE IT.

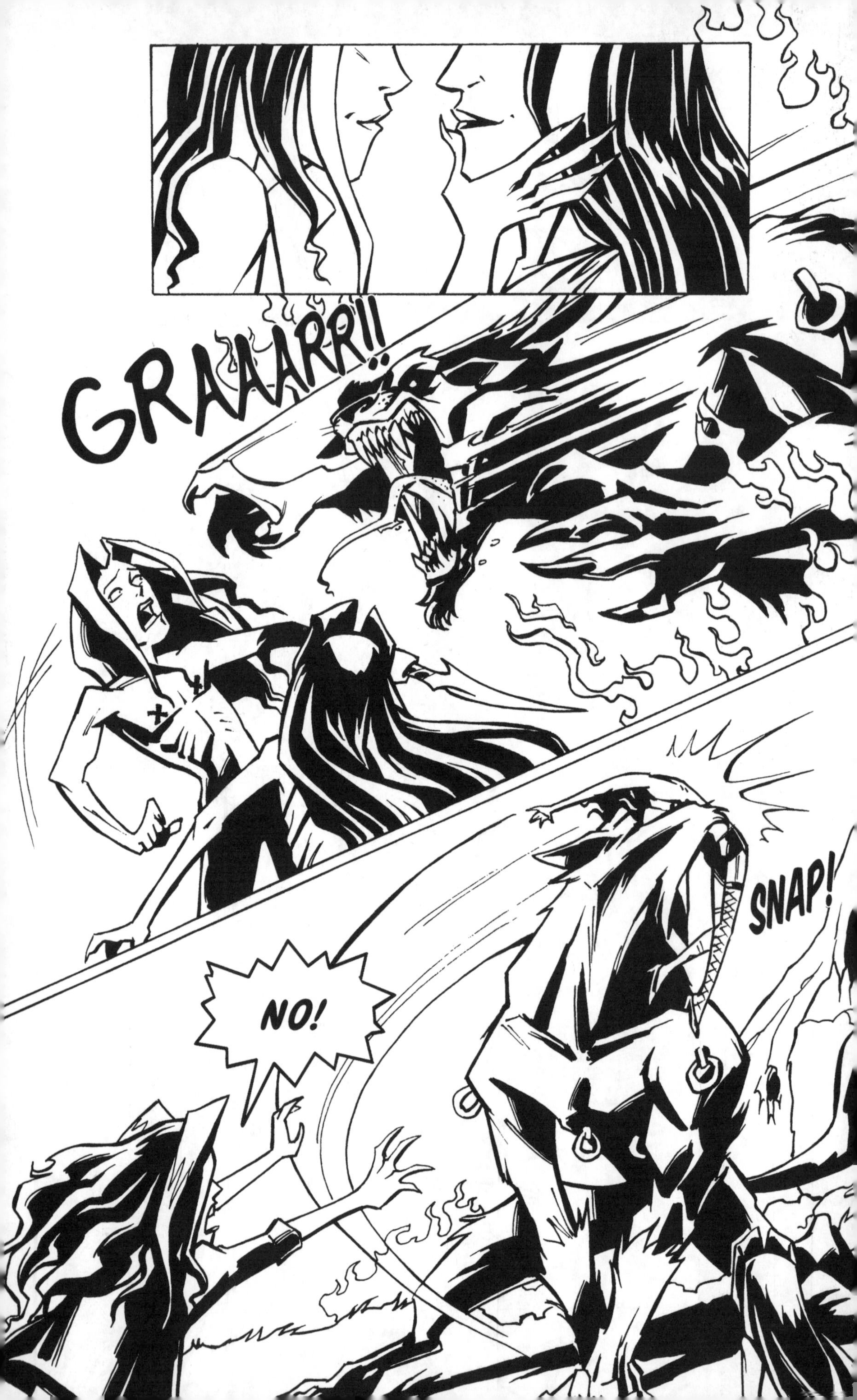
GRAAARR!!
SNAP!
NO!

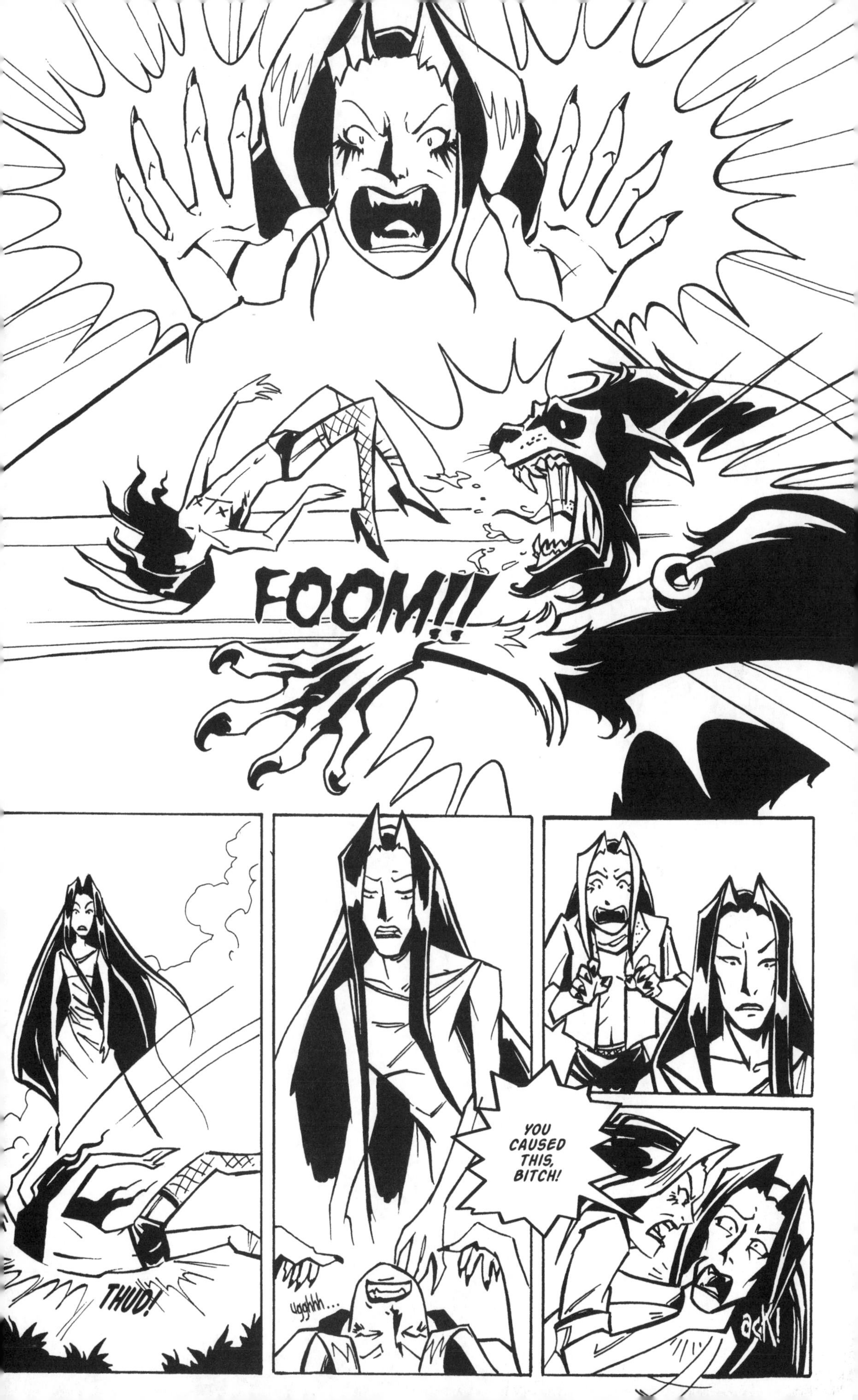
FOOM!!
THUD!
ugghhh...
YOU CAUSED THIS, BITCH!
ack!

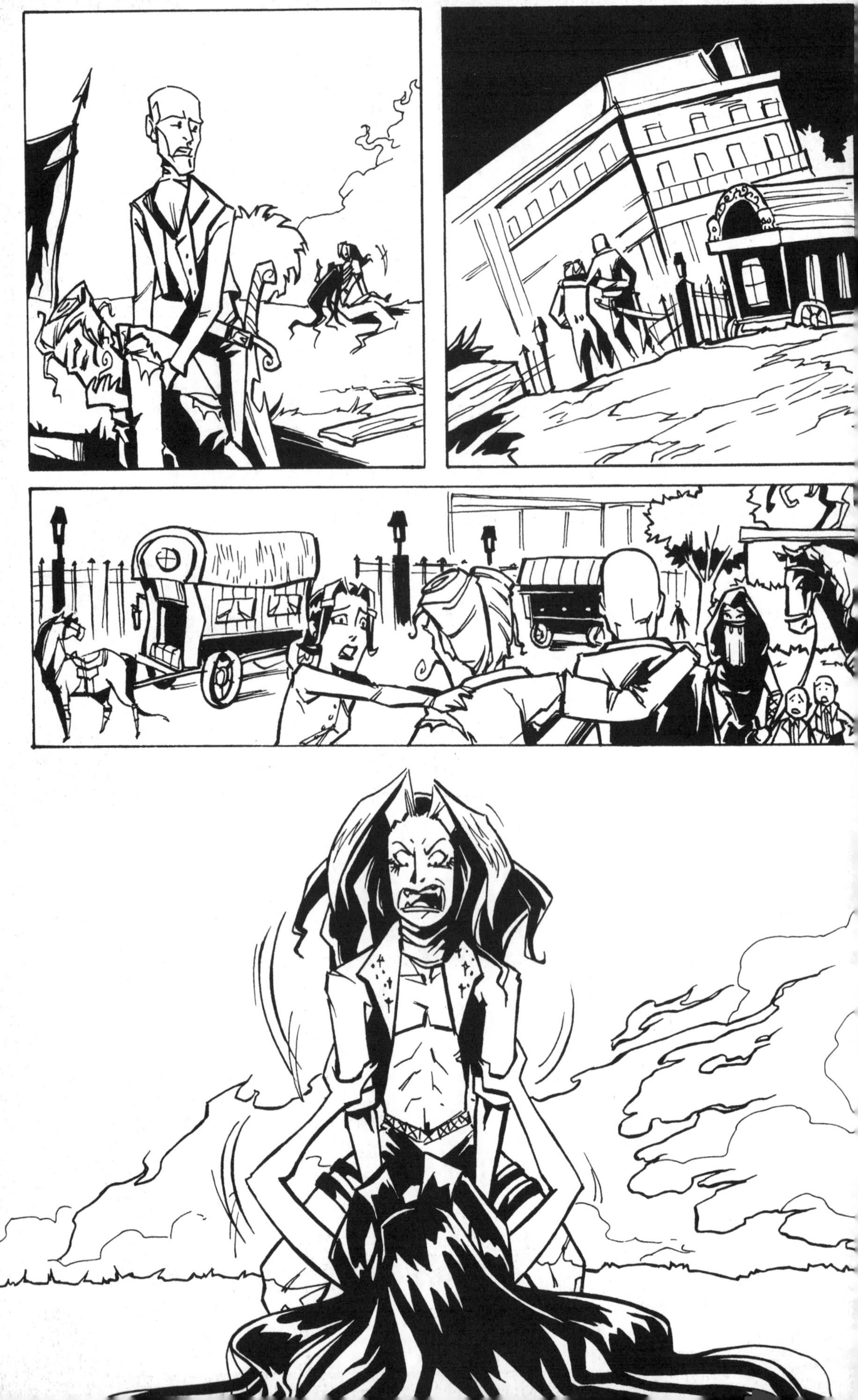

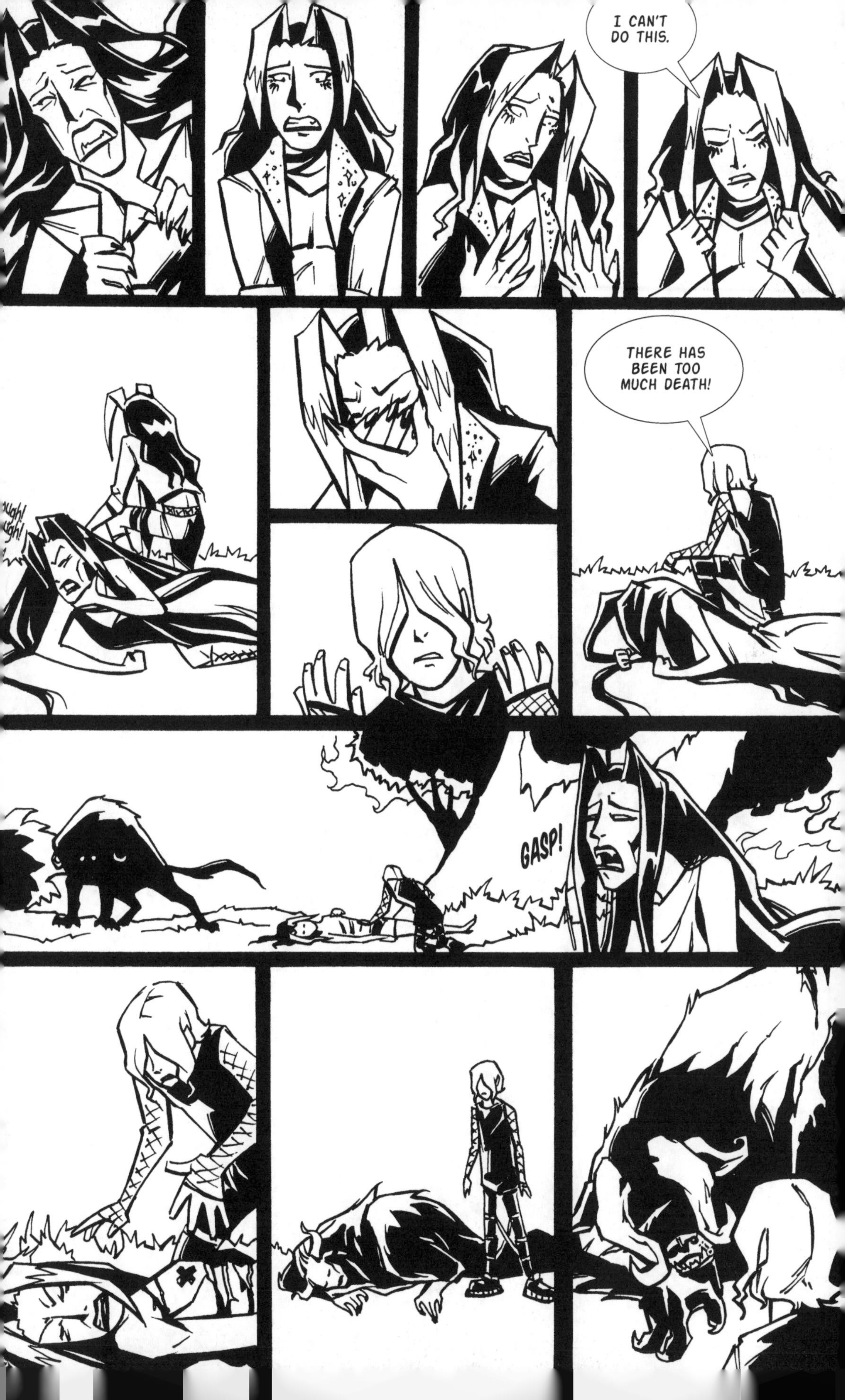
I CAN'T DO THIS.
THERE HAS BEEN TOO MUCH DEATH!
GASP!

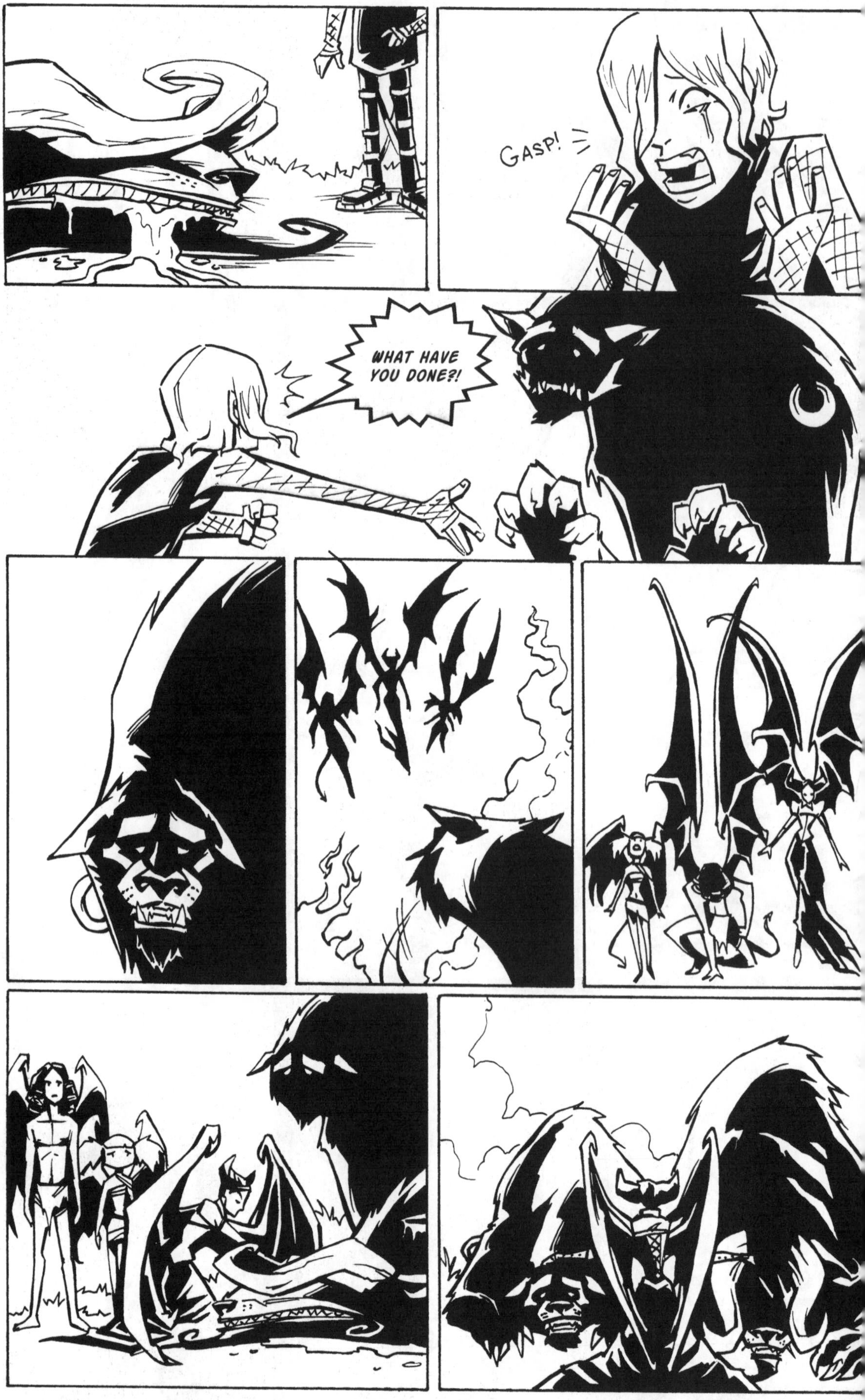
GASP!
WHAT HAVE YOU DONE?!

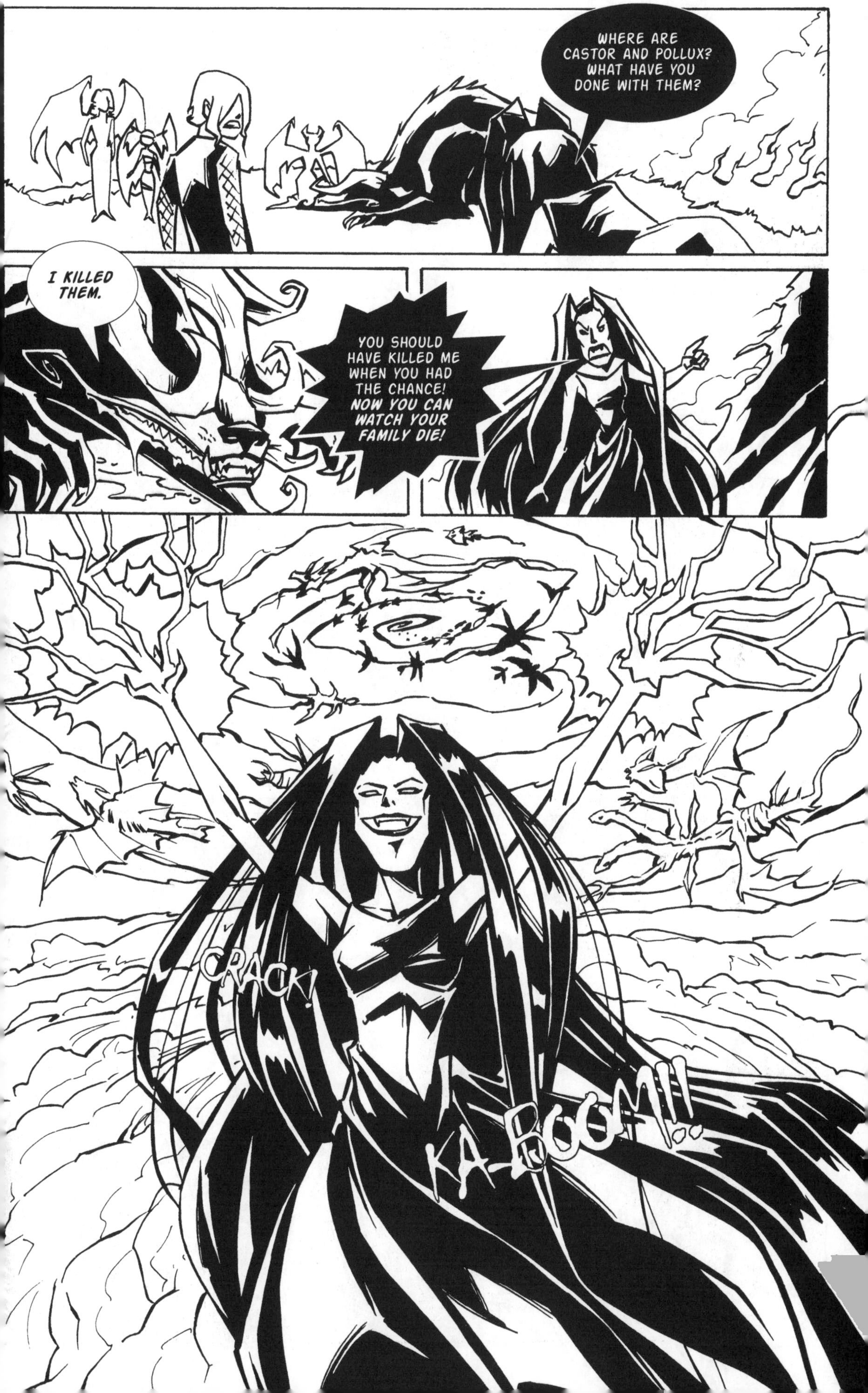
WHERE ARE CASTOR AND POLLUX? WHAT HAVE YOU DONE WITH THEM?
I KILLED THEM.
YOU SHOULD HAVE KILLED ME WHEN YOU HAD THE CHANCE! NOW YOU CAN WATCH YOUR FAMILY DIE!
CRACK!
KA-BOOM!!

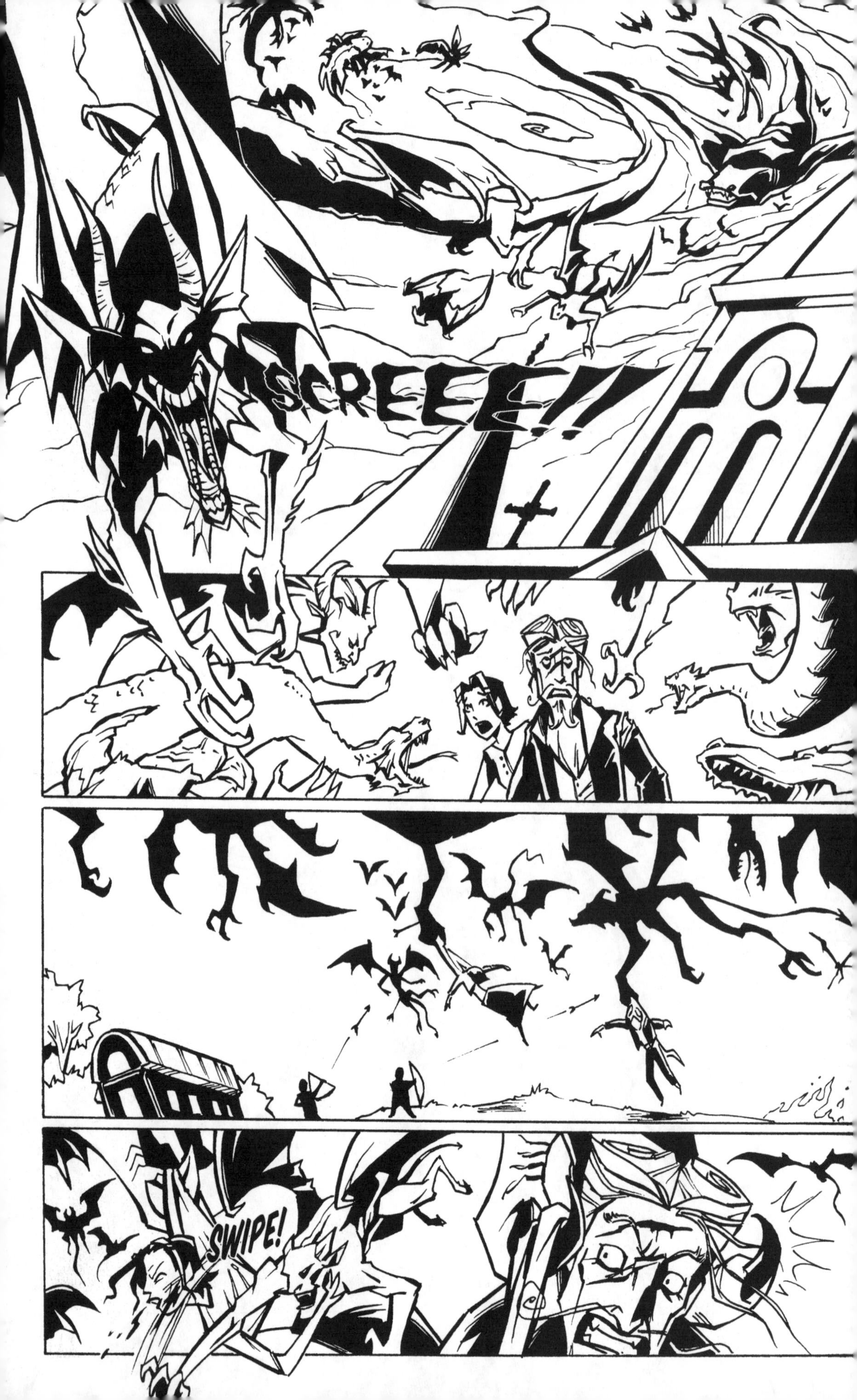
SCREEE!!
SWIPE!

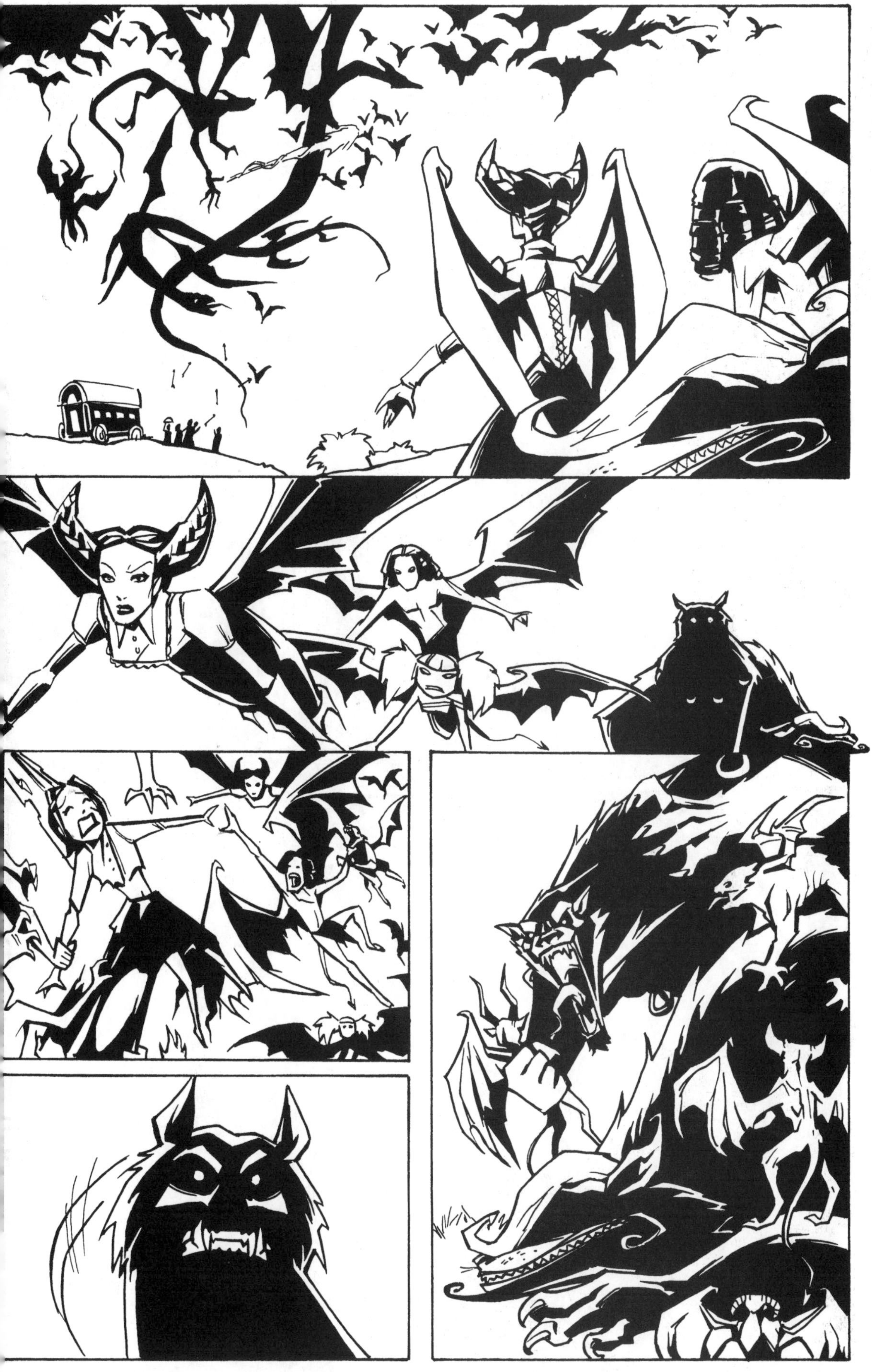

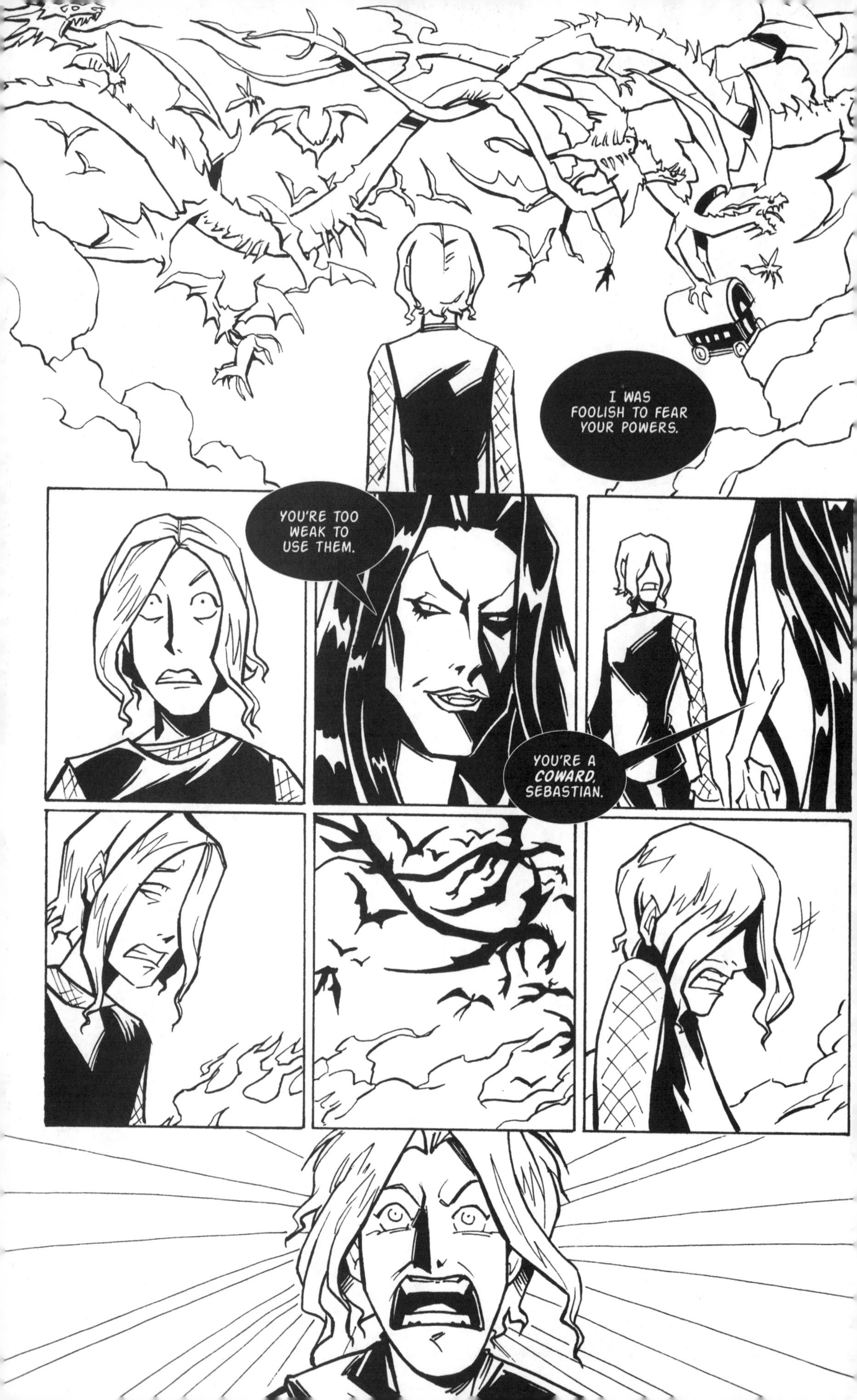
I WAS FOOLISH TO FEAR YOUR POWERS.
YOU'RE TOO WEAK TO USE THEM.
YOU'RE A *COWARD*, SEBASTIAN.

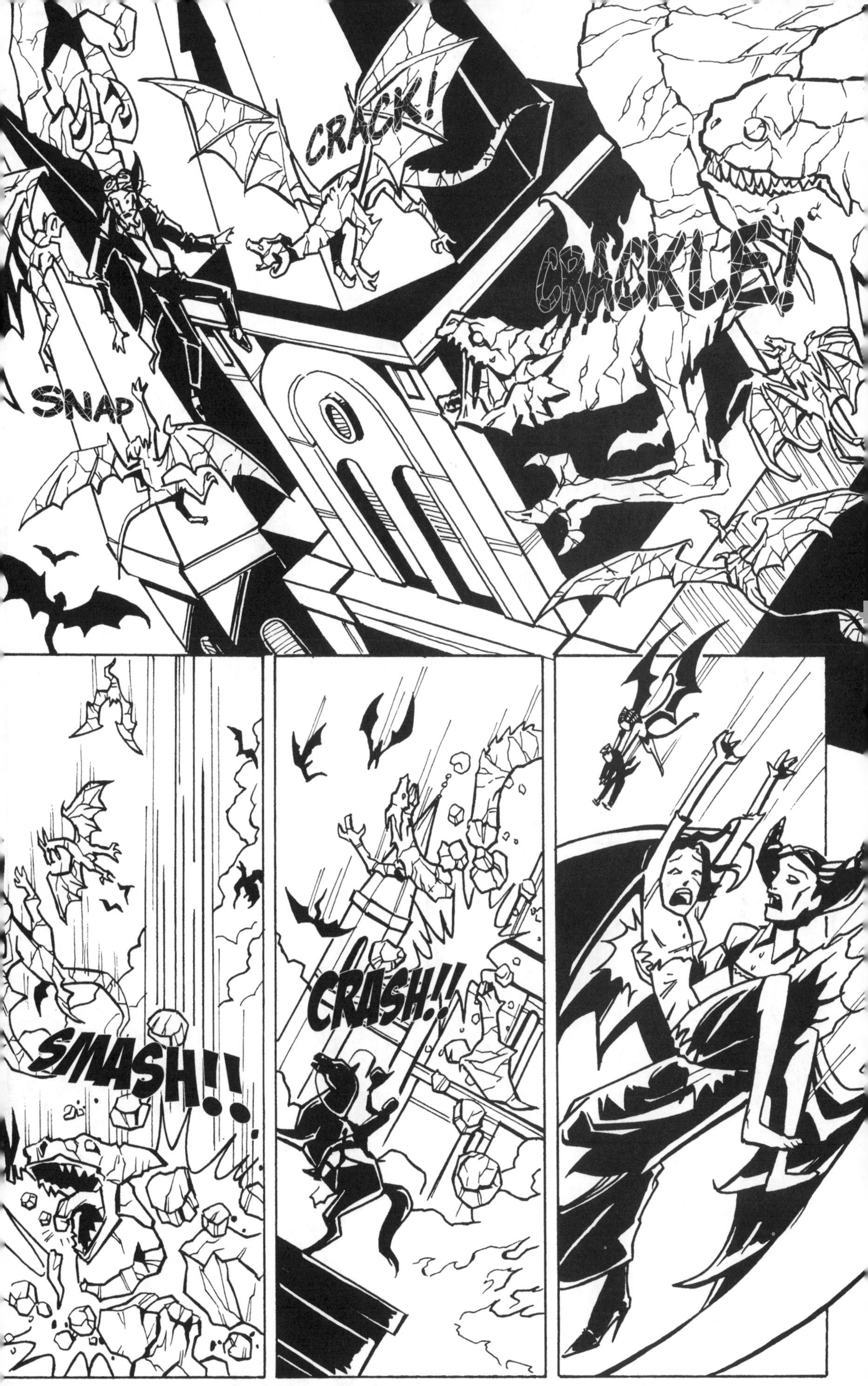
CRACK!
CRACKLE!
SNAP
SMASH!!
CRASH!!

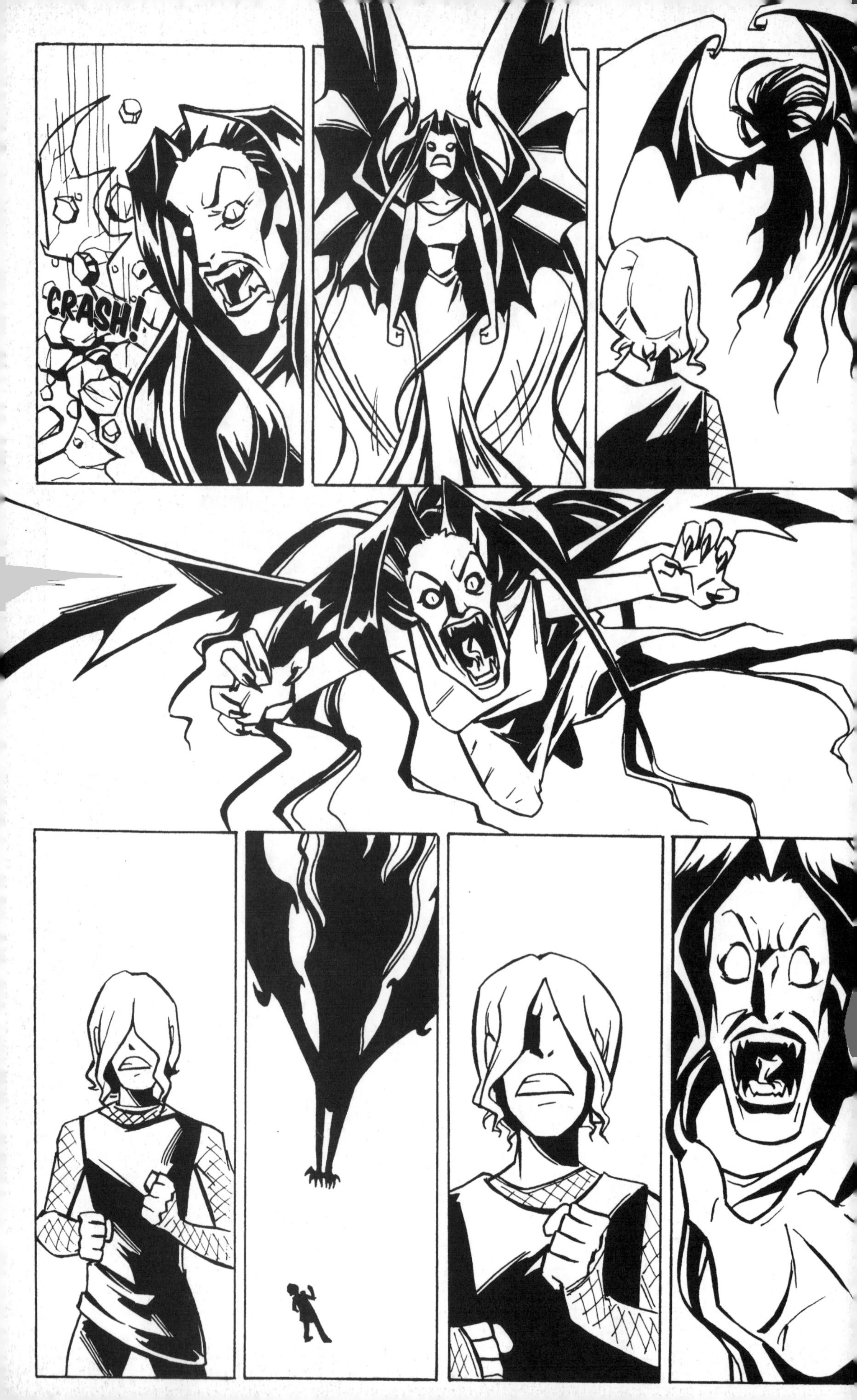
CRASH!

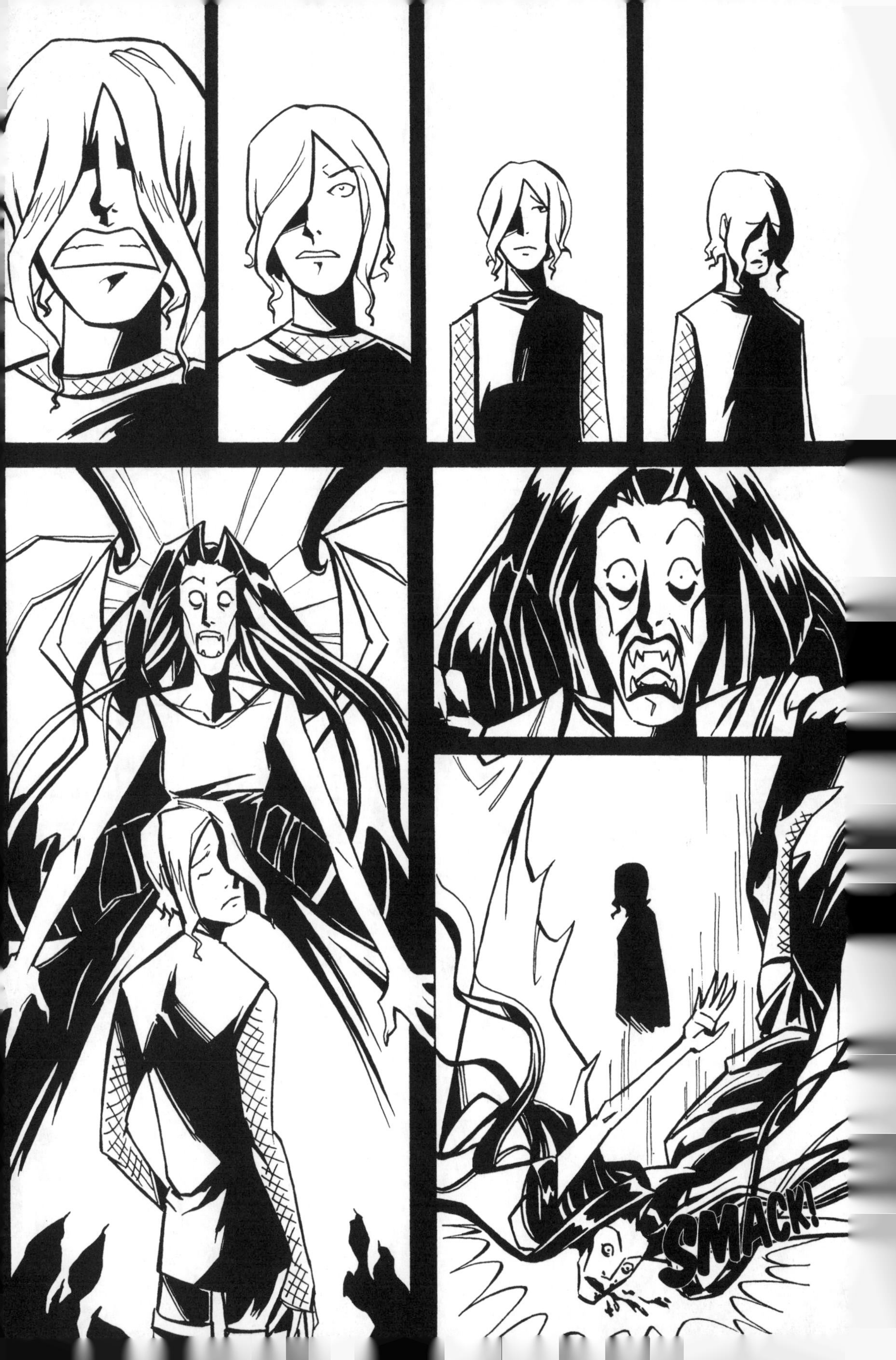
SMACK!

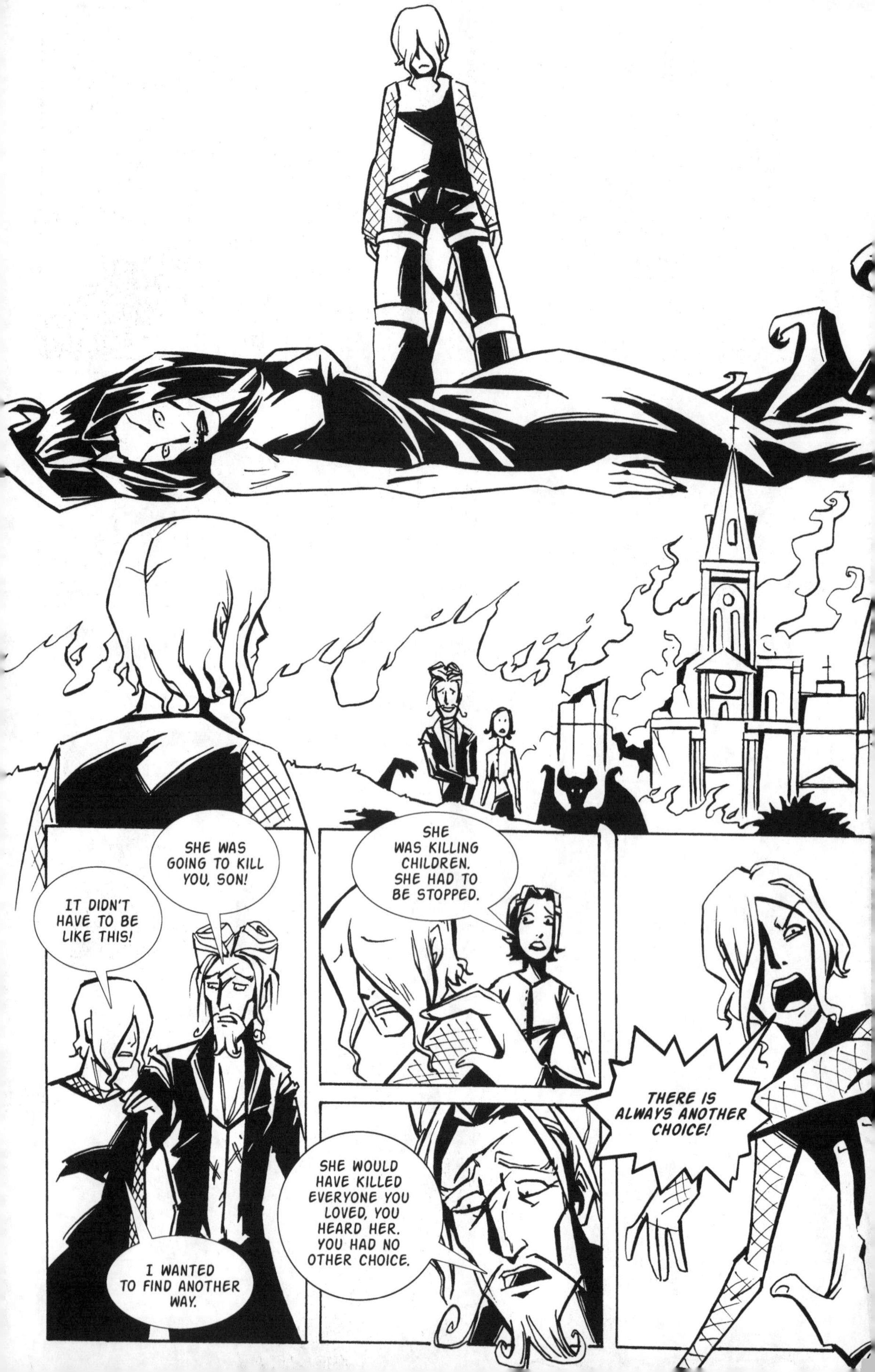
IT DIDN'T HAVE TO BE LIKE THIS!
SHE WAS GOING TO KILL YOU, SON!
I WANTED TO FIND ANOTHER WAY.
SHE WAS KILLING CHILDREN. SHE HAD TO BE STOPPED.
SHE WOULD HAVE KILLED EVERYONE YOU LOVED, YOU HEARD HER. YOU HAD NO OTHER CHOICE.
THERE IS ALWAYS ANOTHER CHOICE!

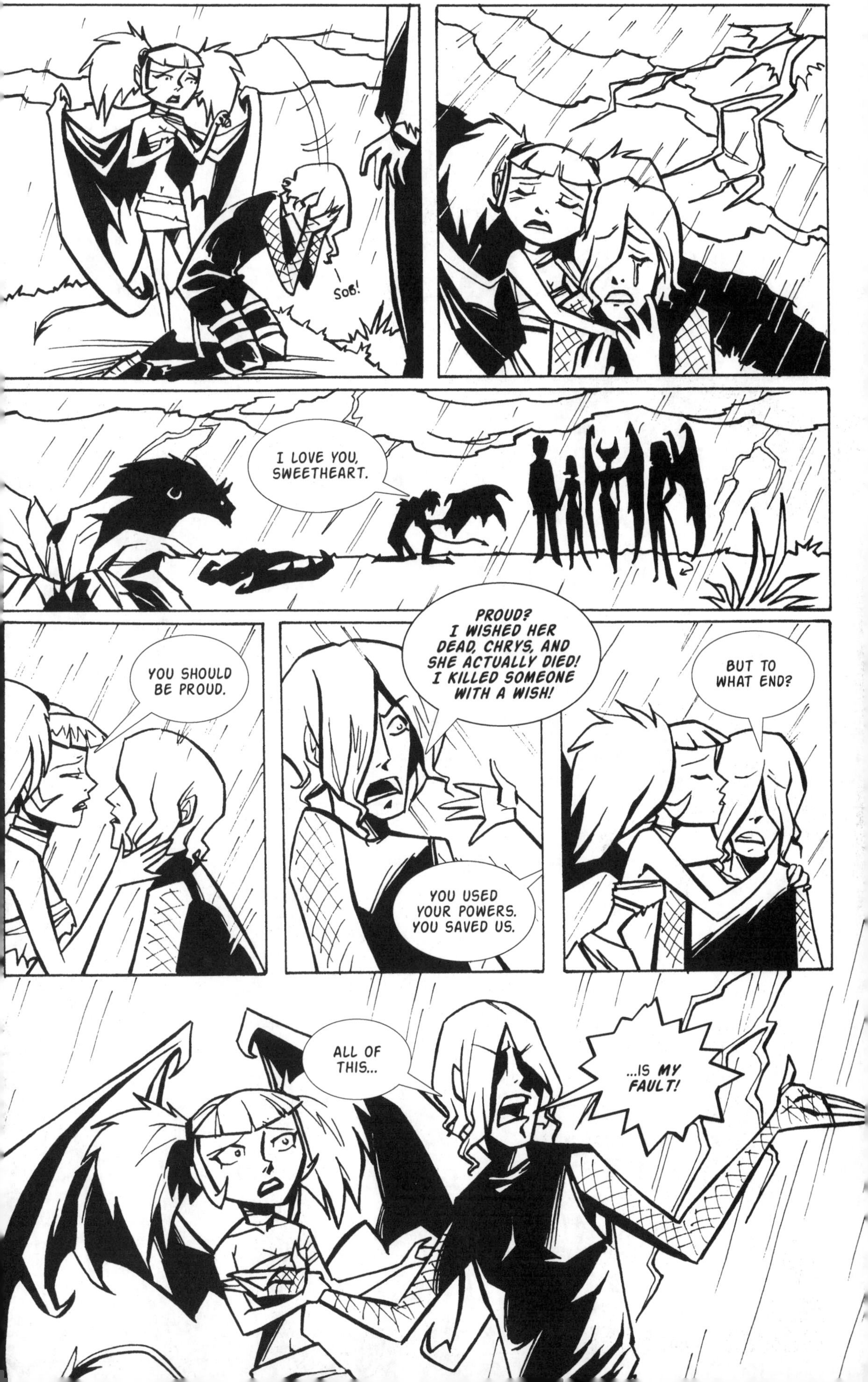
SOB!
I LOVE YOU, SWEETHEART.
YOU SHOULD BE PROUD.
PROUD? I WISHED HER DEAD, CHRYS, AND SHE ACTUALLY DIED! I KILLED SOMEONE WITH A WISH!
YOU USED YOUR POWERS. YOU SAVED US.
BUT TO WHAT END?
ALL OF THIS...
...IS MY FAULT!

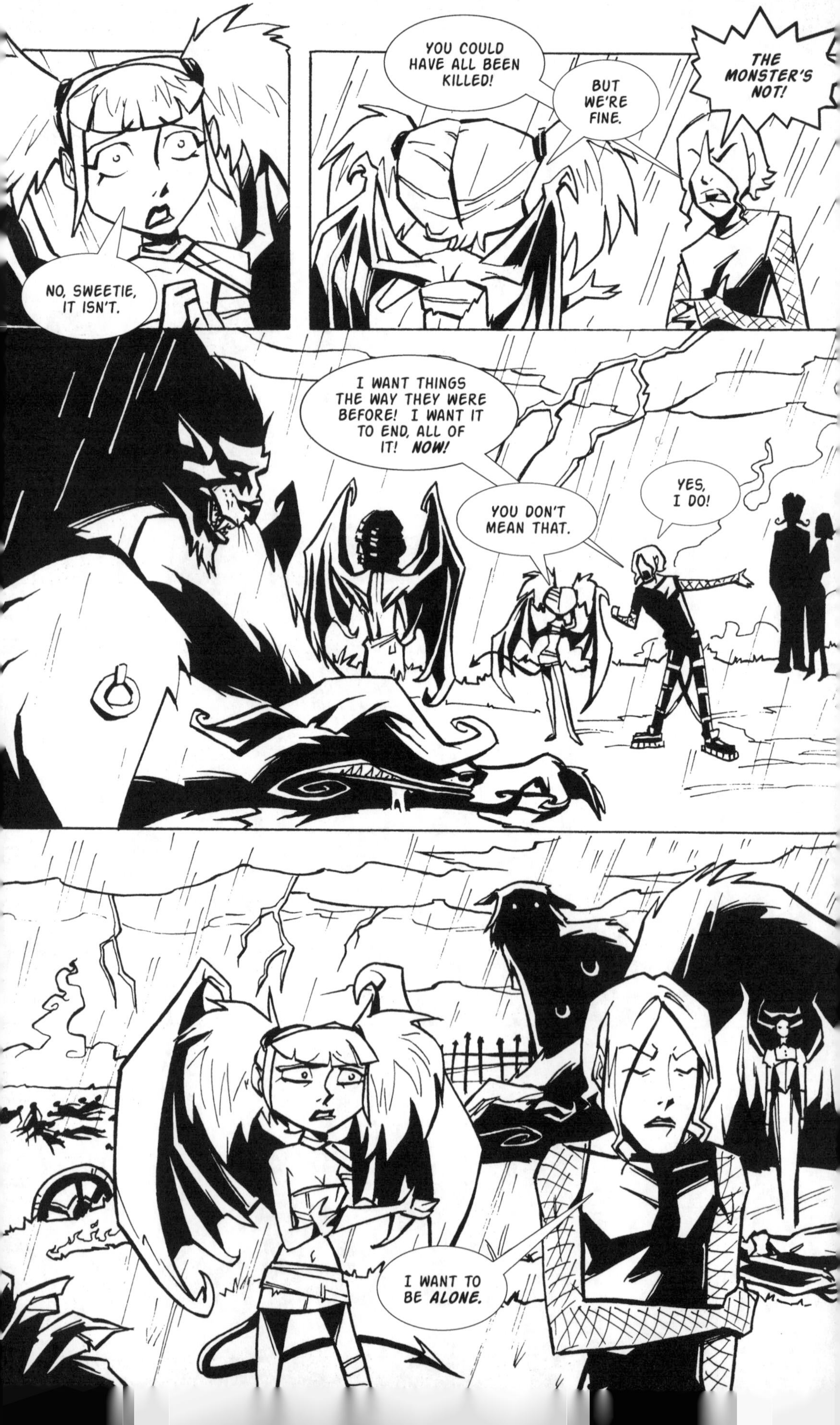
NO, SWEETIE, IT ISN'T.
YOU COULD HAVE ALL BEEN KILLED!
BUT WE'RE FINE.
THE MONSTER'S NOT!
I WANT THINGS THE WAY THEY WERE BEFORE! I WANT IT TO END, ALL OF IT! NOW!
YOU DON'T MEAN THAT.
YES, I DO!
I WANT TO BE ALONE.

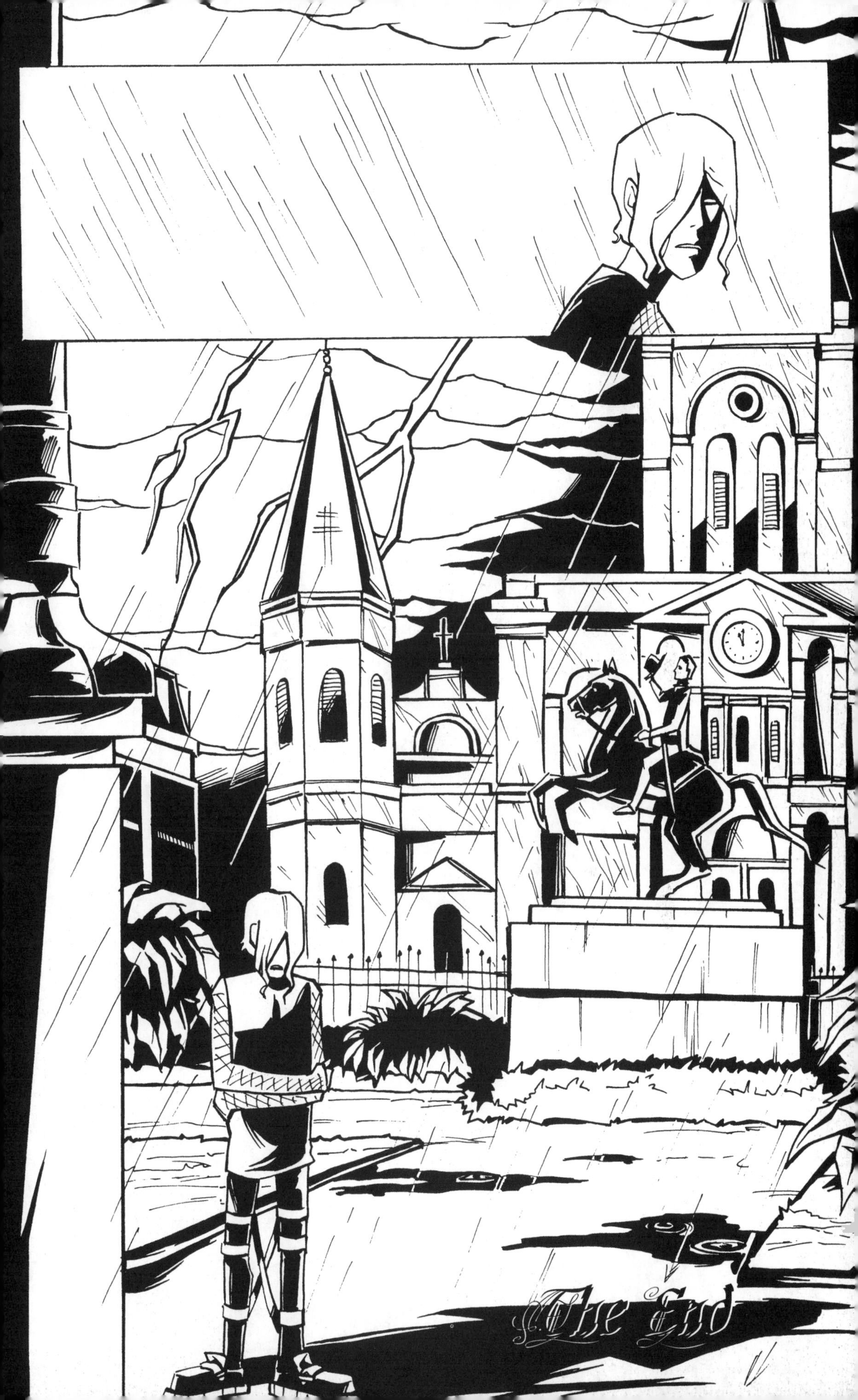
The End

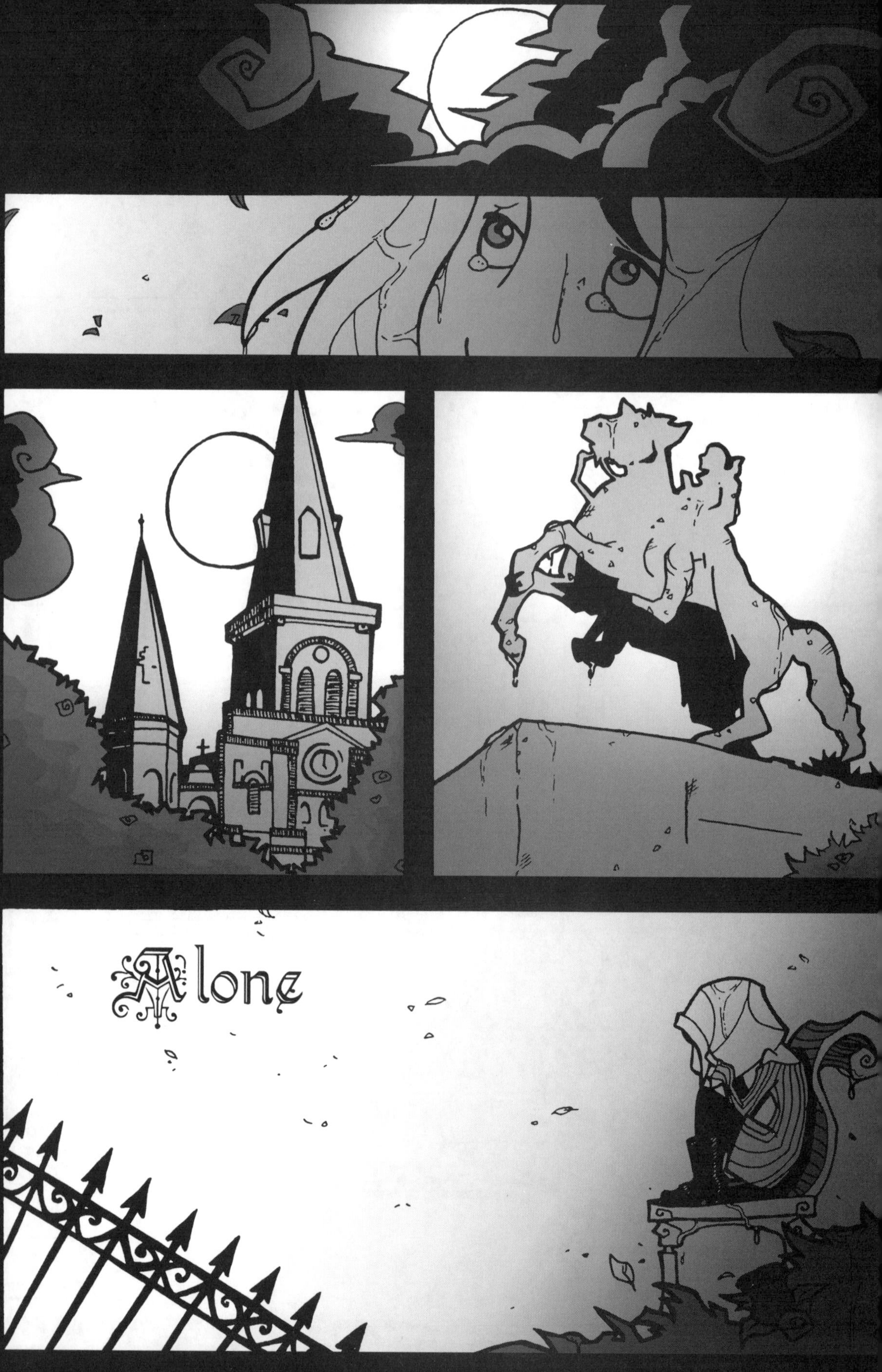
Alone

GloomCookies...

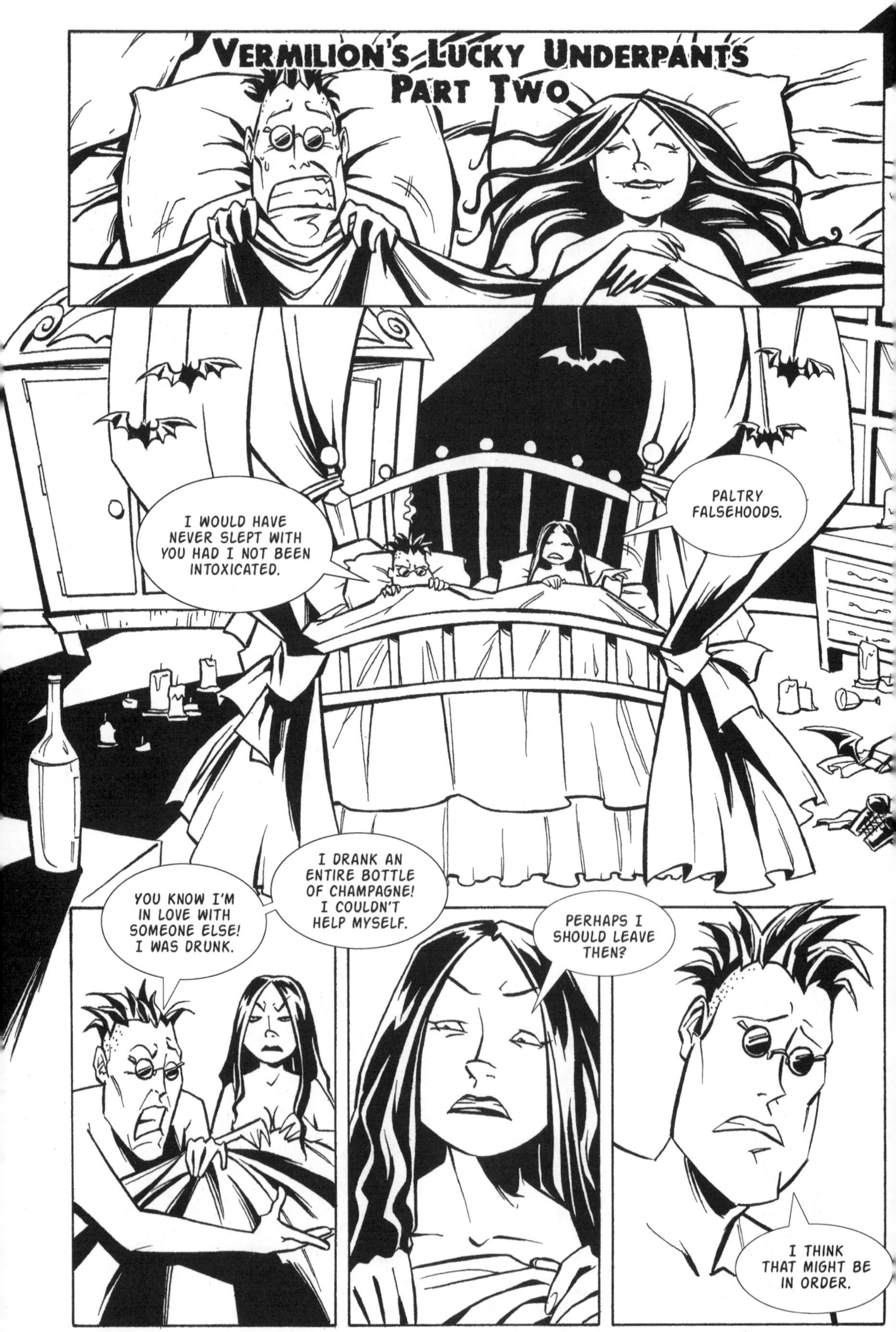
VERMILION'S LUCKY UNDERPANTS
PART TWO
I WOULD HAVE NEVER SLEPT WITH YOU HAD I NOT BEEN INTOXICATED.
PALTRY FALSEHOODS.
YOU KNOW I'M IN LOVE WITH SOMEONE ELSE! I WAS DRUNK.
I DRANK AN ENTIRE BOTTLE OF CHAMPAGNE! I COULDN'T HELP MYSELF.
PERHAPS I SHOULD LEAVE THEN?
I THINK THAT MIGHT BE IN ORDER.

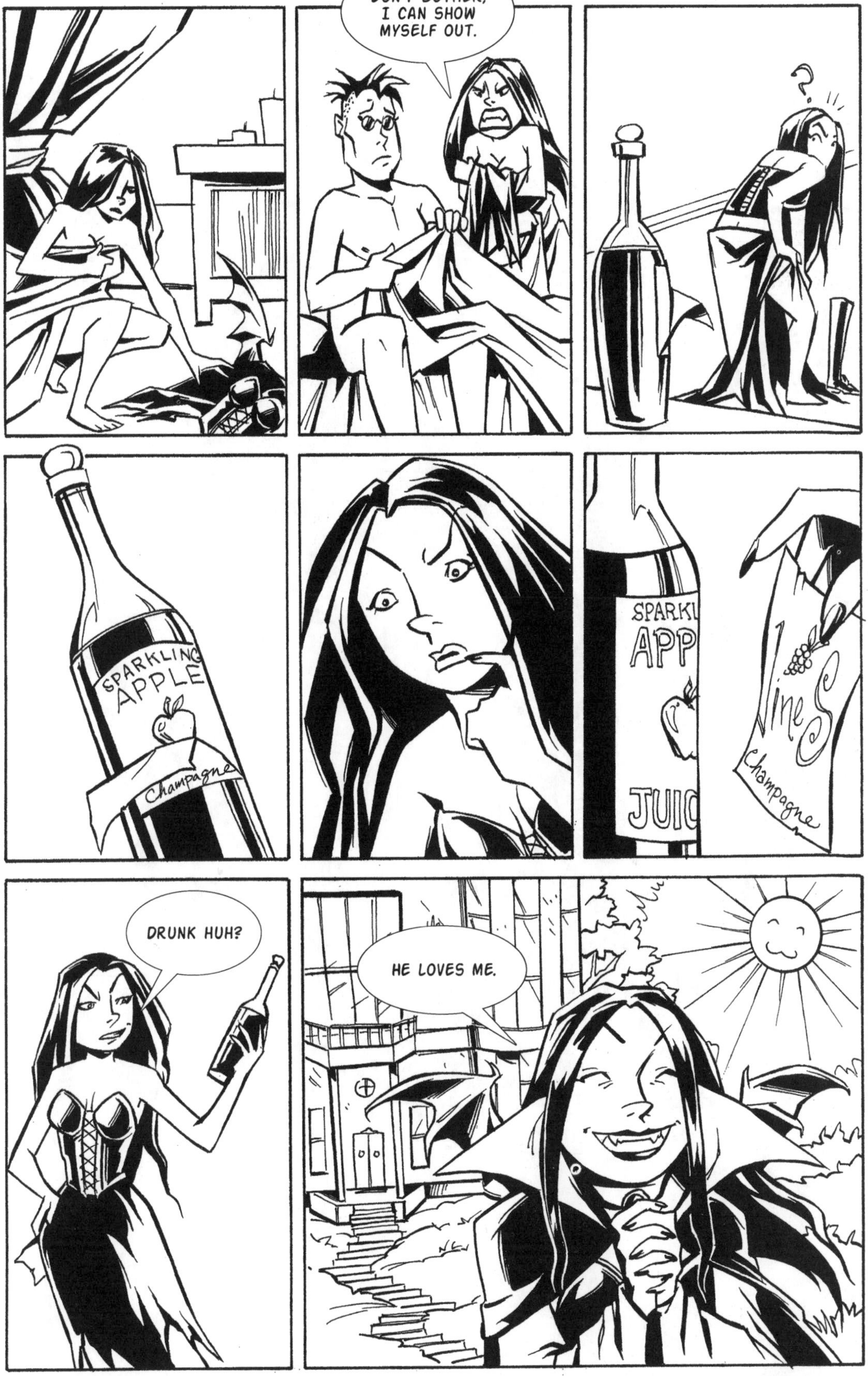
DON'T BOTHER, I CAN SHOW MYSELF OUT.
SPARKLING APPLE
Champagne
Champagne
DRUNK HUH?
HE LOVES ME.

THE END

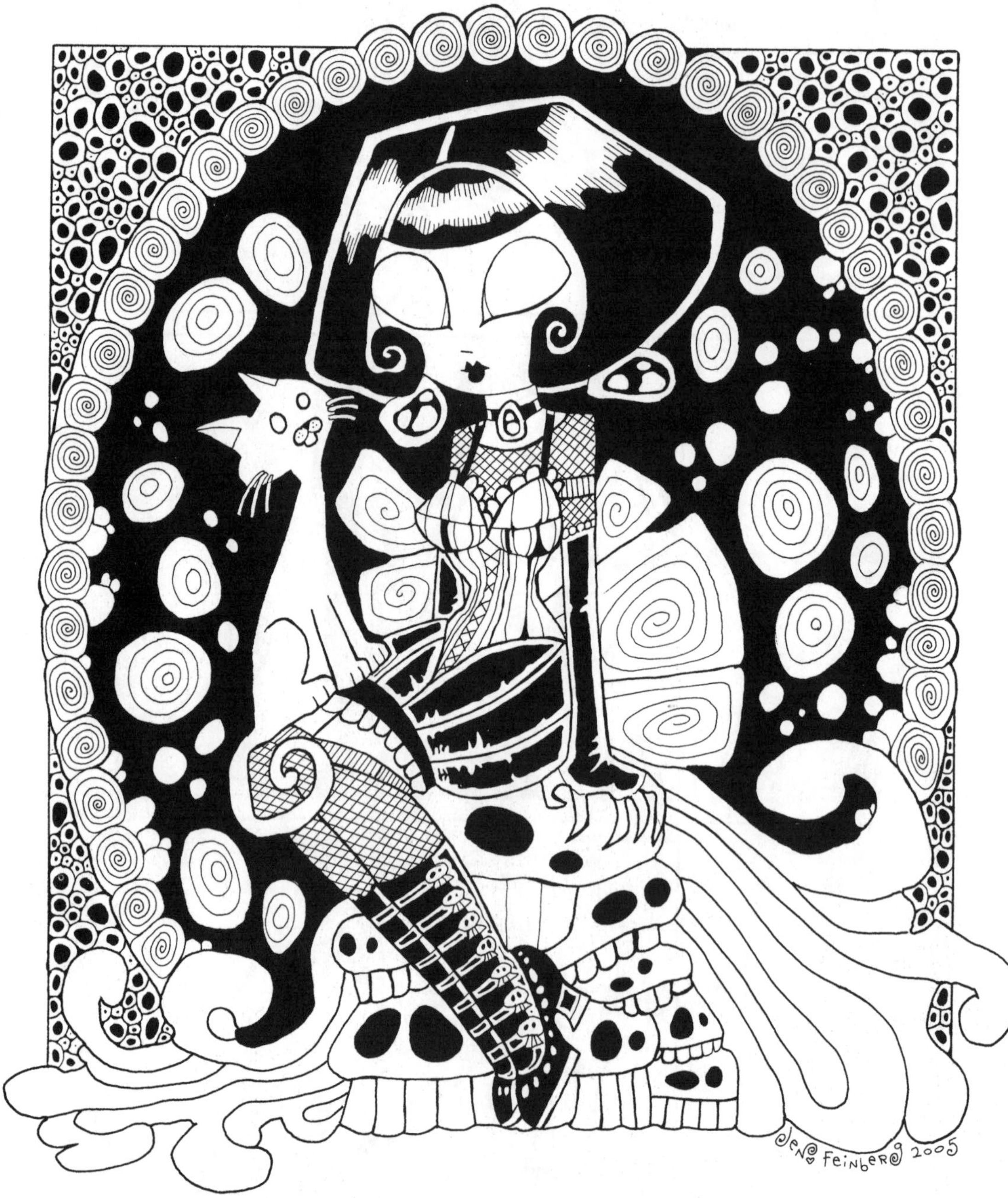
Jen Feinberg 2005

Pin-up by Jennifer Feinberg

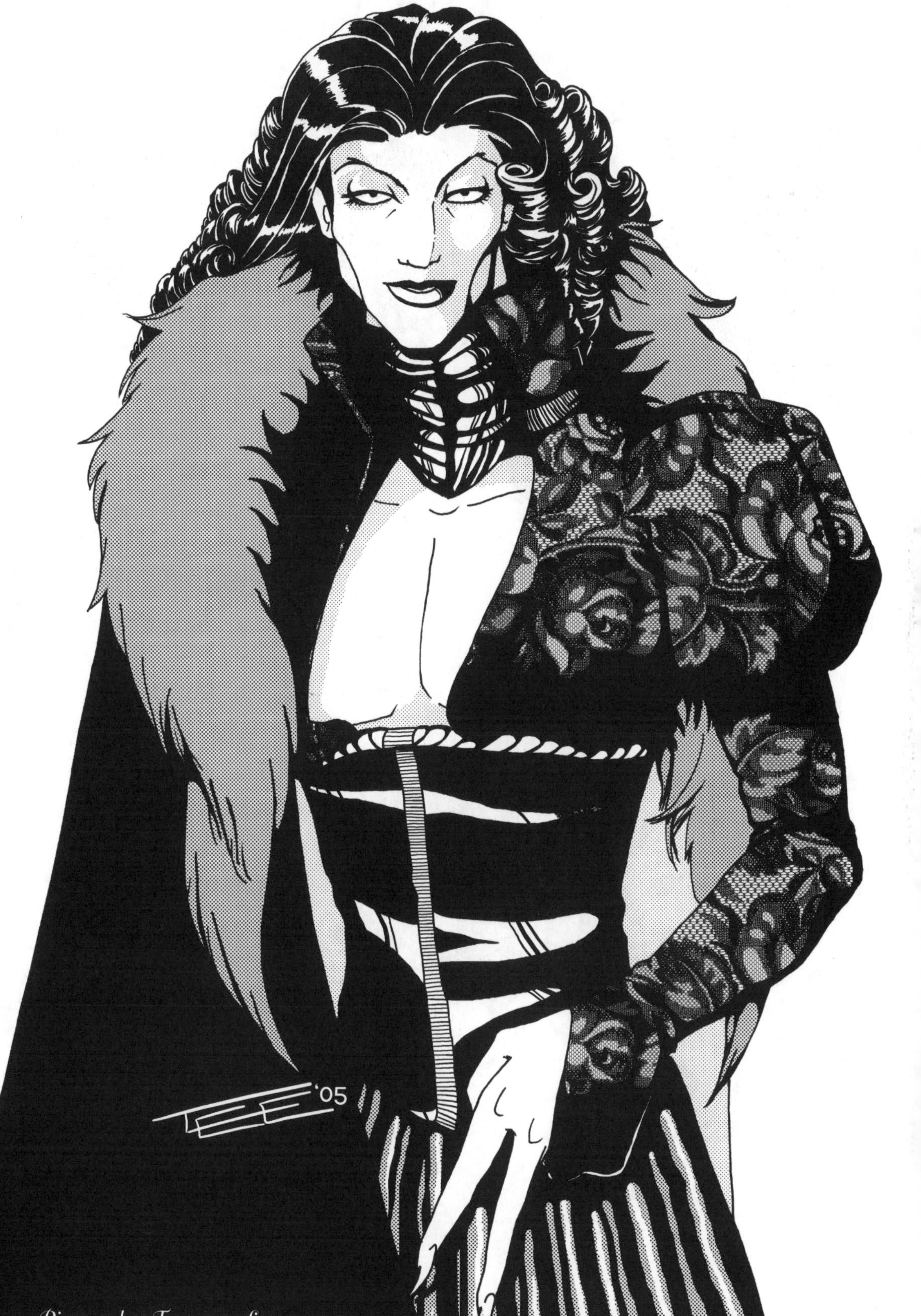
LEE '05

Pin-up by Tammy Lee

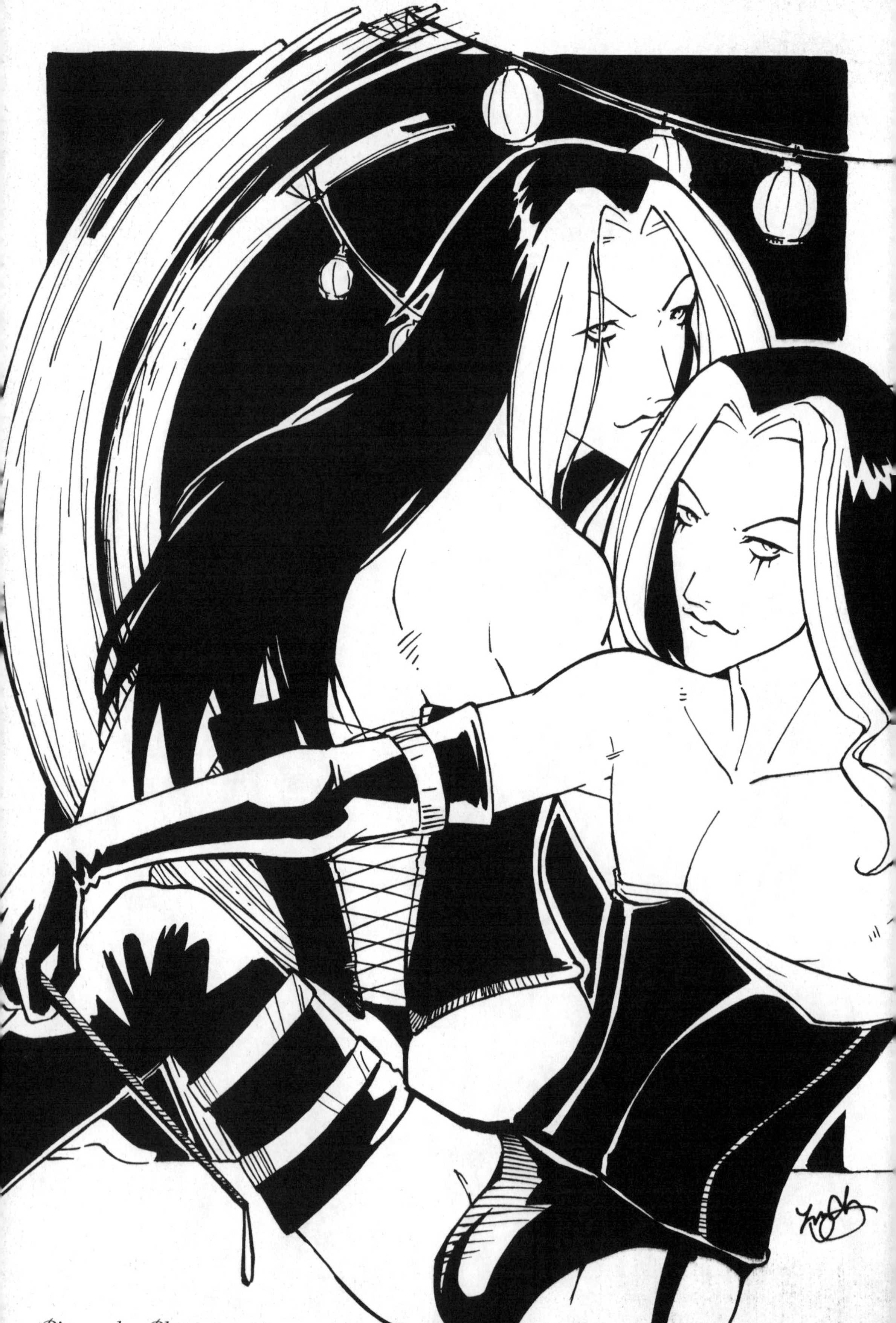

Pin-up by Pluto

Tattoos

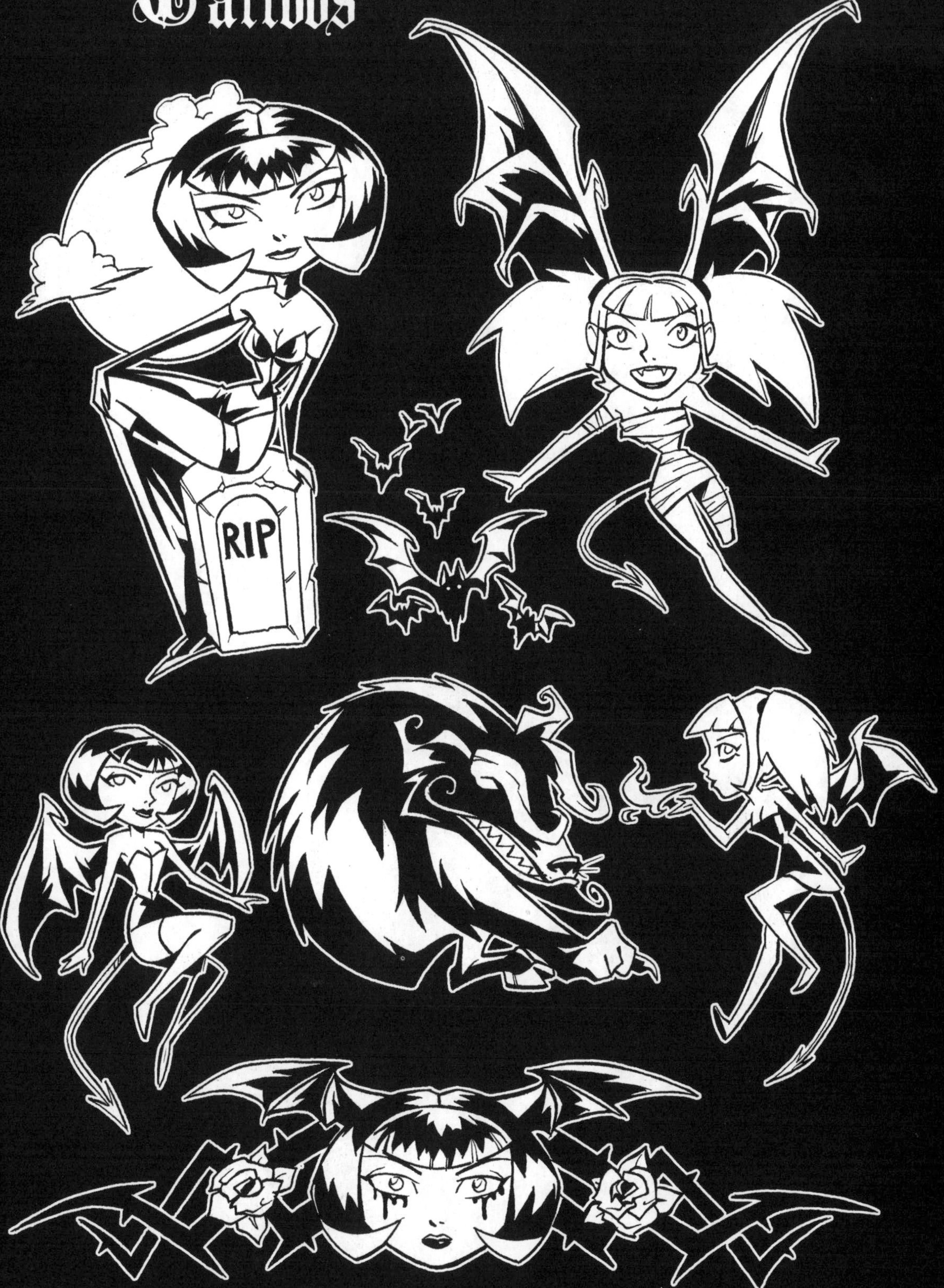
RIP

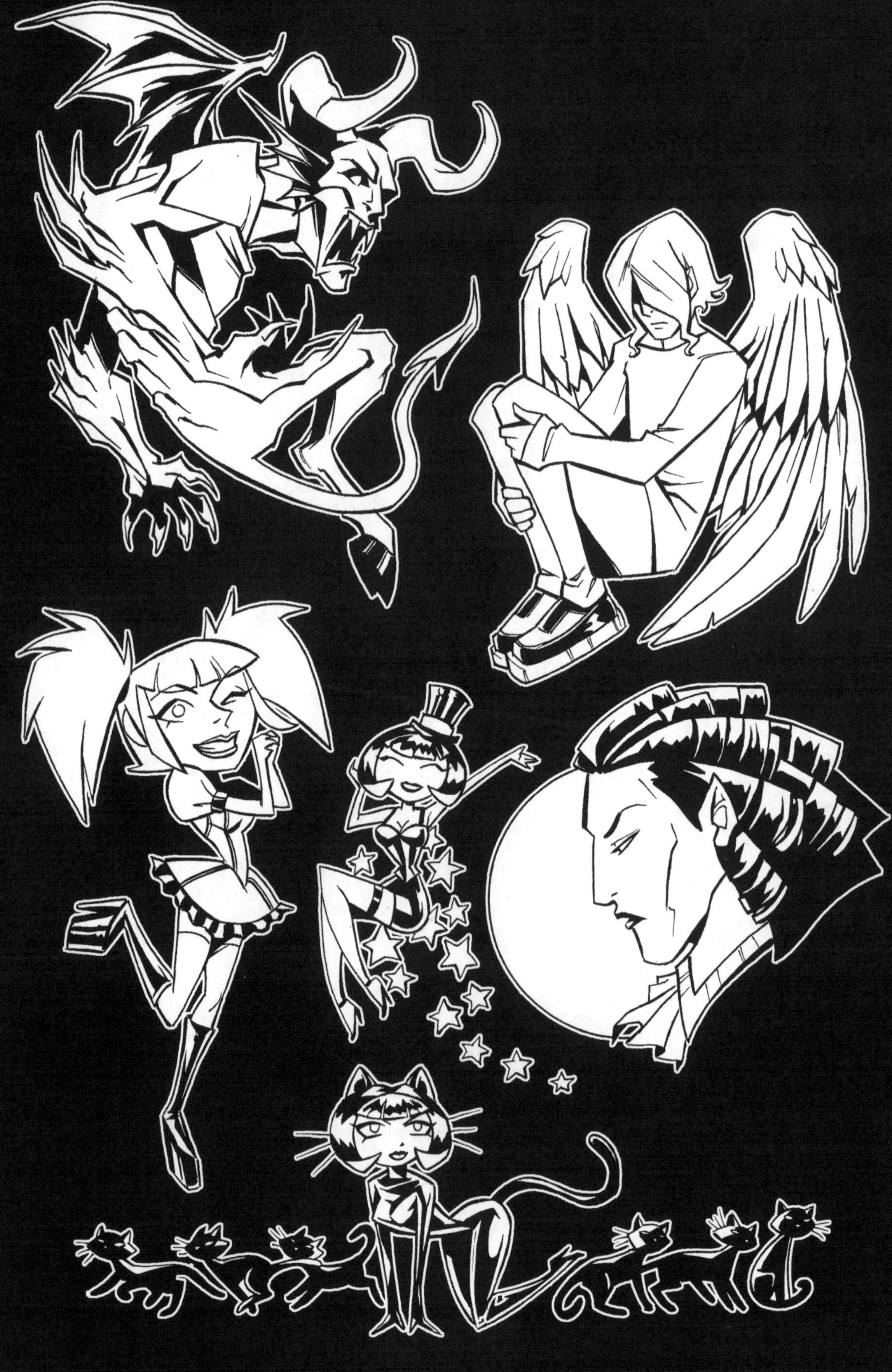

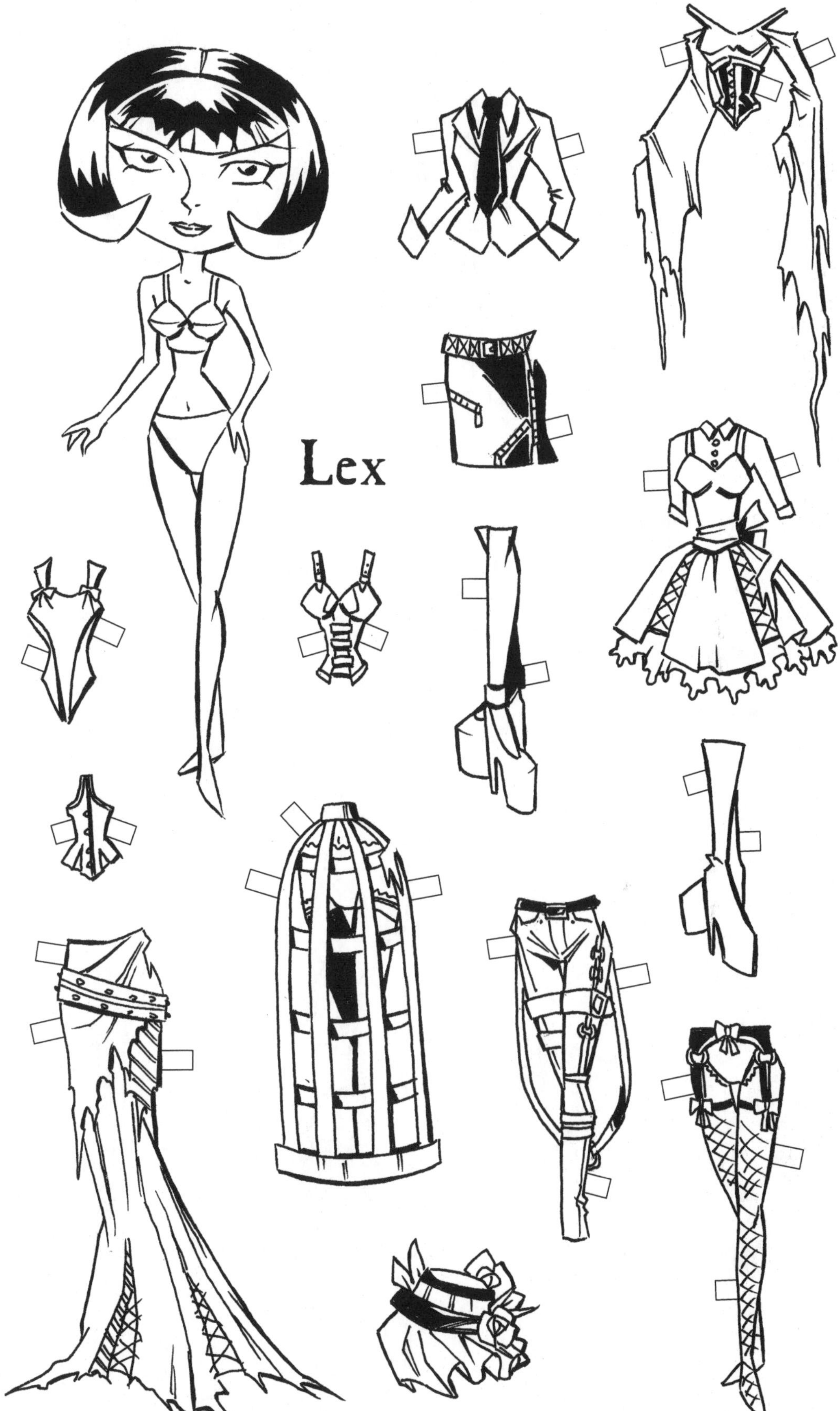
Lex

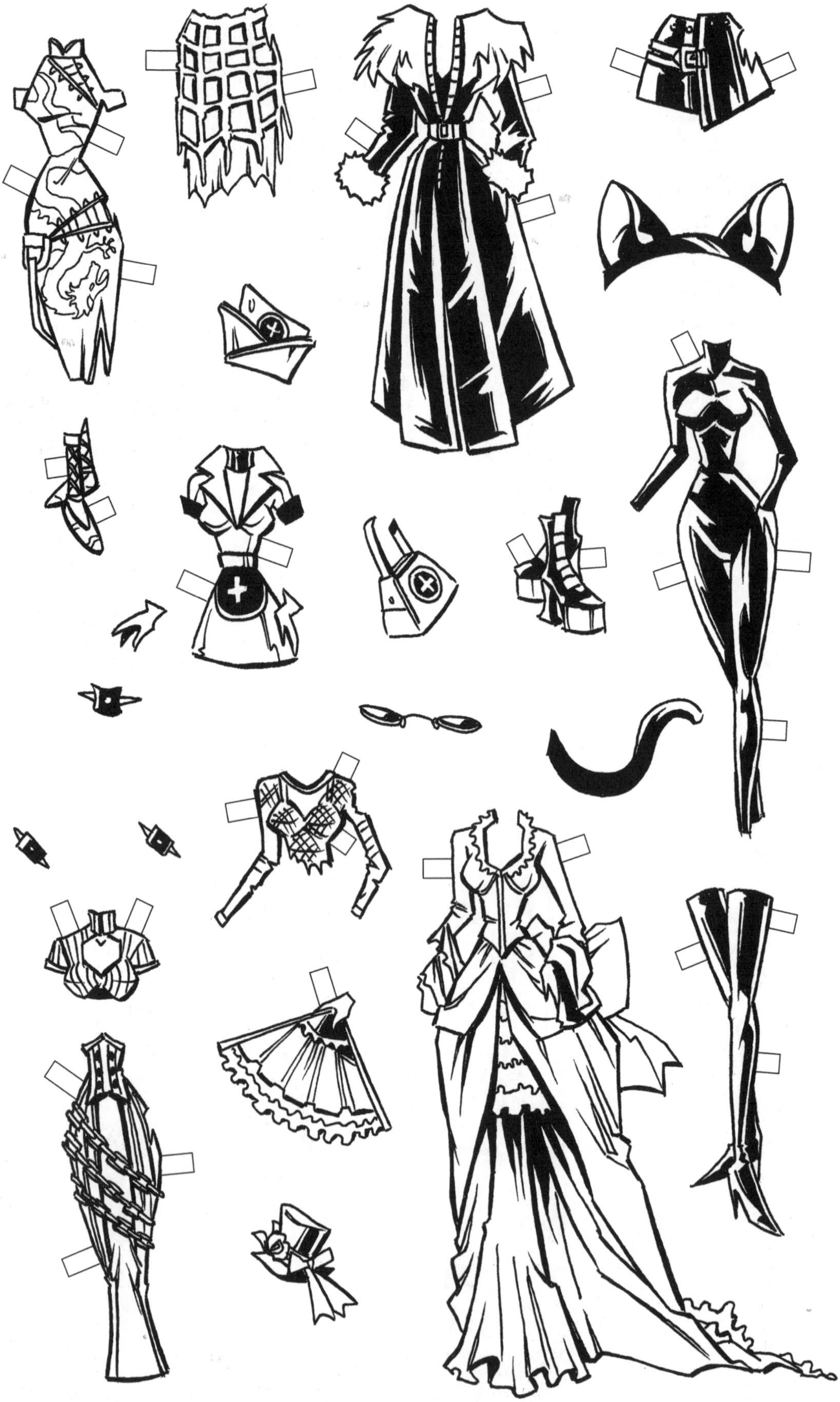

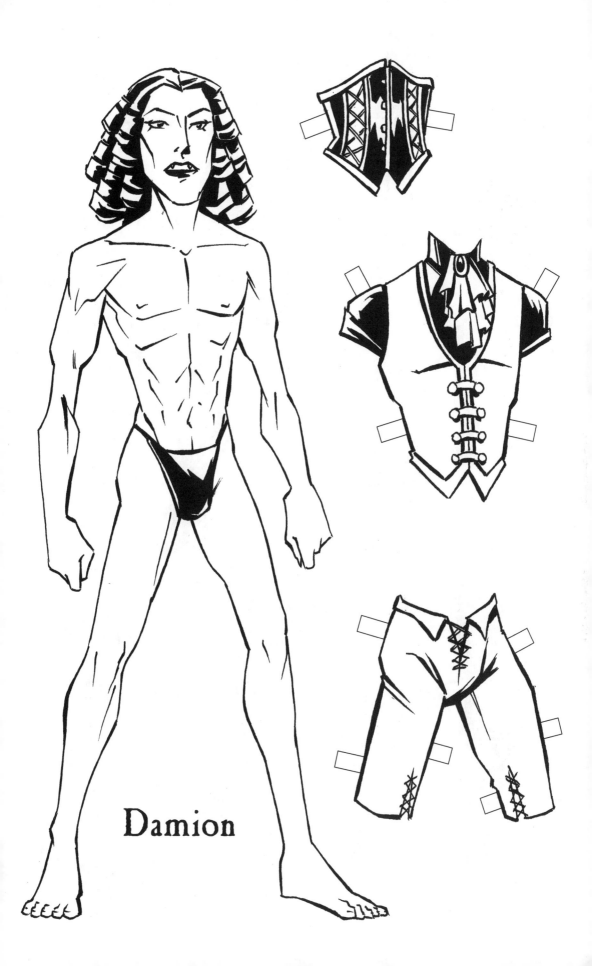

Damion

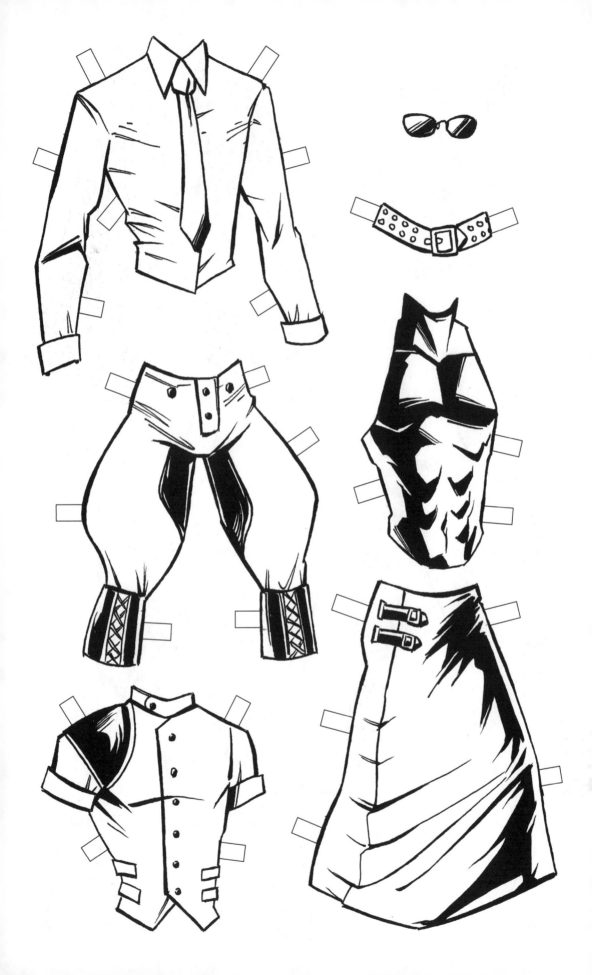

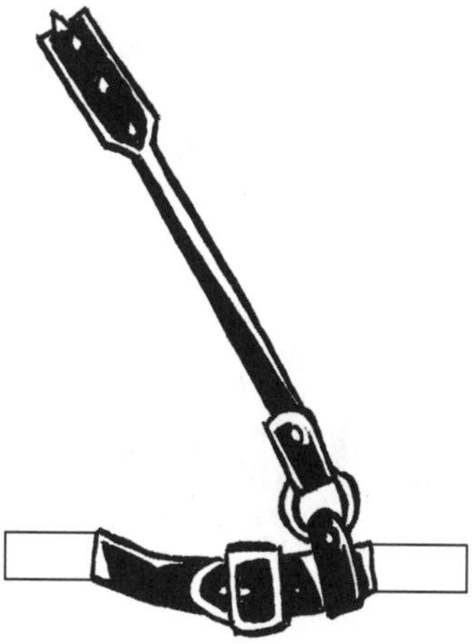
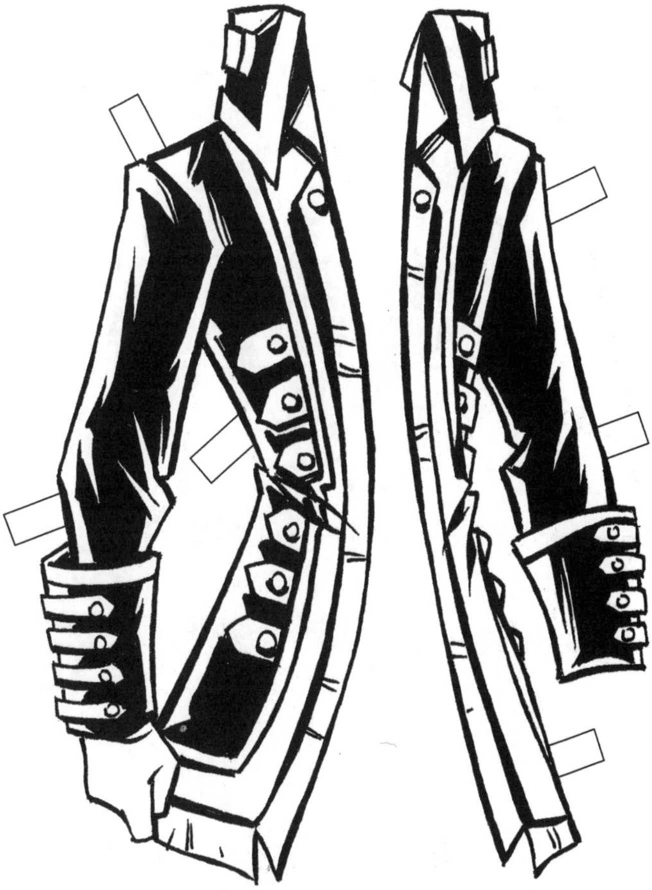
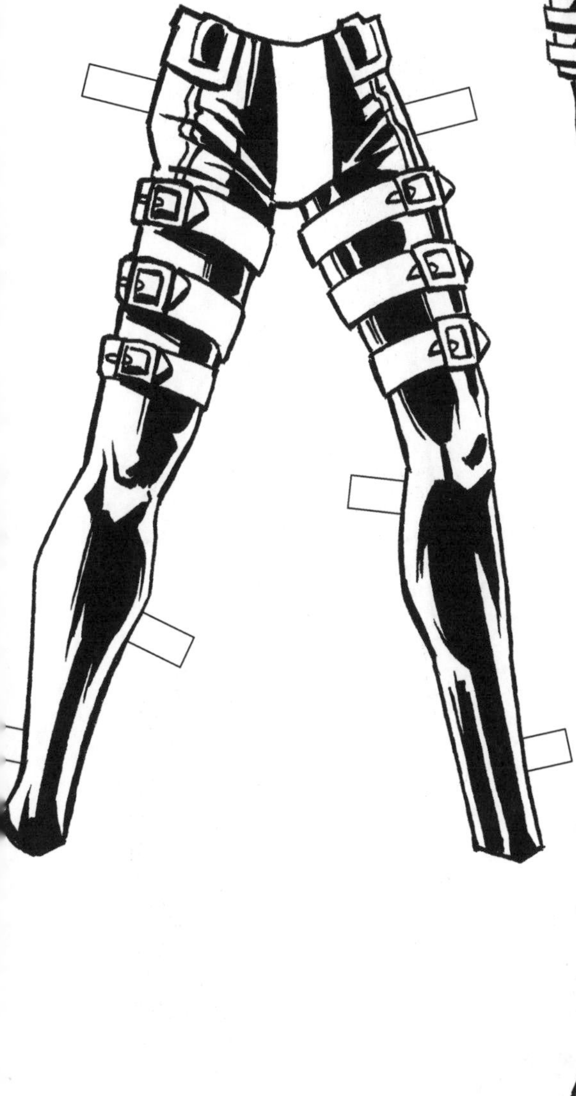
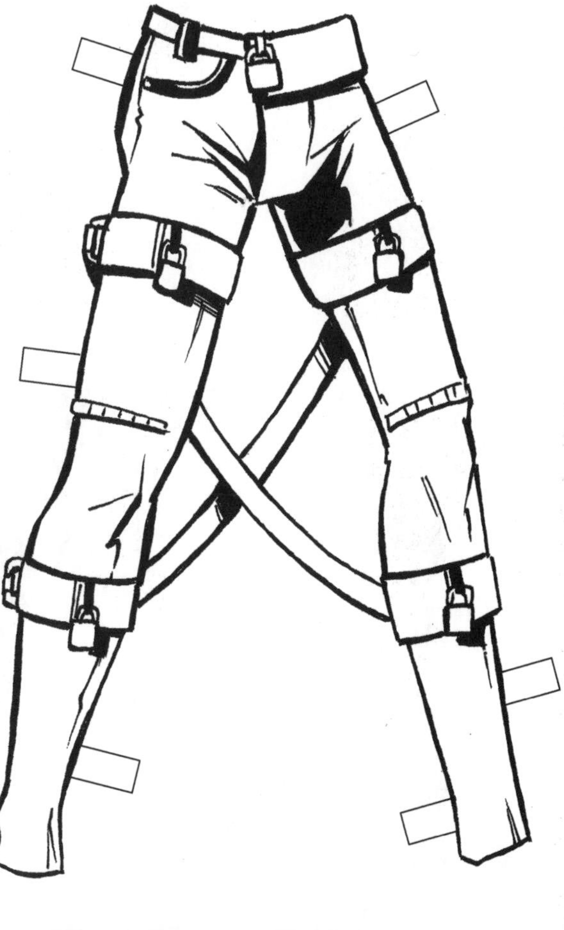

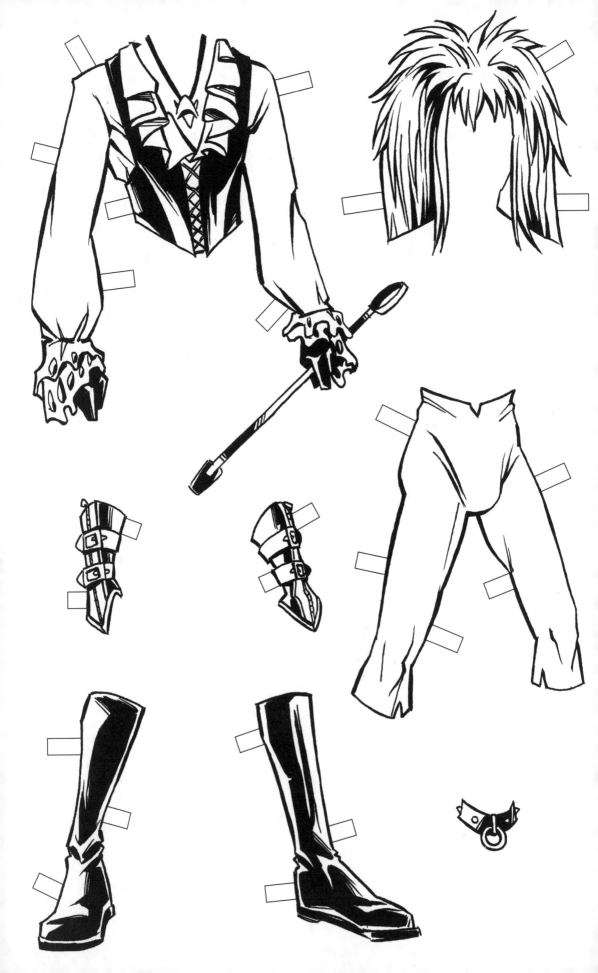

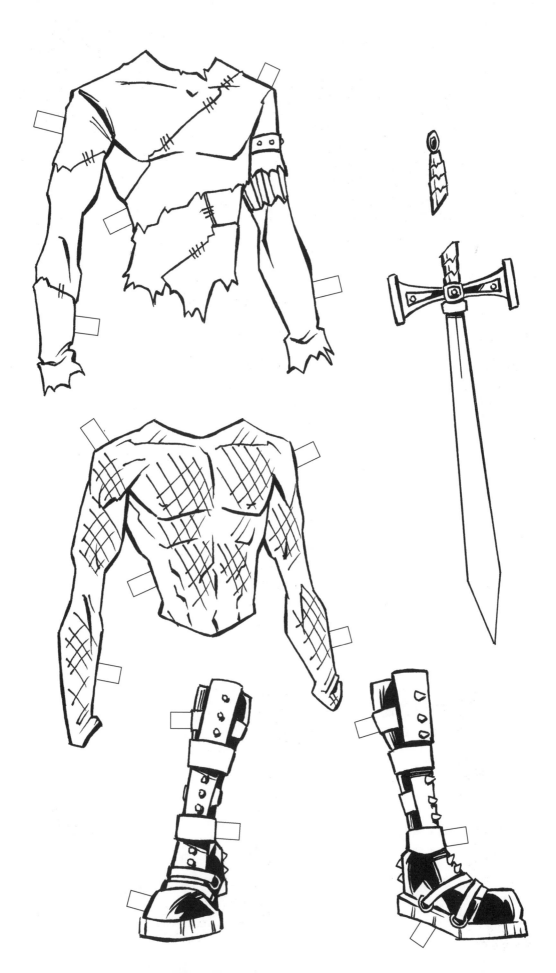

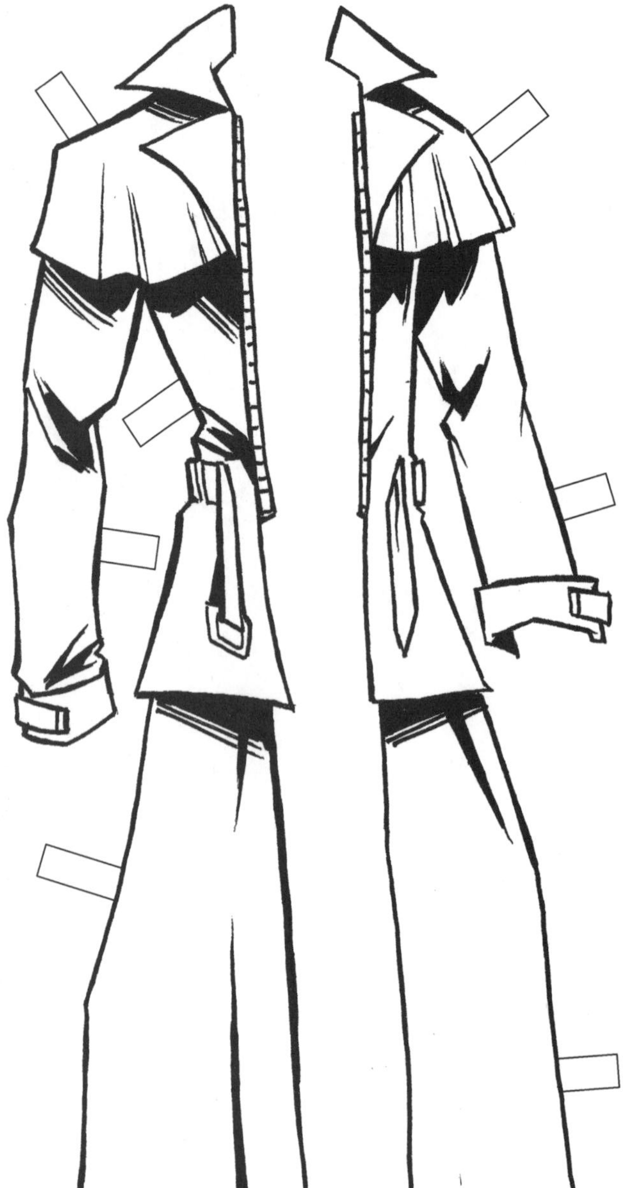

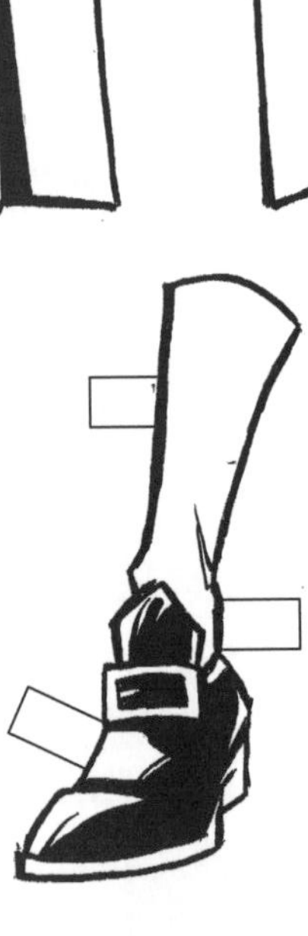

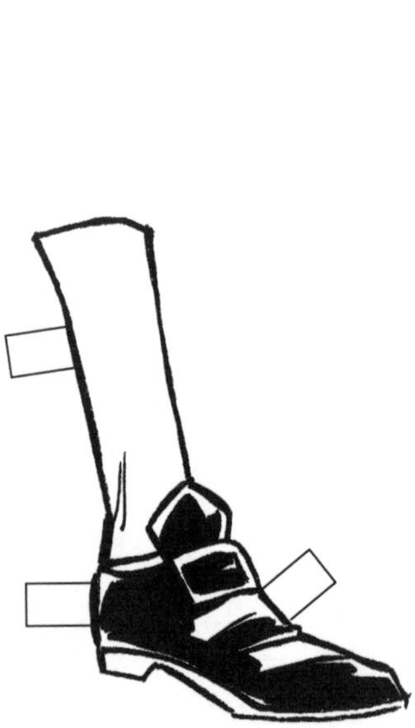

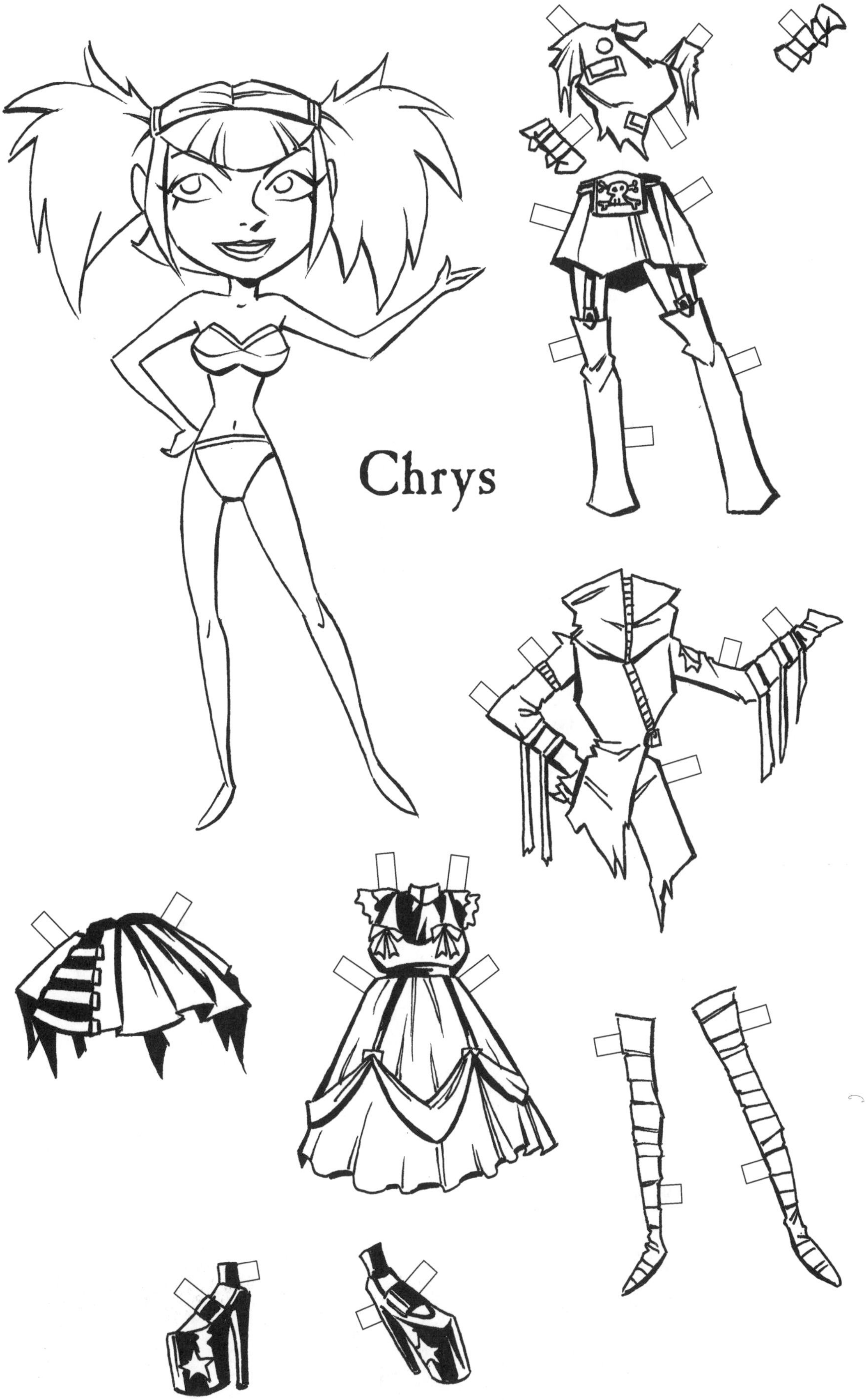
Chrys

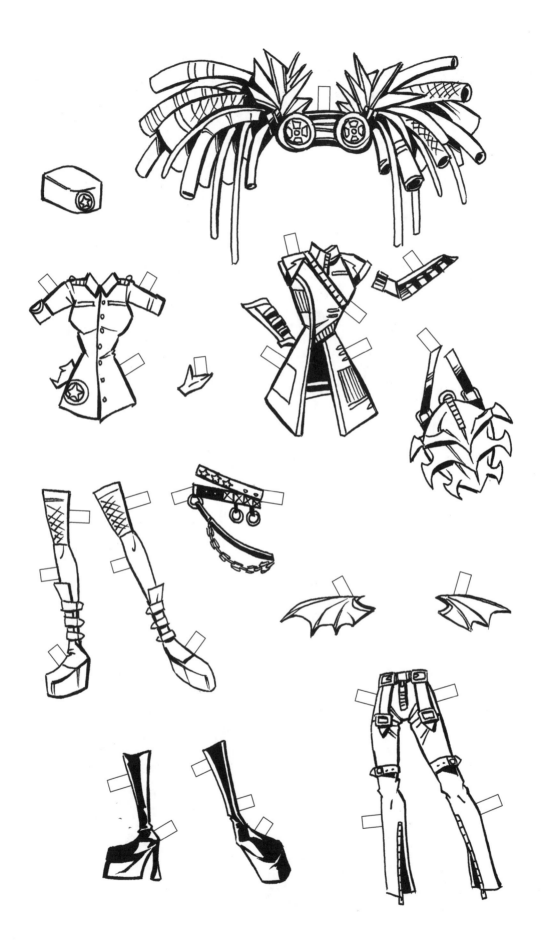

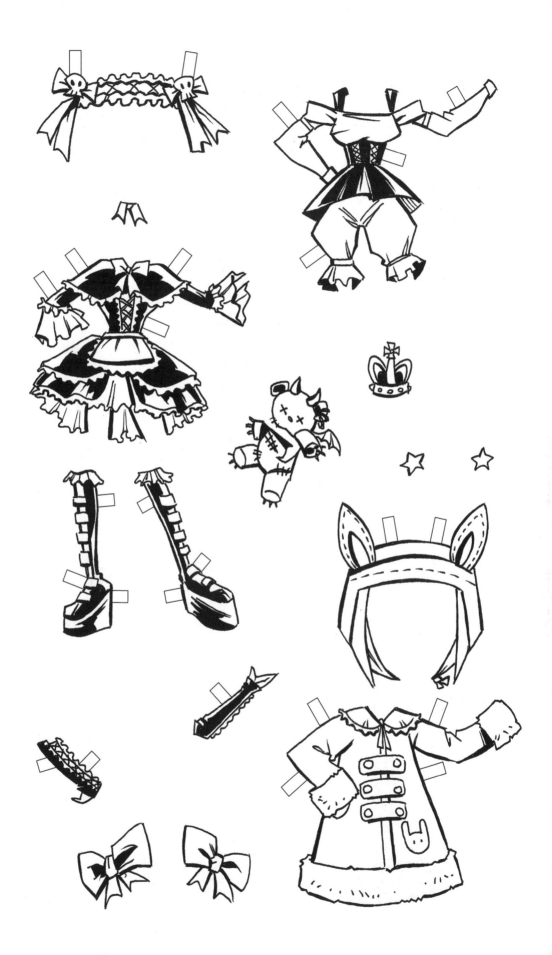

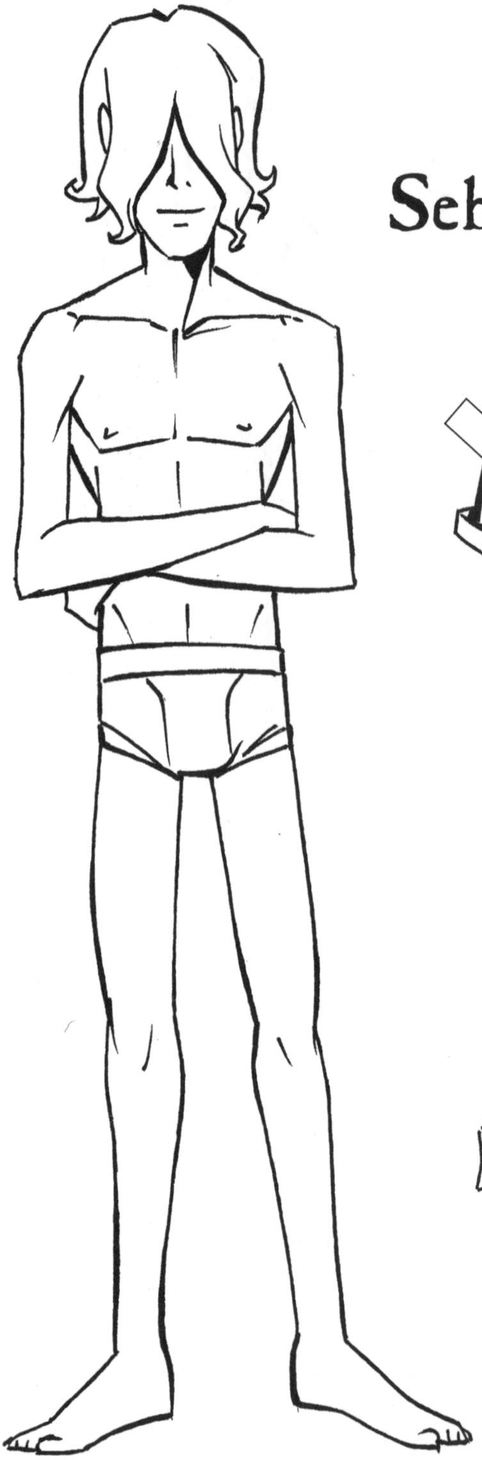

Sebastian

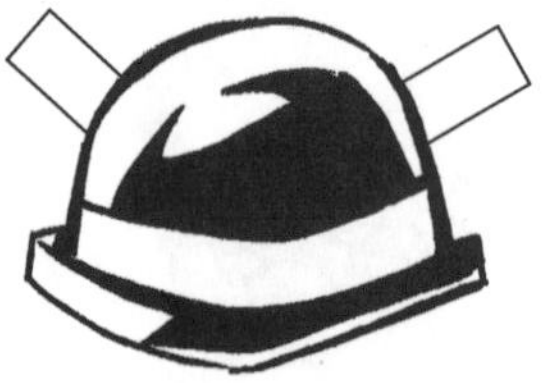

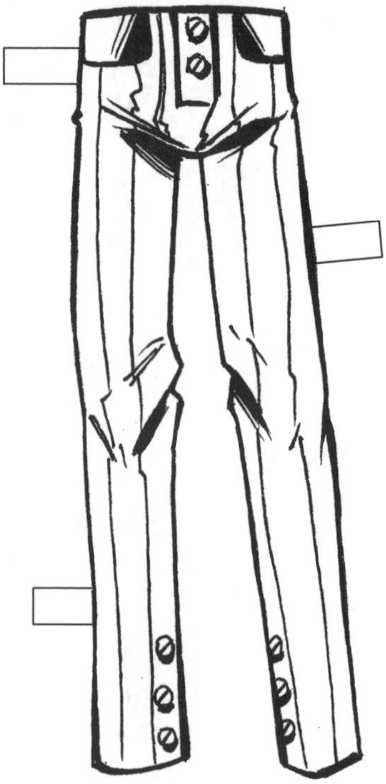

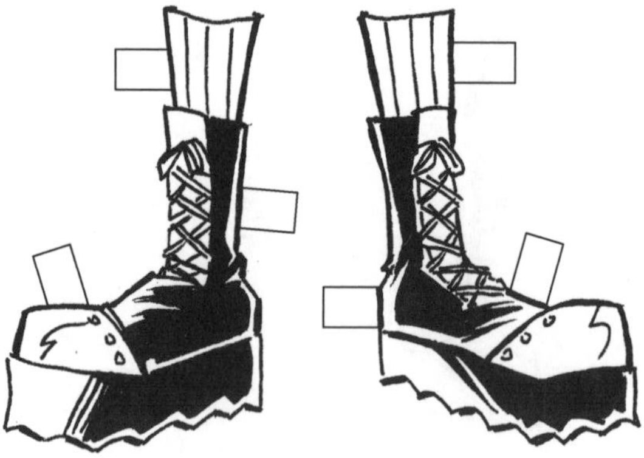

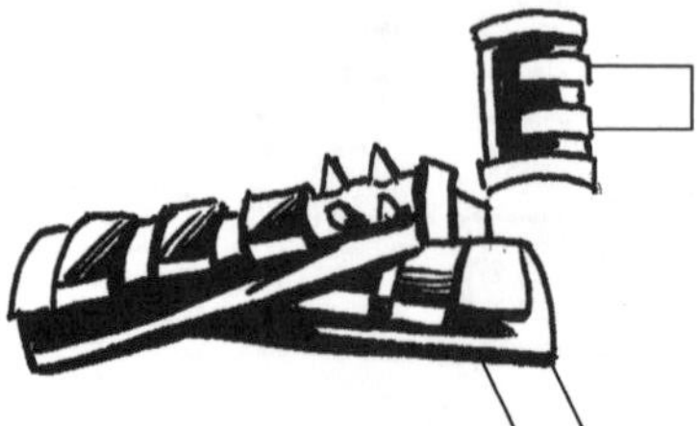

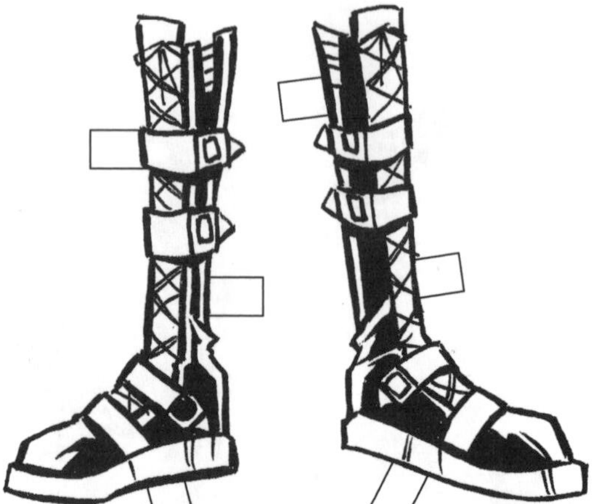

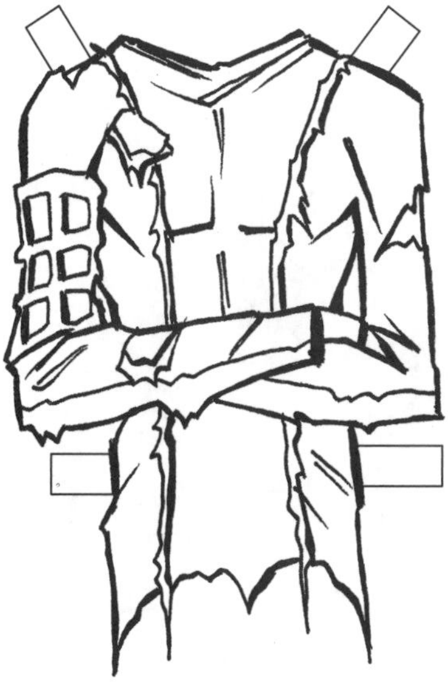
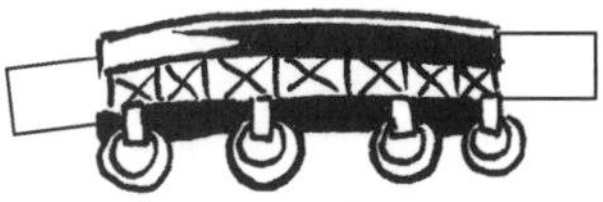
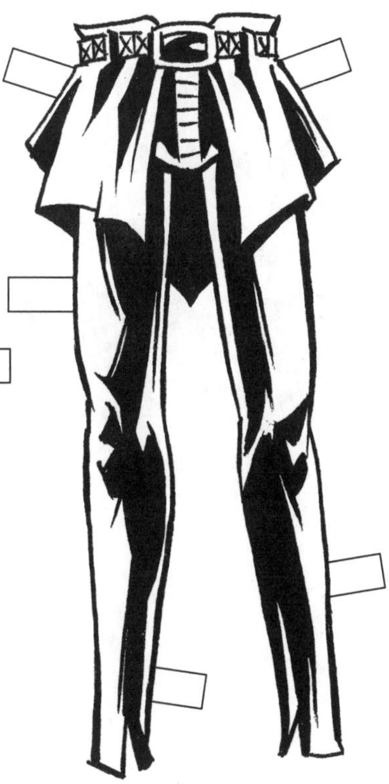
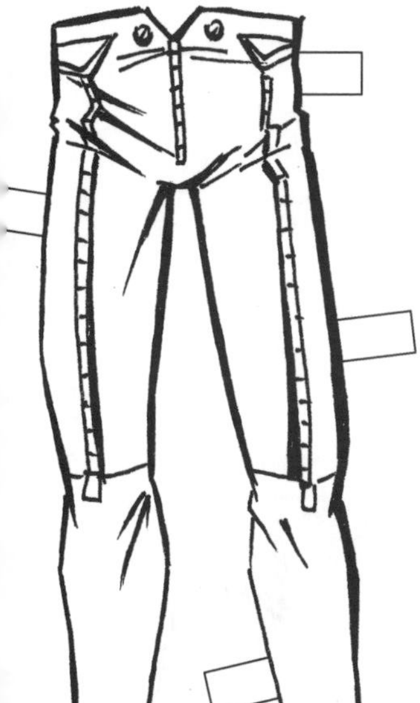
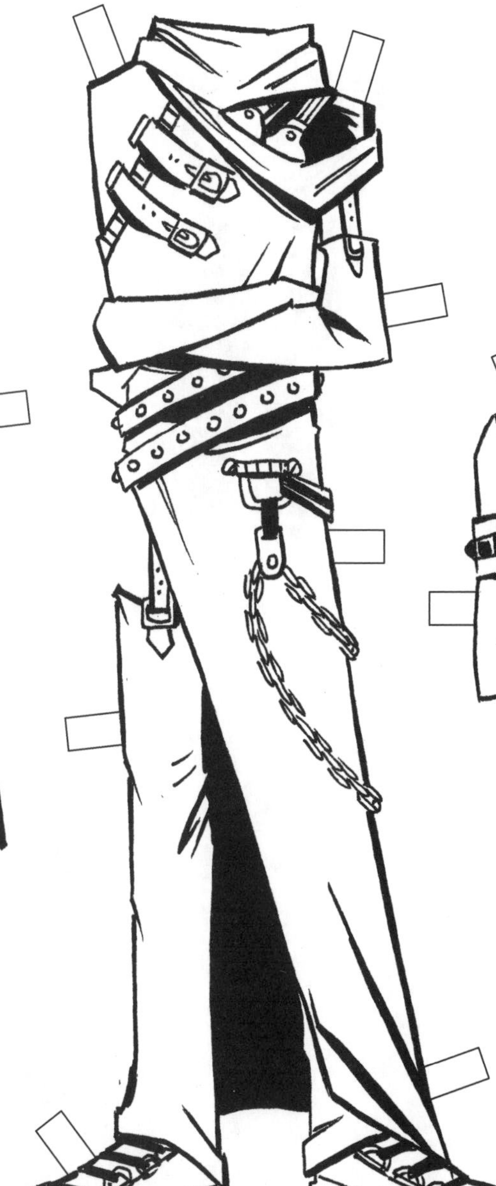
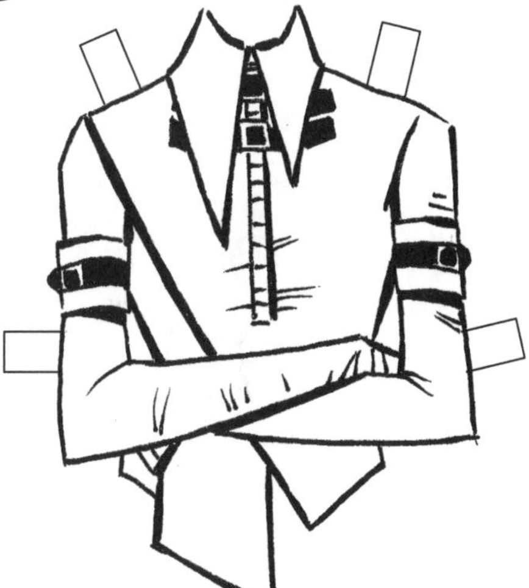

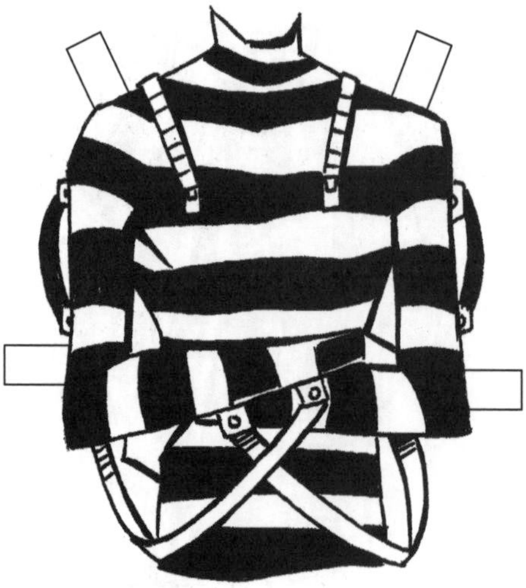

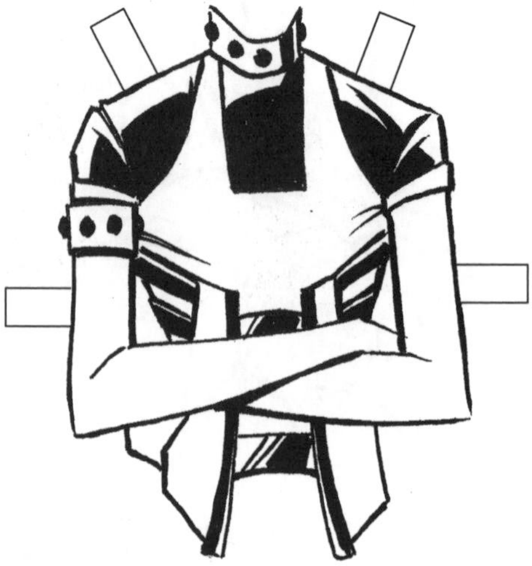

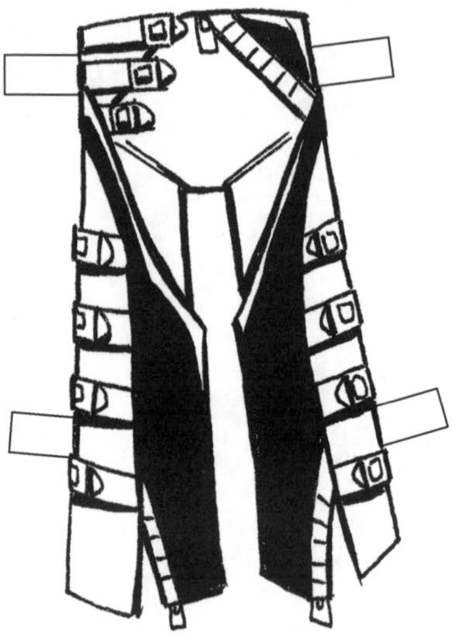

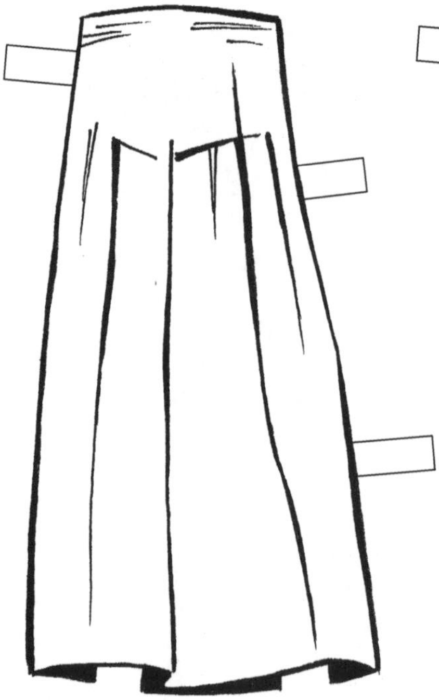

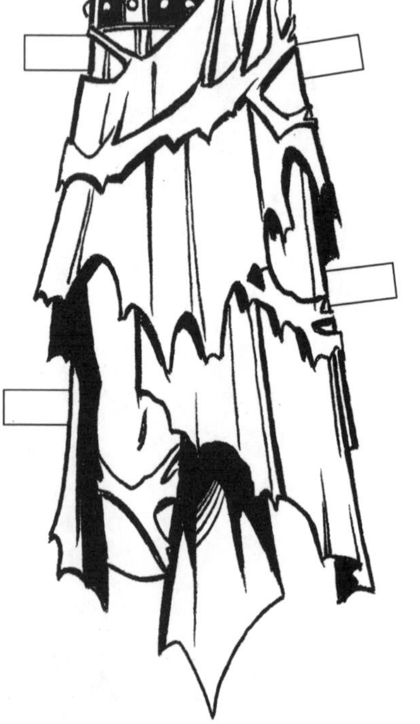

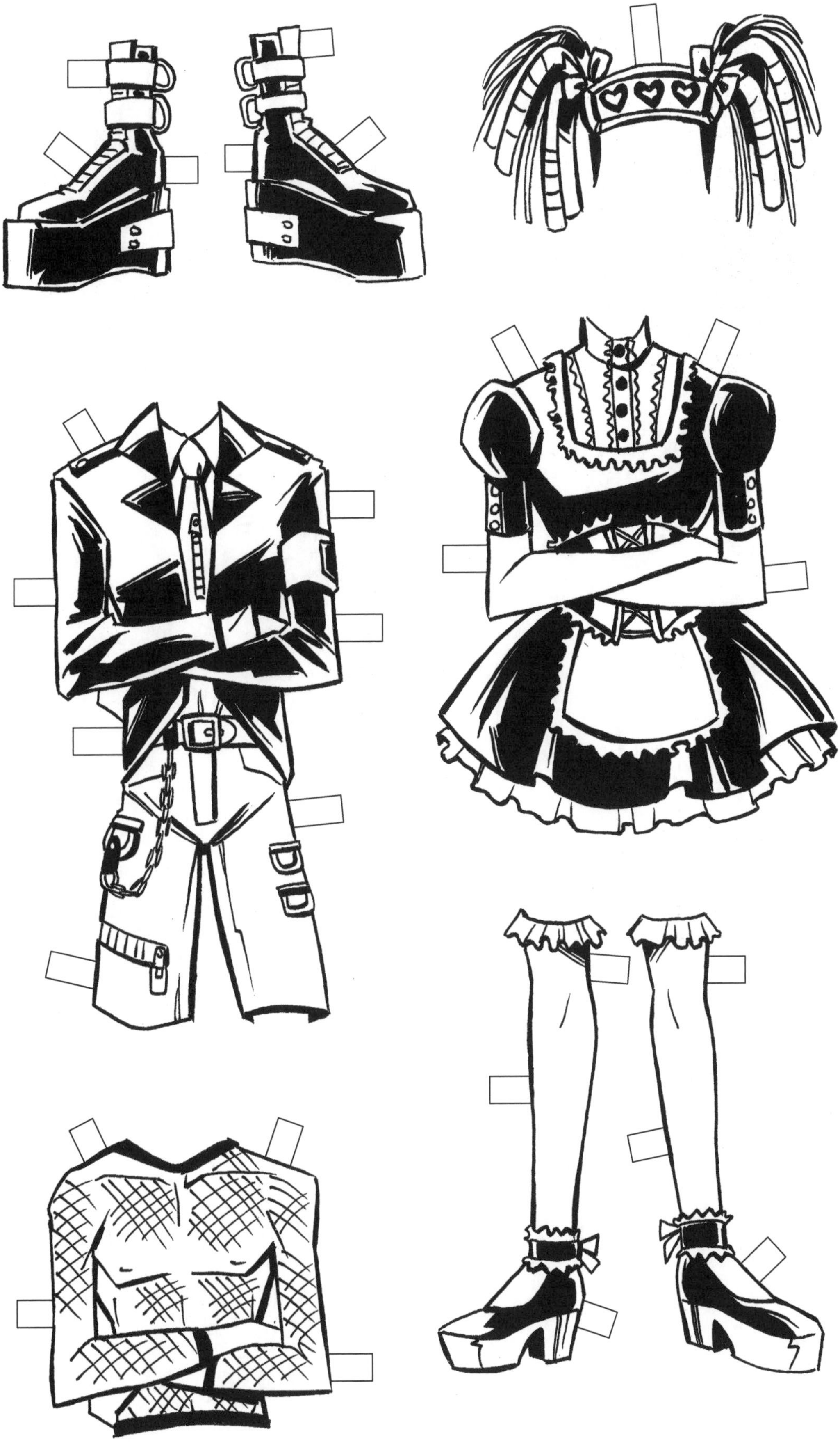

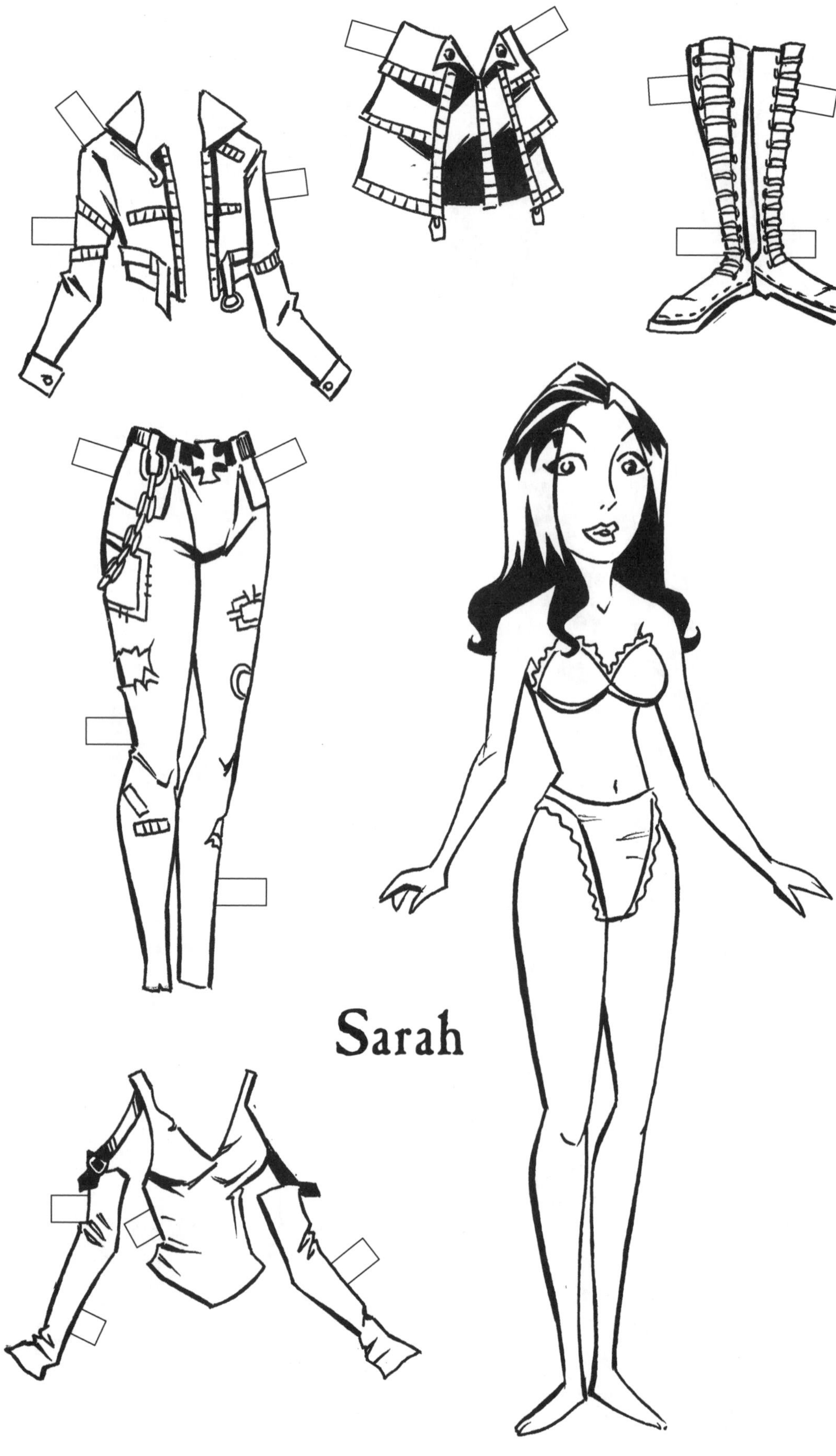
Sarah

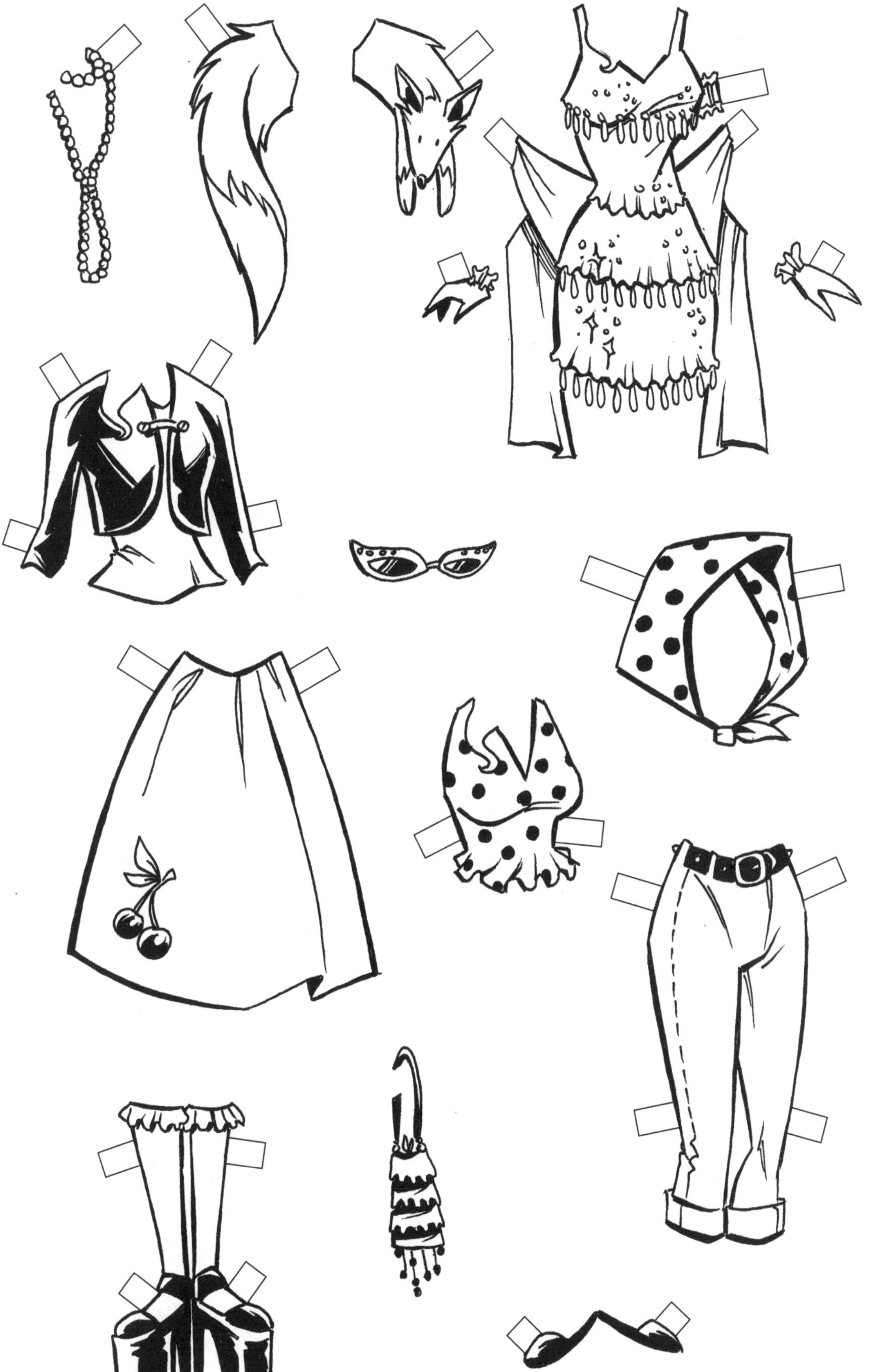

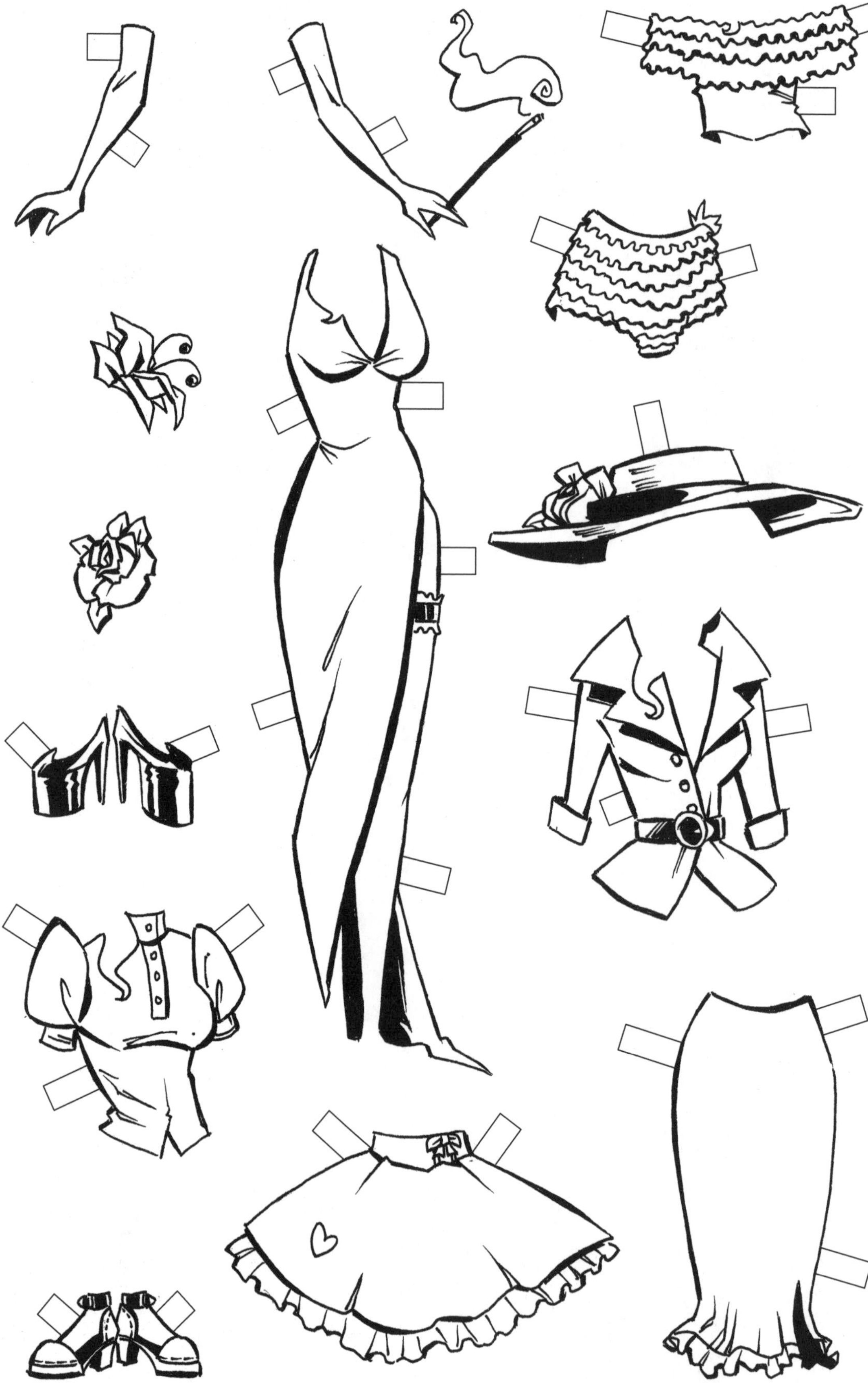

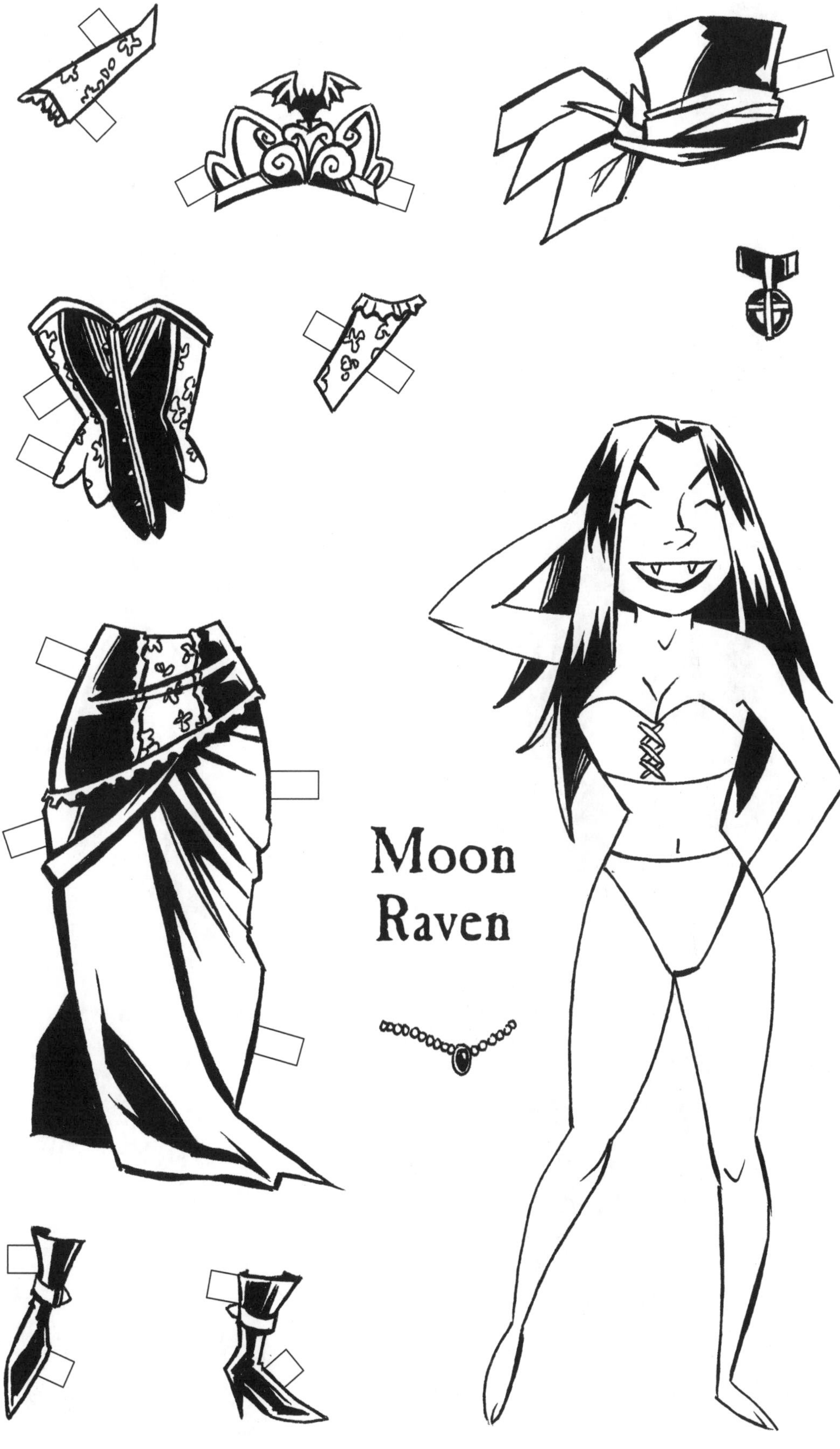
Moon
Raven

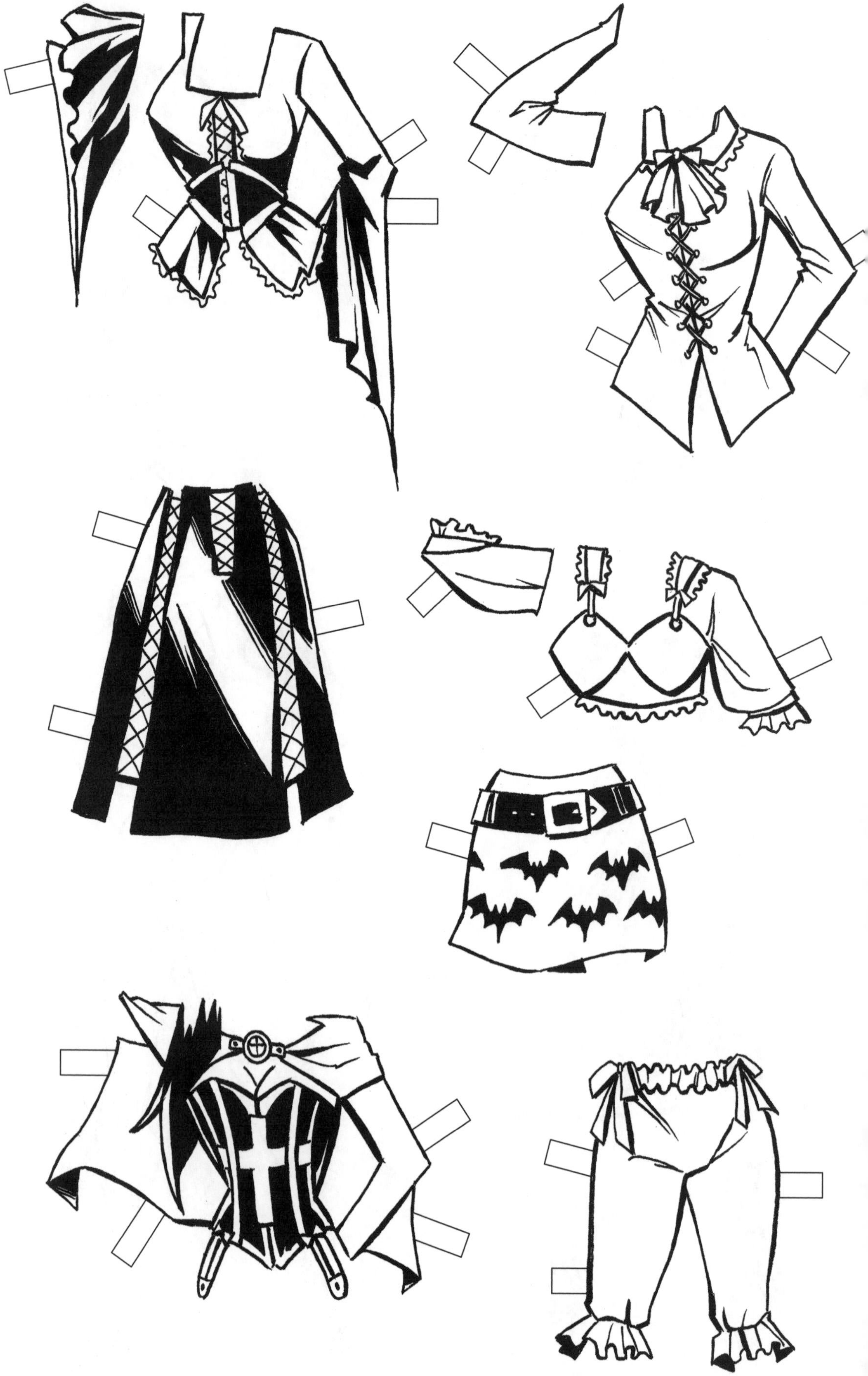

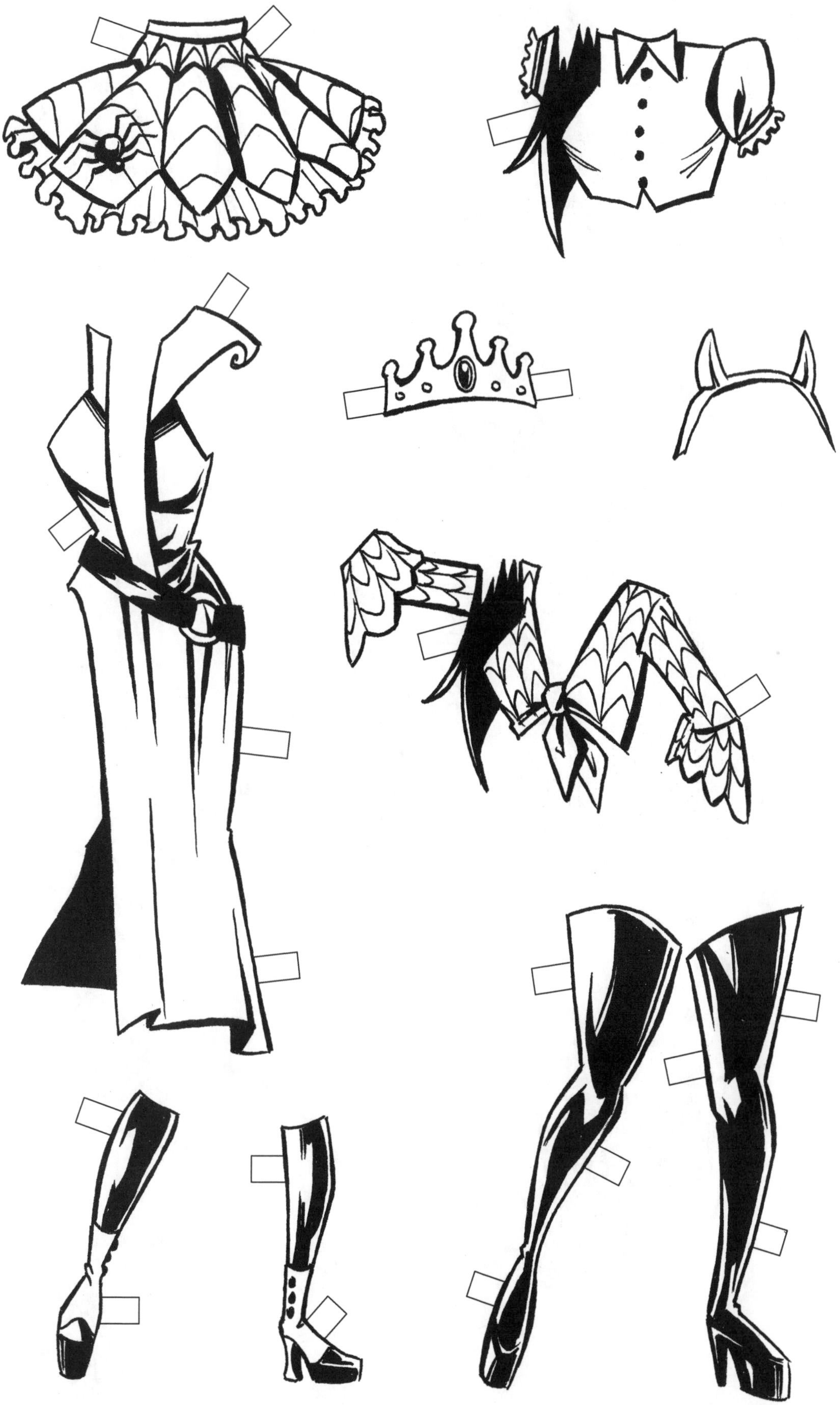

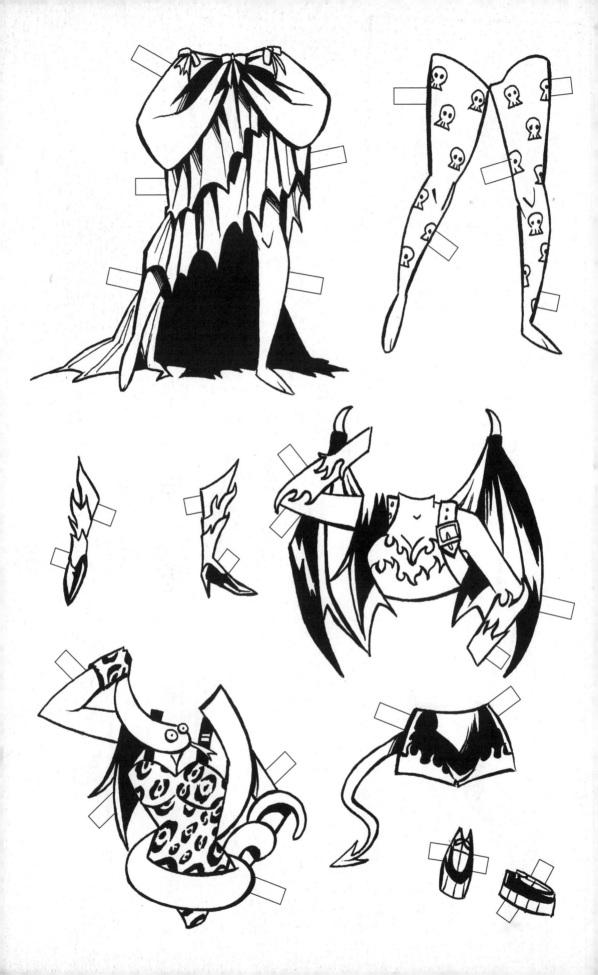

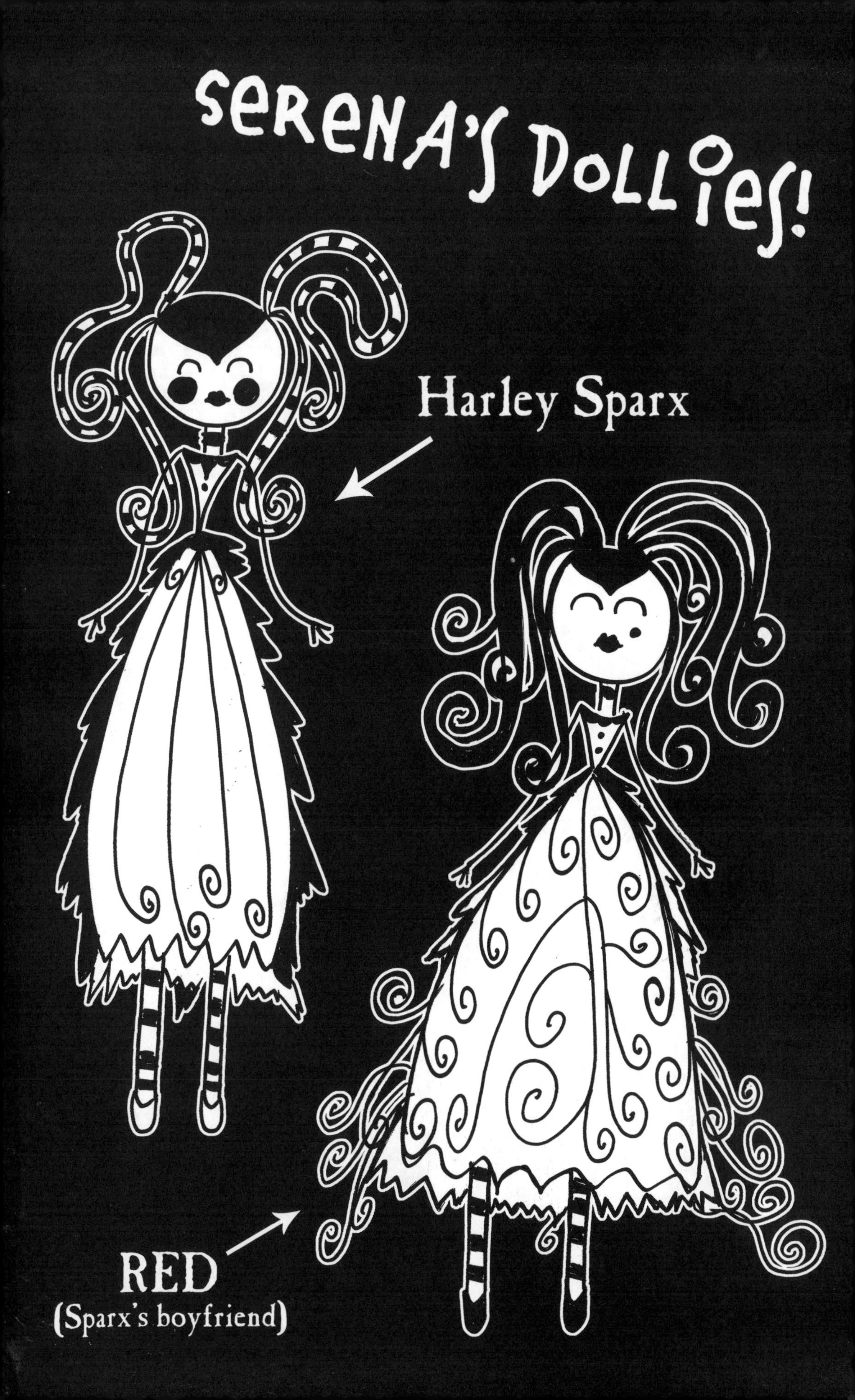
SERENA'S DOLLIES!
Harley Sparx
RED
(Sparx's boyfriend)

The Monster

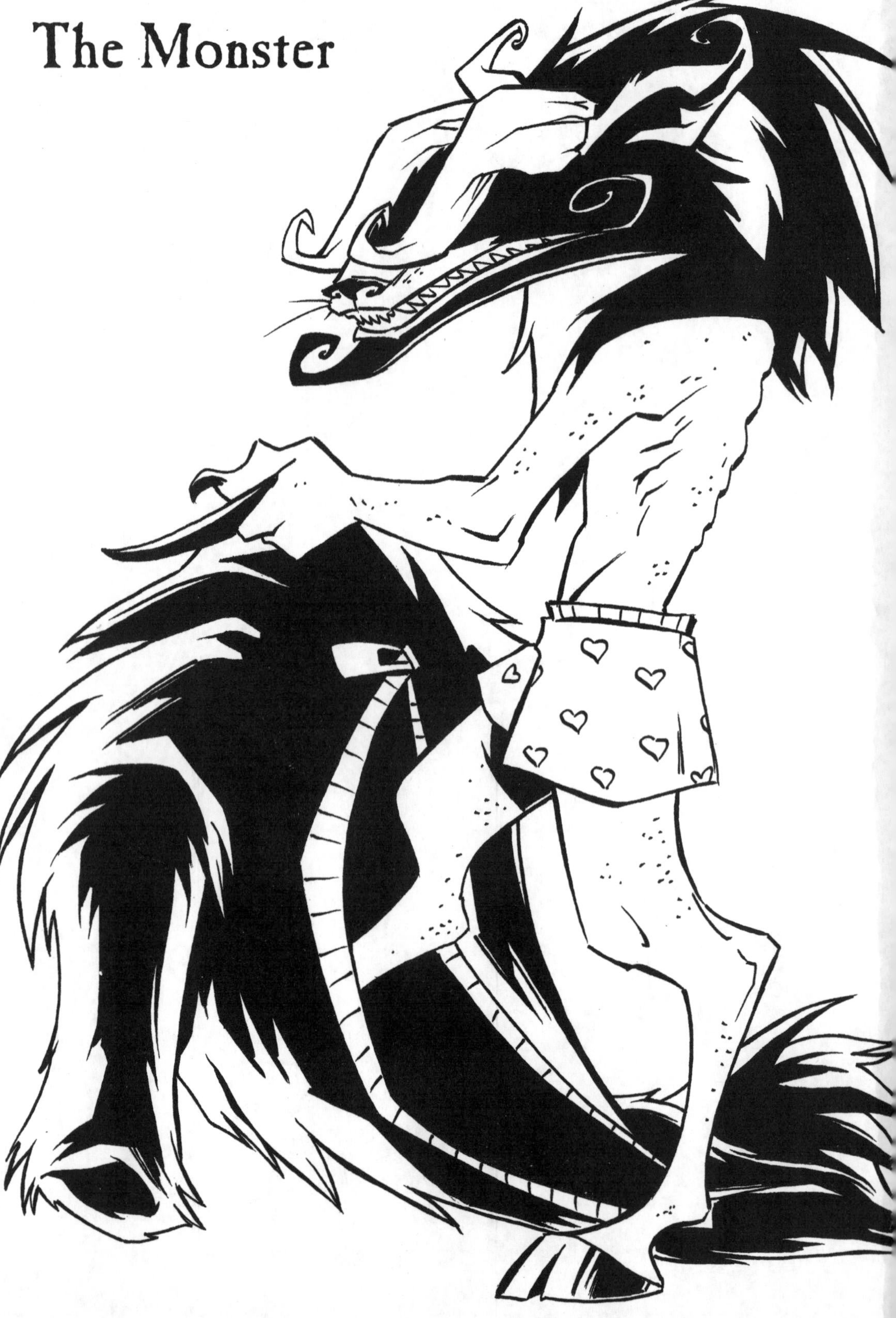